HEGEL AND THE TRADITION:
ESSAYS IN HONOUR OF H.S. HARRIS

Hegel and the Tradition: Essays in Honour of H.S. Harris

EDITED BY MICHAEL BAUR AND
JOHN RUSSON

UNIVERSITY OF TORONTO PRESS
Toronto Buffalo London

© University of Toronto Press Incorporated 1997
Toronto Buffalo London
Printed in Canada

ISBN 0-8020-0927-1

Printed on acid-free paper

Toronto Studies in Philosophy
Editors: James R. Brown and Calvin Normore

Canadian Cataloguing in Publication Data

Main entry under title:

Hegel and the tradition : essays in honour of H.S. Harris

Includes index.
ISBN 0-8020-0927-1

1. Hegel, Georg Wilhelm Friedrich, 1770–1831.   I. Harris, H.S. (Henry Silton), 1926–   .   II. Baur, Michael, 1963–   .   III. Russon, John Edward, 1960–   .

B2948.H43 1997   193   C97-931225-6

Frontispiece: Photo of H.S. Harris courtesy of Diego Nigro

University of Toronto Press acknowledges the financial assistance to its publishing program of the Canada Council for the Arts and the Ontario Arts Council.

Contents

Acknowledgments   vii
Foreword: Hume, Hegel, and Harris   ix
JOHN W. BURBIDGE

Introduction: Hegel and Tradition   3
JOHN RUSSON

Part One: Philosophy of Right

1 Philosophical History and the Roman Empire   17
   PATRICIA FAGAN

2 Locke, Fichte, and Hegel on the Right to Property   40
   JAY LAMPERT

Part Two: Art

3 Hegel and Hamann: Ideas and Life   77
   JOHN McCUMBER

4 Winckelmann and Hegel on the Imitation of the Greeks   93
   MICHAEL BAUR

5 Hegel as Philosopher of the Temporal [*irdischen*] World:
   On the Dialectics of Narrative   111
   MARTIN DONOUGHO

Part Three: Religion

6 The Identity of the Human and the Divine in the Logic of Speculative Philosophy   143
JEFF MITSCHERLING

7 The Final Name of God   162
DAVID KOLB

8 Hegel's Open Future   176
JOHN W. BURBIDGE

9 Hegel's Encounter with the Christian Tradition, or How Theological Are Hegel's Early Theological Writings?   190
NICHOLAS WALKER

10 'Wie aus der Pistole': Fries and Hegel on Faith and Knowledge   212
GEORGE DI GIOVANNI

Part Four: Philosophy

11 Der Unterschied zwischen 'Differenz' und 'Unterschied': A Re-evaluation of Hegel's *Differenzschrift*   245
SUSAN-JUDITH HOFFMANN

12 Dialectic as Counterpoint: On Philosophical Self-Measure in Plato and Hegel   264
JAMES CROOKS

13 Hegel's 'Freedom of Self-Consciousness' and Early Modern Epistemology   286
JOHN RUSSON

Afterword: Theme and Variations: The Round of Life and the Chorale of Thought   311
H.S. HARRIS

Hegel's Works   325

Publications of H.S. Harris   329
JAMES DEVIN

Contributors   347

Acknowledgments

Bringing this volume into existence was very much a cooperative activity. The co-editorship makes this obvious at one level, but there are many other levels of cooperation that are not so obvious. First, we must thank all the contributors for being willing to shape their contributions around the common theme of 'tradition,' which emerged only through a year of letter-writing and discussion, and for the effort they all put into reading and commenting on each other's pieces in order to lend the volume coherence. Second, we must single out for special thanks John Burbidge, who did a great deal to help us put the volume together and who kindly undertook to write the foreword on Harris. Third, we must thank Ron Schoeffel, editor-in-chief of the University of Toronto Press, who was enormously supportive of our project from the beginning and without whose advice and help the volume would never have come to press.

Fourth, we must thank all those who contributed financially to the project: the Acadia University Faculty Association, Christopher Adair-Toteff, Rolf Ahlers, Karl Ameriks, Kostas Bagakis, Simon Barrington-Ward, Patricia Scavuzzo Bascuas, Jennifer Bates, Gene and Kay Baur, Michael Baur, Bishop's University, Kenneth G. Botsford, Nicholas Boyle, Charles F. Brennan, Harry Brod, Robert F. Brown, Randolph Buchanan, John Burbidge, Graham Caswell, Moon-Gil Chung, Ardis B. Collins, Katharina Comoth, James Connelly, Bernard Cullen, William Desmond, James Devin, George di Giovanni, Andre Doz, Louis Dupré, David A. Duquette, Patricia Fagan, Vincent J. Ferrara, Cinzia Ferrini, Douglas Frame, Peter Fuss, James V. Geisendorfer, Philip Grier, Justus Hartnack, the Hegel Society of America, Peter Hodgson, Michael H. Hoffheimer, E.R. Klein, George L. Kline, James P. Kow, Hayo B.E.D. Krombach, Dominic Le Fave, David Leopold, Eric v.d. Luft, John McCumber, David MacGregor, John Maisonneuve, Bruce Merrill, David Merrill, Giuseppe Micheli, Patricia J. Mills, David Morris, Peter Nicholson, Walter T. Odell, Alan L.T. Paterson, Zbigniew

Pelczynski, Mark C.E. Peterson, Riccardo Pozzo, Harry Prosch, Heidi M. Ravven, Abigail L. Rosenthal, John Russon, William F. Ryan, Dale M. Schlitt, Helmut Schneider, Andrew Shanks, Daniel E. Shannon, Gary Shapiro, William K. Sheridan, Peter Simpson, Larry Stepelevich, Peter G. Stillman, Thomas Suh, William Sweet, Maria Talero, Michael G. Vater, Richard L. Velkley, Florindo Volpacchio, John Walker, Kenneth R. Westphal, and Richard Dien Winfield.

Fifth, we are grateful to John Parry for his careful copy-editing of the entire manuscript.

Finally, we thank H.S. Harris for reading the whole manuscript and writing the afterword.

John Russon
Michael Baur

Foreword:
Hume, Hegel, and Harris

JOHN W. BURBIDGE

Henry Harris established his reputation by writing a massive, two-volume intellectual biography of the young Hegel. For the first time, the scattered texts from Tübingen, Bern, Frankfurt, and Jena were integrated into a single pattern that traced the systematic development of Hegel's thought. It soon became the standard reference for anyone, anywhere, who wanted to understand the relation between the youthful, idealistic tutor and the mature, established professor.

The two volumes of *Hegel's Development – Toward the Sunlight (1770–1801)* and *Night Thoughts (Jena 1801–1806)* – both marked the culmination of Harris's earlier pilgrimage through Gentile and Collingwood to Hegel and served as prolegomena to his primary objective: a full-scale commentary on Hegel's *Phenomenology of Spirit*. It is tempting, then, to think of him as an idealist, a graduate of Oxford, standing in the tradition of Bradley and Bosanquet, McTaggart and Mure. Yet, though an undergraduate at St Edmund's Hall while G.R.G. Mure still held sway at Merton, he never studied with Mure, and his subsequent immersion in Hegelian texts has only confirmed his distance from the right-wing Hegelians who see speculative philosophy as another name for theology. When he comes to the end of *Night Thoughts (Jena 1801–1806)* it is that theological reading that becomes the predominant target for his criticisms.

Harris identifies not with the idealist traditions of Oxford and Cambridge but with the empiricist traditions of David Hume. He is as regular in his attendance at conferences on Hume as he is at gatherings of Hegelians. Even though Hegel devotes barely four paragraphs to Hume in his 1825–6 lectures on the history of philosophy, Harris recognizes that, if he wants to make Hegel speak English (in the same way that Hegel wanted to make philosophy speak German), he must appropriate not only Hume's transparent style but also his philosophical program: 'When therefore we entertain any Suspicion, that a philosophical Term is employ'd without any Meaning or Idea (as is but too frequent) we need but enquire, from what Impression is that suppos'd Idea deriv'd?'[1]

To associate Hume with Hegel seems to be a contradiction in terms. Hume is a sober empiricist, never willing to trust himself to anything that is not confirmed either by experience or by custom, while Hegel is a speculative theoretician, who not only constructs an abstract logic and metaphysics but purports to 'deduce' the elements of nature and society. Yet Harris does succeed in bringing the two together, and in so doing he transforms the conventional view, not only of Hegel, but also of Hume.

There are three themes in Hume's philosophy that throw light on Harris's work. First is the position, originally taken by John Locke, that ideas are to be traced back to direct experience. Second is the appeal to custom and tradition, not only as the ground of our conviction that every event has a cause but also as a basis for moral sentiments. Third is the way in which analogy is used to throw light on the ultimate nature of reality. We consider each of these themes in turn.

First, in *Toward the Sunlight (1770–1801)*, Harris traces Hegel's pilgrimage as the young Swabian prepared himself to become an instructor of the German people. The focus of this development was not philosophy, but the religious beliefs that capture the imagination and heart, as well as the constitutional structures of the political order. The subject matter was specific and determinate – cultural and social experience.

Once Hegel arrived in Jena, however, he turned his attention to philosophy: to the patterns of logical thought as well as the formal categories that do justice to nature, human personality, and society. As his vocabulary became more precise, it became more abstract and theoretical, anticipating the density and obscurity of prose that have bedevilled interpreters ever since.

Night Thoughts (Jena 1801–1806) is an extended commentary on those texts. But as one reads it one would not know that Hegel is almost exclusively using terms such as 'being,' and 'determination,' 'actuality' and 'universal.' Harris looks to human experience to provide an interpretation and explanation of what is going on: the logic of 1804 is talking not about thought but about consciousness, or possibly about the structure of society; the philosophy of nature of 1805 is really a paradigm for the total system of social and self-conscious life. For Harris the abstractness of pure ideas makes sense only if they can be spelled out in the experiences of ordinary people, who are conscious of a world and who interact in families and communities. These are the impressions from which theoretical ideas are derived.

'Experience,' then, is not simply a series of sense impressions, as it was for Hume and his heirs. It is a lived interaction between selves and their world. After all, the appeal to the givens of sense is itself an abstraction from life. Impressions are embedded in individual, conscious beings who are born to, and educated by, human parents and who become participating members of church and state. Experience is this rich tapestry of personal and social development.

So Harris not only puts flesh on the bones of Hegelian philosophy in the manner of a good empiricist. He also transforms the conception of experience so that it includes not just the isolated moments of a patch of blue or a shrill high C, but the network of relationships that weaves such isolated instances into a complex fabric. Harris has learned from the pragmatism of his mentor, Max Fisch.

Second, in extending the range of human experience in this way, Harris is not being unfaithful to Hume. For Hume uses the empiricist presupposition not only to deny that the idea of 'cause' is rooted in sense impressions, but also to affirm that it is based in habit and custom. Experience includes the whole range of human practice. It is this breadth of view that is then incorporated into his moral philosophy. Morality is not a question of ultimate standards that cannot be challenged. It is the product of social interaction, which educates feelings and moral sentiment.

It is this perspective that draws Harris to the young instructor of the German people, who proposes a folk-religion that will not only be grounded on universal reason and tie together all the needs of life but will not send fancy, heart, and sensibility empty away.[2] For the young Hegel as for Hume, the imagination must be captured if philosophy is to transform the social order. Imagination stirs the heart and develops human practice. Reason, for all of its authority, has no such power. What is needed is an intuitive sense of how things fit together into a whole, how the parts interact with each other.

Therefore when Harris comes to the more abstract texts of the Jena period, he appeals to customary and traditional patterns as a key for explanations. The patterns he appeals to will be found in the tradition, in the customs that have been passed on. And the aspects of tradition that are most viable are those that appeal to intuition and sentiment: art and literature. Dante, Sophocles, and Homer present the imagination with a picture of how customary behaviour is integrated into a total perspective.

Harris has not just taught courses on Hegel. He has lectured as well on philosophy and literature – on Sophocles, Dante, and Blake. In the midst of preparing footnotes for his commentary on the *Phenomenology*, he produced an ordinary reader's introduction to Goethe's *Faust*. He draws on his regular attendance in the concert hall to create musical metaphors: variations on a theme, fugues in two and three voices, nature as the counterpoint of spirit.

The 'fit' that combines the many details into a single picture is aesthetic. Often the reader is confounded by Harris's sudden shifts. But these leaps are the results of intuitions that leave more plodding thinkers grasping and struggling to find a connection. The unitary vision of art, not religion, is the immediate precursor of philosophy. Harris has learned from Hume to base his interpretation of Hegel on custom, imagination, and sentiment.

At the same time he has transformed Hume's perspective. Custom is not simply the order of established social practice; it is the whole wealth of Western tradition, reaching back over the centuries to the arcadia of ancient Greece and the excitement of Renaissance Italy. Imagination is not simply an artificial construct of retained impressions; it is the integrative vision of the artist, the fit that sets details into a more comprehensive whole. Sentiment is not just a motive for human action; it is a sense of fulfilment, of feeling life as integrated, not only internally within the individual person, but also within the whole realm of social interaction.

Custom, imagination, and sentiment combine when things fit together. *Toward the Sunlight* is driven by the conviction that all the fragments from Hegel's early years, no matter how diverse, ultimately fit into a coherent development. Time and again in *Night Thoughts* Harris justifies his efforts to flesh out Hegel's abstractions by claiming that they 'fit' all the details. From Kant's *Critique of Judgment*, Harris has learned that understanding can go only so far. It needs to be completed by an intuitive sense of beauty, of how parts are integrated into wholes because there is an intrinsic sense or purpose. Kant's concession to teleology as a regulative principle not only becomes the inspiration for his Romantic and idealist successors. It represents as well the way Harris himself has transformed and enriched Hume's appeal to custom and sentiment.

Third, when Hume comes to ultimate questions about the nature of things – about God as the explanation of all that is – he finds experience and custom too limiting. He recognizes that the only tool we have is argument from analogy. Because such reasoning is fallible, it must be tested in dialogue. The *Dialogues Concerning Natural Religion* portray three friends debating in front of young Pamphilius. His education involves being a silent participant of the debate, which leaves him to make a choice among the options. Analogy, enriched and corrected in social discourse, provides the vehicle for exploring questions of natural religion.

Here as well Harris is a follower of Hume. He delights in drawing analogies between logic and nature, between nature and spirit. Analogies are the way not only of interpreting the difficult texts on his desk but of integrating the wide range of human experience into a comprehensive totality. In this way one can begin to have a sense of all that is, and why it is the way it is.

As well, for Harris 'the "life" of mind itself begins with the surrender of all claims to exercise moral authority.'[3] One needs to accept discipline, to learn how to subjugate one's own interests and unconscious drives, before one is free to enter into genuine converse with others. Where diversity is woven into the social fabric, each one contributes, but each one also listens. While human rationality is a communal consciousness, it does not require consensus or agreement. It respects and thrives on diversity and difference. And that difference is acknowledged in the moment of subjection.

Yet once again, Harris does not just take over Hume. It is Hume cancelled, while preserved. Harris has learned from Hegel and Gentile that philosophy is an intellectual dialogue not only with one's contemporaries but also with people from the past. They must be given a chance to speak for themselves in all their diversity; they must be treated with respect.

To be sure, this dialogue will be conditioned by the interests of the contemporary participant. This is why, like Hume, Harris is not interested in ontology and metaphysics. He wants to take seriously what is actually said; yet he endeavours to find an explanation that will fit into the fabric of our modern world.

As a result, this dialogue of mutual recognition not only challenges us by widening the horizons of the world we must explain, but it also provides the analogue that solves the explanatory puzzle. The pattern of human intercourse, the analogue of dialogue, integrates for Harris all reality into a single whole. For Harris's Hegel, the 'Absolute that knows its own knowing as the end and purpose of all being is just the universal brotherhood of man that comes to consciousness when we can, at last, make Philosophy speak the vulgar tongue.'[4] The transcendent God who is wholly other has died. God has become nothing other than the converse of friends, writ large.

Harris's practice embodies his theory when he approaches Hegel's texts. He subjects himself to an alien master. He listens carefully to every word, straining to catch unfamiliar nuances. He does not recreate the text in his own image. It is that discipline that grounds the rich insight of his interpretation. It has made him free to explore productive analogies.

At the same time he is delightfully collegial, almost always working with fellow scholars when translating: Walter Cerf, T.M. Knox, Peter Hodgson, George di Giovanni, Theo Geraets, to name only a few. He is inevitably to be found front and centre in any colloquium on Hegel, listening intently, and challenging interpretations. Even though he defends the validity of his own contribution to any debate, he encourages the independent judgment of others, whether graduate students developing their theses or young scholars seeking recognition. And he is prepared to change his mind, if convinced. The 'universal brotherhood of man' is not simply an ideal. It is the very nature of Harris's scholarly endeavours. He himself creates the analogue that reveals the nature of the Absolute. Like Hume he is a civil man.

Like Hegel, however, he places his own finitude and his own incompleteness into a larger totality. When he recognizes his own partiality he acknowledges that the universe is an integration of particulars, a concourse of interacting parts in a total community. The education derived from submitting to an alien master teaches that one's limitations are part of a more comprehensive totality. Once again Hume is transformed.

Thus Harris's work involves an ongoing dialogue between Hume and Hegel. He has endeavoured, more than anyone else, to make Hegel speak English and has become the focus of a new 'school' of English-language interpreters. In doing so he has risen above the level of commentary. He has developed a philosophy in his own right.

It is tempting to think that originality is to be found only in creative systems, in which a mind sits down to construct a novel theory. For some, Hegel is such an originator. But Harris has shown that, in all of his work, Hegel has been commenting on his predecessors – on the religions of the past, on the constitutions of his native Germany, on the discoveries of Newton and Kepler, on the insights of Kant and Schelling. It is as a commentator that Hegel has established his originality. It took a long time, with many failed attempts in applying the proposals of others, before the *Phenomenology of Spirit* finally saw the light of day. Hegel was not writing a new philosophy. He was simply articulating and extending the one philosophy that has developed over the centuries.

This, too, is what Harris has done. To be sure, his writings have explicitly been commentaries. They attempt to make the details of diverse texts fit together in an intuitively satisfactory way. He writes no metaphysics, no social theory. Nevertheless, he has thereby made an original contribution to philosophy. Reason and sentiment are to be integrated in a comprehensive social order. The metaphysical quest for ultimates must surrender to the dialogues and disagreements of community. The idealistic quest to comprehend all that is must be rooted in human experience. By bringing the empiricism of Hume to the philosophy of Hegel, Henry Harris has transformed the yearning for sunlight and the dark thoughts of the night into a manifestation of human society – into a phenomenology of spirit.

The essays in this volume all reflect Harris's influence. The tradition of Hegel interpretation, exemplified here, will continue to develop and expand with the publication of *Hegel's Ladder*, Harris's monumental commentary on the *Phenomenology of Spirit* itself.

Notes

1 D. Hume, *Enquiry Concerning Human Understanding* ii, in D. Hume, *The Philosophical Works*, ed. T.H. Green and T.H. Grose (London, 1882), IV, 17.

2 See 'The Tübingen Essay of 1793' in *Hegel's Development I: Toward the Sunlight (1770–1801)* (Oxford: Clarendon Press, 1972), 499.
3 *Toward the Sunlight*, 449.
4 *Hegel's Development II: Night Thoughts (Jena 1801–1806)* (Oxford: Clarendon Press, 1983), 411. Harris was writing before people became sensitive to gender-specific language.

HEGEL AND THE TRADITION:
ESSAYS IN HONOUR OF H.S. HARRIS

Introduction:
Hegel and Tradition

JOHN RUSSON

One of the ideas with which we are most comfortable in our everyday life is the idea that we are self-enclosed, independent beings. We strongly defend our claim to being self-possessed, insisting that 'it's my view, and I have a right to it,' or 'that's mine,' or 'I'll do what I like.' In each case, we identify ourselves as the 'I' who is in charge of its own affairs, which means an 'I' with a unique point of view, with a unique body, and with a unique will to initiate actions. On this view, it is up to each one of us to determine who we are and what we shall do. If this is what we are really like, then tradition has little intrinsic value: if we are in full self-possession, then traditions do not bind us or direct us or generate us, but are at most amusing objects of observation.

This, indeed, is a very traditional view of human identity. In the West, it has its most famous exponents in the Stoics of the Hellenistic world. The Stoics insist on the fundamental distinction between that which each of us finds to be in her power and that which is outside, which means drawing a fundamental boundary between 'me' and 'it,' between self and other, between subject and object. The self is here construed as an independent centre of decision-making that confronts an alien world on which it passes judgment. The other, that on which it passes judgment and acts, thus does not enter into the identity of the self – this other is something the subject *has* but is not what it *is*. When our world is understood in this fashion, relationships within the world are understood in terms of rights and in terms of property – that is, in terms of what attaches intrinsically to the condition of being a choosing self, and what attaches to the condition of being an other to that self; hence the reflection of the Stoic ideal of the Hellenistic world in the Roman law of legal persons and property rights.

Hegel's philosophical investigation of human existence concludes in a way that is in general opposed to this Stoic view of the human self. Hegel argues instead that our identities are essentially dependent on what is 'outside' our immediate selves; in particular, our identities are formed by the way we use powers that we inherit from our traditions to take up the materials handed us by those same traditions. Chapter 1 of this volume, Patricia Fagan's 'Philosophical History and the Roman Empire,' studies Hegel's analysis of the institutions of Roman society precisely in order to show how the Stoic conception of the human self that animates these legal institutions ultimately produces only a human world dominated by violence and precisely by a disrespect for rights and property. In the tradition of H.S. Harris, who has devoted a good part of the last thirty years to demonstrating the viability of Hegel as an interpreter of human history, Fagan claims that only Hegel's philosophical principles give us the grounds for an adequate historical method, for his is the method that allows us to see how the eventual outcome of the Roman Empire had its seeds in the ideals instituted at its inception. She argues that Hegel's analysis does indeed do justice to Roman history, and she demonstrates this for the decisive period from 63 BC to AD 68/9. Her paper shows both how Hegel understands the dialectical contradictions of this Stoic approach to institutional life and how Hegel's analysis is itself an attempt to make sense of his own historical tradition – that is, his attempt to understand the Roman world, which laid the foundations for his own world.

If Hegel is sensitive to his tradition of political history, he is equally sensitive to the philosophical tradition within which he aims to be a contributor. Taking its cue from Harris's 'The Social Ideal of Hegel's Economic Theory,' Jay Lampert's contribution, 'Locke, Fichte, and Hegel on the Right to Property' (chapter 2), studies the dialectic of philosophical argumentation about the nature of persons and property, especially as it is worked out in the modern period. Just as Fagan shows the historically demonstrated contradictions of the institutionally sanctioned conception of the self as a property-bearing and rights-bearing ego, Lampert reveals those contradictions as they are articulated in explicit philosophical discourse. In particular, Lampert argues that the very project of drawing boundaries and setting limits (to self and other, to my property and your property, to 'us' and 'them') already involves overstepping those boundaries, such that the self is always already implicated in what it aims to alienate from itself. Lampert's study of the philosophical underpinnings of the institution of property ends with an explicit discussion of how the subject, as understood by Hegel, is always defined within and through a tradition, which it is always in an act of appropriating and redefining: we exist as a dialogue with our traditions.

With this recognition of the primacy of dialogue, we pass out of the study of the institutions that organize political life (what Hegel calls 'philosophy of right' or 'philosophy of objective spirit') and into the sphere of 'absolute spirit,' for we have moved into the study of communication, which means the philosophy of art and language. If it is primarily through our dialogue with our traditions that our identity is forged, then the limits of how we can express ourselves will mark the limits of who we can be. As John McCumber writes in 'Hegel and Hamann: Ideas and Life' (chapter 3), 'I am, in Hegel's view, what I can say.' McCumber shows Hegel to be the true heir to the concern for language in the work of his predecessor Johann Georg Hamann, for Hegel recognizes the essential role of language, which means the essential role of recognition by others, in our achievement of self-identity. This achievement, like language itself, is always inherently public, again undermining the Stoic conception of the primacy of privacy: language is a shared way of treating the sensible features of experience as expressive, so that, in so far as our self-identity is inherently mediated by language, it is equally inherently intersubjective. But this means that the very language that allows us to engage with our tradition itself belongs to a human tradition that exceeds the singular self who 'uses' it.

We thus find ourselves to be really representatives for, or agents of, our historical, artistic traditions – that is, our traditional institutions of expression. Thus to find out who we are is really to discover which artistic traditions are, by shaping our potentiality for expression, speaking through us. This concern with finding out who we are by determining which artistic traditions we are involved in is what lies behind Michael Baur's 'Winckelmann and Hegel on the Imitation of the Greeks' (chapter 4).

It is the notion that our identity is already shaped by our tradition and that when we speak and act we automatically speak and act as representatives of our traditions – whether or not we so intend – that Baur argues is the key to understanding Hegel's conception of tradition. Following a tradition cannot be 'a matter of following any model which is already given and essentially other than ourselves,' for if this tradition is alien we will always be distorting it through our appropriation of it, for we would only ever be following our own interpretation of that other. Indeed, if traditions are alien to us – as the Stoic model would suggest – we must be absolute sceptics about historical interpretation, for all we will ever find, when we look to the past, is ourselves. If, however, we already are representatives of that very tradition, then, 'in following ourselves, we are really only following the ... legacy which is already alive in us.' This principle, which Baur works out in relation to Hegel's transformation of his predecessor Johann Joachim Winckelmann's project of recognizing our Greek heritage, is crucial to modern debates about ethnocentricity, about historical relativism, and about literary interpretation, for it shows that we cannot avoid engaging in cultural appropriation or interpretation, so that any ideal of unbiasedness is incoherent. We are embedded in traditions that form the substance of our identities, provide us with our methods of approach to our existence, and also automatically form the substance of the objects of our study.

But making our artistic traditions our substance, our method, and our object appears to make art the absolute. Martin Donougho, in 'Hegel as Philosopher of the Temporal [*irdischen*] World: On the Dialectics of Narrative' (chapter 5), takes up this issue of the ultimacy of art by focusing on the notion of allegory. Donougho approaches this matter both by way of a study of Hegel's grappling with Dante (a central figure in Harris's own research) and through an examination of other modern approaches to literary interpretation, which also pivot on studies of Dante and allegory. Donougho concentrates on Dante's 'figural realism,' in which form and content are mutually implicating and in which the elevated message communicated through the image 'never *abolishes* the image ... but preserves the real *sub specie aeternitatis*.' In other words, Dante's literary form is itself meaningful, and the thought that this form essentially embodies is dialectic itself. Dante's narrative form is simultaneously the Christian form par excellence – for the divine is united with the *irdisch*, the flux of human, temporal existence – and the form proper to Hegelian dialectics. 'For Hegel,' Donougho argues, 'the secular is the allegorical,' and it is the allegory of the very 'allegorizing activity of subjectivity, the *I* that can never say what it means yet in failing succeeds all the same in saying ... a great deal to us observers.' At the same time, Donougho inquires about our criteria for the interpretation of this artistry that is the foundation of our very selves. Donougho raises the issue of the 'we,' of the community of subjects who interpret themselves, and with this we are led out of the sphere of art proper and into the second sphere of absolute spirit, religion.

Religion, like art, is a sphere in which humans express themselves, but it is one in which the community doing the expressing claims that its expressions are the unique and absolute truth and does not recognize these expressions as 'art' or as allegory. Now according to Hegel's philosophy, the absolute truth is that the nature of our existence is to be engaged in a process of coming to understand itself, and we self-conscious beings are the agents of this program. This, Hegel argues, is what religion, too, claims; but if religion is unlike art, it is equally unlike philosophy, and this latter unlikeness is precisely that religion does not realize that it is making the same claim as Hegel.

Religion is the activity in which the human community announces to itself its own identity as a community coming to be self-conscious as the traditional, religious community that it is – which is to say, it announces its own activity as the ultimate form of meaningfulness. In this way it operates implicitly according to the insight worked out in Baur's 'Winckelmann and Hegel on the Imitation of the Greeks.' In thus identifying its own activity of coming to self-consciousness as the absolute truth, it likewise presents its own self-identity as the basis of any criterion of truth in interpretation, thereby implicitly answering the question raised in Donougho's 'Hegel as Philosopher of the Temporal World.' But religion does not recognize that this is the activity in which it is engaged, and when it refers to the absolute truth of stories about the divine realm, it does not realize that the divine realm it describes is the realm of its own activity. Religion, as the coming to self-consciousness of the human community, is the communal activity of saying 'we' and saying that 'we are the truth,' but inasmuch as it does not achieve the philosophical realization that it is this activity of self-consciousness, it precisely treats the divine as alien to itself and thus treats what is truly an identity of the human and the divine as a separation of the human and the divine.

It is this matter of the identity of the human and the divine that Jeff Mitscherling concentrates on in 'The Identity of the Human and the Divine in the Logic of Speculative Philosophy' (chapter 6). Christianity has as its central image the identity of the human and the divine in the figure of Christ, but, Mitscherling argues, the tradition of Christian thinkers up to Hegel's time is unable to comprehend the force of this image and uses it to mark the separation of the godhead from individual humans. Hegel, on the contrary, fulfils this tradition by transforming it in the very recognition that it is humanity itself that embodies divinity. Mitscherling contends that Hegel's thinking here operates in the tradition of mystical thinkers from the Alexandrian Neoplatonists through Meister Eckhart to Jacob Böhme, but that none of these thinkers pursues the dialectical identity of the human and divine sufficiently far, for they lack Hegel's dialectical logic. Through his logic of contradiction and reconciliation, Hegel is able to comprehend what the Christian tradition before him had sought, but in thus completing the Christian project Hegel equally radically transforms it, for the very separation of God and humanity is lost. Thus Hegel's Christianity, Mitscherling's text suggests, is as much heretical as it is orthodox. This question of the extent to which Hegel's philosophy is essentially wedded to orthodox Christianity, and the relation of such a marriage to his dialectical logic, are the subject of the debate contained in the next two contributions, from David Kolb and John W. Burbidge.

David Kolb, in 'The Final Name of God' (chapter 7), argues that Hegel's dialectical method of analysis always needs some standard by which to evaluate whatever subject matter it faces and that it is this criterion that the *Science of Logic* provides. The *Logic*, he argues, purports to present systematically all the possible ways for conceptualizing anything whatever and concludes by presenting the very dialectical unity of these various concepts as the ultimate standpoint. The ultimate standpoint then is the one that sees in any subject matter a development from less to more sophistication, in which a conclusion is reached precisely at the point at which that which is developing itself recognizes the necessity and ultimacy of the dialectical unity that animates it. Hegel's method thus always involves recognizing a final stage in whatever it studies.

Kolb argues that this is how Hegel understands Christianity – namely, as the final form of religion; consequently, all other forms of religious life are forced into subordinate positions in a developmental history that leads up to this completion in Christianity. But this subordination, Kolb argues, cannot do justice to non-Christian religious traditions. Hegel's whole project is to analyse anything only according to its own standards and to see its activity as self-determination, but his history of religions amounts to forcing non-Christian faiths to measure up to an alien standard by not allowing the possibility that there might be more than one adequate form of religious life (as, for example, there can be more than one language in which human thought is articulated).

John W. Burbidge, on the contrary, in chapter 8, 'Hegel's Open Future,' argues that the inescapability of Hegel's *Logic* – its very closure – is exactly what makes it possible for there to be anything like novelty, anything like a future. Burbidge shows how it is that the very necessity of comparison, which allows one to recognize that something is novel, or different, demands that one have a point of reference that maintains a constancy, or a sameness, between the new and the old. This need for the new to define itself in terms of the fixity of the old – the need for the novel to be traditional – is the key to the necessity of the eternality of the standpoint of Hegel's *Logic*, in the sense that it guarantees that our future cannot be novel in the sense of incomprehensible to us. But it is equally the key to the feature that defines the ultimacy of 'the absolute religion' – namely, the logic of incarnation.

Like the godhead itself, Hegel's *Logic* must open itself up to the test of actuality and allow itself to be interpreted and redefined by the same material it makes intelligible, and it is this commitment to actuality that is simultaneously why it is 'open' to a future and why it must insist on the ultimacy of a religion that posits the historically individuated identification of the divine and the human. The historical unitying of divine and human, however, is not the distinctive doctrine of Christiantiy alone, Burbidge argues. This doctrine, he maintains, equally characterizes Islam, Judaism, Hinduism, and Buddhism and such 'secular' ideologies as Marxism and liberalism.

Essentially, this doctrine amounts to a commitment to the view that abstract doctrines (of religion or logic) rest on their unambiguous realization in temporal, experienceable events – which is to say, that the actual reveals the truth of what is possible. Harris has maintained that it is necessary for the absolute religion to realize itself in a multiplicity of religions, and Burbidge's account of the nature of closure in Hegel's logical system offers a justification for this. On Burbidge's account, the inescapability of Hegel's *Logic*, the ultimacy of the religion that is committed to the historical realization of its truth in singular events, and the

Introduction: Hegel and Tradition 9

commitment to the plurality of adequate religious forms – present, past and future – are logically inseparable. Absolute truth thus does rest on our participation in a 'we' that practices 'the absolute religion,' but this religion need not be orthodox Christianity.

But if Hegel's philosophy of religion tries to do justice to the variety of religious traditions by some form of impartiality, then one might challenge Hegel with the claim that it does justice to none, since religions demand partiality. Hegel's claim is that philosophy is the highest court of appeal, but since he also argues that philosophy can be vindicated only if that over which it passes judgment concedes to philosophy its primacy, one might thus contend that he ends up failing to do justice to religion, for no religion will concede that it is really replaceable by others and that all really find their truth in philosophy. Nicholas Walker, in 'Hegel's Encounter with the Christian Tradition, or How Theological Are Hegel's Early Theological Writings?' (chapter 9), considers whether Hegel's philosophical investigations are themselves religious labours, and he does so by considering the young Hegel's relation to the Christian religion as exemplified in his writings in Frankfurt. In the tradition of Harris's own research into the stages of Hegel's philosophical development, Walker shows that Hegel was not always Hegel (to speak in the language of Donougho's 'Hegel as Philosopher of the Temporal World') but that his own identity emerged through the dialectically evolving tradition that was his own process of education and development. Walker makes the essential point that 'for Hegel the self-articulating movement of philosophy is always already to be grasped as an intrinsic and necessary moment of religious life itself' – that is, Hegel is committed to showing that philosophy is not an alien judge evaluating religions but is that into which the religious life naturally grows, so that philosophy of religion is the very culmination of religion. Walker demonstrates how that process of religious commitment turning itself into Hegelian philosophy of religion is documented in Hegel's own process of coming to be himself. Hegel would thus be the livinig demonstration of the religious tradition's acknowledging that dialectical phenomenology is its fulfilment.

Our consideration of absolute spirit has taken us from art to religion, and we now see that the truth of religion is that it must complete itself as self-reflective philosophy. George di Giovanni's ' "Wie aus der Pistole": Fries and Hegel on Faith and Knowledge' (chapter 10) studies the necessity for this transition within absolute spirit in terms of the epistemology of faith and reason. He shows that Hegel, like his contemporary Fries, argues (against Enlightenment claims for the ultimacy of abstract reason) that all our experience is grounded in a kind of immediacy – a kind of faith – of which subsequent experience is the clarification. In this way, Hegel is typical of an eighteenth-century German tradition (which includes Hamann, as studied by McCumber) that defends immediacy against reflection.

Di Giovanni shows that unlike Fries, however, Hegel argues that ' "immediacy" and "reflection" are relative terms: there is nothing in actual experience that counts as immediate in one context that cannot also be taken as a result of reflection in another, and we separate the two through abstraction only at the risk of never being able to bring them back together.' In other words, the immediacy of our experience is already interptive and is never an innocent access to an alien reality, while, equally, our reflective life is never simply in our control but is always something that we find ourselves to be engaged in. Consequently we must acknowledge that while the real motive force in our life exceeds our immediate grasp, it is only through our attempts at taking up our experience that it comes to be meaningful to us. Thus there is an ultimacy to the religious insistence on the necessity for faith, but this faith must not define itself in opposition to reason. On the contrary, 'faith is a reflective activity from the beginning. It is essentially a faith seeking knowledge of itself ... It is none other than reason itself.' Whether we speak of the necessity that religious faith transform itself into dialectical phenomenology or of the necessity that the immediacy of our perceptual experience resolve itself into an understanding, the basic relations are the same – our experience is defined by the drive to know itself, and it fulfils its own identity only in achieving this self-comprehension.

Absolute knowing thus is not some alien state achieved by means extraneous to our actual experience but is the living fulfilment of our immediate life. Just as it is essential that our experience complete itself in reflectively self-comprehending absolute knowing, so this absolute, which is 'with us from the start,' as Hegel says, must begin as not fulfilled, in a state of ignorance of itself. In other words, the fact that philosophy is the absolute requires that we begin in a religious faith that fails to comprehend itself. So the faith of which it is claimed that it is inadequately represented by philosophy is really a faith that cannot speak for itself – nor can its defenders legitimately claim to speak on its behalf – since it, in being mute (since philosophy is its reflective voice), is not accessible even to the faithful. Again (as we learned in McCumber's contribution on Hegel and Hamann), we are only what we can say – that is, our own faith is to us only what we can express of it to ourselves, and dialectical phenomenology is the rigorous form of this activity of faithful self-expression.

We began with our everyday sense of ourselves as isolated egos, and we moved to seeing how this self is really not the whole truth of our identity. On the contrary, we found that self-identity had to be located in social relationships of mutual recognition through dialogue. We then discovered that these social identities are themselves grounded in art, in the systems of expression that set the parameters within which we can engage with our social traditions. We found that this art implicitly provides the substance, objects, and resources of our lives – which is to say, it seems to be the absolute. Indeed, art is the absolute, but because it is this only tacitly – because it conceals its own primacy from our view and leads us instead to posit ourselves as independent Stoic selves – art is the absolute as not yet self-conscious. Art is the activity of laying itself out as the absolute, but it does not notice itself as so doing. It is religion that recognizes itself as explicitly positing the absolute, but we have seen that what religion fails to notice is that its own act of positing is this absolute that it posits. Art then is the immediate identity of the absolute with itself, whereas religion is the absolute that posits itself but does not recognize itself as so doing. It is philosophy that recognizes its own act of positing the absolute as being the absolute that it posits.

In our attempt to overcome the Stoic notion of selfhood, we initially saw our rootedness in institutional, social traditions – in 'objective spirit,' in Hegel's language – and this led us in turn to posit the groundedness of objective spirit in absolute spirit. We then pursued the dialectic within absolute spirit itself, and this dialectic has directed us finally to philosophy itself as the activity in which the absolute becomes explicitly self-conscious. As this self-consciousness of the absolute, philosophy must thus look at how it has posited the absolute and see the study of its own historical activity, its own tradition, as its real object.

It is this notion that the Hegelian philosophy is itself the activity of philosophy coming to comprehend its own history as the self-enactment of the self-consciousness of the absolute that Susan Hoffmann addresses in chapter 11, 'Der Unterschied zwischen "Differenz" und "Unterschied": A Re-evaluation of Hegel's *Differenzschrift*.' In his *Differenzschrift*, Hegel studies the philosophical positions of Fichte, Schelling, and Reinhold. The key to this work, Hoffmann argues, is that on Hegel's account the positions are all different developmental stages of one and the same philosophical position. They are not simply positions that are alien to one another and competing for some prize; on the contrary, they stand in relation to each other as anticipation and fulfilment, and the extent to which they are opposed is the extent to which they one-sidedly portray themselves as complete in independence of each other.

The mutual embeddedness of the philosophical traditions is crucial to Hegel's portrayal of philosophy as a human enterprise. According to Hegel, philosophy exists as a tradition in dialogue with itself, where later systems of thought exist only by virtue of the ground opened up by earlier systems and where the animating drive behind the earlier systems is still finding expression in the later. This method of studying the history of one's own philosophical tradition so as to see it as developing to a position of self-consciousness with respect to itself is the distinctive insight that Hegel offers, and with which he closes the history of philosophy. It is this method that can tolerate difference, for it can comprehend difference within the unity of its own act of historical self-comprehension.

Just as Hoffmann studies the demands of comprehending difference, and shows how Hegel's method works to integrate differences into the unity of a self-developing story of a tradition that brings itself to self-consciousness, so James Crooks, in 'Dialectic as Counterpoint: On Philosophical Self-Measure in Plato and Hegel' (chapter 12), studies various strategies for orchestrating the relations of unity and difference, focusing on how Hegel's method, as exemplified in the opening arguments of the *Science of Logic*, comprehends differences dialectically by integrating them into a system. Crooks uses this analysis of the systematic whole that exists only as an integration of self-opposed differences to show that the nature of any subject must be to be self-alienated, and he poses the question of whether this alienation can ultimately be overcome. Like Kolb in 'The Final Name of God,' Crooks considers whether the multiplicity comprehended in the system actually exceeds the systematic comprehension and, if so, whether the unity achieved in the systematization is less unified than it must appear to itself to be. In particular, he considers whether the deed of reflection might necessarily exceed the grasp of that reflection. Must not the dialectic always be open to its own overturning by the very supra-theoretical deed of theorizing that always precedes and exceeds philosophy's grasp?

Responding to this issue raised by Crooks of whether the system can be exceeded, John Russon, in 'Hegel's "Freedom of Self-Consciousness" and Early Modern Epistemology' (chapter 13), argues in a way analogous to Burbidge's response to Kolb, that the system must indeed assume a radically open structure but that this openness is already a determination of meaningfulness – anything even posited as exceeding the system is already conceptualized in terms of the system and thus is already committed to answering to the terms of the system. This is the case even if (as Lampert proposes at the end of 'Locke, Fichte, and Hegel on the Right to Property'), this answering to the system transforms the sense of the system. Returning to the theme of stoicism with which Fagan's study of Rome begins, Russon argues that the sceptic who posits an inherently uncomprehended outside to the system is the logical twin of the Stoic who posits the self as alienated from its own traditions. As Fagan shows in her discussion of philosophical history, and as Baur argues in 'Winckelmann and Hegel on the Imitation of the Greeks,' we are already implicated in what we posit as other, and so our challenge is not to find access somehow to some alien being, but rather to recognize the otherness *within ourselves*. This recognition of otherness within ourselves, Russon argues, is the structure of self-comprehension that characterizes 'Unhappy Consciousness.' Any determinateness, in order to be determinate at all, must situate itself in relation to the tradition that defines the subjectivity for which it is such; even if the novel determinateness transforms the sense of the tradition, it can still be thus novel and transformative only by defining itself in terms of the tradition that it transforms. At the level of the system, this means, as Burbidge says, that it is open to the future, but the future will not be incomprehensible. At the level of the epistemology of single subjects, as Harris maintains, we must ultimately be empiricists, always finding ourselves waiting on experience to allow us to make sense of it, but also always appearing as having been anticipated. The nature of meaningfulness is to define itself always in retrospect as a fulfilment.

Thus the nature of meaningfulness is to show itself as the culmination of a tradition. We thus understand ourselves only when we see ourselves as acting as representatives of a tradition and of having the responsibility to fulfil its expectations. This is perhaps the central doctrine of Hegel's philosophy, and it has been the focus of the teaching of H.S. Harris, which forms the tradition of Hegel interpretation that has informed the research contained in the contributions to this volume.

Harris has devoted himself to situating Hegel's philosophical insights within the context of the history that provided Hegel's tradition, and he has done this to allow us to situate Hegel's teaching into the context of our own tradition. In keeping with this spirit of Harris's work, we have tried throughout this volume to make the notion of tradition an explicit theme and to study Hegel in relation to the various traditions to which he could be said to belong, in order to show how Hegel can be meaningful to us. We are not nineteenth-century German intellectuals, and the political, artistic, religious, and philosophical traditions that form the substance of our life demand of us that we speak in their terms if we are to say anything meaningful. But just as Burbidge argues that Hegel's philosophy speaks as well to Buddhists and Marxists as it does to Christians, Harris has posited that Hegel's philosophical science is universal and can speak our language as well as it could speak that of Hegel's own culture. This volume marks a continuing effort to operate within the tradition of H.S. Harris and to continue the translation of Hegel into the language of our culture.

We have left it to H.S. Harris himself to appraise our work in his 'Afterword' to this volume: 'Theme and Variations: The Round of Life and the Chorale of Thought.'

PART ONE:
PHILOSOPHY OF RIGHT

1

Philosophical History and the Roman Empire

PATRICIA FAGAN

In *The Phenomenology of Spirit*, Hegel traces the development of consciousness from sense-certainty to absolute knowing. In his account, consciousness, in its self-transformations and development, repeats the same kinds of logical moves in each of the states it attains. So, as consciousness moves through Self-consciousness, it sets up relations with other self-consciousnesses and its environment, which it repeats in the social world of Spirit. The world of Spirit is the world in which Self-consciousness is actualized because it is there that Self-consciousness can realize itself through relations with more universal institutions and groups. For Hegel, world history itself works out the development of Spirit as it works itself out in the *Phenomenology*. The task of philosophical history is to show how this development has taken place. So, for Hegel's project to succeed, his account of the development of history in Spirit would have to be true. In what follows, I defend Hegel's account of history by showing that, in interpreting the historical sources for the early Roman Empire, we, as historians as well as philosophers, should reach the same conclusions that Hegel does.

My arguments fall into three parts. First, I discuss how we, as philosophical historians, must approach world history already having an education in dialectics that will allow us to understand how the world develops itself dialectically. Second, I lay out the logic of the transition in Spirit from ethical substance, which generally represents the world of ancient Greece, to legal status, which represents Rome, so that we have this logic ready to hand when we turn to the third section of the paper. Third, I examine in general terms the political structures of the Roman Empire, as set up by the first emperor, Augustus, and how the logic of these structures, designed to ensure the emperor's absolute control over all the workings of his empire, led necessarily to a situation in which the emperor's own armies became the actual source of control over the emperor himself when they assassinated Gaius in AD 41 and themselves chose his successor, Claudius. I conclude briefly by turning back to the *Phenomenology* to examine how the world of Rome – legal status – breaks down and becomes medieval Christian Europe – culture.

I

History is a *pros hen* equivocal, and philosophical history is its paradigmatic instance because it is the history that does the job of history most completely. The job of history is to tell the story that one's evidence compels one to tell, while still recognizing that the *historian* is the one who brings in the categories of analysis and selects the evidence. That is, history in the fullest sense must see its object both as itself and as external to itself – my evidence is me to the extent that I tell the story it allows me to tell (it tells its own story through me), and it is external to me in so far as I can reflect on it and interpret it and bring my thought to bear on it. That is, the object of my study is me, is internal, because it is necessary that *I*, as a historian, already know what I am looking for when I come to my object. My object is external to me in that interpreting it requires not that I make up its story as I go along but that I rely on, examine, evidence.

Simple history (what Hegel calls 'reflective history' in *Lectures on the Philosophy of History*) tends to be too one-sided. It sees only that its object is outside it and insists that it can decide what it wants to study and how. Simple history does not comprehend well enough how its evidence, its object, is itself insistent, has its own logic, and makes demands on the historian. Instead, simple history satisfies itself by 'laying out' events and then trying to explain them by attributing their moving force to particular persons or groups of people that it has chosen in advance. So we see historians of Hellenistic Greece discussing Alexander the Great of Macedonia as the single mover behind the great social and political changes in the Mediterranean of the fourth century BC and trying to understand how Alexander's personality and psychology drove him personally to attempt to create a world empire.

The philosophical historian, in contrast, approaches this same period and area by looking at the larger cultural and social institutions that created Alexander and through which he moved. The philosophical historian comes to her material already working with the presupposition that her object is understood fully only through the understanding of what that object itself puts forth as being essential to it at a foundational level: its founding institutions. The philosophical historian knows that world history is a history not of individual persons but of the more universal bodies and institutions through which individual people move and live. For her, the truth of these individuals is expressed most perfectly in the things to which they commit themselves, which give them a place to grow and transform themselves, and in and through which they interact with other individuals, groups, and institutions.

All this is not to say that the philosophical historian is merely a social historian with an elevated title. Social historians, too, can produce historical interpretations that refuse to allow their objects their own logic and life. The distinguishing mark of the philosophical historian is that when she looks at the world rationally it looks rationally back. Philosophical history regards its object as, first and foremost, rational; it sees its rational object working *itself* out according to the same demands, facing the same problems, as all rational beings. The philosophical historian sees her object as being engaged in a project of *self*-development and *self*-transformation.

The task of philosophical history is thus to discover and explain how world history works itself out in its own terms, how it sets up and resolves its own problems. The philosophical historian recognizes that all rational development is driven by a self-moving dialectic and sees her task as being to expose the dialectical workings of world history as they appear at particular times and places.[1] Philosophical history is history in the fullest sense because it recognizes that its object is, like itself, rational, partaking in the same reason that drives philosophical history, and that it is the job of history to come to its object, interpret it, and make that shared rationality explicit for all to see. In the *Phenomenology*, Hegel can write his philosophical history of Greece and Rome in chapter 6 only because he has already studied the forms of rational self-consciousness in chapter 4 – the master-slave relation, stoicism, and scepticism. In 'Spirit' Hegel shows how the rationality of the individual and the rationality of human societies and cultures are the same.

II

Legal status is that form of Spirit which arises in the ethical realm out of the collapse of ethical substance. Ethical substance is the community in which the individual member finds her own value entirely as a member of the community. The individual is defined entirely by her position within the community and by the traditions and customs of her ancestors. She exists solely *as* a member of that community; she is one with her community. The individual within this community acts always in accordance with its laws and traditions but does so purely from habit (*ethos*). The bond between individual and community is such that the individual member need not refer ever to a code of law, or ponder her own action; simply by acting, she acts as a member of her community, following its laws. The member of the ethical community can ever act only according to the *ethos* of her community, because she is and acts solely as part of that community.

The laws of the ethical community are divided into two kinds: divine and human. Divine law is that which ensures recognition and protection of the individual member in death, as an ancestor. Human law is concerned with the social and political functioning of the community. It exists solely to protect and further the interests of the community. It emerges from the decree of the will of members of the community; divine law, from what the members of ethical substance see as an ethical, universal, unwritten code enforced by the gods. Both sets of laws, however, are fulfilled only through the actions of individuals. The community is the product created by the actions of the individuals and their adherence to the two groups of laws.

These two sets of laws and the dependence of the community on the individual members are the causes of the downfall of ethical substance. This collapse is similar to the downfall of the master-slave relationship in Hegel's discussion of Self-consciousness in chapter 4.[2] Ethical substance falls when two individuals, each professing to follow a different set of laws, meet in conflict. The community, like the master consciousness, is held to be independent from the servile consciousness of its members. The members of the ethical community here believe themselves utterly dependent on the self-sufficient community for existence and meaning. In fact, however, the community is equally dependent on its individual members for its meaning and existence; it is not independent. The community cannot exist without members to inhabit and enact it; it is a living organism, dependent on all its members to maintain its vitality. 'The community is for *itself* by other individualities being *for it*.'[3]

When two individuals, claiming to be serving the community's interests, clash in their support of the two different laws, they destroy each other. The community likewise is destroyed because it cannot exist without these individuals to protect its laws and perform the labours necessary to support its existence. Destroyed individuals cannot act, and it is such action on which the community, in ethical substance or elsewhere, depends.

The problem with the master–slave relationship is that both parties hold the master's consciousness to be the real and determining consciousness – the self-consciousness – and the slave's to be contingent and determined, when, in the actual working out of the relationship, it is the slave who constitutes the truth of their consciousness. The slave is the only one who *acts* in any way. The master orders, and the slave performs; the slave shapes the world according to her own interpretation of the master's orders. The master has no power to act or interpret but can only receive what the slave gives him. Thus the master's own meaning depends on the actions of another. Likewise, in ethical substance, the members of the community treat their community as independent of themselves for its existence and determinative of their own meaning, believing that the community will survive even though they are destroyed themselves. None the less the community is destroyed, because its meaning and existence depend on the actions of its members; when these constituting members die, the community expires along with them.

Hegel's ethical substance corresponds generally to ancient Greece before the Peloponnesian War or perhaps before the rise of Alexander the Great: a land of individual and autonomous city-states, the *poleis*. The downfall of ethical substance *as a world* comes when one of these *poleis* 'kills' the others by subduing them and imposing its own laws on them (*PdG* M289.14–18N; see note 3, above, re abbreviations). Each *polis* has its own set of laws, which developed naturally out of the practices – the acts – of its members. In Greece law arises naturally from practice; there is no essential difference between the two. *Nomos* means both 'law' and 'custom'; law in Greece is that which is sanctioned by long and relatively unreflective practice. It is part of the nature of the community because it is the acts of the individual members of that community, the citizens, that constitute law; law grows up along with the community. Members of an ethical community cannot transgress their laws or actions because their actions *are* the laws. Greek *nomos* is a natural and growing part of the life of the *polis*; it is not, like Roman *lex*, something artificially laid down for or fixed on (which is the essential meaning of *lex*) the members of the community.

However, with the supremacy of one *polis* over all the others, this natural relationship between the *polis* and its *nomoi* disintegrates (289.–4 – .–1). The law of the supreme *polis* is now laid down for the others; it is not a natural part of the other *poleis* through having grown up with them but becomes *lex*, laid down, and fixed *for* them. For the individual members of the *poleis*, law is no longer a natural part of their action. They can no longer act habitually in accordance with their laws. They can no longer find their meaning in their *polis* and its laws. The *polis* itself dies because it no longer forms the ground for the lives of its individual members through its laws.

With the death of the *poleis*, the individual citizens lose their substance (289.–5 – .–4); they no longer find their own content, meaning, and value in their law-full relationship towards their *polis*, because both *polis* and law are dead to them. The citizens no longer share their ground with each other – the great history, the assurance of their lawful standing and function within the *polis*. Each citizen must now stand alone, apart from the others, because the immediate and habitual relationship of the *nomoi* is gone. The *polis*, as a *res publica*, must now be held together by a code of *leges*; the citizens are now separate atoms artificially held together by a legal structure (289.–2 – .1) in the new form of Spirit, legal status.

In his account of ethical substance, Hegel must give two accounts of the breakdown: one for the collapse within the ethical *community*, another for the disintegration of the *world* of ethical substance. This second account is necessary because the world of ethical substance is composed of many discrete ethical communities; ethical substance as a world cannot be destroyed until those communities themselves lose their autonomous natural character. Legal status is a world in which the individual community *is* the entire world; the Roman Empire was a *world* empire. Thus the breakdown of the community, the *res publica*, in legal status is the breakdown of the *world* of legal status.

Legal status is an advance for Spirit over ethical substance because, in it, two great changes take place: law becomes universal and political power becomes incorporated. In legal status individuals are all equal under one law. Individuals were equal in ethical substance as well in that all people were entitled to burial; the problem arose in ethical substance because there was no *one* set of laws and no *one* legal voice. Antigone and Creon destroyed each other and their *polis* because each chose to honour only one set of laws, even though this meant *dis*honouring the other law by not obeying it. Legal status has one universal law and one universal voice. The lord and master of the world is the one person in whom all laws and all decisions of law converge; his will becomes law. The Roman emperor is both man and god; human and divine law should meet in him. They do not, of course, because the emperor is only human after all, and his rule becomes simply the human decree of a Creon. None the less, because the emperor is an individual, law becomes self-conscious in him, which it was not in ethical substance. The emperor recognizes himself in others, and thus law, brought forward, now recognizes itself also. Law in ethical substance was *nomos*, immediate and unreflective; here law incorporated is law that is mediated and recognizes others, even if only to destroy them according to the arbitrary will of the emperor.

Legal status is what characterizes the form of Spirit that arises out of the failure of ethical substance. This downfall comes about from the clash between the proponents of divine law and human law, which destroys the individual ethical community, and from the conquering of all ethical communities by one community, which results in the end of ethical substance as a world determination. The individual members of the community in legal status no longer have immediate relations to their community and substance but are now empty legal persons (290.6 – .8). These legal persons, inasmuch as they deny their meaning as legal persons, correspond to the form of self-consciousness Hegel describes as stoicism (290.–7 – .–6).

Legal status also resembles the sceptical self-consciousness in that both are without content (291.–17 – .–16). The legal person finds her content in the world that lies before her by designating this world 'possession' (291.–10 – .–7).

For the legal person the world is only something to take and to own – an object external to the person. The individual person finds her content in the possessions she has as 'property' (291.–6 – .–5). Property in legal status is that which allows the person to see *herself* as an object and thereby to be self-conscious; the individual has for herself only the meaning of her property. The *personality* of the legal person is embodied in her property; property is what belongs *to her* and is what is proper to her. For the legal person, just as for the thing in chapter 2, property (here, possessions) is what distinguishes one person (or thing) from another and what constitutes her own identity as a person; her possessions are her characteristics.[4]

The legal person, however, despite her dependence on her property for her own meaning, wants to say that her property has *its* value because it belongs to *her* (291.–1 –292.3). What and how much her property is – the content of her property – do not matter to the legal person, because she insists that her worth as a person with rights comes to her simply by existing. The legal person's property and its content do not in fact matter to her because they really belong to another, apart from herself (292.7–.9); this other is the lord and master of the world (292.–17). The lord of the world is the real possessor of the property of the legal person because he is the will of the law and thereby passes judgment on all those things and persons that fall under the law. Because he is the one who determines what the content of all property is, he is the one to determine the value of the legal person. The legal person is only a thing with rights; possessing no content of its own, it is an empty formal unity and can be determined by the will of the lord of the world.

In the early days of the Roman Republic, to own land was to be the very best, most 'righted' kind of person; nobility at that time was the nobility of property. Slowly the unpropertied class, the *plebs*, emerged, and the nobility of political office began to take precedence over the nobility of the landed aristocracy. Finally, under the empire, a freed slave, once property himself, could have as much value and authority as a patrician of the oldest family, according to the whim of the emperor. Likewise, the emperor could, if he so chose, confiscate all the property of whomever he chose and have them executed under the law of *maiestas*, which allowed the emperor to deal as he pleased with those whom he judged had acted in a way designed to undermine the authority of the imperial name. The rights and property of the legal persons in the empire became dependent entirely on the will of the emperor.

This lord of the world, who is in one manifestation the Roman emperor, because all property and right converge in him, is for legal status the real content and essence of the legal person, though he himself is still only one person (292.–14 – .–13). The lord of the world has absolute power over the legal persons, even though they believe their own personhood to be absolute and sacrosanct. Likewise the lord of the world holds himself to be 'the absolute person' (292.–16) – he is personhood completely fulfilled, and he is the one real person who stands alone in the face of the multitude of unreal legal persons (292.–13). The lord of the world, like the Roman emperor, believes himself a god. (As the absolute person – the one in whom the legal status of persons is most fully realized – he represents as a god what the legal persons believe themselves to be, just as the gods of ethical substance represent to the members of the ethical community what they believe themselves to be.)

Despite his divinity and absolute personhood, despite his being able to confiscate and kill, the lord of the world, as the universal form of the discrete persons whom he dominates, is equally dependent on the persons for his own reality (292.–12 – .–10). His own personhood and role as lord of the world depend on the many individual persons and their obedience to him. Without the multitude of obedient persons behind him, this power is 'unreal and impotent' (292.–9). The emperor remains emperor only as long as he has the support of his people, especially the legions.

III

In this aspect of being both dependent and independent, legal status particularly resembles the sceptical consciousness. Just as stoicism and scepticism pass over into the unhappy consciousness, so legal status passes over into culture, which is the world of the unhappy consciousness. The unhappy consciousness is the truth of stoicism, and so culture – the realm of self-alienated Spirit – is the truth of legal personality (293.–6 – .–4). The human and divine laws of ethical substance meet in the person of the lord of the world because he is both man and god, a universal and an individual; but because he is only a person, dependent on other people for his reality, the universal and the particular are not met in him. His will is only the continued rule of the will of Creon – arbitrary and human. Legal person and lord of the world recognize this break, and both look to another place to find the real universal authority which they once believed the lord of the world possessed (293.–3 – :–2). This turning away from the human ruler and the human world is the turn made in culture and earlier in the unhappy consciousness. What must now be examined more thoroughly is the manner in which the transition from legal status to culture exemplifies the transition from stoicism and scepticism to the unhappy consciousness.

In legal status the citizen who previously thought of herself as a *Greek* is now the Roman who thinks of herself as an 'I,' an individual of absolute worth. The individual in the world of legal status now finds her substance – her underlying meaning and content – not in her community through its laws, but in herself. She is now a legal person, and her value is to be a person with rights under the law, regardless of any other factors. In legal status, all persons are equal under the law (290.7). Their community is nothing to these legal persons except the arena for their own legal personhood and rights. The legal person in legal status possesses her own being-for-self (290.5); she is an atom, dependent on nothing else for her existence as a legal person. Legal persons are persons possessing absolute and untouchable rights simply by existing.

The legal person finds her substantiality in the recognition of her rights by other legal persons (290.–14); her rights are rights and she is a person with rights only if her rights are acknowledged and accepted by others. None the less she insists that she is in and for herself; she insists that she is independent, possessing intrinsic merit, which is supported only by *her own* existence. The Roman citizen's rights are so firmly entrenched that Cicero, the saviour of the Roman people during the conspiracy of Catiline, is forced into exile because he refused civil rights to men who had conspired against the *res publica*. Even with the full support of the senate and *senatus consultum ultimum* (the order from the senate stating that the consuls should take care to prevent any harm coming to the republic), even though the conspirators had engaged in plotting the worst crime imaginable – the overthrow of aristocratic rule – the conspirators still possessed rights. The conspirators simply *were* Roman citizens possessing the right to trial and appeal. This fact alone ensures their rights even in light of their *actions*. Cicero did not respect these rights, and so he was forced to pay the legal penalty for that refusal.

Hegel likens the independence of consciousness of legal personality to that of the stoical consciousness in chapter 4, saying that legal personality is the actualization of the renunciation of the world found in stoicism (290.–2 – .–1). In stoicism, the slave consciousness withdrew from the determinations of the external world by claiming that these were unimportant to the real individual that the slave was in thought (119.–8 – .–5); they could never touch the 'real her,' because her mind and her thought were her own. In legal status, the person likewise insists that despite all other determinations she is primarily a person with rights and that this quality of hers can never be touched or taken from her. Both the stoical consciousness and the legal person claim that their real meaning does not come from, is not granted by, anything external to themselves; the world does not matter – they are who and what they are simply by existing. Stoicism says, '*I* have control over my own thoughts'; the legal person says, '*I* have legal rights'; the *thought* of independence is actualized in legal status. In legal status, the person's rights accrue to her from her *oneness* (291.10–.11) – from her being a single person, apart from any other factor external to her simple being.

However, while the stoical consciousness withdraws from the external and determined world to the inner, undetermined, and universal world of thought (121.14–.21), legal status essentially moves out into that world and declares the inner world meaningless. The individual legal person finds her meaning not so much in herself, as the stoical consciousness does, but in the outward and imposed *leges* of legal status. These *leges* all function around the notion of 'property' – of things, objects. The legal person is her things; she without her things does not exist. The legal person as an individual self-consciousness is not meaningful; what is meaningful is the law or status given her by the alien lord and master. Just as the stoical consciousness wants to insist that the real world is the world in its thoughts, legal status wants to claim that all that exists is what is external to the legal person.

Legal status actualizes the sceptical consciousness as well as the stoical. Scepticism is the 'contradiction of a consciousness which is at once independent and dependent' (291.20 –.22) because the sceptical consciousness, while insisting on its absolute freedom and independence from everything external to its own thought, still depends on this external world to provide the content it needs to deny in order to be a *sceptical* consciousness. Legal status manifests this same contradictory dependence and independence in two respects – for the individual legal person and her rights, and for the universal lord and master of the world and his position as lord of the world.

First, then, the individual legal person manifests the dependence and independence of scepticism in that she is independent because her legal rights accrue to her simply because of her being a legal person, regardless of any external consideration. This independence resembles the sceptical confusion of thought in which all objects were dissolved because in legal status the absolute being is held to be the empty legal person (291.–17 – .–16). The content that the individual possessed in ethical substance as a citizen immediately related to her *polis* is no longer determined by its relation to the *polis* and its *nomoi*. The world in legal status exists as an undetermined *object* for the legal person; she determines this object by calling it 'possession' or 'property' (291.–8 – .–5). The legal person, just like the sceptical consciousness, insists that the world has value only if she gives it value. The sceptical consciousness asserts its power over the external objective world by denying it; the legal person asserts herself by calling everything that she sees before her her own 'property.'

However, both the legal person and the sceptical consciousness are dependent on the external, objective world for their own identities because the legal person's content as a legal person is determined by her property and the sceptical consciousness needs the content provided by the world in order to deny it. In legal status the relation between the person and her property is more complicated than that between the sceptical consciousness and its objects because the legal

Philosophical History and the Roman Empire   27

person, as a member of a society in Spirit, also has relations with other members of her society – specifically with the lord and master of the world. The lord of the world is the one who actually determines the value of the content of all legal persons because he has absolute control over the world and its role as property (292.7 – .9; .14 – .18). This seemingly independent legal person is in fact dependent not only on her property to provide her content but on the lord of the world to determine the value of that property and her legal status.

This lord of the world now appears to be the independent member of the society of legal status because of his supreme power over all the legal persons, their property, and their rights. However, he too manifests the independence and dependence of scepticism. In order to maintain his position and identity as the lord and master of the world he depends on his subjects' obedience and acquiescence in his rule. His real authority comes from their acceptance of his absolute person (292.–13 – .–12). 'The single individual is true only as a universal multiplicity of single individuals' (292.–12 – .–10). The lord of the world is, after all, a single person among other persons; he is the absolute person, however, and as such he embodies and fulfils legal personhood. He provides the unity of the state and the law in legal status; he contains the content of all the rights and all the property of his subjects. He can no longer be the lord of the world if he no longer possesses all their content himself. The universal lord and master of the world is utterly dependent on his individual subjects for his meaning and his role as lord of the world. This situation was manifested in the Roman Empire by the legions' insistence that they be the ones to choose the emperor. Imperial power comes to consist of having the legions loyal to oneself; if the emperor died or was unable to control the legions, civil war erupted and was settled only when an emperor was found of whom the legions approved. After the suicide of Nero in AD 68, Italy was almost destroyed by the civil wars of the following year, which came to be known as the year of the four emperors. Ultimately, Vespasian was able to gain and keep the *imperium* because he was the only one of the emperors able to keep the legions' loyalty and support. The Roman emperor wants to maintain that his legions are his property and depend on himself for their meaning. None the less he is unable to control them, and his very position depends on their support, which can be removed in an instant.

One finds a perfect example of the dependence of the lord and master of the world on the acquiescence of his subjects in the accession of the emperor Claudius after the assassination of his nephew, Gaius (Caligula), in AD 41. Not only was Gaius killed by his legions – more specifically the Praetorian Guard – and Claudius selected as the new emperor by these same legions, but these things *had* to happen, given the way Augustus, the first Roman lord and master of the world, set up his empire. That is, the changes that Augustus made to the power structure of Rome had certain potentials that were realized fully by the Praetorian Guard in AD 41 when they killed Gaius and chose Claudius as his successor. We see in this assassination and the selection of a successor for the dead emperor the necessary working out of the logic of the political structure of the Roman Empire. We see also how this process bears out Hegel's analysis of legal status in every respect.

One great problem faced by the late Roman Republic was the concentration of military power in the hands of the few men who were in charge of various Roman provinces. This military power – *imperium* – was granted legally at Rome, but, once away from the city, these governors had forces at their disposal sufficient to allow them to move against Rome itself. Julius Caesar was the governor who was able to reap the full potential of *imperium* when he marched onto Italy from Gaul, crossing the Rubicon, in 49 BC. Caesar's actions here triggered the civil wars that resulted in his own victory and establishment as sole power at Rome until his death in 44 BC. (Here, in brief, we see the institutions of the republic leading to its downfall and transformation into empire.) When Augustus at last achieved victory in the struggle for power following Caesar's death, he reworked the administration of his empire so as to guard against the possibility of one of his governors holding sufficient power to challenge his own. A key move in this reworking was to ensure that all of the legions were dependent on and loyal to no one but himself. Augustus accomplished this goal in part by refusing to allow men of senatorial rank (the traditional Republican holders of *imperium*) to have access to certain key provinces and legions – *imperium* was to be no longer the possession of the Roman political elite.

The legions were needed in the provinces in order to keep the peace and ensure that these areas were content to remain provinces. Augustus divided the republican provinces between himself (the imperial provinces) and the Senate (the senatorial provinces). Those of long-standing peace Augustus put in the hands of senatorial governors without legions to support them.[5] More recent or more troublesome acquisitions were governed by imperial appointees in charge of legions. Augustus made it a crime for a man of senatorial rank to enter Egypt without the emperor's permission,[6] in part to ensure that no man with any personal authority or power could get close enough to the armies there to take control of them. Ultimately the Senate had no control or authority over any of the legions; the army was entirely in the hands of men who were dependent on the emperor's favour for their position, and no armed force was allowed in Italy except for the emperor's own Praetorian Guard.

The Praetorian Guard under Augustus had developed from the practice of generals of the republic who had kept their own private bodyguards. In 27 BC, Augustus created a permanent guard of nine cohorts of one thousand men each, which were under the command of prefects of equestrian rank appointed by the emperor (beginning in 2 BC, but originally under Augustus's sole control)[7]; they were really the emperor's personal troops. As Augustus eventually had no need to leave Italy (and did not, after 13 BC), with all the imperial provinces in the hands of his own men,[8] the Praetorians themselves also remained in Italy and would never see active service unless the emperor or a member of his family went to battle. Augustus kept three Praetorian cohorts stationed at Rome, and six others in various Italian towns.[9] (Tiberius, Augustus's successor, in AD 23 concentrated all the Praetorian cohorts in one barrack just outside Rome;[10] this act was significant for the balance of power between *princeps* and Senate.)

With this particular disposition of armed forces Augustus ensured that no one in the Senate had access to any kind of well-trained or well-armed military force anywhere in the empire and that he himself was the only one in Italy with an army. The Praetorian cohorts were a constant reminder to the Senate and the citizens of Rome of the emperor's privileged status and of his personal power and authority. Moreover, Augustus created in the Praetorian Guard a large, standing military force loyal not to Rome, the Senate, or the empire, but to himself, to the *princeps*. No one had authority over these military resources aside from Augustus and those he chose to represent him.

As well as removing military power and thus the making of war and peace from the hands of the Senate, Augustus began the work of rendering the Senate and the *Comitia* (a larger, more general assembly of Roman citizens, not merely those of senatorial rank, which voted on such issues as enacting laws, electing magistrates, declaring war and peace, and the inflicting of the death penalty) ineffectual. Already under the late republic the *Comitia* had lost most of its legislative powers and had given way to the authority of the Senate.[11] Augustus, and Tiberius after him, brought about complete loss of authority for both bodies. Augustus chiefly undermined the authority of the Senate by the institution of the *consilium* in 27 BC;[12] this body of men chosen from among the senators would discuss matters before they were brought before the full Senate in order to remove the need for a full debate. In AD 13, the *consilium* was enlarged and given the power to decide matters without any need for discussion or approval from the Senate.[13] Augustus also began to issue edicts of his own will, which the Senate would then ratify.[14] In effect, all government was in the hands of the emperor, though Augustus and Tiberius both kept up some semblance of a partnership between *princeps* and Senate. Certainly by the time of Gaius the Senate had become a body void of authority, which existed seemingly to carry on debates about matters of no importance to anyone.[15]

Augustus also undermined the traditional senatorial magistracies.[16] While he allowed these magistracies to continue and permitted men of senatorial rank to make their way through the traditional republican *cursus honorum*, Augustus began to appoint imperial officials to take over the duties of the senatorial magistracies.[17] This action had two effects: first, it resulted in still more removal of authority and power from the Senate, and second, it created magistrates with no practical administrative experience. Such men could stand no chance of being appointed by the emperor to positions of real responsibility because they were given no opportunity to prove or to better their ability. Augustus managed by devices of this kind to create out of the former ruling body of Rome a class of men with no power, no authority, and no ability or hope of advancement. The Senate became under Augustus a body detached from the real questions of government and administration and later, after the assassination of Gaius, incapable of taking control of an empire without an emperor.

In short, the various changes wrought by Augustus produced a feeble Senate, a strong army, and a *princeps* who possessed all the real power and authority in the empire. The emperor's will was in fact the law of the empire. Men such as Augustus, and, to a lesser extent, Tiberius, chose to allow their will to be bound by already existing law. Under Gaius, however, this pretence was given up, and the full extent of the power of the *princeps* was explored and exercised. The *princeps* had the life and the property of every citizen at his disposal, and his word dictated the course of court battles, private affairs, public disposal of funds, foreign affairs, of every aspect of life in the empire.[18] His ability to enforce his will rested largely on the presence and loyalty of his armed forces; because no private individual or governing body could match the forces at the emperor's disposal, no serious resistance to him was possible. The position of the *princeps* was not entirely secure, however; without the loyalty of his armies, he had no authority or power. If the armies chose to revolt, then the emperor was lost. Gaius was removed not so much because members of the Senate conspired against him but because members of his private army, the Praetorian Guard, chose to remove him. In AD 69, the empire eventually fell to Vespasian, a victorious and experienced general, able to carry battles and win over the legions of his opponents. Political power came to rest on the favour of the armies; Gaius's assassination and Claudius's accession are the first example of events that became the pattern for imperial successions. Gaius's army removed him and replaced him with their own choice, Claudius. The Senate really had no role to play in this bid for power. Removed from active and serious political and administrative life, it became an organ devoted to flattering the *princeps* and providing the occasional officer for his armies or governor for his provinces. Individual senators may have played some part in the struggles between emperor and army, but generally as free agents, not as functionaries of senatorial government. The Senate itself as a governing body was moribund, having nothing to do with government, military affairs, or the choice of *princeps*.

Gaius was the *princeps* to be removed and then replaced by a successor chosen by the Praetorian Guard because he was the *princeps* who refused to stay within the limits set by his predecessors. Augustus and Tiberius had elected not to exercise fully the power they possessed as *principes*.[19] Gaius chose to use that power and even to abuse it. His position legally was not particularly different from those of Augustus or Tiberius, except in so far as he had the precedent of two emperors before him who had on occasion chosen to use their real imperial power. Gaius knew that there was no power in the empire that could challenge his own and no authority before which he had to bow down.[20] He was the law of Rome and chose also to be its god.

Gaius was popular with the armies when he took power both because of his Julian ancestry on his mother's side and because of his father's successful record as a general.[21] Raised among the German legions, Gaius was the darling of the armies and thus a natural successor to Tiberius. His membership in the imperial family and his being named co-heir along with the Emperor Tiberius's grandson, Tiberius Gemellus, made his succession a smooth one. Tiberius's extended absence from Rome and the treason trials of the last few years of his reign made the presence of the young Gaius all the more welcome to the citizens and Senate of Rome. In addition, according to one ancient source, Josephus, the members of the army stated their willingness to die so that Gaius could become emperor.[22]

That Gaius began his reign by exercising his power openly seems to have bothered no one because he exercised it in ways guaranteed to win favour from the inhabitants of Rome. He recalled those banished under Tiberius and burned the documents relating to the trial of his mother and brothers,[23] acts that our sources portray as generous and noble; yet the second especially (given the importance of these particular documents and the Roman insistence on keeping careful public records of all matters) seems to be the act of one determined to assert his own authority not only over the present and future of Rome, but over its past as well. Gaius is said also to have revived Augustus's practice of publishing the accounts of the empire, given up by Tiberius, and of having returned elections of magistrates to the *Comitia*.[24]

This publication of the accounts and election of magistrates, while appearing to be a step towards re-establishing some sort of republican government, go hand in hand with Gaius's refusal on his return from Germany in AD 40 to have any more dealings with the Senate. He would govern and be the *princeps* only of the equestrian order and of the common people.[25] Turning the elections back to the *Comitia*, while he did so before his trip to Germany, withdrew a privilege of the already-ineffectual Senate; having no real power, the Senate had to content itself with privileges of this nature. By his refusal to acknowledge the Senate, Gaius made clear its real status. He had no need to deal with or acknowledge it because it could do nothing; he was himself the power. The Senate therefore was compelled to attempt to rid itself of this *princeps* because it had not yet accepted that this ineffectualness was to be its true role under the empire. An emperor more along the lines of Augustus or Tiberius was needed, or no emperor at all.

As well as earning the hatred of the Senate, Gaius managed to alienate even the common people of Rome by mid-40 with the numerous and heavy taxes he began to levy towards the end of his reign.[26] Even the Praetorian Guard, the body most naturally allied with and loyal to the *princeps*, grew dissatisfied with Gaius, as the involvement of its officers in the successful conspiracy against Gaius and the guard's easy acceptance of Gaius's death attest. Suetonius, Josephus, and Dio tell us that Cassius Chaerea, a tribune of the guard, had a personal grudge against Gaius and was for that reason involved in the assassination,[27] but this story, if true, does not explain the general attitude of the Praetorians to Gaius's murder. In part this attitude can be accounted for by appealing only to pragmatism on the part of the guard: with one *princeps* dead, it was necessary to find a successor before attending or not attending to punishment or revenge for the assassins.[28] In addition, Gaius seems to have been attempting to remove some of the privileges of the military now, and not merely those of civilians. While in Germany, Gaius halved the donative paid to soldiers on completion of military service,[29] and he wanted to kill all the legions that had revolted against his father.[30] The military has never taken kindly to attempts to reduce its own privileges, and Gaius's Praetorian Guard was no exception; threats to the regular army could easily have become threats to the Praetorians. At any rate, Gaius was, after his death at least, deemed expendable by the Praetorian Guard and by the people of Rome.

The combined enmity of the Senate and the Praetorian Guard was what removed Gaius from power. It is typical of both of these groups that the initiators of the deed were the members of the Guard, while the senators involved waited for their lead.[31] The Senate had become ineffectual to the point of being unable to carry out its own conspiracy, relying on the military to do the action and ultimately to resolve the situation created by the assassination.

After Gaius was removed, it was necessary that some decision be made about the future government of the empire. The Senate was discussing whether to restore the republic or to choose a new *princeps* from among various candidates.[32] Not surprisingly, given the Senate's lack of involvement in government and military affairs, it was unable to reach any decision and lacked the power or authority to carry out and enforce any decision it did make. The Praetorian Guard, in contrast, was able to make a decision and act on it immediately.

With one *princeps* gone, the Praetorians needed another in order to justify their own continued existence in the military forces of the empire.[33] The Praetorians were a privileged, elite group among the regular legions, receiving more pay, earlier retirement, larger donatives, and better living conditions, and rarely being forced to go into active war service, since they were stationed at Rome.[34] Their chief officers were men of considerable influence and power in Rome and could, as Sejanus and Macro did under Tiberius, have great influence on the political life of all corners of the empire. No one would have been too willing to give up the prerogatives and rewards of belonging to the guard in any capacity, and the one way for the Praetorians to ensure absolutely that they maintained these things was to make certain that the principate continued, and under someone they knew would rely on them as previous emperors had.[35]

The guard chose Claudius, and though some sources present his choice as *princeps* as having been quite arbitrary and fortuitous, there are some justifications for it from the point of view of the Praetorian Guard. Claudius, while not himself a successful general, came from a family with a tradition of military successes, being the brother of Germanicus and the son of Drusus Nero. The enthusiasm felt for Germanicus in particular seems to have extended to Claudius also.[36] Quite possibly the Praetorians would not have wanted a particularly warminded *princeps*, because that could have resulted in their own involvement in battle. Claudius, then, was a good choice; as a man with no military experience, he would have been less eager to undertake large-scale, dangerous military operations. Though not directly a member of the imperial family, Claudius belonged to the imperial household and was a man of consular rank; technically, he was the equal of the possible successors being discussed by the Senate. Claudius was also popular among the citizens of Rome, particularly among the equestrian order,[37] having himself been an *eques* before Gaius made him his colleague as consul.[38] He was not a man who would be too strongly resisted by anyone at Rome as the new *princeps*, especially with the force of the Praetorian Guard behind him.

The Senate, when informed of the Praetorian Guard's action in choosing a new emperor, had no option but to capitulate. The senators had no real alternative of their own to offer, the Praetorians were the only group at Rome with the power to enforce their own decisions, and further delays could lead to civil war. Quickly and quietly, the Senate gave in and accepted the soldiers' choice of emperor.[39] Claudius proclaimed to the Senate that he knew that it feared the rule of one person because of the abuses of past *principes* but that under himself government would be open to all. In this same proclamation, Claudius promised each member of the Praetorian Guard 15,000 sesterces for his allegiance, and the same amount to all members of the other legions,[40] thereby demonstrating that he recognized the reality of his own situation in a way that his predecessors did not. Though the favour of the legions had always been important to secure maintenance of imperial power, Claudius's succession to Gaius was the first incident of that power's resting entirely in the hands of the soldiers, and the first instance of the military's self-conscious use of the political power that it possessed. After Claudius, everyone knew that, personal authority and popularity aside, what put a *princeps* in power and kept him there was the support of his legions and his Praetorian Guard.[41]

The events surrounding Gaius's assassination and Claudius's accession were largely determined by the way in which Augustus set up the administration of his empire. Given the distribution of power Augustus put in place, something like these events had to take place eventually. When all the effective power of the empire was put into the hands of one man and removed from the body that had previously held it, it was inevitable that that body, the Senate, would eventually be unable to take control of government when a crisis such as Gaius's assassination arose. When one interest group, the Senate, did not have the power to enforce its own wishes, another one, the Praetorian Guard, did. The power of the guard was closely allied with the institution of the principate, and so the guard had to maintain that institution. Claudius's accession was the first of many to come in which the deciding factor in the choice of a *princeps* was not birth, or wealth, or political success, but the will and support of the military.

IV

The collapse of legal status comes about through the legal person's recognition that she is not an independent being-for-self but is dependent entirely on the will of the lord of the world, who is quite outside her. The lord of the world becomes fully aware of this power through his ability to destroy the self of his subjects (293.5–.7). His subjects, believing in their own absolute independence, 'exclude any continuity with others from their unyielding atomicity' (293.11–.12). The lord of the world, because he possesses their real essence and content, provides this continuity; all legal persons may look to him to see what they themselves really are. The legal persons refuse to see themselves in the lord of the world and so exclude him from their own rigid absoluteness. However, he can assert his destructive power over the legal persons and can thereby deprive them of their supposed being-for-self (293.16–.19). He tells his subjects that, because he alone possesses their essence and content, they are not independent and self-sufficient but depend for their very existence on his whim. He can take their property, which provides their content, and he can kill them, which contravenes their rights. The legal person is a person with rights not simply by existing but because the lord of the world chooses to acknowledge these rights; if he wishes, he can completely ignore these rights.

The legal person learns of her own emptiness and dependence through the lord of the world's destructive power; she recognizes that this power outside and hostile to herself is what determines who and what she is. Seneca committed suicide at Nero's request because he saw that his emperor was in fact the real power in his life and that his own existence depended not on his legal rights as a citizen but on the will of the emperor.

This life-and-death power of the lord of the world is what makes him conscious of his own authority. This consciousness 'is really the abandonment of its own self-consciousness' (293.−13) because he, as a legal person, also refuses to see himself in others. He chooses instead to see his subjects as simple objects, alien to himself, with whom he may do as he pleases; in his eyes they have no relationship to himself and his power. His destruction of his subjects is the act of a sceptical consciousness, because by destroying his subjects he completely denies their value and importance to him. He insists that everything external to himself is *simply* objective and external and cannot touch his own value. This destruction is also the act of primitive and unself-conscious desire, which asserts itself by destroying its surroundings through eating them. At any rate, legal status can no longer sustain itself because the very germ out of which it develops reveals its true nature; the independence of the legal person is completely empty and is dependent entirely on the will of another.

Legal status destroys itself when the legal person, now convinced of her own meaninglessness and inessentiality, withdraws into the world of thought from the actual world (293.−11 − .−9). This withdrawal is the '*actual* truth' of the view of the stoical consciousness (293.−4); what emerges here is the alienation of consciousness from the '*universally acknowledged authority* of self-consciousness' (293.−3 − .−2). What takes place in legal status is the actualization of the self. In ethical substance the individual is merely subsumed in her community and her ancestors; she herself counts for nothing as an individual. Legal status exalts the individual, by entrenching personal legal rights in its constitution. In legal status the individual self derives its meaning not from its immediate relation to its community but from itself; the legal person's primary meaning comes from her *being a* legal person, not from being a member of a group. However, because of the legal person's real contingency on the will of the lord of the world, who is the universal authority and the only real self in legal status, the legal person comes to recognize her own lack of value and meaning. Both the legal person and the lord of the world are without essence or content because each depends on the other for content, and yet both are empty. The legal person's content comes from her property, which is actually possessed by the lord of the world. The lord of the world has his content in the multitude of his subjects, who are all empty legal persons and are dependent on him.

Neither the individual legal person nor the lord of the world is able to find meaning in their relationship or in the world of legal status, which is based on external relations. The person and the lord are both determined in legal status by their relations to objects. When these objects can no longer satisfy them, they retreat into themselves. Neither is able to see herself or himself in the other or in the world. The legal person sees that the *leges* are not herself, that her property is not herself, and that the divine lord of the world is not herself. She seeks and finds her value in another world, which is outside her own world, and in which she really does possess absolute value as an immortal soul. The world of ethical substance, in which human and divine live harmoniously side by side, has become the world of unhappy consciousness, or culture, in which human and divine inhabit two separate worlds (294.2–.5).

The world of culture, as the world of medieval Christianity, is a self-divided world, just as the unhappy consciousness is a self-divided consciousness (295.–19 – .–18). It splits into two worlds: the real, temporal world, and the eternal world of pure consciousness (296.–1–297.3). The temporal world in culture is a meaningless world that receives its actuality only from that world which is beyond it (295.–10 – .–8). Everything, including the individuals inhabiting this world, has its being in the eternal world that is outside itself and opposite to it (295.–6 – .–4). The world of culture is 'self-alienated actuality' (296.1). In culture, the individual now insists that she herself is meaningless in the face of the other eternal, divine world. The world in which she lives is one determined by its relations to the other world, to which the individual will go after her own death. The human world, now separated from the divine world, has lost its meaning because it is a changeable, temporal world, not an unchangeable and eternal one. This separation into two distinct worlds is not a separation that really exists but is the form in which the world of culture chooses to understand itself.

Culture is an advance for spirit from the ethical realm because the world of culture now recognizes that the self is not sufficient unto itself for the creation of its own meaning and content. Ethical substance does not recognize the individual self as anything of importance. The individual is what her community and family make of her; she is completely determined by her relations to these two institutions. Legal status insists that the individual is of real value in and of herself; she needs no other relations to determine her. Culture in one sense merges these two forms; it recognizes the need for an other for self-consciousness and yet allows the individual absolute value. The individual in culture claims that her own real being does not subsist entirely in herself but that there is an other outside of herself, who is more meaningful than herself and who gives her meaning. Because the individual is now an immortal soul as well as a member of the temporal world, she sees herself as a single consciousness, which has at its core something that cannot be taken from her and that really defines her own being. Culture is an advance for spirit because in culture the dependence of the individual on the universal is recognized, and yet the individual, as immortal soul, is still allowed to possess some kind of discrete meaning. Culture is the arena in which the proper form of the relationship between the individual and his society will be worked out.

Legal status in the ethical realm does after all follow the same pattern of development that occurs in stoicism, scepticism, and the unhappy consciousness. Ethical substance is the master-slave relationship of spirit; when it breaks down, the stoical and sceptical world of legal status comes into being. These developments are the actualization of the developments within self-consciousness because they no longer occur in the thought of an individual self-consciousness but are played out as shapes of the human world, as we have seen in the discussion of Gaius, Claudius, and the political structure of the early Roman Empire. Legal status does show itself to break down for the same reason that the stoical and sceptical consciousnesses break down: because of the insistence on the absolute value of the individual and on his power over the external world. Just as Scepticism broke down into the divided world of the unhappy consciousness, legal status collapses into the divided world of culture. This transition, like all transitions in the *Phenomenology of Spirit*, shows itself to be an advance for spirit and part of its working out its proper shape for itself.

Thus we have seen how, for Hegel, the dialectical self-transformation of self-consciousness from stoicism and scepticism to the unhappy consciousness is actualized in the transformation in spirit from ethical substance to legal status to culture. We have seen also how Hegel's likening of these moves in spirit has been actually worked out in world history in the self-development and transformation of the Roman Empire. History itself does indeed move from and through the same rational, dialectical drives and demands as the individual self-consciousness as Hegel lays them out for us in *The Phenomenology of Spirit*. Only by becoming students of dialectic can we see how this development works, how the world itself has worked itself out in the same way that we, as rational beings, work ourselves out. The practice of philosophical history allows us to recognize ourselves in the traditions and institutions that have formed us and that provide the grounds for all our activity, because it alone demands that we treat our world and the objects of our study with the respect and recognition that we desire for ourselves: the recognition that it, like us, can and does grow and live according to its own needs and desires in a self-conscious way.[42]

Notes

1 The philosophical historian must practise what John Russon in his essay in this

volume (chapter 13) describes as 'active empiricism' – an examination of one's object that regards that object as a self-determining process and seeks to ask the object how it works itself out.

2 John Russon has discussed this parallel in *The Self and the Body in Hegel's Phenomenology* (Toronto: University of Toronto Press, 1997), chap. 4.

3 G.W.F. Hegel, *Phenomenology of Spirit*, trans. A.V. Miller (Oxford: Oxford University Press, 1977), 288. Hereafter, references to this volume are included in parentheses in the text, and a decimal after the page number indicates the precise line numbers from which a quotation was taken, with negative numbers indicating lines counted up from the bottom of the page; this reference would be 288.–6 – .–5.

4 Compare Jay Lampert's discussion of the origin of the notion of a 'right' in chapter 2, below. There we see that right must first take the form of property because right must first be something that is immediately graspable – clearly objective and open to being possessed. On correlations of person and property, see G.W.F. Hegel, *Philosophy of Right*, trans. T.M. Knox (Oxford: Oxford University Press, 1967), 42, 45, 52–3.

5 Alban Dewes Winspear and Lenore Kramp Geweke, *Augustus and the Reconstruction of Roman Government and Society* (New York: Russell and Russell, 1935), 94–5. Ronald Syme, *The Roman Revolution* (London: Oxford University Press, 1939), 314–15. Suetonius, *Lives of the Caesars*, Loeb Classical Library (Cambridge: Harvard University Press, 1970), *Augustus*, 38, 47, 49.

6 H.H. Scullard, *From the Gracchi to Nero* (London: Methuen and Co. Ltd., 1970), 259.

7 Ibid., 251.

8 Suetonius, *Augustus*, 20.

9 Ibid., 49.

10 Cassius Dio, *Roman History*, Loeb Classical Library (Cambridge: Harvard University Press, 1961), LVII.19. Suetonius, *Tiberius*, 37.

11 Winspear and Geweke, *Augustus*, 88.

12 Dio, *Roman*, LII.21. Suetonius, *Augustus*, 35.

13 Dio, *Roman*, LVI.28.

14 Ibid., LVII.8. Winspear and Geweke, *Augustus*, 90–1.

15 Albino Garzetti, *From Tiberius to the Antonines: A History of the Roman Empire, AD 14–192*, trans. J.R. Foster (London: Methuen and Co., 1974), 99.

16 Tacitus, *Annals of Imperial Rome*, ed. C.D. Fisher (Oxford: Oxford University Press, 1986), I.2, XI.5.

17 Winspear and Geweke, *Augustus*, 93.

18 For example, Dio, *Roman*, LIX.8, 14, 15, 22, 28. Suetonius, *Gaius*, 26, 29, 40.

19 Garzetti, *From Tiberius*, 103.

20 Suetonius, *Gaius*, 29.
21 Flavius Josephus, *Jewish Antiquities*, Loeb Classical Library (Cambridge: Harvard University Press, 1962), XVIII.166, 206.
22 Ibid., XVIII.210.
23 Suetonius, *Gaius*, 15.
24 Dio, *Roman*, LIX.9. Suetonius, *Gaius*, 16.
25 Garzetti, *From Tiberius*, 99. Suetonius, *Gaius*, 49.
26 Garzetti, *From Tiberius*, 101. Josephus, *Antiquities*, XIX 24–5. Suetonius, *Gaius*, 40.
27 Dio, *Roman*, LIX.29. Josephus, *Antiquities*, XIX *passim*. Suetonius, *Gaius*, 56.
28 Josephus, *Antiquities*, XIX.151–2.
29 Suetonius, *Gaius*, 44.
30 Ibid., 48.
31 Dio, *Roman*, LIX.29. Josephus, *Antiquities*, XIX.61–4. Suetonius, *Gaius*, 56.
32 Josephus, *Antiquities*, XIX.158–61. Suetonius, *Gaius*, 60.
33 J.P.V.D. Balsdon, *The Emperor Gaius* (London: Oxford University Press, 1934), p. 105.
34 Scullard, *From the Gracchi*, 252–3. Tacitus, *Annals*, I.17.
35 Josephus, *Antiquities*, XIX.162–4.
36 Ibid., 223. Suetonius, *Claudius*, 7.
37 Scullard, *From the Gracchi*, 300. Suetonius, *Claudius*, 6.
38 Dio, *Roman*, LIX.6. Suetonius, *Claudius*, 7.
39 Suetonius, *Claudius*, 10.
40 Josephus, *Antiquities*, XIX.246–7. Suetonius, *Claudius*, 10.
41 Balsdon, *Emperor Gaius*, 109. Suetonius, *Claudius*, 10. Claudius was the first emperor to resort to bribing the troops.
42 I would like to thank Michael Baur, T.D. Barnes, John Russon, and K.L. Schmitz for their remarks and reflections on earlier versions of this paper. I am quite confident that I have not yet even begun to address the majority of their insights. Illicit and anonymous attendance at H.S. Harris's graduate seminar on Hegel's *Phenomenology* at York University and University of Toronto from 1988 to 1989 influenced my reading of this text immensely, and I take this opportunity to offer Professor Harris my profound thanks.

2

Locke, Fichte, and Hegel on the Right to Property

JAY LAMPERT

The Argument for Property Rights

There is a tradition, beginning roughly with Locke, hitting its peak in Fichte, and perfected, and hence destroyed, in Hegel, of deriving the right to property from the fact that consciousness grasps objects in the world. It is Fichte who has the most straightforward argument – that the self, in distinguishing itself from the not-self, constitutes a boundary between itself and the world and further, by manifesting that boundary *within* the world, establishes a kind of fence between what belongs to it in the world and what does not. The differences between Hegel and Locke and Fichte appear not in the beginnings of their individual texts, since Hegel's *Philosophy of Right* (1821) essentially begins with property rights in the same way as does Fichte's *Science of Right* (1796) and Locke's *Second Treatise of Government* (1690); they emerge rather in the way that property is treated in the parts of the book that follow those beginnings. Property continues to be a determining category of political relations in Fichte and Locke, but it loses value in Hegel once relations between citizens take more complete forms. We then see what presuppositions underlay property for Hegel when it arose as the first social act.

In the commentaries on Hegel's conception of property we find a range of views from Wilfred ver Eecke's idea, that Hegel is a staunch supporter of property rights,[1] through Peter G. Stillman's, that Hegel thinks property will always play a role in society but will be subordinated to more cultured forms of ethical life,[2] to H.S. Harris's argument that Hegel thinks that the property relation, at least in capitalism, leads to a social division of wealth, power, and moral demands: 'In other words, he [Hegel] is expecting a social revolution, and his economic and judicial "syllogisms" require a conclusion that he knows how to write, but must be enacted by the world-spirit before it can be the concern of the philosopher.'³ In so far as the vocabulary of liberalism, social revolution, and even private property itself has different connotations in contemporary European, American, and Canadian contexts, Harris's interpretation could be thought of as the heart of the Canadian school of Hegel studies. In this sense, I would like to think of the present paper as written in the spirit of the Harris tradition.

Perhaps there was no single concept of property before the time of Locke. In fact, it is extremely difficult to think of the phenomenon in a unified way, or to conceive a single paradigm of property. Should we think of the paradigmatic piece of property as land, as an unmovable place in which a person lives beyond the interference of others? Or is the paradigmatic case rather a movable thing, where the issue of property is one of exchangable objects measurable by some universal standard of value? Or is property rather first and foremost *self-possession*, control over one's body or one's mind, such that property in external things is secondary or even unimportant? Or should we even define property as starting with private property, instead of looking for the paradigm in public property, as in the mutual responsibilities of society's members? For that matter, do we have to think of humans as the paradigmatic property-owners, instead of conceiving of humans as themselves paradigmatically property of the gods or of the land or of a culture?

On the broadest possible construction, categories of property cover the relation between a conscious being and a structured field of objects, where that structure also calls into play some forms of contact with other conscious beings. On a more narrow view, more closely connected to ordinary language, categories of property involve individual, conscious beings making exclusive claims on divisible portions of the field of objects, marking those objects as their private concern, and erecting barriers, laws, and police forces to control those lines of exclusion.

I try to show below how the traditional arguments for the right to property validly entail the right to property only in the broad sense. These arguments then take the case of property in the narrow sense as the natural first expression of the right to property – a step that may still be legitimate. But what has to be seen in the end (something that Locke does not acknowledge, Fichte only begins to accept, and Hegel systematically attempts to recognize, though he is unable to shake off the last remnants of the tradition) is that once the process of conscious beings relating to the field of objects progresses to its completion – once the categories of property in the broad sense are fulfilled – the narrow categories of property will have been surpassed.

In this chapter, I develop parallel analyses of the texts of Locke, Fichte, and Hegel, examining the steps in each argument that lead from the concept of the self, through the grounding of property rights, to the partial overcoming of property rights in larger social structures. For each philosopher, I analyse a series of progressively more complex categories of property, commenting on particular points along the way. My systematic argument is that for each philosopher, the more thoroughly property works its way through the social structure, the more the categories of property have to be overcome in other forms of social relations. This development is least pronounced (though it is suggested) in Locke, and most explicit in Hegel.

For Hegel, property reaches its most advanced level in society when it is stolen. To anticipate his culminating example of property, Hegel argues that intellectual property, though protected by copyright law, is ultimately fulfilled only once it is appropriated by those readers who are able to make better intellectual work out of it. But while I am arguing on the whole that Hegel's analysis of property and the state shows that the state must ultimately reject the categories of private property, I conclude that Hegel's analysis leaves a remnant of the property relation behind. The remnant is not so much in that he allows individuals to own small amounts of private property on the side – in a peaceful state he does allow that, but in the wars between cultures that he anticipates as a healthful and inevitable growth of world-spirit, he argues, private citizens' property can justly be plundered. Rather, the remnant of the property relation in Hegel's analysis of the state shows itself in his account of the right of advanced states to make use of less-advanced states. That is, something too much like the property relation governs Hegel's analysis of cross-cultural contact, even at a point of the text after Hegel has shown that property relations must be overcome in favour of larger social relations.

While most of this paper is a defence of Hegel's analysis of property as the form of individuality that citizens must first achieve but must subsequently rid themselves of, Hegel's text is finally not able to rid itself of the last remnant of the category of property – namely, its possessivist construal of cross-cultural relations.

Locke: Getting Something under One's Power

The State of Nature: Power, Use, and Labour

Locke's analysis of the origin of property rights begins with a general analysis of power, or 'dominion over the world' (*Second Treatise of Government*, chap. 1).[4] The starting point for Locke's treatise involves a cluster of concepts including power, life, and property:[5] 'Political power, then, I take to be a right of making laws with penalties of death, and consequently, all lesser penalties for the regulating and preserving of property, and of employing the force of the community in the execution of such laws and in the defence of the commonwealth from foreign injury; and all this only for the public good' (chap. 1, sec. 3). Political power is specifically the power over life and, consequently, property; this suggests the scheme prevalent in much of Locke's discourse – namely, that property is in the same category as life, only in a lesser form. To explain what it means to have a 'right' to life or to property, we have to look briefly at Locke's account of the state of nature.

The 'state of nature' or the 'state of liberty' is a state of 'perfect freedom,' a state of equality, in which no one has more jurisdiction than anyone else. The 'law' of the state of nature, which is nothing other than 'reason,' teaches that 'being all equal and independent, no one ought to harm another in his life, health, liberty, or possessions' (2.6). From this statement alone it would be difficult to tell whether the state of nature permits no property, or insists on equal property, or just restricts the theft of another's property. Indeed, we still need to explain how 'possessions' arise in the state of nature in the first place.

Locke's account of possession begins with God's creation. When God creates something, He makes it for His use, or for His pleasure (2.6). It is therefore His 'property.' If we think of the property of humans in the same way, then there are three aspects to Locke's definition of property in the state of nature: (a) products are property of the producer, (b) the inferior is the property of the superior, and (c) the usable is the property of whoever's use it was made for. The latter does not quite say that whoever *can* use something owns it, but even so there is an ambiguity here over the relation between the production of something and the right to use it. Still, the model of the autonomous producer does begin to offer a definition of right.

It has become common in modern moral philosophy to treat rights as mysterious properties with some sort of other-wordly origins, so that sceptics can ask, 'Where do these rights *come from*?' But in the tradition of Locke (and Fichte and Hegel), rights are not thought of as deontologized absolute qualities somehow attached to a human being but are descriptive of the natural state of human activity. A person has the right to do something as long as it is the sort of thing a person would naturally do if she weren't prevented from doing so by coercive societies or madmen and criminals.

To have a right in the state of nature is thus not so much an attribute as a type of activity, a function of executing one's will. In the state of nature everyone has the right to execute the laws that govern his own activity. 'What any man may do in prosecution of that law, everyone must needs have a right to do' (2.7). Right thus emerges as the lack of jurisdiction among individuals, and the freedom that exists for each individual is first of all his freedom to keep his freedom. Here right has a kind of ontological ground in the momentum that a free condition has to continue itself. A right is at root a ground not to do something contrary to existing circumstances but just to live as one has been living. Now, if someone should threaten a person's freedom, that potential victim is free to restrain the offender, to demand reparation, or even to exercise dominion over him so long as the threat exists (2.8–10). Anyone can kill a murderer in the state of nature, since the murderer has renounced reason ('the common rule and measure God has given to mankind,' 2.11). Reason itself is therefore the paradigmatic case of something humans possess. Freedom, and hence reason, which allow a person to exercise freedom, are so tied to a person that to remove them would be to destroy the person. We might see this as a ground of the right to property in general, though it would not yet justify the right to property in things whose removal would not kill the owner.

The Person, the War, and the Fence

When one person declares an intention against another in the state of nature, it is like declaring war, since no forum for negotiation is assumed. In this event, the victim is free to react against the aggressor. To attack a person in any way is to imply an overall threat that 'attempts to get another man into his absolute power' – i.e., 'to make me his slave' (3.17). To take his freedom is to take the 'foundation of all the rest' that a man has, to destroy the 'fence' of security around the person. It is not surprising, once the freedom-person-power-property identity has been made, to find that enslaving someone is the most dangerous of offences, since it threatens to steal the self both in its inner rational faculties to act freely and in its outer resources that the person could make use of to exercise that freedom.

But a peculiarity develops when Locke argues that a man cannot forfeit absolute power over himself, either in committing suicide or in selling himself into slavery. His argument is that one cannot forfeit a power one did not already have. But this first limitation on the right to use oneself highlights an ambiguity over whether the right to one's self is absolutely given with birth or depends on using one's powers appropriately. Is the right to property grounded in a person's *right to use* whatever is available (which would allow enslavement of a death-row prisoner whose life is owed to the state and is therefore available) or in the freedom to act that exists *within* any rational being (in which case the prisoner retains his freedom). Locke seemed to want to define property as the product of use, but his rejection of slavery requires limiting that definition by appeal to a self that cannot be the property of others. And if there is a restriction on grasping the self of another person (along with a corresponding rule against letting go of one's own self), then the emergence of property rights from the state of nature is also the emergence of limitations on grasping objects in general. An analysis of property is not just an examination of the act of acquisition but must also be an analysis of who precisely can acquire precisely what.

Need, Use, Labour, and Exclusivity

The naturally free and rational self has a fortiori a natural right to make use of nature in general, but what Locke wants to explain is how individual men 'come to have a property in anything' (5.25). Two things have to be explained: how particular men gain a right to exclusive use of particular things, and how the right to appropriate things out of the common resource is to be limited (chap. 5).

Locke explains the first of these points by means of notions of labour and the body (5.27): 'Though the earth and all inferior creatures be common to all men, yet every man has a property in his own person; this nobody has any right to but himself. The labour of his body and the work of his hands, we may say, are properly his. Whatsoever then he removes out of the state that nature has provided and left it in, he has mixed his own labor with, and joined to it something that is his own, and thereby makes it his property. It being by him removed from the common state nature has placed it in, it has by this labour something annexed to it that excludes the common right of other men. For this labour being the unquestionable property of the labourer, no man but he can have a right to what that is once joined to, at least where there is enough and as good left in common for others.'

The first property of each person is 'his own person' – namely, his body. The second property, derivative of the body, is his labour. Somehow the person's freedom, which was the ground for settling issues of slavery and natural right, has become the body. But even if one's body is one's own, it is not clear why it should follow that one's labour is one's own as well. If we could conceive of labour as simple bodily movement, then we might think that having power over one's body entails having power over where one puts it. But labour seems to be more than simple bodily movement. At the very least it involves altering the world shared by other people, and in fact it involves whole economic systems of production and social relations. It is therefore not clear why the labourer should have an exclusive right to the products of activities in which other people had at least indirectly participated.

Locke's argument for the general premise – that exclusive property in one's labour entails exclusive property in the products of one's labour – depends on a mixed metaphor. First, he argues that if a man 'mixes his labour' with a thing, given that his labour is his own, the thing also becomes his own, since it has something of his own mixed into it. It seems rather odd logic to say that if one owns a part of a thing one therefore owns the whole thing. If, by my labour, I 'annex something to it,' why does that 'exclude the right of other men'? In fact, the argument depends on the other side of the metaphor: the labourer 'removes [the object] out of the state that nature has provided and left it in.' Instead of the labourer entering the common realm and adding a new piece to it, he removes a part of the thing, takes it away with him, and works on it in a private space. The metaphor of mixing with something sounds like a positive contribution to the common state; the metaphor of removing something from the common state suggests rather a loss from the standpoint of the common state and a repulsion of the rights of others.

This second, negative point, which shows that acquisition of property is something that a person does in relation to other people – something rather violent at that – is crucial to Locke's argument, but it is a point on which he himself has a blind eye. This ambiguity between acquisition as autonomous labour and acquisition as the deprivation of others becomes especially sharp in his attempts to account for a limitation to the right to property. We now consider how Locke gets entangled in the ambiguities of the limit.

Limit – Spoilage and Other People's Needs

The problem of the relation between the individual's labour and the forms of mutual conditioning and mutual recognition that are presupposed by that labour comes to the fore in limitations on an individual's right to property.

One aspect of this issue arises in cases in which several people have 'mixed' their labour with the same thing and the thing has to be divided up among its various owners. Locke's talk of 'the labour of his body and the work of his hands' (5.27) has the ring of individual craftsmen making things autonomously, but if one thinks of labouring on an object using an instrument made by someone else, it is clear that the work of others, and the work of social institutions from transportation systems to licensing bureaus, is involved almost every time one's own labour is at issue. The problem is not just how to distribute fair shares of the product; it is the deeper one of Locke's neglecting the forms of will, recognition, and violence that operate as the preconditions of acquisition of property.

But the most serious problem for Locke's account is his interest in seeing a limit placed on how much each individual has a right to seize (5.31). If we think of the right as created by the free act of mixing one's labour with something, it would hardly make sense to limit a person's right to appropriate things. One would have the right to own as much as one could lay one's hands on. Locke tries to set a stricter limit on acquisition by saying that a person may take only as much as he can use or 'enjoy' before it spoils. But even if Locke is right to introduce enjoyment as a condition of the right to property, it does not really limit acquisition. It does not exclude seizing property and allowing it to spoil as long as the spoilage is enjoyable. It is odd also that Locke does not consider the stockpiling of goods in such a way as to preserve them from spoiling. He wants to define the limitation on the right to property in a way that implicates only the individual and his personal use of it, and for this reason he defines overpossession according to what that individual cannot use before spoilage; but almost in spite of himself he has to notice that the reason overpossession is bad is that others have to go without, and this is not ruled out in cases where an owner hoards goods but keeps them from spoiling. The prohibition on spoilage, which turns out not really to limit property at all, is in effect a prohibition against harming others by possessing what they need. Up until now, Locke says, there has been plenty of property of all kinds in the common store, so there has been 'little room for quarrels' about whether a person has taken too much (5.31). The paradigmatic case of acquiring property is a case in which there is an infinite ready supply.[6]

Money and the Nation's Efficiency: The Problem of the Common

The idea that one person's acquisition of property does not affect other people assumes that someone without property can always go somewhere else to get some. Locke says that in the 'first ages of the world,' this would not have been a problem at all (5.36), and even now (Locke's time), one can go to America, or even Spain. Locke is often thought here to be criticizing particularly the land fenced off by hereditary aristocrats who are not using all of the products of that land, but in fact his primary aim here is to justify seizing the land in America whose present inhabitants are underusing it. Locke's apology for seizing land in America involves a certain contradiction: the reference to 'the wild woods and uncultivated waste of America' (5.37) suggests that no one is currently inhabiting them, thus leaving them free for inhabitation, while the reference to 'waste' assumes that people are in fact there but not maximizing use. It is here for the first time that Locke suggests that a person may have a right to his possessions only if he can maximize their use.

Again, Locke has competing arguments. On the one hand, he suggests that freedom implies a responsibility to exercise freedom, hence that the capacity to produce useful things implies a responsibility to be industrious (for example, 5.34). On the other hand, 'The benefit mankind receives from [an acre of land that bears twenty bushels of wheat] in a year is worth L5, and from [another acre in America] possibly not a penny if all the profit an Indian received from it were to be valued and sold here' (5.43). The first argument is based on the individual's exercise of free activity, and the second on the benefit to mankind as a whole (though Locke is being somewhat disingenuous in promoting seizure of someone's land on the grounds that he is not getting enough enjoyment out of it). The first of these versions of the duty to maximize use seems individualistic; but while it blames the inefficient individual, it does not suggest that his goods be expropriated by more efficient users. The second version seems to promote the welfare of all mankind, but it sets the stage for expropriating the property of any society with a smaller-scale economy. The issue of efficiency thus leads also to the origins of territorial government.

A prince should rule not by virtue of power or party affiliation but by regulating employment and encouraging industry (5.42). Systems of production have had the result that 'communities settled the bounds of their distinct territories' and agreed not to claim land within the other communitees' territories (5.45). The origin of government in Locke's philosophy is based not just on the negative desire of individuals to preserve their freedom by instituting a common legal system against offenders but also on the positive exercise of maximally efficient freedom – maximally efficient production of objects for consumption. The first of these two foundations of government – the desire for mutual protection – would seem to lead ultimately to a desire for the most universal government possible; only if the foundation of government is based on the desire for the most efficient production is there a reason for one community to fence itself off from another.

Now if efficiency increases, Locke's account needs some way of consuming the excess. (Otherwise, the Indian might be following the law of reason more by producing only his daily needs than the Englishman is, with his twenty bushels.) That is, if there is a duty to produce more than one requires, there must be a right to own more than one needs, so Locke should expand the limits of the right to private property. But at the same time, the government is now being relied on to increase efficiency, and the government itself functions as a kind of community property. These two seemingly opposite requirements of Locke's account – public cooperation and private excess – are both satisfied by the phenomenon of money.

In the remainder of this section, we see that Locke's account of private property implies a need for public property and, more important, for mutual recognition of intersubjective interests, but rarely does he more than hint at these implications.

As to the role of community property, Locke says that in times of scarcity, distribution of land would leave some without, and in that case, the commoners would have to hold land in common. In fact, it is difficult to see how Locke could consider any private property acceptable in times of such scarcity. In any case, the commonality of property is made reasonable by scarcity, but it is made possible by government. And this is not only because government passes the law, as if it were putting up a fence with a sign on it saying 'no fences allowed,' but, more significant, because government controls money and commerce. Money constitutes the general ability to regulate an economy, as well as the specific ability to distribute privately consumable property from a common store.

From the standpoint of increased private wealth, money allows a kind of stockpiling that never spoils. Since a person has a right to a thing as long as it does not perish, then assuming he can gather a ton of berries, he has several choices (5.46). He can eat them all, or he can give some away, or he can exchange them for nuts (which last longer), or he can exchange them for gold, which lasts for ever. He can then keep as much gold as he wants, until such time as somebody else wants to exchange his perishable goods for that gold. The complicated issues of exchange, contract, and consent are not analysed by Locke here, but the gold exchange radically expands the right to property.

There is in effect absolutely no limit any longer to the possession of goods, and so the definition of property as something one can use becomes irrelevant. Money means that one can hoard property that one is not using at all, especially in such common phenomena as a person who possesses a quantity of money that, if exchanged for certain perishable goods, would feed the hungry and if not exchanged for those perishable goods would mean that those goods would spoil. This type of scenario is after all the common complaint against the hoarding of private property in general: that wealthy persons hoard while others go hungry. Locke seems to accept the complaint as valid if the wealthy person is hoarding berries, but if Locke denies the complaint when the person is hoarding the exchange value of berries in money, nothing is left of his original sense that property rights are limited by the needs of others.

Now, in so far as Locke can convincingly argue that money is just the substitute for a commodity one has laboured for, then the right to money-property has the same ground as the right to berry-property. But once there is a trade in money, so that some people can make money as interest on capital, or can use money to hire others to create value for them, and so on, then property can no longer be tied to the labour of producing usable goods. The attempt to ground the right to property in bodily activity seems entirely beside the point.

Now, Locke does end his chapter on property with the account of money, and he begins the next chapter with the issue of 'paternal power.' We *might* then attribute to him the view that property is only the *first* product of power that sets the limits of the exercise of a person's power in relation to both nature and other persons' power; but that property is not an appropriate category for analysing political relations once property is universalized beyond immediate consumable commodities into a monetary standard of exchange values. That is, we might say that property for Locke is sublated in power. However, it does not seem that he ever abandons the right to private property that money carries beyond limits, and in the process, at least on my reading, undermines.

The basic problem in Locke's account of property is that he settles for unresolved ambiguities – between the positive right to seize property and the negative right to live in a world where some goods have always not yet been seized by others, between private consumption of property and public organization and production of it, and between autonomous acts of the individual owner and the forms of mutual recognition (often, or perhaps always, violent) among people engaged in the system of acquiring, using, and exchanging property. To see how these oppositions are synthesized, and to see how mutual recognition and structures of community contribute to the origin of property, we turn to Fichte.

Fichte: Recognition, Limit, the House, and the Border Patrol

As it does for Locke, property for Fichte emerges as the expression of rational consciousness. But whereas for Locke, property is grounded on autonomous activity, for Fichte, property is grounded in a prior mutual social recognition, and this precondition allows consciousness to proceed to a subsequent commonality of social distribution. Yet while Locke understates the role of mutual recognition in the constitution of property rights, we see below that Fichte overstates it.

Fichte's *Science of Rights*[7] investigates 'how a community of free beings is possible' (p. 126). Fichte has offered the basis for his account in his *Science of Knowledge*. To summarize the first three principles of that text: the ego posits itself freely, unconditionally; the ego posits the not-self as its object; as a result, the ego posits, or recognizes, a mutual limitation of self and not-self. Fichte analyses the ways in which the ego unfolds both its own freely self-developed constitution and its capacity to find itself determined by the not-self. It turns out that the drive of the knower to reidentify the self and the not-self requires that the not-self appear as itself having the structure of selfhood. That is, each self must know, and limit itself in accordance with, another self, and this mutual limitation must be in part external, in the form of a community, and in part internal, in the form of moral conscience.

Perception and Line-Drawing: The Articulated Body

The ego first recognizes itself in nature and posits itself as extended in space and time; its first activity is to interpret itself as delimited by physical surroundings:

Locke, Fichte, and Hegel on the Right to Property

'The Ego in contemplating itself as activity contemplates its own activity as a *line-drawing*. This is the original scheme of activity in general, as every one will discover who wishes to excite in himself that highest contemplation' (89–90). The ego posits itself as having a specific location, it extends the realm of its concern, knowledge, and activity around itself in determinate directions according to determinate plans. In short, to act is to draw a line from oneself into the world – a line directed outwards from oneself, which at the same time circumscribes oneself and connects oneself with the world around. This phenomenology of line-drawing develops into the right to property. The cognitive activity of determining a point and generating spatial extensions becomes the projective activity of determining oneself as a body and moving through space, which becomes the communicative activity of putting up a fence around one's property and engaging in systems of exchange and mutual protection.

Causality and the Right to Property: Mutual Recognition and Exclusivity

Like Locke, Fichte defines 'right' as the natural activity of a rational being. In its positive sense, right is will determining itself (205). On the negative side, right is the right to compel others to accepts one's own will (141). Where Locke simply threw together the positive sense of right as self-chosen activies and the negative sense of right as mutual limitation, Fichte grounds both together: 'Here lies the ground of all *right of property*. That part of the sensuous world which is known to me, and has been subjected by me, though only in thought, to my purposes, is *originally* my property (originally, I say, not in a *community*.) And being thus my property, no other person can have causality upon it without checking the freedom of my causality' (166).

In relation to property, Fichte characterizes the positive sense of right as the 'right to free acts in the sensuous world' (213), hence to control, and in that sense to possess, things in the physical world. In the negative sense, a controller of an object has a right to limit the control that another person can have on it. This requirement that others leave my goods alone demands first that each person must 'declare his possessions' (179), and second that there be a universally acknowledged arbitrator of disputes.

The Property Compact and the Open Road

It is in this light that Fichte uses the trope of the social contract. The presumption is that each person has his own will that he is prepared to limit in relation to others. In fact, this point leads Fichte into the striking judgment that 'each citizen of a state has, therefore, necessarily a property; for if the other had not guaranteed him his property, he would not have guaranteed theirs' (214).

The contract will have three forms. The first is the 'Property Compact' – that 'each, therefore, pledges all his property as security that he will not violate the property of all others' (215). We are to imagine here a world where each sees to the end of his property and sees the material outside that limit as the expression of some other will not his own. There is a telling detail in Fichte's account when he notes that public property includes the roads through which anyone can travel through open space to sell goods, visit other households, and so on. Much of Fichte's model of the spatiality of property suggests a filled plenum, where everything is the expression of somebody's will (in contrast to Locke's sense that the world is still mostly unclaimed land), but in fact the criss-crossing of open roads is probably necessary for the very notion of property. If there were no open roads, and a person had to enter somebody else's will in order to move anywhere, the objective world would collapse altogether.

The second, positive form of the agreement is the 'Protection Compact,' whereby each agrees to act to protect the specified property of others (219). In order to protect another's property, one must *know* exactly what the other possesses and must always be informed as soon as another is attacked (219). The 'Union Compact' expresses the fact that the whole of property is articulated into parts (227). As each citizen's property is grounded in the protection of another, each experiences a 'return to self' from the acts and promises of the other (232–3). Whereas Locke essentially casts property as a private activity with minor public consequences, Fichte regards privacy itself as a result of a history of the relationship between individual and social conditions.

Property Law and the Problem of Distribution

The right to property does not belong to individuals prior to the social contract or to the laws that express the contract. Civil law is coextensive with legal right, which is coextensive with the Property Compact (289). One consequence is that if a given person does not have enough property to live on, he is not in a position to agree to this contract, so the contract of all with all would collapse. Hence the possibility of law as such requires that each person have a minimum amount of property. When some people fall below that minimum, the property of others belongs no longer to them, but to the poor (293). The universality of the property contract implies the limitation on the absoluteness of private property in the form of redistributive taxation.

Once the person needs the recognition of others, he needs it to be uninterrupted. To be recognized as a person, each individual must announce his eligibility to be a person to the state and must be approved as such. Specifically, he must state what his property is and exactly how he intends to live off it; he must declare his occupation (294). 'There must be no indeterminacy in a state organization' (295). This statement serves as an overview of the Fichtean state in the most worrying sense. (Worry itself is a characteristic of the Fichtean citizen.) But there is no suggestion that the criterion of entry into society – namely, minimal life support – should also limit the right to property to that minimum. It is as if the property owner justifies his right to property on grounds that would justify only minimum property and then conveniently forgets the nature of that justification once he expands his possessions. Like Locke's, Fichte's defence of property rights vacillates between defence of satisfying needs and defence of enjoying acquisitions.

It seems clear, both in analysing Fichte (or Locke or Hegel) and in general, that there are many different types of property, each of which can be justified to varying degrees, limited to differing quantities, related to various social relations, analysed for varying ontological categories, and so on. For Fichte, different types of property can be analysed as a series of phenomena that progressively reveal the essential function of property – namely, to transform the human possession of objects into a set of intersubjective social relations. As we look at a series of types of property, we see below how the desire for possessions becomes a desire for a certain kind of sign or mark of recognition, though we also learn how Fichte takes the category of the mark too far.

Seven Forms of Property from Food to Names: The Problem of the Mark

Land: The Mark of the Fence
The state organizes men to grow plants on the land. 'The lands of the commonwealth are chosen by the individuals and guaranteed by the state to each. Their limits are designated by fences or other marks, so that they may always be known. To wantonly remove such marks is a crime, because it leads to endless law disputes' (299). Different kinds of property have to be free from interference in their own ways; farmland requires that no one interfere between planting and reaping time (298). The right to property in land extends only to this determinately limited cultivation of a field (carefully fenced off, or the limit and the law collapse) for personal use.

Mineral Land: The Mark of Government
Since mining is a risky venture, unlike farming, no individual can be guaranteed a living from it. Consequently, only a corporation, which can afford to wait for profits, has a right to own mineral land. Indeed the state is best equipped for such tasks, so mineral lands should be state property (301). The future has the form of public ownership, which alone makes long-term planning possible.

Animals: The Mark of the Brand

Property in animals is acceptable to the extent that a person can make an animal subservient to him (302). The only thing that Fichte sees as a problem in the owning of livestock is that of making known which animal belongs to whom (304). The answer is threefold: the owner should keep the animals on his land; fortunately, animals desire to come back home if they happen to stray; and, lest they wander off or are rustled, the owner should brand the object with his 'mark' (305). This kind of property, which possesses the power of self-locomotion, is beyond Locke's sense of property as only that which one grasps with one's bodily limbs. In some ways, this property wants its freedom, but once tamed, it is property that comes to its owner.

Industry: The Mark of Market Planning

Society is made up of 'producers' of raw materials, and 'artists' who manufacture artificial goods. As usual, the state decides what needs to be produced, distributes work among its labourers, and then buys their wares (312–13). There is to be no unmediated market, and the hand that guides the economy must be highly visible at all times (316). It is not surprising by now that the state has moved from being the witness to being the actual signator of every contract.

Money: The Mark of Pure Form

When the state buys the products it has commissioned from artists and producers, it pays them not in commodities but in money. Fichte sees the source of money not in the attractiveness of gold but in the neutrality of a common marker and the violence of forcing the sale (318–20). After the product-money exchange, the artist/producer is left with two kinds of property: money and items for personal use (such as furniture and jewellery) – pure signs and pure luxuries, respectively – but not his own productions. Though in a sense he still possesses his instruments, his labour power, his land, and other raw materials, these things somehow slip out of Fichte's account. The real issues of economic life have ceased to be a matter of possessions (what Locke naturally thinks of as property) and have begun to be a matter of another kind of power altogether – namely, the power to control marks and signs, the power to control the recognition of others.

The House, the Lock, and the Wilderness: The Mark of the Surrogate

The house comes up here not as a question of immediate surroundings but as one of how to know which pieces of money belong to which person. For the state to know whom to protect in case of thieves after coins, which are not officially marked with the names of the temporary owners, the state would have to keep track of how much each person has. Since that degree of knowledge is impossible (with credit cards it may become possible) the owner must ensure that his coins are 'inseparably connected' with something 'expressly posited as the symbol of all absolute property' (322). One could just keep one's money in one's pockets. But if one wants to use the money later, one could keep it in the 'surrogate of the body' – namely, the house (323). Now, the state knows that the house is mine (though Fichte does not make it clear how this is so), but it is not allowed to look inside at my specific goods (324). 'The lock is the boundary-line between the power of the government and my own private power.' In some circumstances, the state can seize my house as punishment (324), but it cannot enter my house or punish me inside my own house (325). For that matter, if I enter another's house, I do so under *his* private authority and must trust him not to attack me.

It is clear that something very strange is happening here to Fichte's account of property. What began as a relation of reciprocity synthesizing self and other has become a demand for signs justifying other signs, where the ultimate signifier, the house, is desperately invested with a sense of pure privacy, a wild space where any crime is possible. The issue of property has become one of controlling the marks of selfhood.

The Good Name
This is the mark of the owner of the mark. The final form of property is one's good name, the mark as such. The state cannot always prevent overly trusting people from signing contracts with untrustworthy types, beyond the eye of the government (326). So how to protect citizens against infamous characters? By 'warning all citizens against men known to be infamous' (327). The problem of patrolling the good name takes us to the end of Fichte's analysis of property.

Police, Passport, Signature, and Border Patrol

In general, the state's job is to protect people. If violators (whatever the crime) can be made to expiate without being made pure outlaws, that is acceptable (344). A prisoner, on entry into the penal system, should suggest a date by which he will have been reformed. If he meets the deadline, he gains unconditional freedom and full citizenship; if he misses it, he is sent into exile (362). During confinement, the criminal must labour, and earn property, and this will prove his desire to rejoin the Property Compact (362). The proof, oddly enough, that property comes from labour emerges while Fichte speaks of forced labour.

Police mediate between state and citizens; they execute law and protect travellers and traders (375). Since the police themselves are responsible for any crime in their precinct, they must put up a sign in any unsafe neighbourhood as a warning (376). The chief principle of police law is 'that each citizen shall be at all times and places when it may be necessary, *recognized* as this or that particular person.' To this end, 'each one must always carry a pass with him, signed by his immediate government official, in which his person is accurately described. There must be no exceptions to this rule. In the case of important persons, who can afford to pay for it, it may be well to use their portrait (photograph) in the place of word descriptions, which are always more or less insufficient. No person should be received at any place who can not thus make known by his pass his last place of residence and his name' (379).

Obviously the passes can be forged. At this point, Fichte is writing as though he is just clearing up a few unrelated loose ends, but the problem of the guarantee of recognition has taken over. How to test the pass? The government official endorses it (381). How to find the endorser to interrogate him? We can force the pass-holder to declare his last residence, where the endorser lived (381). But what if the whole thing was forged (381), and the endorser either doesn't exist or is a liar too? We could make special paper so that making single forgeries would be too expensive for anyone to bother with (382). But what if somebody does bother, to counterfeit passes or currency (recognition and property finally showing themselves to have the same structure exactly)? A seal should be stamped on legitimate passes (383). Forgers may try anyway, so the state should 'strictly watch' who receives materials that could be used for counterfeiting and check those persons' passes (383). The pass, in short, is to be guaranteed by the state's prevention of counterfeit passes, which it does, circularly, by checking suspicious persons' passes.

According to Fichte, all law then depends on 'detection.' We need more police. If we had enough proper police, we would not need so many undercover spies and informants. Police could wear uniforms – a new and sometimes ridiculed idea, Fichte says, but a good one. After all, spies just pretend that citizens are not watched. But why would citizens not want to be watched? If they are innocent, that is (387).

Fichte's text has degenerated into some kind of nightmarish parody of recognition, where intersubjectivity has been replaced by mutual surveillance. The need for recognition by other people has become a moment-by-moment phobia of not being seen and has as a corollary the phobia of a silent intruder sneaking into one's house.

Locke ignored the role of reciprocal action in the acquisition of property. Fichte grounds property in mutual recognition, but the reciprocity of that recognition is infinitely deferred. Hegel seeks to systematize the reciprocities that constitute property and the state and thereby to synthesize Locke's model of property as product and Fichte's model of property as a recognition contract.

What we have seen so far is that property is not just a category of individual rights but a category of social relations. Property relations develop into relations of mutual recognition; but if property is not understood in this way, it can instead inhibit social reciprocities by encouraging individuals and groups to expropriate possessions from less efficient possessors, as we see in Locke. Fichte does show how property relations develop into higher forms of recognition, but he lets the forms of desire for recognition drift so far from actual production and state institutions that they degenerate into longing and frustration.

Hegel's task is to show how property can transform into mutual recognition, in a way that accomplishes the synthesis of individual and community. This means overcoming the essence of what we usually think of as property – namely, the category of individual possessiveness. At the same time, Hegel attempts to show that the transformation from property into sociality does not leave actuality behind in favour of impossible idealizations of perfect mutuality. The challenge is to retain a sense of productive actuality in a theory of the state, but without allowing remnants of possessive individualism to undermine the universalization of intersubjective recognition. To transform property into recognition without either idealized mutuality or destructive remnants of property – we see below how far Hegel succeeds.

Hegel: Violence and Getting Rid of Things; Copyright and World History

Property is the thing that societies are trying to get rid of, but it sticks to our hands in the form of contingency. That is, on Hegel's account of will, individuals find their nature and end in social relations institutionalized in the state. The state in a sense precedes the emergence of individuals, yet, though property is the immediate form of the social relation, as Locke and Fichte said, it undergoes modification, perhaps abandonment, as the state comes to comprehend itself.

This section is a reading of Hegel's *Philosophy of Right*.[8] I look both at the sections dealing specifically with property rights, and at the subsequent sections in which remnants of the category of property continue to play a role in articulating higher social relations. At the border between property as such and the indirect role of property in higher relations, is Hegel's discussion of intellectual property (sec. 69). It is with copyright law that we see whether property is tranformed into something else or alternatively is left behind when other phenomena are added.

Externalized Will Is the Right to Property

I begin with a brief summary of Hegel's account of the emergence of property rights from will, an argument that carries on the tradition of Locke and Fichte. Mind asserts itself in its freedom and translates itself into existence – which is to say, will (sec. 4). Will develops from being an indeterminate reflection on (hence negation of) surroundings (sec. 5), through to positing determinate content for both self and other (sec. 6), to unifying a constant yet changing agent as an individual (sec. 7). 'An existent of any sort embodying the free will, this is what right is' (sec. 29).

Right is at first seized or claimed as an immediate possession, in the form of property; when internalized and reflected on, it is morality; and when expressed through and through by the whole of society and its parts, it exists in actuality as the state in world history (sec. 33). It is not so much that there is *a* right to property, but that that right *is* at first property.

As a will confronting the world, the person embodies abstract rights. With determinate ends, and determined by natural desires, yet of infinite value as a self-determining subject, it is a 'personality' (sec. 35). As an independent person in a world, the imperative is: 'Be a person and respect others as persons' (sec. 36). In so far as all make the same demands, the rule, both universal and yet restrictive, is: 'Do not infringe on personality and what personality entails' (sec. 38). As in Fichte, in order to exist *for itself* in a world context, the person 'claims the external world as its own' (sec. 39). Right is by definition the abstract form of human directedness – abstract both as a form of claiming the right to objects (seizing them as property rather than constructing a common world out of them) and as a form of claiming a right to the recognition of others (signing a contract with them rather than working together with them).

Now, externalization by definition means that the externalizer finds his end in something other than himself. To draw that conclusion, Hegel argues not so much that the will deserves to have power over objects but that it makes the objects depend on it for their existence (sec. 44). It sounds as though Hegel is only repeating Locke here, but it is only Hegel's premise that the will takes away the object's independence that makes valid Locke's deduction of the right to a thing from the power over the thing. Hegel, in giving the argument that is the condition of his predecessor's argument, puts that predecessor under his power; he makes that argument dependent on him – he makes Locke's philosophy his property, as we see below.

In so far as one's will is externalized in an object, that object itself is set apart from other objects that do not have one's will in it. It is private property (sec. 46). The idea of altogether shared property, which Hegel sees in Plato's *Republic* (sec. 46), misunderstands the moment of individuality in will.

When Locke grounds property in what the body can use, there is an obvious

Locke, Fichte, and Hegel on the Right to Property 59

sense of the limits of the right to property, having to do with the borders of the body. But for Hegel, the body grounds property not as the first consumer of property but as the first instrument for seizing property (sec. 48), so for Hegel the question of the limits of property is not decided by the nature of property (sec. 49). Once property is grounded in the individual's externalization, no characteristic of the individual can stem its momentum. Even if external conditions were imposed, the right to property would be duty bound to violate them. Whereas Locke would like to limit the amount of property a person can have without changing the nature of property, Hegel's argument is that as long as there is private property it cannot have limits in principle. If property has to be limited, that could only be by substituting some other category for property as a whole. The way in which Hegel aims to solve the problem of limit without introducing an external force is by arguing that the logic of taking property entails the need to get rid of it.

Hegel distinguishes three stages in the dialectic of property: the positive moment of taking possession of a thing, the negative moment of using it up, and the 'infinite' moment of 'alienating' forms of exchange and renunciation.

Possession

Possession can take three forms: grasping, forming, and marking. Grasping is direct and immediate. The paradigm is picking up a sensible object that one can hold in one's hand, though grasping is extended by instruments or receptacles, or by conjunction, as when owning land includes owning mineral rights (sec. 55). In grasping, one takes hold of a piece of something (a handle) that has other pieces attached to it on the other side. Here the paradigm keeps a kind of distance from the object even when grasping it by its handle.

Forming an object is possession in the sense of having free reign over changes in the object, as in growing crops or taming animals (sec. 57). By making the object dependent on oneself, one gives the object a new kind of existence for itself. Slavery is a special case here, Hegel says, in that while one forms the slave's mind and body (by feeding and education), one can never own an absolutely free person.

To possess something not by hand but by mark is to universalize the ownership relation beyond physical grasping into a kind of cognitive and institutional representing (sec. 58). Even the acts of grasping and forming, which seem to deal primarily with a subject doing something to an object, deal essentially with the subject doing something to the other subjects observing those acts. The paradigmatic instance of property has quickly shifted from occupying plots of land to controlling the meaning of essences – processing information. The further property acquisition proceeds beyond handfuls of earth, the more property becomes an issue of transformation rather than of simple possession.

Use

The fact that a person has a positive relation to an object, in possessing it, implies that he has a negative relation towards it, namely in changing it. Hegel says that it would be going too far to say (with Locke) that I possess something only while I am changing it, since the point of changing it is that it is dependent on my will, so it is still mine during the times I will to leave it as is (sec. 59). If a person were to claim something that he could not possibly make use of, as if I were to stake a claim to Buckingham Palace (sec. 62), that would be tantamount to claiming to live a life that I could not live, or to have a personality that I can not express, or, worse, to let somebody else's will intrude on my own. Having the freedom to make use of objects does not as a rule mean that usage is arbitrary, since each person's use of objects expresses that person's inherent character. Even when usage is relatively arbitrary, which Hegel accepts as a possibility, it is an arbitrariness that only a project-making, rational being could think up. Arbitrary usage is not a danger to selfhood as long as it is only one's use of personal property that is arbitrary. But continuation of the same kind of arbitrariness into state organization will make property the principal threat in the state.

Now, since the object is universalized in use – destroyed in its particularity in order to serve as one of my satisfactions – it is exchangable for any like object that could satisfy my needs just as well (sec. 63). Grasping dismembers the object; forming changes it; marking abstracts from it; using negates its independent value; money exchanges it for something else – the project of taking property is directed step by step towards getting rid of it. To be sure, there are some social phenomena in history that discourage abandonment of property, as the archaic, irrational law that in early Greece prevented families from selling family land (sec. 63Z). But such a law is possible only when families take precedence over the free personalities of individuals and when people feel that the debt to ancestors takes precedence over mercantile debts. Family land is thus possible only before true property exists. Conversely, the only kind of family that can exist in a world where property exists is the bourgeois family, which has no mausoleum, only a joint bank account (secs. 162–174).

Alienation of Property

Some property is owned for a specified limited amount of time (sec. 64). But in a way, Hegel argues, all property is in principle possessed only to the extent that one can give it up. What is graspable can be thrown away. And once it has fallen out of private use, it is open to public use or to redistribution.

Hegel's examples of this last point are striking. When private tombs are no longer observed, he says, they can be bought as souvenirs; after the Reformation, the Catholics' instruments of the Mass become secular trinkets; when Turkey was overrun, its art treasures were, quite properly, Hegel thinks, auctioned off; and when copyrights run out, texts enter into the public domain (sec. 64). Hegel shows no sense of loss at the destruction of cultures. The standpoint of property is indifferent to previous ownership. Hegel does not explore the possibility that the paradigmatic sense of property might be the booty seized in war or that property right is grounded in cultural conquest. But he does focus on the logic of alienable labour.

The phenomenon that Hegel appeals to is that I can let my property fall into dereliction, or hand it over to others, since it was mine only while my will was in it, at least 'provided the thing in question is a thing external by nature' (sec. 65). This latter qualification seems at first a bit odd, in suggesting the empiricist notion that I can withdraw will from the thing on any moment's notice, as if my acts of will are context-free. In a way, though, the concept of property is this deliberately naïve, externalist misunderstanding of the self–other relation. It is not just that empiricists approve of the property relation as a defining relation of the social contract; rather the property relation is the embodiment of the standpoint of empiricism within the actuality of human society.

The qualification above is that when property consists of one's very personality, such as one's personal ethical or religious convictions, or one's free will, it is inalienable (sec. 66). This exception seems odd. People do commit suicide, bureaucrats become men without qualities, and so on. But Hegel says that they do so only at the risk of creating a schism within their personalities, making themselves deny what they are – in short, by being 'wrong' according to their own principles (sec. 66).

But Hegel approves of some versions of the articulated division of personality into pieces, some of which are alienated. He argues that one does have a right to give away single products of one's skill or to give others limited use of one's abilities for a limited time (sec. 67). This might seem like an ad hoc exception for the sake of capitalist practice of a phenomenon that otherwise violates Hegel's principles. But in fact it arises from a paradox inherent in the will's ability to gives things up without giving itself up. Hegel's idea seems to be that while a slave is committed to a lifetime of willessness, a day labourer can choose to stop any time he wants (sec. 67Z). But this seems an unlikely account of the phenomenology of employment. The only way to make sense of Hegel's example of 'freely' selling one's labour time to 'make a living' is to interpret this right to sell one's time as a consequence of the category of externalization brought to its extreme. Hegel defends the possibility of selling one's time – parts of one's life – not because it is socially just or personally fulfilling but only in that it is consistent with the form of life governed by the categories of property. As a form of life, it is essential for the development of human society, but in its own consequences it begins to show its limitations. The consequence that Hegel is pointing up here is that the externality of property relative to the owner cannot help but be alienating for the maker of property. There is no way to avoid dividing one's self, and treating one's time and even one's self as a kind of property, when one is engaged in the act of making property.

Hegel's next point is that if one can give up part of one's labour, one can give up part of one's mental productions – one's inventions, one's books, in general one's 'methods of expressing oneself' (sec. 68). One might speculate on whether Hegel's text would have taken a different direction had Hegel begun not with externalization as occupancy of land but with externalization as artistic expression. That would have been to follow the tradition of Rousseau and Herder rather than Locke and Fichte. However, such a romantic reading of property would not make any difference. Even if one did share oneself in art, the logic of sending the art into the world would make it possible for any non-romantic to grab it. And in that case, externality takes its revenge on the artist who wanted to include some of his own inwardization with the finished product.

The idea that even one's artistic expression, once externalized as property, is alienating to the producer makes it clear that the category of property as such is an ultimate danger to selfhood (even though the origin of selfhood depended at first on the ability to grasp and shape property). To be sure, we would have liked to be able to express ourselves spiritually and to own property. But Hegel's argument shows that the self-externality of a life devoted to production of property cannot be overcome by producing a more spiritual kind of property; it can be overcome only by turning the whole property relation into a different kind of social relation.

Copyright

Normally, when a person purchases a copy of an artwork, a book, or an invention and gets full rights to the copy, the author retains the right to the original text as a 'capital asset,' along with the exclusive right to make additional copies (s. 69). This is the issue of copyright per se, which becomes for Hegel the paradigmatic case of alienated mental property, and thereby the paradigm of all property. For in some ways even the transfer of physical objects is a transfer of the mental conditions of producing, owning, and reproducing that object. And sending something into the world is not just ridding oneself of it; it is also sending representatives of oneself into the world, communicating with others, and constituting a system of mutual recollections among senders and receivers.

According to Hegel, it is in general a good thing for intellectual development if authors can keep the rights to their ideas. It gives them incentive and security (sec. 69). Hegel's paradigmatic instance of property is the book. The right to property in one's original ideas consists, for example, in Hegel's exclusive right to write Hegel books. Critics have frequently suspected that Hegel's system of the process of absolute spirit is modelled on the process of Hegel writing a book. This might even be what makes the system true. At any rate, the author's right to his book is only half of Hegel's theory of books. The other half is that Hegel, to write his book, has to infiltrate the books of others. Locke and Fichte have to give up to Hegel the exclusive rights to their books, so that he can rewrite their books into his own system. The purpose here of mental production is that readers understand and make those ideas 'possessions' first by memory and then by thought (sec. 69). If mental production is the paradigmatic case of externalizing will, and hence of generating property, the paradigmatic owner is not in fact the producer, but the persons to whom the producer alienates those products.

Each new possessor rethinks the ideas in a 'special form,' so that the ideas then become their capital assets for their own books. In a sense each new possessor possesses the property more than the last. The job of a teacher is to be a kind of 'fence' for alienated – that is to say, stolen – ideas. The important point that Hegel draws from copyright is that a person cannot really expect to keep his abstract right to his property. For Locke, theft is an anomaly. For Fichte, it is an everpresent threat. For Hegel, property is crying out to be stolen.

Property thus turns into something else: first the intersubjectivity of making deals (contract), then a moral duty to take things or give them away, then the state's right to organize material conditions for the sake of rational development.

Hegel's last point in the sections on property consists of his final argument against suicide. Just as one has no right to become a slave, one has no right to sacrifice one's life. Death 'must come from without, either by natural causes, or else, in the service of the Idea, by the hand of a foreigner' (sec. 70). Indeed, since one has rights only to what is subordinate, it makes no sense to talk of having a 'right over oneself' (sec. 70Z). This right over oneself – the very principle with which Locke began, the principle that seemed to be at the heart of Hegel's adoption of the Locke-Fichte tradition of grounding property on self-consciousness – is in the end of the tradition explicitly violated. We have seen on many particular issues that at the very points where Hegel takes Locke or Fichte as a predecessor, he gives the arguments behind (and the consequences ahead of) those predecessors. In this sense, to take someone as a historical predecessor is to become that author's logical predecessor. It is as if the successor is trailing the author home, slipping in behind him as he walks in the door, remaining as an infiltrator, a squatter, and a parasite, and slowly turning it into his own house without the original author ever noticing.

In short, Hegel used Locke and now he abandons him. Locke ends up in the family's funeral urn after all, the philosopher's property, killed, in the service of the Idea, at the hands of the foreigner. All property is destined to be killed by this foreigner.

Contract: Exchange for Its Own Sake

The production and possession of property can only be alienating. Hence, the only way to achieve selfhood once objects come into one's possession is by trading those objects away and by making that act of trade fulfil a need for social relations. To complete an analysis of property, we need to follow the development of those social relations that are no longer exactly property relations but which make transformative use of property relations. In a sense, every topic in political philosophy at least indirectly implicates a function of property. In the remainder of this paper, I look at Hegel's analysis of those post-property categories in which he most explicitly shows how property categories contribute to, transform into, and in some cases hinder progressive development of the state. The primary development in Hegel's argument is that development of the state depends on systematically dismantling property relations. But we also see below that at key points Hegel himself fails to dismantle completely the property categories in his own thinking and that this creates problems for his own analysis of the development of the state.

Contract agreements in some ways seem to be just a more sophisticated structure and guarantor of property rights, and in some passages Hegel himself seems to treat contract in this way. But, in fact, contracts are introduced only at the point where property can no longer be considered a private matter.

As soon as objects are recognized to be inherently exchangeable, each person must recognize that he has his property as a consequence of a negotiation with other people's desires and efforts. The will, the freedom, and the property of each presuppose mutual recognition and can exist only with their 'participation in a common will' (sec. 71). Indeed, though individuals may believe that they contract with others in a Lockean sense only for 'needs, benevolence, advantage, etc.,' it is really reason that signs the contracts. The contradiction of contract is that to see myself as exclusive owner I must identify with a common will, but then the things ought to be common, and not just mine (sec. 72). The community thus deals jointly with an object, while under the somewhat illusory guise of claiming that only one person is dealing with it at a time.

It is odd, albeit traditional, that Hegel considers contract under the assumption that parties to a contract start off on equal footing. In some ways the contract relation is better suited to the categories of master-slave. Nietzsche, for example, thinks of the creditor–debtor relation as the first mark of inequality in human affairs; the paradigmatic contract would then be one where one party is forced into an agreement with another. Yet while Hegel presupposes equal starting points, he seems not to be thinking of contract as motivated by desire for something one does not have, for which one is willing to give up what one does have. Instead, he seems to be thinking of contract (like potlach) as exchange for the pure sake of exchange. On this model, the objects of property themselves are merely instruments for establishing social relations that ultimately have little to do with property. Contract relations allow people to trade away the exclusivity of individuality, to share in a common rationality and a common system of exchange – that is, to trade property for civil society.

Civil Society: The Construction of Needs and the Division of Labour

Political economy exhibits the rationality that works itself out in the midst of the apparently unconnected relations of need and satisfaction that hold among men, each with their own interests, some vigorous, some lazy, some lucky, and so on (sec. 182). Men have needs – for example, for food, housing, and respect – and to satisfy these needs, they work out strategies of labour (secs. 190–1). Hegel points out that others can make us feel needs in order that they may 'profit' by selling things to us (sec. 191Z). Since each person is thereby determining the needs of others, and each is involved in the satisfaction of each, each person is not just setting himself to labour but is setting others to work as well, so that the system as a whole is fulfilling the needs of all at once (sec. 192). 'Everything private becomes something social' (sec. 192Z). Property, fulfilled, is not private, but social.

In effect, what is consumed is not an object in nature but a product of human labour, indeed a product of somebody else's labour (sec. 196). From the standpoint of individuals, some people will feel 'needy' no matter how much luxury they have (sec. 195), some will suck others dry, and so on. But from the standpoint of the system, the political economist observes a vast pool of capital from which each person 'draws a share,' and by his labour puts something (perhaps not exactly the same amount) back (sec. 199). This may be an act of violence for the individual, but it is neutral for capital. Because individuality is not lost, there are bound to be inequalities both in possessions and – more

66   Jay Lampert

important – among the agricultural, business, and civil-servant classes (sec. 201). Even if in a sense civil society is entirely devoted to production and consumption, the issue, Hegel argues, shifts away from possession towards satisfaction, away from property towards human organization, towards the issue of law and justice. The problem that I am marking from this point on is the way in which remnants of property rights frustrate emergence of the universal in civil society. At the same time, Hegel's own ambiguity over whether he expects property rights to disappear frustrates his ability to describe a fulfilled state.

The Judicial System: Contingency (the Remnant of Property) in Decision-Making

The primary concern of law is 'the endlessly growing complexity and subdivision of social ties and the different species of property and contract within the society' (sec. 213). But Hegel's section on law does not concentrate on what property law should consist of. It focuses on how administration of a legal system can avoid arbitrary application contingent on the arbitrary will of judges. That is, contingency in division of property across society carries over into contingency in society's decision-making.

Case law cannot be 'deduced' from positive law (sec. 212), and while judicial precedents anticipate, but underdetermine, subsequent cases (sec. 211), and while judicial discretion is inevitable (sec. 211Z), and while specific punishments have to be set in each case individually (sec. 214), Hegel argues that the fact that the concepts behind the law are recognized prevents the judges from counting as legislators (sec. 211). It seems unlikely that Hegel thought that his own solution to arbitrariness was complete. Law is supposed to regulate property, thereby to raise the contingencies of private property to the social universal. But the contingency of the law itself – the very contingent character of property, which now attaches itself to the law that was supposed to curtail that contingency – perpetuates the contingencies – of property. And to the extent that precedents are the legal property of society (the way books are its intellectual property), we can say that the frustration of civil society consists in the way in which it must, but cannot, unite with its property. There is an element of case-by-case, on-the-spot contingency of judgment and enforcement that cannot be excluded. To this extent, responsibility for generating a unity of society under law falls not to the courts but to the police.

Police and Public Utilities

In one sense the police do not interfere in private property. 'Given good laws, a state can flourish, and freedom of property is a fundamental condition of its prosperity' (sec. 229Z). Police are to prevent crime, which in effect means that they prevent injury to persons and property (sec. 231). But to prevent injury before it happens, the police do have to interfere in private actions before those private actions actually consist of public violations. But once the police have been given powers to intervene in advance of injury (sec. 234), and given that the state has an interest in 'prosperity' (sec. 229Z), it follows that the police have the power to step into the marketplace in advance of all transactions in order to maximize efficiency. Hence the police should have the power to run the marketplace as a kind of public utility (s. 235). The point is to assure in advance that the contingency of the private not interfere with the unity of the public.

It is clear for Hegel that the private (in property), the contingent (in judgment), and the arbitrary (in will) never disappear even once everyone recognizes that 'unity is the chief of all desiderata' (sec. 300Z). Nevertheless all the power of the state is devoted to turning private interests public. It would be inappropriate to make a utopian argument that Hegel should have found a way to remove interests of private property and contingent will from the unified state. However, it is incorrect to interpret Hegel as being benignly 'making room' for private property or allowing for inevitable contingency. The dialectic of the overcoming of property in Hegel's text is precisely that property must be overcome and that it cannot be. The individual must have his own house, his own food, and his own choices, while at the same time the individual finds his space, his needs, and his ends in systematic relations with others. The state needs him to need his property, but the individual wills the state to will his property transformed.

Solving the Problem of Poverty: Colonies or Corporations

Whatever individuals may or may not still possess privately, the essential structure of property is to be transformed by law, by justice, and by economics into public utility and mutual recognition. But since a conscious being never simply loses its sense of individuality, even when it develops systematic, self-conscious relations in a community, Hegel recognizes that individual property never disappears. There will always be a tendency for some members of a society to expropriate the property of others, to leave behind a whole class in a state of poverty. By being left out of the propertied society, by not having enough property, the poor are the last members of society to be defined especially by property categories. The capacity to do away with poverty, the last remnant of property categories, is the ultimate test of civil society as a whole.

Hegel recognizes therefore not only that the enjoyment of property can be an act of violence but that as profit-motivated industry increases, and the division of labour becomes extreme, a whole class will fall into 'dependence and distress' and will lose access to both physical and intellectual enjoyment (sec. 243). If the poor slip into a state of resentment, despair, undirected anger, and frivolity, the society has collapsed (sec. 244Z).

Hegel offers two solutions to poverty. Charity is not a solution, since it robs recipients of self-respect; public works projects are almost a solution, but they result in overproduction of commodities (sec. 245). To resolve the problem of overproduction specific to public works projects, Hegel observes that civil society goes to sea. It seeks markets abroad that are 'deficient in the goods it has overproduced, or else generally backward in industry' (sec. 246). (Obviously this solution can work only as long as some societies are behind others [though Hegel's account of world history does assume this, as we see below], and obviously the backward country's poverty is exacerbated [though Hegel says nothing about that].) International trade is thus essentially colonialization, in which 'progressive peoples' take to the sea and backward, superstitious ones stay inland (sec. 247). ('Progressive' peoples inevitably lose control of their societies and so have to ship the detritus of their economic practices elsewhere.) To the colonies they send their excess labourers. Where the excess labour will go when the world has been grabbed up is not clear from Hegel's text. And Hegel's account of the relation between the colonial homeland and the emigrants who found the colony abroad essentially omits the indiginous peoples altogether. We return shortly to the problem of national borders and the possession of colonies, but it is clear that colonialization in itself will not solve the problem of poverty on a world scale. The internationalist element of Hegel's first solution to poverty cannot succeed without an element of mutual responsibility, and this latter is suggested in Hegel's second solution.

Hegel's second solution to poverty involves the 'corporation' – a kind of trade union or industrial association. It handles its members' interests, membership drives, insurance, training, and so on (sec. 252). The problem of wealth and poverty is solved: since success will be measured by effort within the group, individuals will not require idiosyncratic excess to prove their worth, and the poor will have the right to work within their corporation and so will earn their way out of poverty. People in a society, especially those engaged in industry, where there is a tendency to think that the highest end is private property, must realize that the work they do is always 'work with a public character' (sec. 255Z). They must think of themselves as a 'we.' Private property here is effectively a minor byproduct of distributed power sharing in the state.

This second solution in a way is univeralist. Why does Hegel allow it to be undermined by the colonial borders involved in the first solution? This is the key moment, close to the end of the *Philosophy of Right*, at which the development of the state seems to be leading to a kind of global civil society, a totality of syntheses of individual and universal will. Something prevents Hegel from drawing that conclusion, which would be natural to the logic of the entire text. Some category from an unsynthesized stage of the dialectic is preventing the dialectic from reaching its own fulfilment. Something about the structure of property is persisting in Hegel's analysis of the relations between nations and cultures.

World History and the Border

Hegel begins his account of nationality by suggesting that people have to be willing to sacrifice their property altogether in order to protect their state. Whereas civil society protects property against personal arbitrariness, the sovereign state calls for citizens to sacrifice property and even life in the interests of the united people (sec. 324). Yet Hegel is in a way just pushing the role of the private one step up, into the autonomy of the state itself in relation to other states. At this level, the private is once again made to be violated, in war. 'Perpetual peace' in the Kantian ideal would lead just to corruption, Hegel says, whereas war purifies by its 'indifference to the stabilization of finite institutions' (sec. 324). The state's stable success will be expressed in the military-industrial complex that in the end sweeps the state away. 'To be sure, war produces insecurity of property, but this insecurity of things is nothing but their transience – which is inevitable' (sec. 324Z). Up to this point, Hegel reaffirms the position that possessive individualism, even including the possession by a national state of its own institutions, must be subordinated to the sweep of world culture.

But Hegel's suggestion of globalism hits a limit. The contact of states, he says, as expressions of self-knowledge, ought to be governed by some kind of international law. But Hegel goes on to say that, unfortunately, there can be no highest world arbitrator, so international law must always remain at the level of an 'ought' (sec. 330Z). Hegel's reason for backing away from international law seems based on a romanticization of peoples over rationality. Yet if Hegel argues that families dissolve into the state, why does he not conclude that states dissolve into world politics? The answer lies in Hegel's theory that world history does not develop throughout the world simultaneously. In this last issue of Hegel's text, his own account of the history of forward and backward nations is itself a product of remnants of property categories that have stuck to Hegel's analysis even when he thought he was overcoming them.

Hegel's immanent critique of the theory of property rights from Locke to Fichte, and his correct analysis of the way property categories must be overcome in the progressive development of systematic social relations, are finally left incomplete by the remnants of property categories in his account of world history.

World history, he says, is the mind's rational 'interpretation of itself to itself' in stages, rejecting lower forms for higher (sec. 343). The history of an individual nation is of philosophical interest only in so far as nations are the clothing of mind (sec. 346). But once a nation has served its purpose, it has lost for ever its place in world history. It sounds as if we citizens are the property of mind, rather than vice versa, and that mind withdraws its possession of us when we are used up. In so far as the most advanced nation is the one embodying mind, that nation is in effect the world subject, and other nations become the objects for the consciousness of that subject. The civilized nations have a right 'to treat as barbarians those who lag behind them' (sec. 351). To the victor of history, go the others as spoils, in the same way that a person's memories become a part of him.

Why does overcoming the categories of property by the state have to end for Hegel with nations treating other nations as barbarians?

The claim of state autonomy and national borders, which was never really given a rational foundation in Hegel's text, and which was acceptable for the sake of the argument only as long as we could think of it as a remnant of arbitrary property-parcelling that still needed to be overcome, persists in Hegel's account to the very end. However, it does not seem impossible to rewrite the last chapter of Hegel's text. In the big picture, the relation of a person to his environment is caught up in much bigger systems than can be accounted for by the categories of grasping and trading. So if in world history the relation of individuals to objects is not really a property relation, we ought to conclude (following Hegel's principles but against his conclusion), then neither is the relation of states to one another. Just as war destroys property when it is time for the infusion of new ideas, so history must destroy borders. From the largest standpoint, should someone in the Hegelian tradition not think of the different nations as each willing a different element or perspective of the world mind, where some kind of cross-cultural hermeneutic constitutes the principle of progress, rather than as following a rather linear, one-nation-at-a-time model? Hegel seems stuck in the model of the relation between superior and subordinate, the model that first justified property rights, even though his own exemplar of the end of property in copyright violations suggested that he was about to work out a model involving the joint dialogue of authors. If the latter were treated as the paradigm of world history, the categories of property would have been more fully overcome, as seemed to be promised earlier in the text.

In the tradition of Locke, Fichte, and Hegel on the issue of property rights, the problem of the national border is consistently a bell-wether topic, though none of the three highlights it specifically as an issue of property. For Locke, the topic slips in in the form of guarding a community against the inefficient use of property carried on outside its borders. For Fichte, it slips in in the form of sending outlaws into exile so that they will not interfere with the mutual recognition of property owners within the borders. For Hegel, the border is the persistence of the element of private will that entered the world in the form of property and will not leave.

Yet in all three cases the implied material on the other side of the border ought to, but does not, undermine the sense the philosopher has of property within the border. For Locke, the American Indians on the other side of the border ought to have given the occasion to rethink the conception of efficiency. For Fichte, the countries into which exiles would be sent, and which would thereby have to have treaties with the exiling state, ought to have provided an occasion to reformulate the conception of recognition without constant spying. And for Hegel, the historical contributions of parts of the world such as Africa, concerning which Hegel has a notorious blind spot, ought to have created an opportunity to complete the transformation of property into the history of self-knowing. This is no doubt the most difficult blind spot for any philosopher either of property or of borders. The ultimate boundary of a culture's borders are those beyond which there is not just somebody else's territory and somebody else's property, but those beyond which there is a culture that does not measure by property or by borders at all.

Since Hegel especially is concerned to trace the transformation of property into something that is not property, in order to trace the history that unites the world mind, Hegel cannot afford to assume that communities that dismiss property rights and state borders are lagging behind those that have not yet overcome those forms of arbitrary individuality. This is not to say in advance that every community has an equally successful or rational way of negotiating the relation between the private and the public. But it is to say that for a Hegelian (and of course being in the tradition of Hegel might mean treating Hegel as conquerors treat their prey – namely, by plundering their treasures and hanging them on a new wall), the borders of one's home state must be torn down even if one is not sure whether what will flow in will increase the quantity of recognizable material or transform it utterly.

Conclusion

I conclude with a brief remark concerning the relation between this essay and two other contributions to this volume, the fine pieces by James Crooks (chapter 12) and David Kolb (chapter 7). I think that all three of our papers deal with the transformation from free-playing individualities to the structured necessity of systematic totality. Crooks is trying to show how the road to system is blocked by some aspects of the musical play of fugue – because it is essentially a deed rather than a theory, and because it is ironical and dialogical rather than synthetic. I think that Crooks hopes that, by finding something that the system cannot systematize, he can show that there is room for a kind of individual play that systematic Hegelianism would remove. Kolb is concerned that the closure of the system of logical categories would imply that the various religious voices in world history would have to be closed into a developmental history. In the absence of a clear axis by which to rate religions for degree of advancement, Kolb suggests an '"open" Hegelianism,' though he notes also that if there is no scheme of advancement, then there is no determinate negation, and then no Hegelianism at all.

Within the concerns of both Crooks and Kolb is the modernist concern that the integrity of individual voices and cultures may be lost if the system closes. In this sense, one might be concerned that the system would exclude private property as well. The fact that Hegel does not exclude a role for private property might therefore seem consoling. But the problem here is that the unsystematized material is not benign; it is not a way of blowing off steam or singing in private for one's own amusement or praying that one's culture be left alone. For a phenomenon to claim resistance to synthesis is for it to threaten its own kind of hegemony. This is clear in the case of private property, whose claim is to 'leave room' for the individual but whose meaning is to monopolize power in a system of production. Similarly, fugue seems like irony at first, but it soon develops the sneer of a prince. And Kolb points out that every religion reinterprets world-historical phenomena in its own images and thereby pre-empts the rights of others to do the same. There is no neutral space for individuality to settle into. Property, fugue, and cultural autonomy are not just looser forms of organization that allow some room for social harmony and some room for individuality; they are instead active opponents of the social.

But perhaps the appearance that the world is too restrictive if the synthesis is closed and too dangerous if it is not is the result of conceiving of both the closed system and the open one on a model that treats viewpoints as pieces of property and systematic relations as border crossings. On the property model, the system can look only like some army swarming across borders (temporal as well as spatial and ideational) and imposing its will on us. Similarly, individuality can appear on this model only as holding something back (which neither Crooks nor Kolb is advocating). And the development of world history can appear to each nation only as something that happens for it. Yet thinking of the system as a kind of authority involves drawing the model of system from the model of a possessive individual – a singularity that dominates the things that it owns – which is to think of the system on a model that is precisely what the system overcomes. But if the property model of interpreting the system's control over its material could be induced to transform finally into a social organization model, then the system itself would appear as a dialogue, a community, and a text in the public domain where the whole system of parts would develop together. History would not be more for our sake than for theirs, but we could say that whatever is is part of the same stage of development. Our open listening and free-playing engagement would be not for the sake of avoiding system but for making it mean something more than any one person could own.

Notes

1 Wilfred Ver Eecke, 'Hegel on Freedom, Economics, and the State,' in William Maker, ed., *Hegel on Economics and Freedom* (Macon, Ga: Mercer University Press, 1987), 127–57.
2 Peter G. Stillman, 'Property, Contract, and Ethical Life in Hegel's *Philosophy of Right*, in Drucilla Cornell, Michel Rosenfeld, and David Gray Carlson, eds., *Hegel and Legal Theory* (New York: Routledge, 1991), 205–27.
3 H.S. Harris, 'The Social Ideal of Hegel's Economic Theory,' in L.S. Stepelevich and David Lamb, eds., *Hegel's Theory of Action* (Atlantic Highlands, NJ: Humanities Press, 1983), 49–74.
4 John Locke, *The Second Treatise of Government* (Indianapolis: Bobbs-Merrill Company, Inc., 1952).
5 For a philosopher usually thought of as an empiricist, there is almost nothing in Locke's definitions that brings power and the other terms back to sense impressions. If Locke is an empiricist in his political philosophy, it is in the sense that he is a philosopher of positive relations, of externalities in Hegel's sense, a philosopher of abstract right. Burbidge shows in his introduction to this volume how Harris makes Hegel speak English and so turns empiricism into Hegelianism. In the present paper, the development of the idea of property exhibits within itself the same transformation from the empiricist to the systematic standpoint.
6 Heidegger in 'The Question Concerning Technology' argues that the idea that all the objects in the world exist as a ready supply, or a standing reserve, is a defining idea of the technological worldview. In Martin Heidegger, *Basic Writings*, ed. David Farrell Krell (New York: Harper and Row, 1977), 283–317, especially 297–99.
7 Johann Gottlieb Fichte, *Sammtliche Werke Zweite Abteilung, A. Zur Rechts- und Sittenlehre, Herausgegeben von J.H. Fichte* (Berlin: Verlag von Zeit und Comp., 1845), translated as *Science of Rights (Grundlage des Naturrechts nach Principien der Wissenschaftslehre)*, trans. A.E. Kroeger (London: Routledge and Kegan Paul, 1889). The translation is old and often takes liberties with the text.
8 Georg Wilhelm Friedrich Hegel, *Grundlinien der Philosophie des Rechts* (Hamburg: Verlag von Felix Meiner, 1967), translated as *Hegel's Philosophy of Right*, trans. T.M. Knox (London: Oxford University Press, 1967).

PART TWO: ART

3

Hegel and Hamann: Ideas and Life

JOHN McCUMBER

I

With his Aristotelian affinities and Kantian descent, Hegel thinks that philosophy is our highest task, and he would not be pleased to admit that there is any larger: 'If, as Aristotle says, theory is the most blessed and the best among good things, those who participate in that pleasure know what they gain from it – the satisfaction of the necessity of their spiritual nature. They can hold back from making demands on others, and can content themselves with their own needs (*Bedürfnisse*) and the satisfactions which they obtain for them.'[1] Other passages where this end is decked out in reams of Hegelian encomium are not difficult to find – indeed, are often hard to avoid. And so it seems that, for Hegel, philosophy need not contribute to life beyond philosophy: it is an end in itself, and the highest there is; *um so schlecter für das Leben*. But Hegel also knew that philosophy would always be a primary interest of just a very few people.[2]

There are places where Hegel thinks of philosophy not as the culmination of the entire human enterprise but as part of it. One such is in his remarkable essay of 1828 on the religious writer and cultural *Ungeheuer* Johann Georg Hamann. According to Hegel, Hamann was unusual partly because, though an obvious genius, he felt no need (*Bedürfnis*) for philosophy: 'the need for scientificality itself, the need to become conscious of one's ideas (*Gehalt*) in thought, to see that content develop itself in thought, and just as much to confirm itself in that form, to satisfy itself as thought itself, was completely foreign to him.'[3] Hamann felt no need of philosophy – but his whole life manifested it. As the word *Geschmack* ('taste') in a similar passage on page 280 indicates, what Hegel has in mind when he writes of the 'development of a content' has something in common with Kant's principles of enlarged thought. In such thought, we undertake to test the results of our judgment against the opinions of others (and against the possible views of those whom we cannot actually consult), ready to learn from them and revise our views if need be.[4] The thought in which content must develop is then that not of an individual but of a community.

Unwilling to submit his thought to others in this way, Hamann 'persisted in the profound concentration of his particularity' – indulged himself in the purest, and hence most idiosyncratic, forms of self-expression. 'He, who should have become one our best writers, was seduced by the desire to be original and became one of the most reproachable.' Full of private jokes and allusions, Hamann's writings are incapable of reaching a broad public: some love them, others hate them, none understands them.[5]

Hamann's lack of interest in the concrete expression of his thought also allowed its core to remain very abstract indeed. His version of Christianity was intensely and deeply meaningful – for him. But it was without any doctrine, community, or moral guidance, bereft even of the command to love:[6] 'Hamann utterly failed to appreciate that the living reality of divine Spirit does not keep itself in such contraction but is its own development (*Ausführung*) to a world and a creation, and is this only by way of the production of distinctions whose limitations, yes, but also whose legitimacy and necessity in the life of finite spirit must be granted recognition.[7] Hamann's reduction of Christianity to his own rhapsodies – to the 'actuality of [his own] individual presence'[8] – was in a sense liberating, for it enabled him to see through all sorts of fixed dogma, including various separations and distinctions that Kant claimed to have established as ultimate. But it deprived him, we have seen, of a public: And this meant that he relied greatly on his private circle: on his friends.[9]

There, too, Hamann's unreceptivity to philosophy caused him trouble. In his earlier years, he took it on himself – as a 'divine vocation'[10] – to help his friends to self-knowledge by scolding them for their every failing. This project produced a series of wrecked relationships, which Hegel recounts in several places and at painful length.[11] Eventually – aided by the abstract and nebulous nature of his Christianity, which enabled him to tolerate a great many things that more sober Christians regard as failings – Hamann abandoned his scolding. But his inner personal core did not come to expression at all: it remained foreign to his own everday life, and hence foreign to his friends.[12] The keynote of his later life was that his friendships dissolved, no longer in dispute, but in mutual incomprehension:

> and incomprehension is in this perhaps worse than disagreement, that it is [always] connected and afflicted with misunderstanding of oneself, while disagreement may be directed against others alone ... If sentiments, thoughts, representations, interests, principles, beliefs, and perceptions (*Empfindungen*) are communicable among hu-

man beings, in the view of [Hamann's] circle there remained, *beyond* and *behind* all such concrete individuality the naked and concentrated intensity of feeling, of faith. This simple and ultimate element alone was supposed to have absolute worth, and could only be found, known, and enjoyed through the living presence (*lebendige Gegenwart*) of a trustful interiority that held nothing back, gave itself wholly ...

Since in this kind of relationship the distinctiveness and particularity of various viewpoints comes to the fore – and does so in unclarity, since the entire situation here is unclarity itself – and since this appearance as such does not correspond to the supposedly *ineffable* interiority which is sought for and demanded to be seen, the soul does not yield itself to comprehension and the result is *indéfinissable*, and incomprehensibility and unsatisfied yearning: a mood in which people, without really being able to say why, find themselves separate and foreign to one another, instead of having found one another – which they thought was the only possibility.[13]

The problem with Hamann and his circle, then, was a failure of dialogue: they were unable to discuss what was important. The opinions and representations that they shared were considered by them to be trivialities, while their deeper natures were manifested in mute devotion or in the immediate, idiosyncratic 'expectorations' found, for example, in Hamann's writings on Kant.[14] There was no attempt to find a common ground of intelligibility – no effort to articulate words in which, though they might disagree, they might at least understand one another.

Systematic philosophy, if this is what Hamann so deeply lacked, is in the first instance necessary for a certain type of friendship. As such it is directed not against disagreement but against a more profound malaise – the separation and foreignness that remain a mere feeling because people 'cannot really say why' they find themselves in it. Systematic philosophy is thus a temporal process in which participants gain the words they can use to understand one another – in which they create for themselves, and for their community, a company of words.

Misunderstanding is, Hegel notes, to be distinguished from disagreement. If you and I disagree, it is possible for me to be wholly clear about my own opinion, and even perhaps wholly justified in it. But if I do not understand you, it is because I do not have words that would enable me to do so. And to be missing the right words is, for the *zoon logon echon*, always a problem. It means being incapable of articulating not only another's but one's own thoughts on certain issues; unable to formulate, let alone decide, certain questions; barred from entering into certain communal practices, from playing certain games.

This does not mean that philosophy has no role in resolving disagreements. In the year of the essay on Hamann, Hegel writes (with reference to C.W.F. Solger), 'Most, indeed all disagreements and contradictions (*Widersprüche*) must be resolvable through the seemingly easy tactic of setting before oneself what one has actually said, simply examining it, and comparing it with the rest of what one similarly maintains. Knowing what one is saying is much rarer than we think.'[15] This stance of course is exaggerated, and Hegel knew it. Two pages earlier he had written, 'There is one species of incomprehension which, it can be directly demanded, ought not to exist, namely, incorrectness (*Unrichtigkeit*) as regards what is actually the case ... Philosophy must at least complain, where justified, about the false statement of the facts, and if one looks closely this species [of incomprehension] is, surprisingly, the most common, and sometimes attains unbelievable dimensions.'[16] Empirical disagreements exist, indeed predominate. But the philosophically more respectable and interesting controversies result from 'not knowing what one says.' They are to be overcome not by empirical investigation but by what we would call analysis of the terms in which those controversies are couched.

I am, in Hegel's view, what I can say: for Hamann and his circle to have the kind of friendship they wanted, they needed a different kind of language, a different sort of self. They needed to be the kind of person who neither identifies so utterly with her opinions and values that to reject them is to reject her (as with the younger Hamann) nor holds her ownmost essence aloof from interaction (as with the older Hamann). To enter into the kind of friendship that Hegel here advocates is thus to have a self that is able both (1) to articulate itself completely and (2) to abandon wrong or unintelligible ideas, habits, practices, and so on, without abandoning itself.

The completeness claim in (1) needs qualification. Hegel does not believe that everything about us and our experiences is articulable: the opening pages of the *Phenomenology* teach that the sheer immediacy of sensory experience is not.[17] And since Hegel, like a good empiricist, holds (as the *Encyclopaedia*'s Introduction puts it) that *nihil est in intellectu quod non fuerit in sensu*,[18] this ineffability continues to shadow all articulation – all the way, perhaps, to the system itself. Where Hamann went wrong was not in recognizing that certain aspects of himself were ineffable but in positing that ineffable dimension as his own essence and making it the governing factor in his relationships with others.

It is easy to recognize the kind of self that Hegel implicitly advocates here as the 'consolidated self' I have elsewhere argued was the *telos* of the *Phenomenology*:[19] a self that is in harmony between the unity that makes it 'a' self at all and the multiplicity that makes it rich and dynamic. The consolidation of the self is thus an achievement of harmony over diversity or, as Hegel puts it in the *Lectures on the Philosophy of Religion*, of healing a rupture (*Entzweiung*): '[The need for truth] presupposes that in subjective spirit the demand is present to cognize absolute truth. Such need means immediately that the subject is [currently] in untruth; as spirit, however, the subject is something over and above this untruth, and hence its untruth is something that is to be overcome. The untruth [of the soul] is, more precisely, that the subject is split within itself, and need expresses itself to the extent that this rupture be sublated ... and this reconciliation can only be reconciliation with the truth.'[20]

Such consolidated selves are a condition for the formation of all sorts of human groups, as well as for society itself. As Jürgen Habermas has maintained, and more clearly than Hegel, language is not merely a private affair but is the fundamental social means by which we coordinate actions. The nature of a society and the groups it contains can be understood from the sorts of interaction that it, and they, sanction and seek.[21] A self that is to any degree inarticulate is then, like the older Hamann, asocial. One who cannot give up old beliefs and old ways is, like the younger Hamann, anti-social.

II

Hamann's unrecognized need for philosophy thus manifested itself throughout his life: in confilict with friends and in his inability to be understood by them. Hamann's writings, by contrast, concern a need that Hamann did indeed recognize, and which in Hegel's view should have called forth – but again, did not – the need for philosophy: the need for language. Hamann claims that the need is, in the first instance, that of reason, which requires language as a sort of material basis. Kant had viewed reason as alinguistic, and Hamann opposes this 'purism' with a Berkeleian conception of sense impressions as a divine language.

Hamann begins his *Metacritique: On the Purism of Pure Reason* by giving what for him is the core lesson of the empiricists, citing Hume's version of Berkeley's critique of Locke:[22] 'Ein großer Philosoph hat behauptet, daß allgemeine und abstrakte Ideen nichts als Besondere sind, aber an ein gewisses Wort *gebunden*, welches ihrer Bedeutung mehr Umfang oder Ausdehnung giebt und zugleich uns jener bei einzelnen Dingen erinnert.'[23] I have quoted the German because it contains a pregnant mistranslation. In the passage Hamann quotes, Humes speaks – as did Locke – of an idea being 'annexed' to a term. This use of 'annexation' calls for investigations that I cannot pursue here; but it is clear that, for Locke and Hume, if an idea is 'annexed' to a name, then their connection can be undone so that we can break through to what Berkeley called 'naked ideas.'[24] Thus for Locke annexation is the 'voluntary connexion' of a word and a complex idea.[25] It is not bondage: if it is voluntarily done, it can voluntarily be undone. Similarly for Hume: 'The word,' he writes, 'raises up an individual idea, along with a certain custom.' The custom here is just the habit of referring to a variey of different impressions with a single name and is not necessarily permanent: the same idea may at different times be annexed to different words.[26]

But Hamann fatefully translates 'annexed' not for example with *beigefügt* but with *gebunden*, so that general ideas are bound to the words that stand for them as we are, for example, 'bound' to an oath (*an eine Eide gebunden*). Ideas are thus from the start word-bound for Hamann, as they are not for the empiricists: to think without words – which is precisely what the *große Philosoph*, Berkeley, made essential to philosophical method – is for Hamann senseless.

Ideas are not merely 'bound' to words for Hamann: they may even be created by them. This is illustrated, two pages later, by the word 'metaphysics.' Hamann accepts the traditional view, now discredited, that the name is a mistake: that early editors of Aristotle introduced it to cover a number of treatises they placed following ('meta') the *Physics* in the order of his works. Once the name was in place, however, it inevitably resulted in those treatises being viewed as constituting a single investigation, aiming at completing the *Physics*'s account of natural phenomena by investigating what lies beyond (again, 'meta') them.[27] The name thus created the idea – one of the central ideas in the Western tradition.

Hamann's own 'metacritique' aims at continuing Kant's critique of reason by exposing and investigating what lies beyond the purity of Kantian pure reason: language itself.[28] We become aware of this, Hamann argues, by seeing that pure reason is not simply given but has been constituted by a twofold purification.[29] The first stage was the attempt, associated with Descartes,[30] to make reason independent of all tradition, including cultural heritage and religious faith. The second, clearly attempted by Kant, was to make reason independent of experience altogether. But these two purifications cannot be completed without a third: reason must be made independent of language, for a language conveys the tradition and heritage of its speakers, as well as the more or less scientific results of the inductions that its speakers have performed over history. Thus when Kant claims, for example, that the concept of freedom is entirely independent of sensory expereience and so can be given no sensible display, it is inconsistent of him to go on and define it in the ancient words of philosophical German. At least as wrong was the idea of deriving the 'pure concepts of the Understanding,' or the categories, from consideration of the basic forms of predication; language, writes Hamann, has no other credentials than usage and tradition.[31]

Hence, as Günter Wohlfahrt points out, none of the three purifications is possible for Hamann.[32] Reason for Hamann is never pure, but at most a concrete formative power whose material is language. Philosophical discourse, correspondingly, is not a pure description or argumentative consideration of ultimate facts, but a series of transformations of words – the rekneading of old leaven.[33] It is this creative transformation of language that is carried out by what Josef

Simon calls the 'concrete reason' that Hamann defends against what he sees as the artificially purified version put forward by Kant.[34] Such reason takes its 'pure a priori forms,' or its elements, from words and letters[35] – or, for Hamann, as we see below, from the basic sounds and visual forms of the sensory world. Articulating these into what we ordinarily understand as words, it creates something midway between sense and intellect: 'Words thus have [both] aesthetic and logical capacities. As visible and sensible objects, they belong with their elements to sensibility and intuition, but according to the spirit of their institutionalization (*Einsetzung*) and meaning, to the Understanding and to concepts.'[36]

Reason needs language thus not merely as its material basis but in order to overcome the great split in Kant's account of the human mind – that between sensibility and the *a priori* faculties (Reason and the Understanding). But the capacity of language to heal dualisms goes beyond this. For it seems that Hamann actually crosses and undoes two basic Kantian dichotomies: that between the empirical and the *a priori* and that between intuition and concepts. As empirical intuitions, words are the basic sounds and visual forms we experience, and as such they direct the distinctions we form. But as set up or 'instituted' by human beings, words are also pure intuitions, because they have no role in determining the meaning attached to them: the arbitrariness of the designator is thus its purity from the very empirical distinctions that its meaning aims to capture. In their arbitrary meaninglessness, words are merely 'indeterminate objects of empirical concepts': it is only through their association with such concepts that they become determinate objects for the Understanding.[37] Hence the only sense in which words can be 'pure' or 'a priori' follows from their arbitrariness. The view that there is a truly *a priori* realm, in Kant's sense, is the *proton pseudos*, the first falsehood, of his transcendental philosophy.[38]

Words thus play their unifying role for Hamann in virtue of a deeper doubleness in their nature. On the one hand, they grow up from the basic, elementary forms of sensory experience and direct formation of concepts. On the other hand, they are entirely subservient to concepts, because as mere sounds they cannot determine the meanings that they are given. These two aspects of language coincide for Hamann. In one of the most demented moments of the *Metacritique* (itself a far more demented text than my account here dares to portray it), he asks the reader to imagine a ladder on which armies of intuitions climb into the 'fortress' of reason, while armies of concepts descend into the 'deepest abysses of the most intensely felt sensibility.' When the two hosts meet, they fall on one another with 'wanton need' – a hypostatic union whose manifest image is to be found, Hamann claims, in the dynamics of ordinary language.[39] So language is not merely a need of reason. We ourselves, as concrete individuals, must have language if we are to exist in harmony with ourselves.

But how can words be going both ways at once? How can they both depend on and guide our concepts? If ideas are 'bound to' words, how can words be unable to determine their own meaning? To answer this, we must arrive at the deepest of language's healing powers: its capacity to close the gap between God and man. I have said that the elements of language for Hamannn are the basic visual and aural forms of our sensory experience. It is this language – Berkeley's language of the Author of Nature[40] – that ascends the ladder, guiding our empirical distinctions. This is the origin of all language and was taught to Adam in the Garden of Eden. There, 'every appearance of nature was a word – the sign, sensible image, and pledge of a new, secret, ineffable, but all the more internal unification, communication, and community of divine energies and ideas. Everything that man in the beginning heard, saw, contemplated and touched was a living word: for God was the word.'[41]

It is here that Hamann undoes the subservience that language had to ideas in British empiricism. Now the two are no longer radically different sorts of thing, as they were even for Berkeley, but the same; where Berkeley viewed divine language (ideas) as radically other than human language, Hamann has merged the two – and into words, not ideas. The one ultimate word of this divine language of nature, which is also its one definite meaning, is God himself.[42] As such, God unites all oppositions and is the 'coincidence of opposites' – including the hypostatic union of sensible and intellectual that humans achieve in meaningful speech. But human theory, as opposed to human speech, cannot achieve this. Our language is only a 'translation' from the divine language of nature.[43] It goes astray when transcendentalists such as Kant create abstract terms that Berkeley had shown were impossible, in the service of a reason that Hume had revealed as impotent. All that human reason can do is highlight the oppositions that run through our existence, while pointing beyond them to God.[44]

To say that thoughts are 'bound' to words is thus to say that they are bound to mysterious and partial manifestations of God. To say that words cannot determine their own meanings is not to contradict this statement but in a way to repeat it: the arbitrary signs of human language are bound to the meanings given by God in the original, divine language. But – in a final twist – human language and divine language are not wholly separate types, or even strata, of language. If God speaks to us in the sights and sounds of sensory experience, he also does so in human language, in the Bible: 'Holy scripture should be our dictionary, our art of language, on which are founded all concepts and discourse of the Christian.'[45]

Hamann's mistranslation of Hume is thus religiously motivated. At the beginning of the *Metacritique* (*Mk* 285/215), Hamann suggests that Hume's scepticism owes an infinite debt to Berkeley's idealism. We now see that Hamann has in fact accepted Hume's famous demonstration of the impotence of reason[46] and has combined with it Berkeley's view of nature as a divine language – with the result that language is not for 'natural philosophers,' or anyone else, to decipher. Hence philosophy as a rational development – as a systematic unfolding of the unity of the Word behind the plurality of words – is impossible. The human mind can deliver only the 'balled fist' of the truth, in the form of images and words that cannot be brought together into any kind of unity. No human, not even the philosopher, can unfold the fingers.[47]

As with Berkeley, and in the words of Fritz Blanke, 'Hamann's "philosophy" of language is entirely in the service of theology. The Magus hardly occupied himself with the social side of language, and its psychological basic concepts.'[48] But if language cannot be deciphered, then we cannot use it to build community – a small loss, according to Hamann's ideas. But Hamann's life, on Hegel's account, revealed the loss's true magnitude. It showed that we cannot speak to each other in ciphers or build friendship and community on 'expectorations.' Life thus needs language, as Hamann knew; but unless language is to be purely idiosyncratic (and hence, as Wittgenstein showed, not truly 'language' at all), it in turn needs the decipherings of philosophy.

Erwin Metzge has shown what, on Hamann's views, such philosophical deciphering would look like. First, in order to clarify the presence of God in language, the divine language of sensory experience must be seen as at once fragmented (from the human side) and yet unitary (from the side of the divine word), in such a way as to reconcile the fragmentation with the unity.[49] Linguistically conceived, this reconciliation can consist, on one level, only in showing how the manifold of diverse and incompatible words contained in a given language can be ordered into a single, dynamic whole. Since divine language does not merely tell us what is but informs us of what to do, the dichotomy of practical and theoretical must also be overcome, so that words are not neutrally theoretical but are grasped as deeds.[50] In this endeavour, the language of nature – purified sounds and forms, themselves united into unitary wholes – will be shown to have an identity with the freely instituted meanings created by human reason.[51]

Metzge concludes his statement of how things would have to be for Hamann's program to be fulfilled: 'The great tasks which Hamann imposed upon thought ... have not been brought notably nearer to a solution by anyone.'[52] Metzge's account is persuasive, indeed saddening. But perhaps the great tasks are closer to accomplishment than we think.

III

The Preface to the second edition of the *Science of Logic*, which I refer to as the

'Second Preface,' is dated a week before Hegel's death. In it, philosophical thought is the rational ordering of *Denkformen* – forms of thought that themselves are primarily manifested in language: 'Into all that becomes something inward for men, an image or conception (*Vorstellung*) as such, into all that he makes his own, language has penetrated, and everything that he has transformed into language and expresses in it contains a category.'[53] Moreover, Hegel continues, 'in a [philosophically mature] language, thought determinations are displayed as substantives and verbs and hence stamped with the form of objectivity.'[54] If words provide objectivity to forms of thought, does not language function as something very like their material basis? What else could Hegel be thinking when he wrote, in the 1827 edition of the *Encyclopaedia*, 'It is in names that we think'? What else could he have meant when he said, as the *Zusatz* to that paragraph has it, 'We only know our thoughts – only have determinate, actual thoughts – when we give them the form of ... the articulated tone, the word'?[55]

Words are thus the objective, public manifestation of thought itself. They are a manifestation to which, moreover, we are in some respects bound, for (as the Second Preface has it) the thought determinations conveyed in our words are our very selves: 'What is there more in *us* as against them, how shall *we*, how shall *I*, set myself up as more universal than they, which are themselves the universal as such?'[56] The manifestation of thought in words is necessary; words are the objective, ethereal, but still physical or material basis for thought.

But if we are bound to our words, we are not bound to the disorder with which they present themselves to us when we use them in everyday or even scientific discourse. Philosophy presents the realm of thought, which words render objective, 'in its own immanent activity, or (what is the same) in its necessary development.'[57] The 'Necessity' here can be, as immanent, nothing other than rational freedom itself: the Systematic whole of words develops as a free institution of reason.

Moreover, philosophical words do not have any meaning or nature over and above their contribution to this development. A *Denkform* that has been Systematically comprehended is what Hegel calls a moment, and in the 1831 revision of the *Science of Logic* he specifies that to be a 'moment' is to enter dynamically into a unity of effect with one's opposite.[58] To be a moment of the System then is basically to have a certain sort of effect – moments, or Systematic words, are here construed pragmatically: as deeds (*Wortestaten*) – or, to speak anachronistically, as moves in a language game.

Finally, if the System is to be a single, rationally ordered whole of words, that is because words do not first present themselves in such an order: they are, in the first instance, isolated and in that sense fragmentary, familiar but unknown, used everywhere but never examined: 'These categories, which are effective only as instinctually as drives, and are first brought to consciousness as isolated and therefore variable and mutually confusing ... are to be purified and raised to freedom and truth; this is the higher business of logic.'[59] Finally, Hegel's doctrine of determinate negation is manifestly intended to do justice to this enriching play of diversity and opposition among our ordinary categories.[60] It allows words to assume, dialectically, their most varied, even contradictory, senses – all the while remaining in speculative order.

Thus, at least for the late Hegel, language is an objective basis for thought, to which we are bound, as Hamann also believes. And, as with Hamann, language presents itself in two ways – as a unified (or, for Hegel, rationally ordered) whole, and as the fragmentary *Denkformen* that we mortals use in speech. In Hegel's Systematic comprehension of words as moments, words function not merely cognitively but as actions – as deeds, *Wortestaten*. In that comprehension, the language of nature – that in which we describe and articulate the political, personal, and even the natural sides of our lives – is brought to an identity with meanings as free institutions of reason. And this, too, in a way, unites the human and the divine. 'As Homer gives, for certain stars, the names they have among the immortal gods, and the other names they have among mortal humans; so the language of representation is different from that of the Concept ... and science is not merely to inscribe its figurations into abstract realms, abstracter indeed in which those gods lived ... but must also show their *incarnation*, ... the existence that they have in actual Spirit – and this is representation.'[61]

Philosophy brings the language of the Concept – the ordered System of words – into identity with the language of representation – of the historical world in which we live. In so doing, it manifests a sort of incarnation (*Menschenwerdung*) by which the divine (which here is only a sort of language) becomes human – a linguistic reconciliation of human and divine language.

In his last writings, the Great Systematizer thus leaves us with a number of suggestive fragments, in which philosophy is put forth as a linguistic enterprise that takes words not merely for its medium (as all philosophy does) but for its 'objects' as well. The philosophical enterprise, so construed, looks much like one that would satisfy the unspoken needs of Hamann's life and ideas.

But did it? Did Hegel's artful System, in and of words, achieve for him what Hamann's expectorations so signally failed to do? Did Hegel find a way to articulate himself without provoking outrage or incomprehension?

In the summer of 1831, cholera broke out in Berlin. Hegel, who was nothing if not cautious, took his family to the nearby village of Kreuzberg to wait out the epidemic. There he received a letter, in the form of a poem, from one of his

88   John McCumber

younger associates, Heinrich Stieglitz. Stieglitz reported that Hegel's disciples had fallen to fighting among themselves, and he asked that Hegel send a word to put things right – 'the right word, in which alone the magic dwells.' Hegel responded with a poem of his own:[62]

> How welcome to me is my friend's greeting
> Nor greeting only, but a demand that I resolve
> Upon a deed of words (*Wortestat*), to address
> The many – also friends – who are aroused to madness!
> Yet of what crime do you accuse them,
> But that each wants to hear himself, and to speak above the rest?
> Thus would the word, which ought to ward off evil,
> Become itself merely a means to increase it.
> But should that word break forth as it has long driven me,
> Then your call would bind me to dare again,
> In hopes that spirits would come forth to meet that word,
> That it would not die away in empty accusations,
> That they would bear it to the people,
> To work.

The epidemic was still raging when classes resumed. Hegel, who was nothing if not dutiful, returned to the city to teach and to write the Second Preface, with its linguistic emphasis.

The cholera took him on 14 November. The strife over his teaching went on – has continued in fact until today. So, like Hamann, Hegel never found the words that he needed to articulate himself adequately to others; he never achieved his 'company of words.' But unlike Hamann, he died trying.

Notes

1 Preface to the Second Edition of the *Encyclopaedia*, at Hegel, *Werke*, ed. Eva Moldenhauer and Karl Markus Michel, 20 vols. (Frankfurt/Main: Suhrkamp, 1970–1). In what follows, references to this edition will be given by Roman numeral: VIII, 38. It is in the spirit of the view that philosophy simply is the final end of human reason that Hegel so often assures us that it simply must be a system; for a discussion of such passages, cf. Manfred Baum, 'Anmerkungen zum verhältnis von Systematik und Dialektik bei Hegel,' in Dieter Henrich, ed., *Hegels Wissenschaft der Logik: Formation und Rekonstruktion* (Stuttgart: Klett-Cotta, 1986), 65ff.
2 See the letter to van Ghert of 16 December 1809, in Johannes Hoffmeister, ed., *Briefe von und an Hegel*, 3rd ed., 4 vols. (Hamburg: Meiner, 1969) I 299(No. 152)/

English translation in Clark Butler and Christiane Seiler, eds. and trans., *Hegel: The Letters* (Bloomington, Ind.: Indiana University Press, 1984), 588. (All translations in this paper are my own.)

3 XI, 331; also 280, 346.
4 Immanuel Kant, *Kritik der Urteilskraft*, in Kant, *Werkausgabe*, (ed. Wilhelm Weschedel) 12 vols. (Frankfurt: Suhrkamp, 1978); X, 226f./ English translation at Kant, *Critique of Judgment*, trans. Werner S. Pluhar (Indianapolis: Hackett, 1987) 160f.
5 XI, 318, 332, 336; also see 318, 320f.
6 XI, 309, 323.
7 XI, 323f.
8 XI, 317.
9 For the importance of friendship to Hegel's Hamann, see XI, 285ff., 294, 297f., 310f.
10 XI, 297.
11 XI, 285ff., 308f., 314.
12 XI, 309.
13 XI, 343f.
14 XI, 327, 329.
15 Hegel, 'Solgers Nachgelassene Schriften und Briefwechsel,' XI, 248f.
16 XI, 246.
17 III (*Phenomenology of Spirit*), 82–92/English translation, Hegel, *Phenomenology of Spirit*, trans. A.V. Miller (Oxford: Clarendon Press, 1977), 58–66.
18 VIII, 51f. (*Encyclopaedia* No. 8 Anm.)/12.
19 See John McCumber, *Poetic Interaction* (Chicago: University of Chicago Press, 1989), 301ff.
20 XVII, 250. If we accept the view that Anthony Storr attributes to a broad spectrum of psychoanalytical and other forms of psychotherapy – that mental 'health and happiness depend entirely upon the maintenance of intimate personal relationships,' we can see that a consolidated self is also an analytically mature one. Its friendships are intimate because everything can be articulated in them, and they are sustainable because they are always changing. Anthony Storr, *Solitude* (New York: Ballantine Books, 1988), 7ff. Many of the most important examples that Storr uses to argue against this view are philosophers such as Kant, Spinoza, and Wittgenstein. In this respect Hegel, who as we see below was in many ways a veritable Sphinx, remained true to his profession: he perhaps exalted the value of intimate friendships because he himself had so few of them.
21 See the essays in Jürgen Habermas, *Communication and the Evolution of Society*, trans. Thomas McCarthy (Boston: Beacon, 1979); also Habermas, *Theory of Communicative Action*, trans. Thomas McCarthy, 2 vols. (Boston: Beacon, 1984–7).

22 The *Metacritique* (hereinafter Mk) is a seven-page essay that Hamann wrote in 1784 but was not published until after his death in 1800. It can be found at Johann Georg Hamann, *Sämtliche Werke*, ed. Josef Nadler, 6 vols. (Wien: Herder Verlag, 1949–53), IV (1951) 283–9. All references to Hamann's works are to this edition, the pagination of which is maintained in the useful collection Hamann, *Schriften zur Sprache*, ed. Josef Simon (Frankfurt: Suhrkamp, 1967), English translation, R.G. Smith, *J.G. Hamann* (London: Collins, 1960), 213–21.

23 Mk 283/213; emphasis added.

24 'It were, therefore, much to be wished that everyone would use his utmost endeavours to obtain a clear view of the ideas he would consider; separating them from all that dress and incumbrance of words which so much contribute to blind the judgment and divide the attention ... We need only draw the curtain of words, to behold the fairest tree of knowledge, whose fruit is excellent, and within the reach of our hand.' George Berkeley, *The Principles of Human Knowledge*, in David M. Armstrong, ed., *Berkeley's Philosophical Writings* (New York: Collier, 1965), 58–60.

25 David Hume, *A Treatise of Human Nature*, ed. L.A. Selby-Bigge (Oxford: Clarendon, 1896), 17; John Locke, *An Essay Concerning Human Understanding*, ed. Alexander Campbell Fraser, 2 vols. (New York: Dover, 1959), II.29.10.

26 Hume, *Treatice*, 20f.

27 Mk 285/215. For this tradition and its fate see Joseph Owens, *The Doctrine of Being in the Aristotelian Metaphysics*, 2nd ed., rev. (Toronto: Pontifical Institute of Medieval Studies, 1963), 74, and the literature referred to there in note 18.

28 Günter Wohlfahrt has illuminated the degree of Kant's blindness to language and listed some of the isolated themes in Kant's *Critique of Judgment* that might have been brought together had Kant, like Hamann, understood the linguistic nature of reason. These themes include such important ones as the (linguistic) inner continuity of reflection and determination, the (linguistic) interchanges between intuition and concept, the *comprehensio aesthetica* (bringing together in an intuition), and the *comprehensio logica* (bringing together in a concept). Günter Wohlfahrt, *Denken der Sprache* (Freiburg/Munich: Alber, 1984).

29 Mk 284/214f.

30 Günter Wohlfahrt, 'Hamanns Kantkritik,' *Kant-Studien*, 75 (1984), 408.

31 See, for example, Kant, *Kritik der reinen Vernunft* (Akademie-Ausgabe) B 95–109, 369ff.; *Mk* 2284/215.

32 Wohlfahrt, *Denken der Sprache*, 147. Focusing on Kierkegaard's critique of Hegel, Hermann J. Cloeren has traced its background in an entire 'analytical' tradition in eighteenth- and nineteenth-century German philosophy, including Hamann and O.F. Gruppe: Hermann J. Cloeren, 'The Linguistic Turn in Kierkegaard's Attack on Hegel,' *International Studies in Philosophy*, 17 (1985), 1–13.

33 Mk 284f./215.
34 Josef Simon, 'Introduction,' in Hamann, *Schriften zur Sprache*, 71ff.
35 Mk 286/217.
36 Ibid., 288/219.
37 Ibid.
38 Mk 289/220.
39 Mk 287/218f.
40 Our ideas, for Berkeley, cannot be shown to be caused by external substances, or at least by unintelligent ones: they are all caused directly by God: Berkeley, *Principles*, 71f. But if an intelligent God is the sole cause of our sensations, then those sensations count as a sort of divine, visual language, in which the Author of Nature instructs us about what to expect, especially in the way of tactile impressions: I see the fire from a distance, in order that I not be burned. The tactile impression, following regularly on the visual one, is, so to speak, its 'meaning': see Berkeley, 'Towards a New Theory of Vision,' in Armstrong, ed., *Writing*, 343f.
41 Hamann, 'Des Ritters von Rosenkreuz Letzte Willensmeinung ...' in Hamann, *Werke*, III 32; also in Hamann, *Schriften zur Sprache*.
42 See Robert E. Butts, 'The Grammar of Reason: Hamann's Challenge to Kant,' *Synthèse*, 75 (1988) 251–83.
43 Hamann, *Aesthetica in Nuce,* in Hamann, *Werke*, II 261; also, with identical pagination, in Hamann, *Schriften zur Sprache,* ed. Simon.
44 For more on this see H.A. Salmony, *J. G. Hamanns metakritische Philosophie* (Zollikon: Evangelischer Verlag, 1958), 185–92.
45 Hamann, *Werke,* I 243; also see Fritz Blanke, 'Gottessprache und Menschensprache bei J.G. Hamann,' in Blanke, *Hamann-Studien* (Zürich: Zwingli-Verlag, 1956), 53–97.
46 For Hamann and Hume, see James C. O'Flaherty, *Unity and Language: A Study in the Philosophy of Johann Georg Hamann* (Chapel Hill: University of North Carolina Press, 1952) 60f.
47 Mk 289/220.
48 Blanke, 'Gottessprache,' 96f. For a partial corrective, see Butts, 'Grammar,' 262f.
49 Erwin Metzge, *J.G. Hamann's Stellung in der Philosophie des 18. Jahrhunderts* (Darmstadt: Wissenschaftliche Buchgesellschaft, 1967), 243.
50 Ibid., 251.
51 Ibid., 242.
52 Ibid., 252.
53 VI, 20/English translation, Hegel, *Science of Logic,* trans. A.V. Miller (New York: Humanities Press, 1969), 31.
54 VI, 20/32.

55 Cited after M.J. Petry, ed. and trans., *Hegel's Philosophy of Subjective Spirit*, 3 vols. (Dordrecht: Reidel, 1978), III, 203.
56 V, 25/35.
57 V, 19/31.
58 See V, 114/107; the passage is clearly late, for it has a footnote referring to the 1830 *Encyclopaedia*.
59 V, 27/37.
60 V, 49, 51/54, 55.
61 Hegel, review of Karl Frierich Göschel, *Aphorismen über Nichtwissen und absoilutes Wissen* ... (1829), in XI 378. For an illuminating discussion see Emil Fackenheim, *The Religious Dimension in Hegel's Thought* (Boston: Beacon, 1967), 191ff.
62 The poem can be found in Johannes Hoffmeister, ed., *Briefe von und an Hegel*, 3rd ed., 4 vols. (Hamburg: Meiner, 1969), III, 346f. The biographical context is supplied in Clark Butler and Christiane Seiler, ed. and trans., *Hegel: The Letters* (Bloomington, Ind.: Indiana University Press, 1984), 678ff; a different translation of the poem is on p. 680.

4

Winckelmann and Hegel on the Imitation of the Greeks

MICHAEL BAUR

Johann Joachim Winckelmann (1717–1768) is generally acknowledged to be the founder of German neoclassicism – and with good reason. It was largely under the spell of his writings that many German thinkers, including those who went on to influence Hegel, began to develop an appreciation for the ancient Greeks. Herder, for example, recalls the invigorating effect that Winckelmann's writings had on him: 'I read them with a feeling like that of a youth on a fine morning, like the letter of a far-distant bride, from a happy time that is past, from a happy zone.'[1] In his autobiographical work, *Dichtung und Wahrheit*, Goethe recalls the period of excitement during which anyone interested in art or antiquity 'always had Winckelmann before his eyes';[2] and during his famous trip to Italy, Goethe carried Winckelmann's *History of Ancient Art* with him as his constant travelling companion. Lessing also marked his indebtedness when – after hearing of Winckelmann's untimely death – he wrote that he would have gladly given several years of his own life so that the great man himself might live longer.[3] While Winckelmann was not the first to recognize the significance of ancient Greece, he certainly articulated the meaning of the Greeks more vividly and convincingly than anyone had done before him. Without him, there would be no sense to Goethe's dictum: 'Jeder sei auf seine Art ein Grieche, aber er sei's.'[4]

While few would dispute the far-reaching influence that Winckelmann had on the German intellectual climate of the eighteenth and nineteenth centuries, some would question whether this influence allowed for a genuinely healthy understanding and appropriation of the Greek legacy. Indeed, a number of facts seem to suggest that Winckelmann's own comprehension of the Greek ideal was rather shallow and empty. For example, Winckelmann continually emphasized direct experience over book-learning; but he never actually reached Greece in his travels, even when he was given the opportunity to do so. In his analysis and evaluation of classical Greek art, he relied almost entirely on Roman copies, and in many cases he misidentified the works in question. Most significant of all is his misidentification of the group sculpture called the *Laocoön*. Winckelmann praised the *Laocoön* as one of the greatest and most representative examples of classical excellence, but this work does not date from the classical period at all.[5]

According to some critics, the putative superficiality of Winckelmann's appropriation of the Greek legacy is just one instance of the emptiness that characterizes the appropriation of the Greeks by the Germans in general. Thus Eliza Maria Butler has spoken of the 'tyranny of Greece over Germany': 'If the Greeks are tyrants, the Germans are predestined slaves ... The Germans have imitated the Greeks more slavishly; they have been obsessed by them more utterly, and they have assimilated them less than any other race.'[6]

Not coincidentally, the putative freedom or unfreedom of one's appropriation of the Greek ideal is one of the basic problems at issue in this chapter. In the following pages, I argue that Winckelmann not only understood this basic problem but also touched on its actual solution, albeit in an inadequate, aesthetic manner. I go on to suggest that Hegel articulated this solution in an adequate and properly philosophical manner. But before addressing these larger issues, we must first consider the reasons for Winckelmann's admiration of the Greeks and the substance of his 'Greek ideal.'

It should be no surprise that what Winckelmann admired about the Greeks depended largely on how he approached them in the first place; part of his achievement lay in his ability to teach the Germans how to look at the Greeks in the right way. Combating what was a dominant tendency at the time, Winckelmann showed that art history should be much more than an arid taxonomy of cataloguing, numbering, and describing. For him, art should be treated as the spontaneous self-expression that arises from a people's particular situation, not as an external production that transpires above and beyond the flow of life itself. Thus in his two great works – *Reflections on the Imitation of Greek Works in Painting and Sculpture* and *History of Ancient Art* – he shows that genuine appreciation of art cannot abstract itself from the historical, ethnic, geographical, climatic, social, and political conditions that give rise to art in the first place.

In spite of his sensitivity to the situatedness of the Greeks' self-expression in art, Winckelmann believed that any merely relativistic or subjectivistic understanding of artistic production would be entirely inadequate. For him, the Greek expression of beauty – though conditioned by many factors – is not to be understood as something arbitrary and idiosyncratic; classical Greek art is imbued with universal significance, and even truth. Accordingly, he despised the subjectivistic and eccentric art of the seventeenth and early eighteenth centuries, especially that of Bernini and his followers. This kind of art tries to portray itself as being genuinely free and spontaneous, but it really only manifests the false freedom of caprice and conceit. Thus Winckelmann speaks of contemporary artists with disdain: 'Nothing gains their approbation but contorted postures and action in which bold passion prevails. This they call art executed with spirit, or *franchezza*. Their favorite term is *contraposto*, which represents for them the essence of a perfect work of art. In their figures they demand a soul which shoots like a comet out of their midst.'[7]

The bivalence that Winckelmann knew and admired in Greek art – its situatedness and universality – points to the unique and overriding feature, which, according to him, made the Greeks great as a people. This was their enjoyment of what we might call 'situated freedom.' The freedom of the Greeks was not an empty and abstract ideal that had to be imposed on an otherwise unfree actual life; the Greeks' freedom was an essentially rooted freedom, growing naturally out of their lived sense of harmony with the world. This is why it expressed itself as spontaneous joy and love for life. The Greeks were great because theirs was a concrete universality and freedom that allowed for – in fact, implied – feeling and attachment. This unique harmony of self-determination and passion, composure and vitality, is what Winckelmann meant by the 'noble simplicity and quiet grandeur' (*edle Einfalt und stille Grösse*) of the Greeks.[8]

Given the substance of his Greek ideal, it is no wonder that Winckelmann continued to think of the Greeks on the basis of an essentially aesthetic paradigm. As Winckelmann showed, the freedom of the Greeks was natural and spontaneous, requiring no theoretical mediation or justification; and so it expressed itself naturally in the form of art. In his attachment to the Greeks, Winckelmann never departed from this aesthetic paradigm.

While many of Winckelmann's early followers may have had questions about the historical accuracy of his writings, few would have challenged the desirability of what he was espousing in those writings, namely, the harmonious unity of feeling and universality. The Greeks were great because of their situated freedom: what the Greeks knew as rational, free beings stood in natural harmony with what they felt as living, breathing beings. Though Winckelmann articulated his Greek ideal mainly in relation to the art of the Greeks, few contemporary Germans could resist thinking about this ideal in relation to their own society and its possible regeneration. Thus a common issue for Germany's contemporary *Volkserzieher* was that of overcoming the sense of alienation and purposelessness that accompanied modern detachment and artificiality.

As a young man, Hegel also aspired to be a *Volkserzieher* in the tradition of thinkers such as Mendelssohn, Lessing, and Schiller – all admirers of Winckelmann. And thus it is not surprising that Winckelmann's vision of Hellenic 'noble simplicity' should have found expression in the writings of the young Hegel. In a school essay from August 1788 ('On some characteristics which distinguish ancient writers ...'), Hegel borrows several ideas from Christian Garve – another follower of Winckelmann – to express the essential difference between the Greeks and the moderns. The naturalness and simplicity of the Greeks, Hegel writes, make them superior to us moderns; while the Greeks could freely breathe the ether of their own, home-grown categories, we moderns must live on the alien and artificial turf of borrowed categories: 'Their whole system of education and *Bildung* was so constituted that everyone had derived his ideas from direct experience and 'the cold book-learning that is just expressed with dead signs in one's mind' they knew nothing of ... We learn, from our youth up, the current mass of words and signs of ideas, and they rest in our heads without activity and without use; only bit by bit through experience do we first come to know what a treasure we have and to think something with the words, although they are forms for us according to which we model our ideas; they already have their established range and limits, and are relations according to which we are accustomed to see everything.'[9]

Throughout his life, Hegel continued to be interested in the difference between the naturalness of the Greeks and the detachment of the moderns. In the 'Preface' to his *Phenomenology of Spirit*, Hegel once again asserts this distinction: 'The manner of study in ancient times differed from that of the modern age in that the former was the proper and complete formation of the natural consciousness. Putting itself to the test at every point of its existence, and philosophizing about everything it came across, it made itself into a universality that was active through and through. In modern times, however, the individual finds the abstract form ready-made.'[10]

While reaffirming the basic difference between ancients and moderns, the author of the *Phenomenology* does not merely reiterate what he had claimed before. Now, instead of conceding the superiority of the Greeks, Hegel goes on to argue that modern abstractness and indirectness constitute a potential advantage. Clearly, some significant change took place in Hegel's thought between 1788 and 1807. The *Bildungsroman* that tells the complete story of that change is the two-volume work by H.S. Harris, *Hegel's Development*. While the scope of the present chapter does not allow for any detailed treatment of that development, the trajectory of this development helps us understand Hegel's unique appropriation of Winckelmann's 'Greek ideal.' Two of Hegel's works from the 1790s can serve as signposts for us.

In his 'Tübingen Essay of 1793' (*Religion ist eine ...*), Hegel grapples with the question of how a folk-religion ought to be constituted. Among other things, Hegel writes, 'Its doctrines must be grounded on universal Reason,' but 'Fancy, heart, and sensibility must not thereby go away empty.'[11] Clearly, Hegel's basic concern here is the possibility of recapturing, or perhaps even in some sense imitating, the original Greek unity of life and thought, of subjectivity and objectivity. After discussing his requirements for a properly constituted folk-religion, Hegel concludes this essay by suggesting a rather stark contrast between the Greeks and the moderns. In the final paragraph, he paints a sorry picture of what the modern world has become: 'A different Genius of the nations has the West hatched – his form is aged – beautiful he never was – but some slight touches of manliness remain still faintly traceable in him – his father [i.e., the historical tradition behind modern society] is bowed [with age] – he dares not stand up straight either to look round gaily at the world nor from a sense of his own dignity – he is short-sighted and can see only little things one at a time – without courage, without confidence in his own strength, he hazards no bold throw, iron fetters raw and ... [end of manuscript].'[12]

It is significant that Hegel returned to this final, unfinished paragraph and deleted it. This deletion suggests that in 1793 Hegel was beginning to realize that such a stark contrast would imply the impossibility of imitating the Greeks; and this in turn would suggest the futility of the *Volkserzieher*'s task. Instead of drawing such pessimistic conclusions, Hegel sought a new way of conceiving the difference between the Greeks and the moderns. It is no accident that this renewed search coincides with an attempt by Hegel to move beyond the Kant-inspired moral-religious paradigm that governs the Tübingen essay.

Three years later, in a poem that he wrote for Hölderlin ('Eleusis,' composed in August 1796), Hegel once again touches on the issue of imitating the Greeks. In the main section of this poem (following the proem addressed to Hölderlin) Hegel addresses Ceres and recognizes that the original spirit of Greece is gone:

Doch deine Hallen sind verstummt, o Göttin!
Geflohen ist der Götter Kreis zurück in den Olymp
Von den geheiligten Altären,
Geflohn von der entweihten Menschheit Grab
Der Unschuld Genius, der her sie zauberte!

The natural wisdom of Greece cannot be recaptured by any 'Forschers Neugier,' or repetition of formulae. But while reflection (*der Gedanke*) is incapable of capturing what has been lost, there is a kind of intimation (*Ahnung*) that can be felt even in the modern period. Hegel thus concludes the poem on a hopeful note, as he senses the everlasting presence of the Goddess:

Du bist der hohe Sinn, der treue Glauben,
Der, eine Gottheit, wenn auch Alles untergeht, nicht wankt.

Hegel's earlier contrast between the Greek world and the modern world is now moderated: while the spirit of Greece is not recoverable as the same actuality that it was for the Greeks, it has not vanished altogether. Furthermore, Hegel is now beginning to think of the possible imitation of the Greeks no longer in terms of a primarily moral-religious paradigm but in terms of an aesthetic paradigm. This aesthetic turn is confirmed not only by the poetic presentation of Hegel's thought here, but also by an observation that he made during that same year: 'I am now convinced that the highest act of Reason, the one through which it encompasses all Ideas, is an aesthetic act, and that *truth and goodness only become sisters in beauty* ... Poetry gains thereby a higher dignity, she becomes at the end once more what she was at the beginning – *the teacher of mankind*.'[13] If Kant's moral-religious outlook was the dominant paradigm for Hegel's expression of the Greek ideal in the Tübingen essay, then it is Schiller who informs Hegel's basic orientation in 1796. Just one year before his composition of 'Eleusis,' Hegel had read Schiller's *Aesthetic Letters* with great enthusiasm and reported to Schelling on this work: 'It is a masterpiece.'[14]

These two works of Hegel from the 1790s suggest the importance of two interrelated questions with which he was struggling, and which helped to determine the eventual direction of his thought. Is it possible for us moderns to be like the Greeks? If so, how is this possibility to be envisioned – morally-religiously, aesthetically, or according to some other paradigm?

Before trying to answer these questions, we should consider the basic difficulty involved in the possible imitation of the Greeks by us moderns. It would seem that the very ideal that makes us admire the Greeks and want to be like them – their situated freedom – also makes it impossible for us to imitate them. When we ask how we can imitate the Greeks, we are asking how we can achieve a harmonious unity of objectivity and subjectivity, life and thought, belonging and universality, situatedness and self-determination. These are the harmonies that are lacking in our artificial modern society; if these were already actualities for us, then there would be no point in asking how we can imitate the Greeks. But since we are unlike the Greeks – and we are indeed unlike them, in so far as we are asking how we can become like them – then our imitating them would seem to rule out the possibility of our being free and self-determining, for following some exemplar that is external to us amounts to heteronomy, or unfreedom. The obvious implication is that we can never succeed in imitating the Greeks: they were free and self-determining, but in the very act of trying to imitate them, we would be heteronomous.

But the difficulty seems even more intractable than just this: even if we grant – for the sake of argument – that our following of the Greek ideal could be called 'free' in some sense, this freedom would be very different from the situated freedom of the Greeks. Their freedom was spontaneous and unreflective (in Schiller's words, 'naïve'), arising naturally out of their lived world. This is why the freedom of the early Greeks stood in natural harmony with a sense of belonging; this is why the early Greeks did not have to address the problem of reconciling thought and passion, universality and attachment, objectivity and subjectivity. Their situated freedom was natural and spontaneous because it did not have to be achieved; it was not the result of any explicit reflection or deliberation. But the situation is quite different for us moderns, who address this issue as an explicit problem. As long as we have already raised the issue of *achieving* a situated freedom, then no matter what we do, any 'freedom' that we achieve will be a *result*; and for this reason, it will necessarily differ from the natural and spontaneous freedom of the Greeks. And without a genuinely situated freedom, there can be no true harmony between thought and passion, universality and attachment, subjectivity and objectivity. Thus no matter how we try, we seem to be condemned to the dualistic bind (in Schiller's terms, the 'sentimentality') that we moderns want to overcome in the first place. In fact, it is our very *trying* that condemns us to be *unlike* the Greeks.[15]

Despite his apparent obliviousness at times, it seems that Winckelmann himself was well aware of this difficulty. In perhaps his most famous statement of all, he presents a paradox: 'The only way for us to become great or, if this be possible, inimitable, is to imitate the Greeks.'[16] Clearly, if we are not yet inimitable, and if we can putatively become so only through our imitation of the Greeks, then it would be impossible for us ever to become inimitable. For if there is not already something about us that makes us inimitable, then the procedure or technique that we would follow in becoming like the Greeks could in principle be followed (imitated) by someone else; and in that case we would not be inimitable. In other words, if we are to become inimitable by imitating the Greeks, then we ourselves could be imitated by someone else – unless, of course, there is already something about us which makes us inimitable; but this is not the case, since the very issue we are addressing is the issue of *becoming* inimitable.

The basic conundrum here is the same as the issue of freedom articulated above: the manner by which we would putatively become like the Greeks is the very thing that guarantees that we can never really be like them. The act (imitation) by which we would seek to be inimitable like the Greeks is the very act that guarantees that we cannot be inimitable (since, if we are not already inimitable, our imitating could itself be imitated). Similarly, the act (imitation) by which we would seek to be free like the Greeks is the very act that guarantees that we cannot be genuinely free (since we would only be following the lead of an exemplar outside ourselves).

If Winckelmann was aware of the basic difficulty at hand, he also seems to have touched on its solution. Ironically, this solution emerges in what appears to be a statement of despair concerning the distance between the Greeks and ourselves. Winckelmann concludes his *History of Ancient Art* with reflections on the decline and disappearance of ancient Greece: 'Although in looking at this decline I felt almost like a person who in writing the history of his own fatherland had to touch on its destruction which he himself had experienced, I could not abstain from following the fates of these works as far as my eye would reach – just as a girl, standing on the shore of the ocean, looks with tears in her eyes after her departing lover, without any hope of ever seeing him again, believing to see his face in the distant sail. Like this girl, we have, as it were, only a shadowgraph of the object of our desire, which for this reason awakens an all the stronger longing.'[17]

There are several points worth noting here. First, by comparing himself to a girl as she watches her beloved sail away, Winckelmann expresses a certain scepticism and despair. Just like the tearful girl on the shore, he has no hope of seeing the object of his desire, no illusions concerning the inevitable pastness of the ancient Greek world. But this despair does not have a merely negative significance. In fact, the scepticism and despair actually point to their own overcoming. For as Winckelmann goes on to say, the very emptiness and insubstantiality of the object as such – the fact that it is a mere 'shadowgraph' for us – arouse our desire for the object all the more. In other words, our desire is not simply caused by an otherwise independent object or substantiality outside us; instead, it is bound up with the very emptiness or nothingness of the object as such.[18] Thus our longing and desire are ultimately a function of who we ourselves are; there is something about us that explains our longing and desire for the lost object. But then who are we?

Winckelmann suggests an answer to this last question when he refers to the lost Greek world as his 'own fatherland.' In other words, we are offspring of the Greeks and already stand within the tradition initiated by them. Accordingly, the very emptiness and nothingness of the desired object – the apparently unfathomable distance between us and the bygone Greek world – tell us that this object does not stand entirely outside us after all. In fact, the feeling of distance and longing is possible for us only because a prior continuum of meaningfulness still binds us to the Greeks. If we did not already stand within such a tradition or continuum – if the object were a completely independent and alien other – then the object would have no significance for us; it would not be an object *for us* at all. But if that were the case, then we could not even appreciate the object, and thus the question of recovering or imitating the 'lost' object would never arise for us in the first place.

With this observation, the entire problematic of 'imitating' the Greeks is transformed. In its immediacy, the notion of 'imitation' implies that there is some independently existing model or exemplar that we might decide to copy. It is precisely this conception of the issue that gave rise to the related problems of heteronomy and artificiality in the first place. But now, starting from Winckelmann's hints, we can see that this conception is wrong-headed; our 'imitation' of the Greeks cannot be a matter of following any model that is already given and essentially other than ourselves. Instead of following any alien other, we really follow only ourselves; but, contrary to the Enlightenment notion of freedom, this following of ourselves is not the hollow pursuit of an empty, abstract, and detached centre of subjectivity. We follow ourselves through the mediation of an other. In following ourselves, we are really only following the Greek legacy that is already alive in us. No matter how we might misconceive our longing for the Greeks, the fact remains that such longing presupposes a fundamental continuity between ourselves and the Greeks. Similarly, no matter how we might misconceive our own freedom, the fact remains that this freedom is already a situated freedom, such that our own self-determination is always actualized by virtue of the hidden legacy of the Greeks. This account thus reconfirms the basic truth already implied by the Platonic doctrine of Recollection: we could not follow the lead of an object outside us if that externality did not resonate with an ideal or exemplar already operative within us; and conversely, we could not recollect the ideal that is operative within us without the help of some external prompting or reminder.

Following Winckelmann's suggestions, we can see that the fundamental problem is the erroneous self-understanding implicit in modern subjectivism. Modern subjectivism sees the individual subject as essentially separate from all tradition and otherness; as a result, any act of freedom and originality by this subjectivity is necessarily understood as an act of arbitrariness or idiosyncrasy. The basic problem of modern subjectivism, then, is its inability to comprehend the essential unity of freedom and tradition, self-determination and otherness, spontaneity and receptivity, subjectivity and objectivity. Of course, Winckelmann does not use such terminology to explain the problem; but he does touch on these issues in his writings on aesthetics. Thus, contrary to modern subjectivism, he tries to express the possibility of a kind of following that is equally a form of self-following. In his 'Remembrance on the Observation of Works of Art,' he distinguishes between mere copying (*Nachahmen*), which is incompatible with genius and originality, and imitation (*Nachahmung*), which is compatible with these.[19] In his *Reflections on the Imitation of Greek Works*, he says that we are genuinely free only in so far as we follow the Greeks; thus the artist, in allowing the 'Greek rules of beauty to guide his hand and mind,' can 'become a rule unto himself.'[20] Does this following of the Greeks mean that we must follow some pre-given method or set of rules? Not at all. We are free and capable of moving beyond any explicit set of guidelines given to us from the outside, precisely because we can recollect the Greek legacy that is already at work in us implicitly. Even Bernini – who erroneously taught his students to seek beauty primarily in nature – learned how to discover such beauty only through his prior acquaintance with Greek-inspired art: 'It was this [Medicean] Venus therefore that taught him to discover beauties in nature which he had previously seen only in the statue and which, without the Venus, he would not have sought in nature.'[21]

Thus the expression of true freedom and originality in art – the ability to move beyond what is merely given in nature – is made possible by virtue of the Greek vision that we have inherited. Conversely, the abstract freedom of modern subjectivism reveals itself ultimately as a false freedom: in so far as it seeks to detach itself from every possible context, modern subjectivity is able to find real content for its own thinking and acting only in sources essentially external to itself. Thus the abstract freedom of modern subjectivism becomes the wayward freedom of detached caprice and conceit.

Winckelmann's writings on art and aesthetics suggest that imitating the Greeks cannot be a matter of following some alien method or set of rules that we arbitrarily happen to adopt; or what amounts to the same thing, such imitation cannot consist in jumping out of our own subjectivity in order to emulate something external. Such an erroneous conception of the issue arises only if imitation is seen as a merely subjective act, which must be accomplished in a hermeneutical vacuum, and not as part of the self-explication of the very tradition to which we already belong. Indeed, if there were no continuum of meaningfulness between the Greeks and ourselves, then we could not imitate them. But then again, if there were no such continuum, we could not even understand the Greeks; and in that case, we could not even appreciate them, and thus the whole question of how we can be like them would never arise in the first place. The point is not to bridge a gulf between our own subjectivity and some external, desired objectivity, but rather to see the essential harmony or continuity of subjectivity and objectivity, of freedom and tradition.

Though Winckelmann had suggested the basic solution to the problem of 'imitating' the Greeks, he did not articulate this solution adequately. Remaining within the limits of his aesthetic paradigm, Winckelmann could express this solution only by pointing to various works of art, praising the Greek ones and criticizing the modern ones. To say that Winckelmann's aesthetic orientation is limited does not mean that it is somehow 'wrong,' nor does it mean that an aesthetic sensibility is not necessary for genuine thought.[22] To say that the aesthetic orientation is limited is to say that it is not adequate to the needs of the time, the needs of the modern period, which presupposes the priority of rational subjectivity. To modern subjectivity, Winckelmann's mere pointing to the excellence of Greek art could only appear as subrational and dogmatic, for such pointing presupposes that the audience already feels the essential harmony of reason and tradition, freedom and belonging; but it is precisely this felt harmony that is missing in the modern world. Winckelmann's aesthetic paradigm is thus inadequate, since it cannot speak to the needs of the time; his mere pointing will appear to the modern mind as aristocratic, impersonal, and antipathetic to individuality and rational protest.

In so far as Winckelmann seeks to show the essential harmony of reason and tradition, subjectivity and objectivity, by merely pointing to great works of art, he remains insufficiently Platonic (in spite of his deep sensitivity to so many Platonic themes and tropes). Unlike Winckelmann, Plato does not begin by presupposing in his intended audience a felt harmony between subjectivity and objectivity. Plato begins rather with the standpoint of the unconverted knower: this is the standpoint of difference, limitedness, and alienation. According to this standpoint, the individual knower claims to possess determinate knowledge about a determinate object which remains essentially different from, and external to, the knower. Plato starts with this assertion of difference and shows how this difference could not be known as a difference (and the unconverted knower could not claim to have knowledge of anything at all) without a prior, non-mediated harmony between the knower and what is knowable. More specifically, Plato's procedure is to begin with the standpoint of alienated, one-sided subjectivity and to show discursively (in terms intelligible to such subjectivity) that such a standpoint is in fact one-sided and partial.

Following Plato, we can make some general observations about the similarities and differences between philosophy and aesthetics. Like the aesthete, the philosopher's task is to present an intuition of the fundamental continuity between the self and its other; but unlike the aesthete, the philosopher must present this intuition in the medium of conceptual articulation (in the medium of discursivity and difference). The philosopher and the aesthete aim towards the same subject–object unity, but the philosopher provides the discursive, conceptual ladder by which the unconverted individual subject might also head towards this goal.[23] It is only with the help of such a ladder that the unconverted individual knower can consciously and deliberately (without ceasing to be an individual knower) think and act in accordance with the subject–object unity that is necessary for its own knowing.

Against what has been said above on behalf of philosophy, the aesthete might argue that the kind of subject–object continuity or unity at issue here is simply incompatible with discursive articulation, that the giving of reasons necessarily conditions, limits, and relativizes a subject–object unity that is supposed to be immediate, underived, and absolute.[24] Accordingly, the aesthete may contend that the philosopher's task of presenting an intuition of the continuity of the self and its other in the medium of conceptual articulation is impossible. If the aesthete's objection holds, then it would indeed be impossible to demonstrate the one-sidedness of modern subjectivity in terms that are intelligible to that subjectivity.

Against the aesthete's objection, the philosopher can have only one proper response: one cannot demonstrate that the philosopher's task is possible without enacting that task as an actuality. To use an Aristotelian turn of phrase: the possibility of the desired presentation is to be shown only by its actuality. This is exactly how Fichte argues in his 'First Introduction to the *Wissenschaftslehre*': 'Proofs of the impossibility of a project that will be accomplished, and in part already is so, are simply ridiculous. One has only to attend to the course of the argument, and examine whether or not it fulfills its promise.'[25]

Following Fichte, we can begin to understand how philosophy is able to present a discursive, conceptual articulation of the subject–object continuity to which Winckelmann merely points. But first, we should not overlook the fact that Winckelmann and Fichte are strikingly similar in their basic questions and answers. Winckelmann's central question is that of how we can be free and yet also follow an ideal or exemplar that is apparently external to and different from ourselves (the ancient Greeks). Fichte's central question concerning the conditions of the possibility of knowledge exhibits the same logical structure as Winckelmann's question. Fichte asks: how can the I be absolutely for-itself, self-related, free, and self-positing (I=I) and yet also have an object (not-I) present to it that apparently provides all determinate content for the I's knowing and acting?

The answers that Winckelmann and Fichte give to their respective questions are fundamentally the same. Winckelmann suggests that we can imitate the Greeks and still be free, because our orientation towards the Greeks is not caused by any alien or independent objectivity; in fact, we could not desire to be like the Greeks if there were not already a continuum of meaning that binds us to them. Our freedom is always a situated freedom, and thus our following of the Greeks is actually a self-following: in following the Greeks, we are really only following the Greek legacy that is already alive in us. Fichte also denies any ultimate difference or discontinuity between subjectivity and its intended object. He argues that the appearance of the otherness of a not-I for the I cannot be explained adequately by an appeal to a thing-in-itself that is completely alien to the self-positing I; if the object were an entirely independent other, then it could never appear as an object for the I. In denying the existence of a thing-in-itself,

Fichte implicitly affirms a fundamental continuity between subjectivity and objectivity. As with Winckelmann, his question is not that of how one can move from within the confines of one's own subjectivity towards an alien object on the outside; it is rather that of how one can articulate (finite) subjectivity properly, in a manner that allows for the fundamental continuity between subjectivity and objectivity.

Both Winckelmann and Fichte affirm that the other could not appear to the self as a genuine other without some prior continuity or unity between subjectivity and objectivity. But while Winckelmann merely points to the existence of this continuity, Fichte (the philosopher) must problematize it. For Fichte, the unqualified assertion of this continuity would imply the destruction of consciousness; for consciousness requires a difference between knower and known, between subjectivity and objectivity. This difference, however, seems to contradict the subject–object continuity that is equally a necessary condition of consciousness. The identity and difference of subjectivity and objectivity (both necessary conditions of conscious selfhood) seem to be fundamentally incompatible; and thus the possibility of consciousness itself appears to be undermined. Fichte's *Wissenschaftslehre* is an extended reflection on how consciousness is possible, if it requires the difference and non-difference of subjectivity and objectivity. And Fichte's answer takes him beyond the limits of Winckelmann's aesthetic intuitionism.

Fichte argues that the fundamental identity-in-difference of subjectivity and objectivity cannot be presented adequately in the form of a simple, fixed intuition or proposition, but can be expressed and conceived only as an ongoing activity. In this regard, Fichte is like Plato, who showed that the Forms could never be encapsulated once and for all in simple, fixed definitions but must be manifest in the ongoing activity of the soul's eternal dialogue with itself. Also like Plato, Fichte argues that the ongoing activity that manifests the fundamental identity-in-difference of subjectivity and objectivity is essentially recollective: the philosopher must always work backward, from conditioned to conditions, and thus Fichte describes his entire *Wissenschaftslehre* as 'a pragmatic history of the human mind.'[26] For both Fichte and Plato, the philosopher's task is to provide a discursive, conceptual articulation of a subject–object unity that is not relative or conditioned, and the only way that this can be achieved is through ongoing, self-recollective activity.

While Fichte moves beyond the limits of Winckelmann's aesthetic presentation of the continuity of subjectivity and objectivity, he falls short of a completely adequate conceptual presentation of that continuity. As we have seen, Fichte's denial of the existence of the thing-in-itself amounts to an affirmation of a fundamental continuity between subjectivity and objectivity; if there is no thing-in-itself, then there can be no absolute divide between subjectivity and objectivity. According to Fichte, however, one can arrive at knowledge of this subject–object continuity (and of the non-existence of the thing-in-itself) only by virtue of a purely subjective act, which is independent of and indifferent to all objectivity; this purely subjective act is not a 'leap' into the aesthetic intuition that Winckelmann affirms, but rather a 'leap' into the 'intellectual intuition' of one's own freedom. Accordingly, Fichte argues that the two philosophies of dogmatism and idealism are absolutely incompatible[27] and that reason itself can provide no principle for choosing between idealism (according to which there is no thing-in-itself) and dogmatism (according to which there is a thing-in-itself).[28]

In arguing this way, Fichte manifests his failure to present a fully adequate, discursive articulation of the continuity between subjectivity and objectivity. Fichte argues against the existence of a thing-in-itself and thus affirms the basic continuity of subjectivity and objectivity; nevertheless, he also argues that the individual's coming to know of such a continuity can take place only through a purely subjective act, entirely independent of and indifferent to the objectivity with which one's subjectivity is allegedly continuous. In arguing for idealism, Fichte affirms the basic continuity of subjectivity and objectivity, but in requiring a 'leap' into the standpoint of idealism he reaffirms their discontinuity. In spite of his great achievement, Fichte remains trapped within the confines of modern subjectivism.

In order to affirm the continuity of subjectivity and objectivity (and do so in a manner consistent with the demands of conceptual articulation), one must show that the individual subject's own coming-to-know of that continuity is not just a purely subjective act (as it is in Fichte), but is equally a development of objectivity itself. Furthermore, if one remains true to the essential continuity of subjectivity and objectivity, then one must also acknowledge that a transformation in one's own self-interpretation (one's own coming-to-see the basic continuity of subjectivity and objectivity) necessarily entails a transformation in the objectivity in relation to which one understands oneself. Just as we moderns are not completely separated from the legacy of the Greeks, so too the content of the Greek experience is not entirely different from the content of our own modern experience.

Thus, contrary to the sentimental view of the Greeks implied above, we must acknowledge that the Greek experience does not preclude all possible struggle and effort. In other words, the situated freedom of the Greeks does not amount to a complete identity of subjectivity and objectivity. Indeed, if the Greek experience entailed the complete identity of subjectivity and objectivity, then it could not be called conscious experience at all. The ancient Greek experience differs from our modern experience, but not because the Greeks were somehow immune to all struggle and effort; the possibility of such struggle and effort is a necessary accompaniment to the unity-in-difference of subjectivity and objectivity, which in turn is the necessary condition of all conscious experience. It is by virtue of this subject-object continuity that both the Greeks and we can enjoy our situated freedom. The real difference between them and us is that we moderns have been alienated from our natural existence and can now articulate and justify the universal validity of such situated freedom over against all other ideals of human knowing and acting.

It is no coincidence that the movement that has just been enacted in this essay replicates the fundamental movement in Hegel's *Phenomenology*. The *Phenomenology* articulates a movement whereby we readers observe the articulated coming-to-be of the identity-in-difference of philosophical (observing) consciousness and the object of philosophical consciousness (ordinary consciousness); but this movement is the same movement that manifests the coming-to-be of the identity-in-difference of ordinary consciousness and the object of ordinary consciousness. In this essay, we have learned of the continuity (identity-in-difference) of ourselves (as modern philosophical consciousness) and the ancient Greeks (as ordinary consciousness). But we could not consistently conceive of this continuity without acknowledging the identity-in-difference of Greek subjectivity (ordinary consciousness) and its objectivity (the object of ordinary consciousness). In acknowledging this latter identity-in-difference, we have had to acknowledge the possibility of struggle, tension, and effort, even within the Greek experience, and thus we have had to abandon our idealized and sentimental notion of the Greeks.[29]

The modern manner of imitating the Greeks must be actualized principally through the comprehension of freedom and tradition together in genuine self-knowledge. This is precisely the approach that is developed in Hegel's 'science of the experience of consciousness.' By 1807, Hegel realized that our possible imitation of the Greeks must be comprehended philosophically. As Socrates had shown over two thousand years ago, the *Volkserzieher* must be a philosopher, for only philosophy adequately combines an intuition of the continuity of ourselves and tradition (subjectivity and objectivity) with conceptual articulation of such continuity (an articulation that presupposes distance and difference). It is significant that Hegel did not learn this lesson directly from Socrates. He developed this position only in the early 1800s, as he was beginning to reconceptualize the meaning of Christianity and its significance for modern self-consciousness.[30] Throughout the 1790s, Hegel had generally felt that the interiority and other-worldliness of Jesus made the Christian ethos inferior to the public life-style of Socrates. But by the early 1800s, Hegel had realized that humanity must follow Jesus in breaking away from its natural and immediate attachment to the world. Consciousness must alienate itself from its natural and unreflective existence in order to know itself in its universality.

This realization also explains another significant transformation in Hegel's thought leading up to 1807. As we saw above, the early Hegel felt that the abstractness and detachment of modern consciousness made it inferior to the natural spontaneity of the Greeks. But now, this abstractness and this detachment are seen to give modern consciousness a potential advantage; for it is only through such separation or alienation that we can grasp consciousness in its universality and absoluteness. We moderns can articulate the meaning of subjectivity with a conceptual universality that was simply not possible for the ancient Greeks.

Because of its lack of reflectivity, the natural consciousness of the ancient Greeks could see the emergence of subjectivity only as a threat to its own life, and so Socrates had to be put to death. Conversely, the French Revolution had to result in the deadly Terror because the empty and abstract subjectivity that inspired it refused to acknowledge the finitude and death that belongs to its own universality. Now, following Hegel, we can comprehend an absolute subjectivity that necessarily acknowledges finitude and death within itself, and it is precisely through this acknowledgment that we can have everlasting life. Ironically, some of the most basic elements of Hegel's Christian philosophy were already suggested by the staunchly pagan and unphilosophical Winckelmann. And thus what Winckelmann wrote of the artist is equally true of his own achievement: he has been able to 'leave our minds with more than he has shown our eyes.'[31]

Notes

1 Johann Gottfried Herder, 'Denkmahl Johann Winckelmanns 1778,' in *Sämmtliche Werke*, hrsg. Bernhard Suphan (Berlin: Weidmannsche Buchhandlung, 1892), VIII, 441.
2 Johann Wolfgang Goethe, *Werkausgabe*, V; *Dichtung und Wahrheit* (Frankfurt am Main: Insel Verlag, 1981), 295.
3 Letter of 5 July 1768 to Friedrich Nicolai, in Gotthold Ephraim Lessing, *Sämmtliche Schriften*, hrsg. Karl Lachmann und Franz Muncker (Stuttgart: Göschen Verlag, 1886–1924), XVII, 255.
4 Quoted in Henry Hatfield, *Aesthetic Paganism in German Literature* (Cambridge, Mass.: Harvard University Press, 1964), 4–5.
5 See Wolfgang Leppmann, *Winckelmann* (New York: Alfred A. Knopf, 1970), 117.

6 E.M. Butler, *The Tyranny of Greece over Germany* (Cambridge: Cambridge University Press, 1935), 6.
7 Johann Joachim Winckelmann, *Reflections on the Imitation of Greek Works in Painting and Sculpture*, trans. Elfriede Heyer and Roger C. Norton (LaSalle, Ill.: Open Court, 1987), 37.
8 Winckelmann, *Reflections*, 33.
9 Quoted in H.S. Harris, *Hegel's Development I: Toward the Sunlight (1770–1801)* (Oxford: Clarendon Press, 1972), 37–8.
10 *Hegel's Phenomenology of Spirit*, trans. A.V. Miller (New York: Oxford University Press, 1977), 19.
11 This essay is printed as an 'Appendix' to Harris, *Toward the Sunlight*, 481–507.
12 Printed in ibid., 152 and 507.
13 G.W.F. Hegel, 'Earliest System-Programme of German Idealism' ('Eine Ethik'), translated and printed as an Appendix to ibid., 510–12.
14 G.W.F. Hegel, Letter of 16 April 1795, in *Briefe von und an Hegel*, hrsg. Johannes Hoffmeister (Hamburg: Meiner, 1952), 1, 24.
15 The question concerning how we should try to imitate the Greeks is similar to Rousseau's question about how the particular will of the individual can fully alienate itself and thereby subject itself entirely to the general will of the body politic. The problem seems intractable: as long as the particular will acts consciously and deliberately (as a particular will) at all, then it falls short of subjecting itself entirely to the general will; for such consciousness and deliberation entail that the particular will withholds at least one thing from the general will – namely, its own decision-making capacity. Variations on this problem appear throughout Hegel's *Phenomenology of Spirit*. See, for example, Hegel's treatment of the Changeable in relation to the Unchangeable (in the section on the Unhappy Consciousness) and his discussion of the 'education' of the individual consciousness to the point of view of universal (cosmopolitan) consciousness (in the section on *Bildung*). In this chapter, I follow Hegel in trying to show that what is antinomic for the understanding (in this case, the notion of imitating the inimitable) can become the starting point for genuinely speculative thought.
16 Winckelmann, *Reflections*, 5.
17 Johann Joachim Winckelmann, *Geschichte der Kunst des Altertums nebst einer Auswahl seiner kleineren Schriften* (Heidelberg: Weiss, 1882), 298.
18 According to some critical observers, this implies that the German fascination with the Greeks is fundamentally narcissistic. The charge of narcissism bears on several significant issues pertaining to neoclassicism, romanticism, and idealism; however, the narrow scope of this chapter does not allow for adequate treatment of these issues.
19 Johann Joachim Winckelmann, 'Erinnerung über die Betrachtung der Werke der

Kunst,' in *Sämmtliche Werke*, hrsg. Joseph Eiselein (Donauöschingen: Verlag deutscher Classiker, 1825–9), I, 206.
20 Winckelmann, *Reflections*, 21–3.
21 Ibid., 19.
22 As H.S. Harris has shown, an aesthetic sensibility is indeed required for genuine thought; Harris has demonstrated this both performatively (through his manner of interpretation) and more specifically in his analysis of Hegel's famous statement of 1796: 'I am now convinced that the highest act of Reason, the one through which it encompasses all Ideas, is an aesthetic act, and that *truth and goodness only become sisters in beauty* – the philosopher must possess just as much aesthetic power as the poet.' In his later thought, Hegel no longer considered the highest act of Reason to be aesthetic, but he 'never retreated from the view that the philosopher must possess as much aesthetic power as a major poet.' See H.S. Harris, 'The Resurrection of Art,' *The Owl of Minerva*, 16 (Fall 1984), 5–20.
23 See *Hegel's Phenomenology of Spirit*, 14.
24 What the aesthete says here about the underived unity of subjectivity and objectivity echoes what (according to Hegel) Sophocles says in *Antigone* about the unwritten and infallible laws of the gods: 'They *are*. If I inquire after their origin and confine them to the point whence they arose, then I have transcended them; for now it is I who am the universal and *they* are the conditioned and limited.' See *Hegel's Phenomenology of Spirit*, 261.
25 J.G. Fichte, *The Science of Knowledge*, trans. Peter Heath and John Lachs (Cambridge: Cambridge University Press, 1982), 28.
26 Ibid., 198–9.
27 Ibid., 13.
28 Ibid., 14.
29 In arguing thus, I am echoing what Patricia Fagan says, in chapter 1, above, about philosophical history: 'History in the fullest sense must see its object both as itself and as external to itself.'
30 See H.S. Harris, *Hegel's Development II: Night Thoughts (Jena 1801–1806)* (Oxford: Clarendon Press, 1983), 558–9. It is possible that Hegel's work on logic during the early 1800s forced him to reconsider the significance of Christianity for modern self-consciousness; however, an exact determination of the relevant influences is a matter for further research.
31 Winckelmann, *Reflections*, 69.

5

Hegel as Philosopher of the Temporal [*irdischen*] World: On the Dialectics of Narrative

MARTIN DONOUGHO

> Nel mezzo del cammin di nostra vita
> mi ritrovai per una selva oscura,
> che la diritta via era smarrita.
> Ahi quanto a dir qual era è cosa dura
> esta selva selvaggia e aspra e forte
> che nel pensier rinova la paura!
> Tant'è amara che poco è più morte.
> Dante, *Inferno*[1]

We start out in the midst of a dark wood – Dante's figure here is a variant on the labyrinth, the image (according to Northrop Frye) of lost direction. Canto 1 is just a prologue, however. Soon enough Dante's poet-cum-pilgrim will find his way forward through the gates of Hell, when both quest and poem will have begun. The advance (for it is that: what mortally pains us is the memory of our aimless and shadowy beginnings) may be read as emblematic of Dante's own poetic achievement, especially as regards narrative technique. By general consent he moved decisively beyond the labyrinthine origins of modern narration in twelfth-century romance. The nature of that achievement, and its bearing on Hegelian dialectic, are the central concerns in this essay.

Yet my chapter is an exercise less in 'poetics' than in what Angus Fletcher terms 'noetics' – the study of 'thought as discriminible dimension of the form and meaning of the poem.'[2] I argue that Dante's narrative realism is not simply 'life-like' but rather stems from a specific movement of thought, which we might label 'allegorical' or 'dialectical.' Here I am following Erich Auerbach's lead, but I also sketch some ambiguities to this line in our modern (and indeed modernist) times. This chapter explores how Hegelian dialectic figures human reality, the lifeworld presented in literature.

It begins by raising the general question as to how dialectic may be called 'narrative' in its logic and proceeds to look at Hegel's own approach to dialectic, as a prelude to asking about his paradoxical theory of 'figural realism' (a term coined by Auerbach). The section following weighs Auerbach's debt to Hegel's lapidary remarks on Dante, as well as his divergence from Hegel's stance: Auerbach borrows on the credit of Romantic allegory, whereas Hegel problematizes such transcendence and adopts an ironic view of secularity. I then turn to Auerbach's own emplotment (in his book *Mimesis*), which amounts to a legitimizing narrative of the coming to be of modernity/modernism. The fourth section considers John Freccero's semiotic explications of Dante as an antidote to such a modernist narrative. The concluding section turns to Walter Benjamin and Paul de Man, witnesses to how allegory may be used to figure modernity and modernism. I hope in the process to demonstrate Hegel's continuing salience to the problem of thinking 'the legitimacy of the modern.'

I need hardly add that the following remarks are meant as indirect homage to H.S. Harris and his achievements in Hegel studies. His modernist humanism, his bid to remain faithful to what we might call 'rational experience' – the spark of reason in the lifeworld – his (so to speak) 'naturalist' perspective on philosophy, his syncretic focus on aesthetic unity, and his love of art and (not least) of Dante all help make Harris an indispensable guide in our secular times.

Hegel, Dialectic, and Narrative

By way of contrast, let me cite a 'noetic' account of narrative origins quite different from Hegel's. It may be be found in Eugene Vance's intriguing study, *From Topos to Tale*.[3] Vance demonstrates how dialectic (in the Aristotelian tradition) might bear on the evolution of narrative techniques. The story runs as follows. As part of logic, and in particular the logic of topics, dialectics lays out the universal, non-contextual reasons by which we judge and place particular episodes – the 'logic' of the tale – even though the link between them is (for the competent reader) wholly tacit. Such a universal mode of argument is, however, inimical to the realist bias of fictional narrative it sponsors. And so the rational paradigm of Porphyry's tree tends to gives way to the model of the labyrinth (characteristic of romantic quest), contrasting moreover with a third model, which Umberto Eco calls the 'heap' – namely, a conglomeration of figures and tropes, which only God can decipher (hence its allegorical and mystical charge). For romance, nature is indeed a forest of symbols. It is against this background that Vance understands Chrétien de Troyes. He served to stretch the bounds of poetic gesture beyond the old constraints of epic, so preparing the way for Dante's even more ambitious intellectual constructions.

Vance's tale is one of rhetorical shifts and semiotic adventure (adventitious and contingent). He understands culture as sign; he especially resists the more or less standard account of medieval literature as documenting the rise of a modern subjectivity.[4] The 'Auerbachian' storyline I propose to follow, by contrast, has a foot in both semiotic and 'subjective' accounts, focusing on subjectivity but looking also at how the self or subject is figured and signified. I take this play of form and content to be central to modern (specifically Hegelian) dialectic. Yet what do we understand by 'modern' (as opposed to 'medieval') dialectic?

For that we should have to turn to Kant, founder of the modern approach, and still more to Hegel, who extracted it from the *Critique of Pure Reason*, in pointed opposition to Fichte's characteristic model of positing and reflexion. What does Hegel understand by the term 'dialectic'? And how does that bear on 'narratology'? Ignoring for the moment any disparity between phenomenological and logical uses of dialectic,[5] we should note that the term is hardly either used or mentioned in his texts, oddly enough (not so odd, some would say, if it really is the central operation or method in Hegel's system). And when Hegel does explicitly discuss the term, it is often in what we might call 'dialectical' mode – that is, he interprets, say, Platonic or Kantian dialectic in revisionary fashion, showing how really they find their truths in his own procedure, which thereby mediates their immediate status. Thus Plato is lauded for his persistence with the subject matter, his dwelling with its own contradictory nature.[6] Kant's 'dialectic of illusion' (*Schein*), as found in the First Critique, is valued for its antithetical method, which again shows up what is implicit in a concept or stance, but with the end of demonstrating its falsity.[7]

The Kantian element comes to the fore in what functions in Hegel as a technical sense of 'dialectic' – that is, 'negative' (as opposed to 'speculative') reflection. This use finds its proper place in Book 2 of the *Logic* – the logic of reflexion or *Schein* – rather than Book 3 – the logic of the concept (*der Begriff*) proper.[8] Yet such reflection ought not, Hegel urges, simply to be equated with scepticism, which stays content (or merely stuck) with a purely negative result. Dialectic involves differentiation, the positing of difference, though one that, in its own terms, collapses once more. Self-contradiction is the motor of progress and ultimately of unification; in this respect it is 'creative' in much the way *inventio media* was for the medieval logic of topics.

Hegel's most direct if also most obscure discussion of dialectic occurs at the end of the *Science of Logic*, in the section called 'The Absolute Idea.' Here we come as close as anywhere to a discussion of his own speculative method. But it turns out to be no method at all, for method would entail a separation of thematic treatment and what it treats of – a splitting apart of subject and object, or topic thematized and the (usually anonymous yet thereby masterful) position from which it is thematized. Separation is precisely what Hegel's 'procedure' anathematizes as being typical of *Verstand*. So dialectic is, first, at least this: the implication of what it is to say something in what is said, or the reflection of the subject of *énonciation* (the act) in the *énoncé* (the resultant formulation). Moreover, the normative charge inherent in judgment enters here: the act of judging is implicated in the judgment proper. In short: judge, that ye be judged.[9]

Second – and to continue the New Testament conceit – dialectic bears tidings that the first shall be last and the last first. In other words, it reverses hierarchies, ironizes the constative order, brings down an antinomial justice or judgment on the parties. Accordingly, beyond any legitimacy that the Hegelian system as a whole might claim, dialectic asserts the *il*legitimacy of any masterful gesture, as in the famous dialectic of master and slave. (Hegelian dialectic could therefore be accused of harbouring a certain *ressentiment*[10] or of *being* the 'Hapless Consciousness' – save that the dynamics of this formation had already been engaged with in the case studies of 'Rameau's Nephew' and the hard-hearted 'Beautiful Soul.')

Besides the reversal of standing, however, there is (in the third place) a reversal of sequential ordering. Dialectic identifies (or rather, uncovers an identity of) origin and end, *Anfang* and *Zweck*, immediate and mediated determination: 'In this way each step *forwards* to further determinations, in a distancing of itself from the indeterminate beginning, is also a *movement backwards* (*Rückannäherung*) to that same beginning; the *retrogressive grounding* of the beginning and its *progressive further determining* coincide and is [*sic*] the same.'[11]

Simple immediacy therefore turns out to be a result – a connection difficult for *Verstand* to grasp. The movement could be called 'quadruple' as much as 'triadic,' according to Hegel.[12] For (i) the initial determination – given, immediate, it simply *is* – harbours (ii) a contradiction, its negation, since determination comprises negation, in Spinoza's phrase. Such negation in turn shows itself to be not merely external but also (ii) self-negating: something is its own other (the paradoxical kernel of Hegel's insight, in my view). Yet – a further irony – this reduction of the original to negativity and self-negating reflection ends (iv) in the restitution of the immediacy found as (i). We are back at the beginning, though with a difference (and, as we have just seen, a vengeance).

There is a good deal of wisdom, not to say wit, in Brecht's account of Hegelian humour: 'His book "The Greater Logic" I read once, when I was down with rheumatism and unable to move. It is one of the greatest humorous works in world literature. It treats of the way of life of concepts – those slippery, unstable, irresponsible existences; how they insult one another and fight with knives and then sit down to supper as if nothing had happened ... The wit of things he calls dialectic. And like all great humorists he presented everything with a deadly serious face ... I have still not met a man lacking in humour who understood Hegel's dialectic.'[13]

Now, I do not propose to partake of the feast, or even to gather a few crumbs from the table. Rather I wish to ask what manner of story the Hegelian diner might tell. It is clear that the three elements I have mentioned – implication of subject of *énonciation* in the *énoncé*, passing of legitimizing/illegitimizing judgment, rendering of beginning as result and vice versa – carry obvious narrative potential. For example, the dialectical 'experience' of implicature is already processual, a pathway of despair (as Hegel calls it in the *Phenomenology*), a passage of trial and error, which at the same time is not just adventitious: in retrospect, the form may be perceived within the content. Or again, the juridical mode[14] typically supposes a scenario or narrative frame: to understand the story is to forgive (or condemn) its participants, we might say.[15] Or lastly, it is no accident that the *Phenomenology* has often been compared with the *Bildungsroman*, or conversely, that many novels, from Goethe to Proust, are cast in dialectical mode: they tell of a coming-to-oneself, through intermediate stages whose unconscious presuppositions are gradually brought home, to the reader if not necessarily to the protagonist.

But there is another respect in which dialectic acquires a narrative charge – namely, in the relation of identity and difference, in its various embodiments as appearance/essence, particular/universal, act/meaning, emotion (or sense) and intellect, human versus divine sanction. This relation is actualized as what we might call 'artistic realism,' whether of setting, action, or character. For Hegel, the Greek achievement was built on such realism, the unity of *soma* with *sema*, as in a different and displaced manner was the post-Hellenic or Christian worldview. Whether in sculptural *Gestalt*, in visual image, or in narrative and dramatic depiction (where fact and act are one), the emphasis is on appearances, on an added truth to life. At the same time, what emerges as we pass from Greek to post-Hellenic worlds is the gap between the phenomenal reality of lived experience and the universal necessity inherent in law, divinity, and fate (a nice summary may be found in the introduction to the 'romantic' artform in the *Aesthetics*[16]). That is where Dante's realism – as Hegel presents it – finds its appointed place in the Hegelian topocosm. Dante's *Commedia* marks the crucial intersection of classical and modern times, the point of separation-cum-unity between words and things, divine essence and secular finitude. The very 'lightness' of Dante's language – as Italo Calvino would phrase it – points to the 'solidity' of the world it inhabits and depicts.[17]

Let me return, belatedly, to my introductory epigraph: those familiar lines from canto I that set the scene for the beginning of the poem proper in canto II and the subsequent descent through the gates of Hell in canto III: 'Midway through the journey of our life I found myself in a dark wood.' Quite apart from the literary figure of the labyrinth already mentioned, various sources have been suggested for this wood, a peculiar region where all signs seem reversed.[18] Is it too fanciful to suggest a parallel with Hegel's 'inverted world,' or at least with the dialectical inversion (*Umkehrung*) that befalls reified thinking at every pass? Fanciful or not, the suggestion encourages us to draw all sorts of parallels between Hegel and Dante. We might note, for example, how the poet retraces in memory the path already traced by the pilgrim – almost as harsh and bitter in repetition – much like the dual perspective of the *Phenomenology* or (in another register) the *Logic*, a duality that nevertheless converges at the last on a unified and total perspective. The path of doubt leading to despair reminds us of the words of obscure import (*senso duro*) written above the gates to Hell, adjuring us to abandon all hope – words which also (as Hegel himself notes) capture the central contradiction between time and eternity.[19] The passage through Hell and Purgatory would accordingly be like negative or dialectical reflection, and that through Paradise, more like speculative reflection. Moreover, the movement of inversion and recognition through reflection parallels Dante's characteristic logic of conversion: dialectic as convers(at)ion! As for the implicature of authorial testament in the events narrated, that has its counterpart in Hegel's appeal to 'our' subjectivity – the play between 'for itself' and 'for us,' for example. And so on.

Interesting though it is to entertain such epical comparisons, my concern here lies in one quite peculiar narrative feature of Hegelian dialectic, as it emerges in Hegel's brief remarks on the *Commedia*: its formulation of aesthetic realism – paradoxically enough – as allegory. Erich Auerbach did much to alert us to this connection (and my title borrows from him). Following his lead, I broaden my focus below so as to consider some problems of modernity and modernism. Today as well we find ourselves in a 'world turned upside down,' where any humanist synthesis of the sort Dante attempted and Hegel and Auerbach celebrated, any attempt at realizing a legitimate order, threatens to become 'just gaming.' That threat emerges clearly in late modernism (or post-modernism), from Walter Benjamin to Joel Fineman and Paul de Man, who throw a new, flickering light on allegory; some of the consequences of this I return to at the end.

Allegory in Auerbach and Hegel

Allegory played an ambiguous role for the Romantics, and the tradition of Dante interpretation they began is in its way a grappling with the consciousness of modernity. Hegel – and much later, Auerbach – continue that tradition. There are just fleeting allusions to Dante in Hegel's early works – *Faith and Knowledge*, *Natural Law*, and the fragment 'ist nur die Form.' None discloses a deep engagement with the text, comparable to that with Greek tragedy or Shakespeare, say.[20] In the *Lectures on Aesthetics*, however, Hegel mentions Dante several times and in various connections. One connection is with allegory as a literary mode: he disparages any attempt to interpret Dante in a narrowly allegorical sense, as though the meaning of every stanza could be deciphered once and for all (312); and later, in a discussion of the thematics of love, he describes the presentation of Beatrice as 'hovering' between allegory and a poetic transformation of subjective feeling (402). Another connection is with the 'romantic' expressiveness of Italian painting: Hegel argues that we can find the same depth of feeling, the same clarity, and similar spiritual concern: 'Dante too, led by his master Virgil, through Hell and Purgatory, sees the most frightful horrors, he is uneasy and is often in floods of tears, but he strides on, tranquil and consoled, without fear and anxiety, without the ill-humour and exasperation that says "things should not be thus." Indeed even his damned souls in Hell still have the bliss of eternity – *io eterno duro* stands over the gates of Hell – they are what they are, without repentance or desire; they say nothing of their torments – these affect neither us nor them, as it were, for they endure for ever – they keep in mind only their disposition and deeds, firm and constant to themselves in their same interests, without lamentation and longing' (874).

However, the main discussion of Dante in the *Lectures on Aesthetics* occurs in two contexts: (i) Dante's historical place within 'romantic' (i.e., post-Hellenic or Christian) art, and (ii) the classification of the *Commedia* as epic poetry. In this latter connection Hegel is speaking about religious thematics, and he refers to the *Commedia* as 'the most solid and the richest work in this sphere, the artistic epic proper to the Christian Catholic Middle Ages, the greatest poem and the one with the greatest material' (1103). He then expands on this claim:

> Instead of a particular event it has for its subject-matter the eternal action, the absolute end and aim, the love of God in its imperishable activity and unalterable sphere, and for its locality Hell, Purgatory, and Paradise; into this changeless existence (*wechsellose Dasein*) it plunges the living world of human action and suffering and, more particularly, the deeds and destinies of individuals. Here, in the face of the absolute grandeur of the ultimate end and aim all things, everything individual and particular in human interests and aims vanishes, and yet there stands there, completely epically, everything otherwise most fleeting and transient in the living world, grounded objectively in its inmost being, judged in its worth or worthlessness by the supreme Concept, i.e. by God. For as individuals *were* in their

passions and sufferings, in their intentions and their accomplishments, so now they are presented for ever, solidified into images of bronze. In this way the poem comprises the entirety of the most objective life: the eternal condition of Hell, Purgatory, and Paradise; and on this indestructible foundation the figures (*Figuren*) of the actual world move in their particular character, or rather, they *have* moved and now in their action and being are frozen in eternal justice, eternal themselves. While the Homeric heroes have been made permanent in *our* memories by the muse, these characters have produced their situation for *themselves*, for their individuality, and are eternal in themselves, not in our representations. The immortality created by Mnemosyne counts here objectively as the very judgement of God in whose name the boldest spirit of his time has pronounced damnation or salvation for the entire present and the past. – This character of the subject-matter, already independently finished, must be followed by the manner of its portrayal. This can only be a journey through realms fixed once and for all, and although they are invented, equipped, and peopled by the same freedom of imagination with which Homer and Hesiod formed their gods, still they are meant to provide a picture and a report on what has really happened: in Hell the movement is energetic but the figures are plastic and stiff in their agony, lit terrifyingly, though the picture is modified by Dante's own mournful sympathy; in Purgatory things are milder but all fully worked out and rounded off; finally, in Paradise all is clear as crystal, a region of eternal thought where external shapes are no more. (1103–4)

Erich Auerbach, citing the phrase 'changeless existence,' remarks that it occurs in 'one of the most beautiful passages ever written on Dante.'[21] This hyperbolic praise comes towards the middle of his great book, *Mimesis: The Representation (Darstellung) of Reality in Western Literature*, in a chapter called 'Farinata and Cavalcante,' dealing with an episode (or a succession of scenes) in canto 10 of 'The Inferno.' As a professional philologist – one of the most influential in recent times – Auerbach pays far more attention than Hegel does to the linguistic and rhetorical *medium* of presentation, or stylistics. Indeed, it is not the least problematic (or honest) features of his project that even in appealing to the neo-classical norm of imitation and the use (for example, by Goethe) of the word '*Darstellung*' to connote representation, he foregrounds the devices, or 'stylistic levels,' used to achieve such a 'reality-effect' (the same ambiguity dogs Ernst Gombrich's *Art and Illusion*). Thus, analysing the rapid succession of scenes between Dante and Farinata or Cavalcanti, Auerbach is at pains to bring out Dante's syntactic adroitness, his avoidance equally of parataxis (juxtaposition) and of mere effect, his achievement of a rare marriage between the vernacular and an elevated, almost Virgilian tone. Yet Auerbach does so to bring out 'how the unity of the transcendental order [which rules all three realms]

Hegel as Philosopher of the Temporal [*irdischen*] World 119

operates as a unity of the elevated style' (190) – that is, to demonstrate how form reflects thematics.

It is especially at this thematic level that Auerbach reveres Hegel, whose comments are said to illustrate the 'astounding paradox of what is called Dante's realism.' The paradox is that not only sensuous actuality but also history are vividly embedded in a universal frame – that of God's judgment. 'Nearly all the characters in the *Comedy* appear in person,' Auerbach writes in an essay on the portrayal of St Francis in canto 11 of *Paradiso*. 'Dante finds them in the place God's justice has appointed for them, and there, direct encounter is developed by question and answer.'[22] Auerbach terms Dante's procedure 'figural realism': both poles – the figure and its fulfilment – retain a concrete historicity and sensuousness, a 'historicity both of the sign and what it signifies,' as he neatly puts it in his 1944 essay 'Figura.'[23] *Figura* is more than allegory, then. Where abstract allegory is typical of classical or pagan thematics, *figura* by contrast is Christian in its emphasis on the 'earthly' and 'temporal.' Auerbach further suggests that allegorical interpretation (especially in accordance with the medieval fourfold of literal, allegorical, ethical, and anagogic) would never have met with the success it had without such a figural logic or teleology, which lends the narrative the density of actual existence. Because it goes beyond straight allegory, we might well dub the *Commedia* 'quasi-allegorical' (in Coleridge's phrase)[24] or 'real allegory' (as Courbet described his 'The Painter in his Studio'). The point and the paradox is that fulfilment never abolishes the image, as allegory tends to do, but preserves the real *sub specie aeternitatis*. (It is no accident that *Mimesis* often borrows the Hegelian language of '*Aufhebung*,' preservation in negation; nor that the paradoxical nature of figural realism has been underestimated – it is semiosis that turns out to be real!)

In the essay on 'Figura' Auerbach claims that this notion provided a systematic foundation for an approach that he had once taken to 'Dante's realism' where he had (he now admits) drawn on some Hegelian themes.[25] He means the interpretation he had offered in his *Dante als Dichter der irdischen Welt* of 1929.[26] Hegel is never mentioned in that earlier work; perhaps the debt was obvious, or more likely it would just not have done for a young scholar to admit such a crossing of disciplinary lines, especially to a *demodé* philosopher. Yet for anyone acqainted with the *Aesthetics* it is evident where Auerbach gets the historical sweep of the first chapter in the *Dante* study, as well as many particulars in the commentary in chapter 3.

Dante als Dichter carries an epigraph from Heraclitus: 'A man's character is his fate (*daimon*).' Auerbach sees in the unity of character and fate as embodied in human existence the kernel of European literary realism, from Homer to the present. Tragic representation precipitates out a fate that cannot be accommodated within the immediate unity of character found in Homeric epic; it is only (for instance) Sophocles' lingering attachment to individual traits that prevents their total effacement before an anonymous fate. With the story of Christ something new came about, however: a focus on the individual for his or her own sake, even though destiny itself is quite other-worldly. This insight of 'Christian realism' took a millennium to be accepted, however, impeded as it was by what Auerbach calls the 'spiritualism' of Neoplatonist and Manichean doctrine, or by the need to simplify the good news for barbarian ears. It was only in the mimetic art of the Middle Ages that the lesson was truly taken to heart – first with the *Minnesänger*, but especially by the troubadors of Provence and their 'dialectic of feeling' – a brief and precarious achievement that soon dwindled into an exclusive elitism.

This historical account leads to Auerbach's main thesis – that 'we find in the *Commedia* an image of the earthly world in all its diversity, transposed into the world of ultimate destiny and perfect order' (134) defined by divine judgment. Individuals are not thereby divested of their earthly character (as in Greek tragedy); rather, they are identified with their fate, and disclose their destiny precisely through their univocal action. Though this realm is out of time and changeless, temporal existence is preserved via memory. Memory serves to bring out an individual's essential character, what s/he was and is, fixed for ever in divine judgment (142–3). Dante thus differs both from ancient epic or tragedy (where the stories told were already known) and from later naturalism (which sets the scene as a prelude to narrating the action). Dante indeed established the European model (Gestalt) of man. Yet his epochal synthesis of intellect and feeling, of human character and transcendent order, did not last. Petrarch soon turned to presenting a poetic self that looks inward to a modern subjectivity rather than upward to the eternal city (176f.); and so begins what might nowadays be called 'Renaissance self-fashioning.'

Auerbach's account is a sophisticated reworking of the Hegelian tale of the emergence of subjectivity (and its complement, a contingent fate) in the post-Hellenic world. The classical unity of shape and meaning, of physical body and spiritual understanding, finds its epitome in sculpture and the properly sculptural theme of the human form. But such 'individuality' must leave unthematized the relation of the two sides, which devolves on a contingent and external fate. Romantic (post-Hellenic) form and thematics attend to the earthly aspects of a supernal God – in the shape first of the Christ story, and following that in the more secular themes of religious love and community. Dante marks the point at which inner subjectivity interpenetrates outer reality. Like Auerbach, Hegel comments on the way in which Dante mixes his own subjective experience with the objective events that he narrates: 'In [the *Commedia*] the epic poet himself is the one individual to whose wanderings through Hell, Purgatory, and Paradise each and every incident is linked, so that he can recount the productions of his imagination as his own experiences and therefore acquires the right ... of interweaving his own feelings and reflections in the objective side of his work' (1066).

Earlier, in a historical account of the 'romantic' art form, Hegel finds a place for Dante under 'the contingency of aims and collisions' (as compared with the classical world and its literary representation of a necessary unity of will and act, of theme and event). It enters under the rubric of 'Adventures,' the second part of the 'romantic' art form/worldview (the first part concerned religious imagery and stories, and above all the story of Christ). Whereas the great adventure of the Christian world was the Crusades or the quest for the Holy Grail, Dante's poem shows us an internalized quest for salvation of the soul. It is only later that the whole world of chivalry is made fun of (in Ariosto and Cervantes) or reduced to comic characters (with Shakespeare's Falstaff). Ultimately medieval epic is displaced (comically, in Hegel's view) into the modern novel or *Bildungsroman*, and then the entire art form/worldview dissolves into the polarity of naturalism (Dutch painting, for example) and subjective humour (Romantics such as Jean Paul and Ludwig Tieck).

Yet Hegel presses further than seeing in the *Commedia* a unity of event and meaning: he ironizes Dante's realism. Dante is said to make himself judge of all mankind, as if his own poetic judgment were God's (564). True, there are plenty of adventures and characters, Hegel allows, 'inasmuch as this work of salvation and damnation comes before us not just absolutely – hence in its universality – but also as a list of individuals practically without number, brought forward in their particular characteristics. Alongside this [however] the *poet* claims for himself the right of the Church, holds the keys of the Kingdom of Heaven in his hands, pronounces salvation and damnation, and so makes himself the world's judge transporting into Hell, Purgatory, or Paradise the best known individuals of the classical and Christian world, poets, citizens, warriors, Cardinals, and Popes' (589). Note the parallel between the way these characters immortalize themselves and Dante's own memorializing activity (Mnemosyne, in the previous passage) – a parallel that emerges even more strongly in the 1823 Lectures: 'The epic of Catholicism is the *Divine Comedy* of Dante. He calls it "comedy" because it is written in the vulgar dialect of Italian, which was at that time not yet the language of learning. This poem presents us with a duality: a condition (*ein Zustand*), and this eternal condition is Hell, Purgatory, and Heaven. Eternal being is there as condition.[27] It consists of fixed conditions; they are presupposed, and the figures move within it according to their particular character – or rather, they have moved, they are rendered immortal. The individuals are represented as they bring about, in and of themselves, their own immortalizing. Their actions are frozen in an everlasting judgement (*Gerechtigkeit*). The immortalizing of men by the poet and by themselves are presented as one.'[28]

Hegel's account of Dantean epic could well be cast as straight allegory: poetic representation (*Vorstellung*) substitutes God, and in turn the poet, for the true meaning – the Concept – and divine/poetic judgment for the Idea of cognition. Yet we could equally reverse this statement. In his emphasis on the interpenetration of finite and infinite, historical and ideal, event and judgment/interpretation of the event, Dante might serve as the exemplar of dialectical reflection. But whether we characterize figural realism as dialectical or dialectics as figural is of little account, in my opinion. What matters is that we see how both the temporal and spatial orders are at once secularized and redeemed by the mode of telling. An objective order is grounded in the subject, which in turn finds itself in the objective order. In the process nature and narrative history alike receive a pseudo-divine sanction.

Auerbach seeks to borrow something of this aura, not merely for his favoured romance literature, but equally for literary narrative in general. As with the fearful symmetries of Northrop Frye's archetypal criticism, a narrative of declension and displacement (from myth through high mimetic and low mimetic modes to naturalism and ultimately irony) can have it both ways, pointing either nostalgically to divine origins, a transcendent order, or with melancholy towards a final dissolution of meaning in the merely sensuous (or further, perhaps, to a *ricorso* via myth, and so on).[29] Allegory, even the 'real' allegory of a figural mode, may well co-opt the aegis of symbol or metaphor.[30]

From another angle, however, Hegel may be seen as problematizing or even debunking this kind of transcendence. Seeing the poet as a guise of God is itself a kind of irony, for it reduces the divine to human terms. That is exactly how Hegel would treat the Christian idea of other-worldliness, and the concomitant idea that nature is in a 'fallen' state. Nature – in its supposed sheer givenness – can never be redeemed, because it is a projection of subjectivity in the first place. Natural contingency had been a problem for medieval cosmology,[31] but, as Hegel would see it, nature comprises the inessential, which is nevertheless essential to the whole – a paradox that lies at the heart of 'the Hapless Consciousness.' So, Dante's *dolce stil novo* was still not quite new enough to capture the full secularity of world, time, and seculum. Hegel thus appears as the dialectical philosopher of the secular world, an ironical presence behind the scenes from the drama of European literature, silently paring his fingernails.

Legitimate Authority

There is little of such irony in Auerbach's *Dante*, perhaps because he was concerned to bring out (and valorize) the humanist fusion of historical individual and eternal order. Auerbach notes how Dante puts himself in the poem, makes his own experience exemplary, in a unique merging of the personal and the public. Moreover, the *Commedia* appears as the culmination of Dante's tendency to make his own self the unified centre of the whole poem (for example, 63–5, 98). Yet, for all these gestures at self-reflexivity, Auerbach does not question Dante's relation to the universal order, or for that matter his own.

Poetic authority and authorial authority are even further hidden in the structural intricacies of *Mimesis*. Instead of a Hegelian grand narrative from Greek to modern selfhood – as in the earlier study – we are now offered an account of successive stylistic levels, leading finally to Flaubertian naturalism and hence to modernist parataxis and the foregrounding of time and consciousness. Nevertheless, we can discern a plot in *Mimesis*, and we can read between the lines a reflection on its own method of composition. Dante's figural realism occurred, the Epilogue to *Mimesis* suggests, in reaction against the high mimetic style of ancient tragedy – a shift already found in accounts of the life of Christ, which stress both his actuality and his divinity. *Mimesis* in fact develops a two-stage narrative: Auerbach perceives a revival of the high style in European (neo)classicism, and a second reaction against it in the shape of nineteenth-century realism and naturalism, which reaches its appointed end (in both senses) as the paratactic impressionism – he also calls it 'perspectivism' – of Joyce and Woolf.[32]

Yet my talk of 'plot' or 'narrative' perhaps claims too much for Auerbach's avowed procedure, which replaces the confident hypotaxis of a Hegelian story with the parataxis or musical 'motifs' characteristic of a modernist perspectivism – as if Auerbach were mimicking the very examples of modernist literature cited at the close of his book. In a penetrating critique, Paul Bové has called this quasi-allusion to his own compositional procedure (as heir to the realist tradition) a political act.[33] In elucidating how modernism came about, Auerbach also borrows some of its authority, thus capitalizing on his cultural inheritance (I note in passing that this implication of narrative voice in the events narrated is highly dialectical, as already pinpointed).

Auerbach himself draws attention to the circumstances under which *Mimesis* was composed – exile from Europe, the Second World War.[34] Its precarious historicism, its sense of humanism under mortal threat, its claims for a still-viable philological tradition all came under further strain in the postwar United States to which he had meanwhile emigrated, in an institutional life world over which new criticism was just then assuming hegemony. He could no longer insert himself into the tradition, as he had so ingeniously at the end of *Mimesis* – putting a finishing touch to the aesthetic picture much like the painter Lily Briscoe's in (but it is also the formal finish of) *To the Lighthouse*.[35] Bové argues that Auerbach had to cast around for an alternative foundation to his historicist method, one less dependent on the apolitical *Bildung* of Goethean humanism or the more statist tendencies of *Geistesgeschichte* (in the tradition of Troeltsch and Meinecke, at least, for it was not always implicated in *Realpolitik*). Bové discerns a shift from idealism (Hegel) to reliance on an institutional and above all linguistic basis (Vico). Dante remains central throughout, however: ' "Dante" becomes a sign for humanity in Auerbach, and modernity might be said to be a battle for Dante's survival,' Bové writes.[36] In the larger view, modernity/modernism threatens to dissolve the humanist tradition inaugurated and (if you will) underwritten by Dante's great synthesis. Yet in the end that very synthesis is phrased in what could be called an optative mood: it is significant less for briefly carving out its own public sphere – a putative '*Weltliteratur*' – than for projecting a possible reception among future generations. Thus Auerbach claims, in *Literary Language and Its Public* (1958), that 'by letting earthly destinies and earthly passions, with all their tragic contents, live on within the divine order, he [Dante] focused attention on man in a new way. Thus he inaugurated modern European literature (or perhaps it would be more accurate to say the modern self-portrayal of man) and began to build up a public that would be receptive to this literature.'[37]

From Epiphany to Semiosis

In retrospect, Auerbach's Dante might seem a little too complacently theocentric ('a secular religion' is how René Wellek characterizes the approach), for all its close attention to mode of presentation in addition to thematics. In part the trouble lies in the elision of stylistic analysis with the text's own troping devices, as if the writer could (by imitation!) borrow legitimacy from history itself. More recent approaches to Dante tend to resist such appeal to quasi-divine authority.[38] The introduction to a collection of John Freccero's essays observes that as 'the awareness of rhetorical strategies that subvert meaning becomes more acute, "aporia" has replaced "epiphany" as the critic's focus'[39] (not only in Dante studies). Emphasis falls nowadays on the sign, writing, textuality – on the 'vo significando' cited in the *Purgatorio*.[40] Freccero speaks of Dante's 'logology' (Kenneth Burke's term for how the coherence of talk about God reflects the coherence of poetry – reflects, but also differs from).[41] He resists celebration of literary mimesis; he maintains that Dante's realism is nowhere near as benign as Auerbach supposes but is rather the calling into question of the very foundations of the reality 'presented.' In a 1983 essay on *The Inferno*, he writes: 'It would not be difficult to reintroduce signification into the examples adduced by Auerbach and thereby ironize his assertion in order to show that his insistence on the human autonomy of the characters at the expense of the divine order is a function of his own mystification. Negating the negation of secular values that is the function of the infernal context inevitably yields a positive portrayal. So Auerbach pictures Cavalcante Cavalcanti in all his spontaneous grief, as though it were God or destiny rather than the poet, subjecting him to his torment.'

In fact (notes Freccero) the phrase Auerbach takes to be most immediate and 'heartrending' alludes to Guido's own verses precisely denying transcendence: 'It would be difficult to find a more ironically contrived verse in the canto, but Auerbach is as blind to its citationality as Cavalcante is blind to the sweet light of allegory' – that is, in failing to recognize Virgil as figural.[42] Freccero accordingly gives a reading of *Inferno* as a text of ironic intent. The true province of the poet is imaginative representation, the locus of which is the *Purgatorio*: the intellectual vision of *Paradiso* goes beyond poetry, while the corporeal vision of the *Inferno* falls short. In part I, therefore, reality must be counterfeited, as if it were there; and that is the mode of irony. With irony (Freccero cites the semiotician Dan Sperber) words are cited as if they were being used to refer; what we are really being given is the reification of words, the letter rather than the spirit. Divine judgment is (from God's perspective) a purely aesthetic matter, a projection of Dante's imagination; the pilgrim's descent is really a journey of interpretation, as through a linguistic graveyard. The figures come to life – yet only thanks to the movement of irony.

Freccero presses further, however, inquiring into the means by which an ironic perspective is stretched out into a linear narrative. His solution is brilliant: 'Autobiography is a tautology – "I am I" – into which a negative is introduced in order to generate a narrative – "I am I, but I was not always so." Such a narrative transforms irony into an allegory of conversion.[43] That insight is worked out at greater length in another 1983 essay, 'The Significance of *Terza Rima*,' which understands the coherence of belief in the whole *Commedia* as simply a projection of the coherence of the poem and its language.[44] History and temporality are pressed into the service of poetic syntax, in short; temporal closure derives from linguistic closure, and paradigmatically from the pattern of *terza rima*. I can't resist citing Freccero's conclusion: 'Like the Hegelian dialectic, its modern analogue, *terza rima* represents a model for the synthesis of time and meaning into history.'[45]

Allegory and the Dialectic of Modernity

The trouble with putting the matter as Freccero does is that the poet is made to undermine his synthesis in the very act of thematizing it. The model itself becomes foregrounded, ironical, 'aporetic,' and the journey is not upward to an 'anagogical' fusion with the divine but downward, *'catagogical'* (to borrow Tony Nuttall's neologism[46]). Or again, if the naturalizing of divine authority and the historicizing (by narrativization) of law are both made derivative of artistic projection, the poet in turn stands in need of legitimacy (one that a Romantic aesthetic of creativity and 'forming form' sought much later to provide). We observed above the ambivalence of Hegel's own narrative of the rise and fall of realist narrative: whereas Auerbach implicates himself in his quasi-tale of stylistic levels, so gaining authority from the tradition, Hegel's self-implication in the genesis of modernity (or Romanticism) is entirely ironical in mode. Does such irony reduce divine logos to mere words, and the cosmos to poetic selfhood? And is that Hegel's final judgment on the modern world – a secularity without end?

To throw light on such questions, let me, by way of conclusion, pursue the theme of modernity/modernism a little further, using for a guide the notion of allegory as it figures in the thinking of Walter Benjamin and Paul de Man. Neither thinker bears an easy relationship to the 'dialectical' tradition, it has to be admitted (yet that itself will prove a good test). Benjamin repudiates its systemic pretensions, speaks rather of 'dialectics at a standstill,' understands history as entropic and discontinuous, while his avant-gardiste tendencies are resolutely anti-mimetic. As for de Man, he seeks in and by his allegorical readings to divest himself of authority (of responsibility, too, some would say). Nevertheless, simply by yoking allegory to dialectic, in the shadow of Auerbach's failing gesture at legitimation, we can better gauge whether Hegelian reflection finds itself in experience, in the lifeworld.

What would allegory that escapes the symbolic mould, or *impresa*, be like? It would see space and time precisely not as divinely ordained but rather as unredeemed and finite. Such a mode is what Benjamin attempted both to historicize and to interpret in his *Ursprung* study.[47] By displacing ancient epic (Benjamin claims), allegory looks backward not so much to recuperate (say) Old Testament into New, but more to safeguard relics as mementi mori: the Owl of Minerva, we might say, transformed into the angel of death, as it blasts a way through the historicist continuum. Allegory brings out the ineradicable temporality of worldly existence; the notion of 'natural history' – almost a contradiction in terms – indicates how history becomes petrified, nature sheerly contingent. Allegorizing stresses breaks rather than continuity, the Baudelairean fugitive moment read as the hallmark of modernity. Most important perhaps is the conventional status of allegory, its emphasis on writing, hieroglyphics, emblematics, and the like, where in the limit visual experience is divorced from universal meaning altogether and the signifier exists on its own account, without further justification.[48]

Benjamin points out that the Romantics themselves went some way to rescuing allegory, understanding it to be more than the negative face of the Romantic symbol; Herder, Schlegel, Görres, and Creuzer all had a hand in this underground movement. It would thus be false to speak (with Gadamer, for instance) of the revival of allegory following the Romantics' over-investment in symbol, since they already had a place for it. The rigid opposing of symbol to allegory has in fact two roots. On the one hand, classicizing tendencies in Romanticism (as in Goethe) played down allegory in favour of the sculptural fusion of meaning and sense Winckelmann had posited in ancient Greek art.[49] On the other hand, a post-Romantic classification ratified the opposition of organic and mechanical (allegorical) form. Interestingly enough, Benjamin tries to demonstrate a dialectic in the symbol itself, between the plastic and the mystic, the organic (or monumental) and the momentary (or illumination as if by lightning, Creuzer says). There would then be a parallel dialectic in allegory, between its stable face (the didactic and Christian tradition of medieval allegorizing) and the mystic depths, where meaning and sense threaten to peel apart entirely. Comparing the second, unstable terms of each, Benjamin writes: 'Whereas in the symbol destruction is idealized and the transfigured face of nature is fleetingly revealed in the light of redemption, in allegory the observer is confronted with the *facies hyppocritica* of history as a petrified, primordial landscape' (166).

If history is Janus-faced, then here we have the obverse (the death's head, or mortification) of figural realism – non-fulfilment of the figure, so to speak. Nor is there any resolution via the parataxis Auerbach sees as typical of modern narrative, which calls for the epiphanic gesture of a brushstroke or individual perception to 'complete' the picture. Creuzer (to whose remarkable *Symbolik* Benjamin often appeals) places allegory in the setting of the symbol, thereby sanitizing it for a Romantic ideology. Yet he also mystifies symbolism, understanding it as the rational translation into aesthetic terms of a meaning that at the same time resists any such closure.

Hegel also appeals to Creuzer (a friend from Heidelberg days), and in his appropriation of the latter's 'Iconology' to his own ends in the *Aesthetics* he too reflects the double nature of Romantic theory.[50] In Hegel's scheme of things, Greece becomes the land of symbol in the sculptural sense, where shape and meaning (*Gestalt* and *Bedeutung*) fuse totally. The mystic and reflexive side comes out in what he calls the 'symbolic' world-view (or art form). Such a gesture seems on the face of it to privilege symbolic unity; but in fact the reverse is the case, for Hegel proceeds to undermine the classical immediacy from within. What was presented as ancillary or unessential to art – the symbolic mode and world-view, which ultimately reduces to the disjunction of figure and symbolized meaning – turns out thus to be its mediating term. The end result in 'romantic' art is a polarization into external shape (naturalism or 'detailism' in painting) and internal meaning (subjective humour or irony), and further, the parody of art as the 'saint' of Humanus.[51] Hegel's emplotment of the classical Ideal of art allows for the kind of negative reading of aesthetic symbolism Benjamin urges on us.

These remarks may allow us to appreciate the force of Paul de Man's challenge to Hegelian dialectic when he sees in it a leaning towards 'totalization.' De Man, it should be noted, bears an even more conflicted relation to past and present than Auerbach (his predecessor in the chair at Yale), yet perhaps for that very reason remains acutely sensitive to the seductions of method. In one of his most insightful essays[52] he remarks on the way genuinely dialectical works of literary history, from Hegel on, bypass the contemporary moment – this 'predictable blindness' being repeated, he says, in Auerbach's *Mimesis* and Benjamin's *Ursprung* study. (He might well have added other dialectical historians such as Clement Greenberg, Northrop Frye – or Fredric Jameson, in whose work until recently modernism figured as the invisible centre, the black hole in which all distinction gets lost. And what of de Man's own ambivalent and complicitous position?) The remark is one of many asides in an elliptical approach to the problem of how it might be possible to write a history of Romanticism that would 'do justice' to its object, when the suspicion is that Romanticism undermines the authority of a genetic account from within. De Man was always 'after Romanticism,' in a double sense, always trying to avoid ideologizing the very thing he was in quest of. Yet could he ever have succeeded in this? It is unclear whether he understands blindness to the present as a defect, or as inevitable – after all, how is a (correct) perspective on a present perspective possible?[53] A dialectical approach will at least be all set to mediate any immediacies that lurk in its own standpoint. But de Man is objecting to a more refractory presumption which he attributes to dialectical thinking: that of having achieved interpretive closure, to have got the whole story or passed a final judgment from a god's eye view – at the last *trompe l'oeil*, so to say!

Romantic aesthetics has its own perspective or 'myth of origin' (Nietzsche) in the model of creativity or self-expression, with its attendant notions of organic process or the punctual happening of truth and worldhood. Hegel adopts an ironic perspective on this view, precisely by historicizing it. But de Man observes that Hegel's own genetic model is itself a product of the Romantic imagination and rhetoric. De Man quotes the Introduction to the *Phenomenology*

– 'Das Resultat ist nur darum dasselbe, was der Anfang, weil der *Anfang Zweck ist*' – and rephrases this model: 'No father, no son can be God, but the history of the struggle between fathers and sons remains in essence divine.' (De Man is here pointing at the claim to authority in the gesture of reversal I identified as the second feature of Hegelian dialectic.) Much literary and indeed aesthetic history remains in pre-Hegelian mode, he adds, and continues to impose a non-dialectical notion of subject-object on its operations and thematics. Things are (after all) what they are and not otherwise.[54] By contrast, the genetic approach adopted by dialectical thinking seeks to intertwine historical event and act of interpretation, not through some conceptual legerdemain (a 'positing' or '*Setzen*' that invokes the immediacy of Romantic reflection) but in a genuine ontology. At the same time, for de Man dialectical thinking supposes a controlling totalization, just as dialectical reversal imposes a fixed frame of reference: it is this closed system that renders the dialectician blind to an ever-open present, de Man suggests.

De Man does not tell us what a post- or non-dialectical perspective would be, though he implies that it is 'genealogical' in Nietzsche's sense – a narrative without end. Presumably it would undermine the myth of origin-end implicit even in dialectics; it would make a point of not claiming to have effected 'closure' (to have grounded one's viewpoint in some objective historical order, and in turn that order in a subjectivity that is absolute). It would perhaps ask for the identity papers belonging to the 'we' – Hegel's '*für uns*' – of the interpretive act: just who do we think we are? And 'we' can surmise, perhaps, that 'we' are (if nothing else) readers of the words on the page, reflecting on if not subject to the rhetorical devices at work there. One of the rhetorical uses to which genetic narratives are put is legitimation; and of course there is plenty of that in Hegel. De Man urges us to be 'literalists of the imagination,' to resist the call to legitimacy. That is what his 'allegories of reading' are called on to do.

Allegory is a slippery figure or trope. Much as with a narrative of origin, it constitutes a primary way in which value may be redeemed. It recaptures a sense of justification even as the literal loses its aura or its intrinsic meaningfulness. But this justification cuts two ways. In demythologizing the gods, allegory (or allegorizing interpretation) tends either to authorize new ones or else to defend poetic form. Whichever way it cuts, the reader is left with no choice in the matter: allegorizing is a power game.[55] It may be true that in literary criticism as in philosophical interpretation there is no choice anyway, as Northrop Frye says: 'All commentary is allegorical interpretation, an attaching of ideas to the structure of poetic imagery.'[56] But de Man's allegories of reading offer interpretations that lay bare their figural and rhetorical bases, yet without reducing either to some linguistic or to an intertextual structure, and moreover, without rooting the hermeutic process in dialectical terms.

It may well be asked whether Hegel himself is wedded to a masterful procedure, imposing an *interpretatio philosophica* (in place of the *interpretatio christiana*) on texts and events, or whether he can or should be read otherwise. Does Hegelian realism devolve after all on the polarity of speculative meaning/verbal construct? Is Hegelian allegory therefore an abstraction, in the last analysis? De Man has an essay on Hegel's own treatment of allegory, 'Sign and Symbol in Hegel's *Aesthetics*,'[57] which usefully weaves commentary on Hegel's texts with polemic about literary theory and history, and I should like (in closing) to take a brief look at it.

Prima facie, Hegel has no time at all for 'allegory'; it is confined to the section of 'the symbolic' entitled 'conscious or comparative symbolics.' De Man cites Peter Szondi's assessment (in an otherwise sympathetic commentary on the *Aesthetics*[58]) as to the aridity of the whole discussion, indicating Hegel's lamentable ignorance of poetics.

De Man's attack is more comprehensive, however. He begins with a text from the *Encyclopaedia* on the use of indexicals in relation to the system: 'If language expresses only what is universal, then I cannot say what I only *mean* (*meinen*) ... when I say "I," I *mean* me as *this one* excluding all others; but what I say ('I') is precisely everyone, an "I" that excludes all others from itself.'[59] This is taken to be emblematic of the entire dialectical procedure Hegel seeks to impress on us. The 'I' – that is, *my* 'I' – has to efface itself, as if (to quote Beckett) 'I can't go on, I'll go on.' De Man proceeds to consider Hegel's documentation of the emergence of memory (*Gedächtnis*) and writing from imaginative and internalizing representation (*Erinnerung*). It is the birth of (conventional) sign from aesthetic symbol, yet of a sign that the spiritual *I* can thereupon take charge of and revive. 'The art, the *techné*, of writing which cannot be separated from thought and from memorization (*Gedächtnis*) can only be preserved in the figural mode of the symbol, the very mode it has to do away with if it is to occur at all,' he comments, adding: 'No wonder, then, that Hegel's *Aesthetics* turns out to be a double and possibly duplicitous text. Dedicated to the preservation and the monumentalization of classical art, it also contains all the elements which make such a preservation impossible from the start. Theoretical reasons prevent the convergence of the apparently historical and the properly theoretical components of the work' (773). He notes that 'in a truly dialectical system such as Hegel's, what appears to be inferior and enslaved (*untergeordnet*) may well turn out to be the master ... Neglected corners in the Hegelian canon are perhaps masterful articulation rather than the all too visible synthetic judgements that are being remembered as the commonplaces of nineteenth-century history' (774–5). The section on 'allegory,' tucked away under the rubric of 'self-conscious' or 'comparative' symbolics, would be a case in point. He concludes: 'Allegory

Hegel as Philosopher of the Temporal [*irdischen*] World   131

functions, categorically and logically, like the defective cornerstone of the entire system' (775).

Nevertheless, if the dialectic functions as de Man thinks it does, why should it result in 'defects'? It is as though he himself requires the opposition of proper/improper, internalizable/excluded, classical/deformed, in order to work his dialectical magic. Isn't Hegel's own magic strong enough? De Man nicely reveals a dynamic of inverted mastery in Hegel's system which (systematically) undermines its constituent categories. But he presupposes or derives a static opposition – indeed, what he terms an allegory of disjunction – 'between philosophy and history, or in our more restrictive concern, between literature and aesthetics, or, more narrowly still, between literary experience and literary theory' (775). He next lays the responsibility for this allegory at the door of language in its materiality – the impossibility of 'saying what *I* mean(s),' of converting sign into symbol – as soon as history congeals into theory. The same line is drawn also in the polemic 'The Resistance to Theory'(60): it is (Hegelian) aesthetics or aesthetic ideology, enacted under the aegis of the symbol – a self-sufficient plenitude and interiority – that is adjudged resistant to theory, in its silent repressing of the pragmatics of rhetorical and figural acts of thought. Moreover, speculative reflection is diagnosed as the revenge of Hegel's prosaic consciousness, of his 'valet' mentality (nobody being 'poetic' to his valet).

There is no room here to go into the inconsistencies of de Man's own position (fascinating though they are); nor can I do more than suggest that Hegel's 'allegory of disjunction' is a figment of the deconstructive imagination, of what Derrida calls 'positional' thinking. For Hegel (as for Goethe) everything transient is just *ein Gleichnis*, an image or figure; in effect, the secular is allegorical. But what is the secular an allegory of? Not some metaphysical basis or core, but rather of the allegorizing activity of subjectivity, the *I* that can never say what it means yet in failing succeeds all the same in saying (or writing) a great deal for us observers, listeners, or readers. Precisely by invoking the metaphor of the presence of subjectivity to itself – like the spectre at the speculative feast – allegory continually fails and defers. Does the 'I' ever arrive at some final 'recognition scene,' seeing itself reflected in the objective or intersubjective order? Can it manage to pronounce (or write) itself, so to speak? That is the question repeatedly raised in the Hegelian quest for truth.

Yet there is something odd about leaving matters there, inasmuch as it suggests a mere thought experiment on the one hand and a focus on the singular ego on the other. Let me return to Freccero's invocation of Dante's ironic logology and its narrative of conversion – 'I am I, but I was not always so' – and link it with Hegel's invocation of the shifter 'I' in the *Encyclopaedia*. Both contexts replay something larger than the Fichtean scenario of 'I = I,' or rather, they would situate it, temporally as well as indexically. This, I take it, is one of the lessons of H.S. Harris's naturalism, and also the reason he lays so much store by 'aesthetic intuition' in Hegel: Hegelian science always seeks to place us in the actual world of imaginative experience. A recognition scene, the ultimate moment is indeed 'a natural perspective' (to which we might add, with Shakespeare, 'that is and is not'). Furthermore, it is a communal subjectivity Hegel speaks of, 'spirit' (*Geist*) as much as consciousness: as the *Phenomenology* has it, an 'I' that is a 'we' ('but we were not always so,' we can now add). Dante too speaks to us of coming to himself in the midst of our life. For Harris, spirit is the fundamental concept of Hegelian (as opposed to Kantian) idealism, by virtue of its surviving the individual ego's death.[61] Still he recognizes just how problematic that has become in modern times, when our narratives are worn paper thin. To Glyndwr's boast that he can 'call spirits from the vasty deep' we (though I can speak only for myself) are more likely nowadays to echo Hotspur: 'But will they come when you do call for them?'[62]

Notes

This essay has benefited from conversations with my colleagues Jerry Hackett and R.I.G. Hughes – both of them seasoned Dante readers as well as former Torontonians.

1 'Midway in the journey of our life I found myself in a dark wood, for the straight way was lost. Ah, how hard it is to tell what that wood was, wild, rugged, harsh; the very thought of it renews the fear! It is so bitter that death itself is hardly more so' (Charles Singleton's translation)
2 Angus Fletcher, *Colors of the Mind: Conjectures on Thinking in Literature* (Cambridge, Mass.: Harvard University Press, 1991), 3.
3 Eugene Vance, *From Topos to Tale: Logic and Narrativity in the Middle Ages* (Minneapolis: University of Minnesota Press, 1987) chap. 2 ('Dialectics and Fictive Truth'), 19f. and 87f. I confess to having somewhat cut Vance's 'narrative,' with its highly diverting episodes.
4 Vance mentions Robert Hanning's *The Individual in Twelfth-Century Romance* (New Haven, Conn.: Yale University Press, 1977), but one can add the classic accounts given by Richard Southern or Norman Cantor.
5 In brief, the former has to do with the 'experience' of phenomenological consciousness, what seemingly befalls it, even though for us consciousness itself is plainly the agent of its fate; the latter operates in the 'ether' of thought rather than the medium of '*Vorstellung*' or consciousness, yet it too involves the dual perspective of the 'for itself'/'for us.'
6 See, for example, Hegel, *Wissenschaft der Logik*, II (1813) (Hamburg: Meiner,

1969), 491. Cf. vol. (1831; 1969), 163, on the 'dialectic' of the One and the Many in the *Parmenides*.
7 *Ibid.*, 493.
8 See Hegel, *Enzyklopädie der philosophischen Wissenschaften* (1830) (Hamburg: Meiner, 1969), Nos. 79–81; and cf. *Wissenschaft der Logik*, 6.
9 The breakthrough to his own model of dialectic takes place in the early Jena period and may be illustrated in the shift between the 1802 essay on 'Natural Law' and the *Phenomenology* of 1806. In the essay Hegel had resorted to a model of an external balance between antithetical interests (positive and divine law), a balance that takes the aesthetic form of tragic fate, or history. The philosopher is a mere spectator of events, in the medium of (aesthetic) intuition of looking on (*Anschauung*). The shift to a dialectical perspective makes the philosopher part of the action.

The *Phenomenology* is less dramatic and tragic in mode than narrative and indeed autobiographical. Moreover, 'dialectic' is there used to mean consciousness's experience (*Erfahrung*) of contradiction, of negation – it 'goes through' (*er-fahrt, ex-perire*) various stages. But these episodes remain adventitious rather than self-generated; as such the phenomenological dialectic resembles the 'negative' reflection mentioned in the *Logic*.
10 Gilles Deleuze's Nietzschean perspective, in his *Nietzsche and Philosophy* (1962) (London: Athlone Press, 1983), (4) 'From *Ressentiment* to the Bad Conscience,' for example, 159: 'The discovery dear to the dialectic is the unhappy consciousness, the deepening, the re-solution and glorification of the unhappy consciousness ... The dialectic is the natural ideology of *ressentiment* and bad conscience. It is thought in the perspective of nihilism and from the standpoint of reactive forces.' Of course, two or more can play this game (de Man is a player also, as we see below) – the game of adjudication.
11 *Wissenschaft der Logik*, ii, 503: they '*is*' the same (for an identity is singular).
12 Ibid.
13 Brecht, *Flüchtlingsgespräche* (Frankfurt: Suhrkamp, 1961), 11 ('Dänemark oder der Humor. Über die Hegelsche Dialektik'), 109–11.
14 On which see Gillian Rose, *Dialectic of Nihilism: Post-Structuralism and Law* (Oxford: Blackwell, 1984), 11–24.
15 William H. Dray brings out the way in which a rational reconstruction of events through narrative is already in some measure a justification; see his *Philosophical Analysis and History* (New York, 1966).
16 Hegel, *Aesthetics. Lectures on Fine Art*, trans. T.M. Knox (Oxford: Oxford University Press, 1975), 526f. (further references are to this edition, though the translation is sometimes modified). Hegel speaks there of the two worlds of the romantic art form, the inner and the outer. Later (593f.) he speaks of its 'dissolution' into imitation of the prosaic and everyday, and subjective humour.

Naomi Schor, in her *Reading in Detail: Aesthetics and the Feminine* (New York: Methuen, 1987), 29, suggests that Christian art – such as the Gothic cathedral – offers an 'aesthetic contract' to the effect that so long as classical order is respected ornament can proliferate. Schor makes an interesting case for how aesthetics has favoured the dominance of a 'masculine' classicism over a 'feminine' tendency towards ornament, the domestically everyday, in short, towards 'detailism' (a term she recovers from G.H. Lewes). She argues (in her second chapter) that Hegel in the last analysis 'sublimates' detail into an idealist and spiritualist unity – he won't see the trees for the wood. I think her own text sublimates Hegel's text, in much the same way as de Man, I argue below.

17 In the first of his (posthumous) *Six Memos for the Next Millennium*, The Charles Eliot Norton Lectures 1985–86 (Cambridge, Mass.: Harvard University Press, 1988), Calvino contrasts Cavalcanti's 'lightness' with the 'solidity' or 'heaviness' of things which Dante was able to evince through his language; see 15f.

18 See John Freccero, 'The Prologue Scene' (1966), in his *Dante: The Poetics of Conversion* (Cambridge, Mass.: Harvard University Press, 1986), 1–28, where two likely candidates suggested are Augustine's 'region of unlikeness' in Book VII of Augustine's *Confessions* and the topsy-turvey world in Plato's *Statesman*. A.D. Nuttall, in his brilliant study *Openings: Narrative Beginnings from the Epic to the Novel* (Oxford: Clarendon, 1992), suggests an echo not just of the Horatian *in medias res* but also of the 'Donatian' opening to Virgil's Aeneid, 'Ille ego ... et egressus silvis' – the poet's subjectivity displaces the authority of the Muses; see 48, and indeed the whole of chapter 2. Nuttall focuses on 'middleness' and poetic authority.

19 *Aesthetics*, 874: 'Even his damned souls in Hell still have the bliss of eternity – *io eterno duro* stands over the gates of Hell – they are what they are.'

20 See the fragment 'ist nur die Form' in Hegel, *System of Ethical Life (1802–03) and First Philosophy of Spirit,* trans. H.S. Harris and T.M. Knox (Albany: SUNY Press, 1979) 251–3, especially 252: 'Character is eternally a wholly powerless past, over which the man who attends on this stage show [*Schauspiel*] can only dissolve in tears.' The editors comment that Hegel probably did not go beyond the *Inferno*. Harris revised his views on the passage in his comments in *Hegel's Development II: Night Thoughts (Jena 1801–1806)* (Oxford: Clarendon Press, 1983), 219–22: there it is argued that Hegel alludes to *Purgatorio* xxx 49–54 – to the fate of Virgil – and more generally that even Purgatory is this-wordly. Cf. *Natural Law* (1802–3), trans. T.M. Knox (Philadelphia: University of Pennsylvania Press, 1975), 105–6; and *Faith and Knowledge* (1802–3) trans. Walter Cerf and H.S. Harris (Albany: SUNY Press, 1977), 146, where Hegel writes of Hell and damnation as tied to one's subjective deeds, and 'a deathless consideration of this possession.'

Harris elsewhere suggested that the '*Phenomenology* should be read (so far as its literary form is concerned) as the "human comedy" in which the great religious symbols of the Passion and Resurrection receive a philosophical significance within the bounds of a logical comprehension of "experience." He does for the age of knowledge what Dante did for the "age of faith"' 'Hegel's Image of Phenomenology' (1984), in Robert Stern, ed., *G.W.F. Hegel: Critical Assessments* (London: Routledge, 1993), III, 73.

21 Auerbach, *Mimesis: The Representation [Darstellung] of Reality in Western Literature* (Princeton, NJ: Princeton University Press, 1953), 191. The same passage is cited in Auerbach's inaugural lecture at Marburg, 'Entdeckung Dantes in der Romantik': 'eine Seite über Dante, die, ... meiner Überzeugung nach das Entscheidende ist, was man synthetisch über die Komödie sagen kann' (1929), in *Gesammelte Ausätze zur romanischen Philologie* (Bern and München: Francke, 1967), 182. With this page, he adds, the rediscovery of Dante by the German Romantics was complete, and all that followed was a mere working out of their insights.

22 Auerbach, 'St. Francis of Assisi in Dante's "Commedia"' (1944), in Auerbach, *Scenes from the Drama of European Literature*, trans. Ralph Manheim (1959); (Minneapolis: University of Minnesota Press, 1984), 80. The passage continues: 'With Francis of Assisi it is otherwise.' He is presented allegorically, as married to Lady Poverty. The presentation of St Francis is nevertheless not an exception to Dante's realism, Auerbach argues: contemporary readers would have 'spontaneously' recognized the figural linkages, where today's find it strained and artificial – the saint lives only 'in the verse of the poet' (98).

23 In ibid., 58.

24 See Angus Fletcher, *Allegory: The Theory of a Symbolic Mode* (Ithaca, NY: Cornell University Press, 1964), 10.

25 Ibid., 71–2.

26 Translated by Ralph Mannheim as *Dante: Poet of the Secular World* (Chicago: University of Chicago Press, 1961) – 'secular' catches only part of the meaning of 'irdisch,' which means earthly, temporal, mortal. (Further page references in the text are to this edition.) Auerbach had named and praised Hegel in the lecture printed the same year; see note 17 above.

27 *Hotho's sidenote*: His condition is the fixed and eternal being of God himself, in which the individuals move. *Ed.*: The duality consists in the temporal condition's also being eternal.

28 I thank Annemarie Gethmann-Siefert for allowing me to see Hotho's lecture notes prior to their publication.

29 It is surely relevant that in a late essay, 'Philologie der Weltliteratur' (1952), in

Gesammelte Aufsätze zur romanischen Philologie (Bern: Francke, 1967), 301–10, Auerbach espouses humanism as a guiding myth that allows us to resolve the problem of synthesis.

30 For example, Quintilian defines allegory as temporally extended metaphor. This is quoted by Joel Fineman, in his 'The Structure of Allegorical Desire,' in *October: The First Decade, 1976–1986*, ed. Michelson, Krauss, Crimp, and Copjec (Cambridge, Mass.: MIT Press, 1987), 372–92. Fineman polemicizes against such rationalizing allegory, which devolves on the symbol.

31 The theme is of great importance. Blumenberg has written of the centrality of 'self-sufficiency' – whether as subjective self-interest or as objective conservation or inertia – to an emergent modernity in science.

32 See the Index under 'perspective, perspectivism,' but especially 546f. See also Auerbach's 'Epilegomena zu *Mimesis*,' *Romanische Forschungen*, 65 (1954), 14.

   I first was made aware of the figural quality of *Mimesis* itself by Hayden White, in a seminar he led at the School for Criticism and Theory, Northwestern University, summer 1984. He pointed out parallels with Vico and with Hegel (though as far as I know he has published nothing on this). The 'emplotment' of the book is brought out also in Timothy Bahti's recent *Allegories of History: Literary Historiography after Hegel* (Baltimore, Md.: Johns Hopkins University Press, 1992), especially chap. 5: 'Auerbach's *Mimesis*: Figural Structure and Historical Narrative,' 137–55. Bahti's account differs from the one offered here. He sees the plot culminating in the two peaks of Dante and Flaubert, the latter being the figural 'fulfilment' of the former, yet in an odd way: the 'reality' of Charles and Emma's life world is so unreal and deluded that we wish (it is said) she could be 'redeemed' from it. Indeed, according to Auerbach, Emma finds redemption of a sort, in Flaubert's language, in literature. Bahti convicts Auerbach of supposing there is a 'real' outside of literary constructions, and of naturalizing literature, as if aesthetics can come to our rescue. I doubt whether Auerbach is that naïve; and Bahti's account fails to mention Auerbach's *dénouement* in modernist parataxis – hardly supporting a belief in uninflected 'reality' or in some literary absolute. I also think that Bahti is tempted to find ideological closure in much the same way as his own mentor, de Man – on which, see my conclusion.

33 Paul Bové, *Intellectuals in Power: A Genealogy of Critical Humanism* (New York: Columbia University Press, 1986), 86.

34 See *Mimesis*, 557, and 'Epilegomena,' 18: '*Mimesis* ist ganz bewußt ein Buch, das ein bestimmter Mensch, in einer bestimmten Lage, zu Anfang der 1940er Jahre geschrieben hat.' He also adds (15) – with pride, I think – 'Es ist aus den Motiven und Motiven der deutschen Geistesgeschichte und Philologie entstanden; es wäre nie geschrieben worden ohne die Einwirkungen, die in meiner Jugend in Deutschland erfahren habe.' The exile's perspective and his method of perspectivism (as it is

labelled in the index) are of course connected.

35 A different light is cast on this example in Wendy Steiner's *Pictures of Romance: Form against Context in Painting and Literature* (Chicago: University of Chicago Press, 1988), 55: 'Lily's static canvas is the product of a story that supplies its ultimate meaning.' In the tradition of romance – the genre that is – formalist artifice is contrasted with realism, narrative, contingency, and eroticism; the statue or picture metamorphoses into life, or vice versa. Compare my remarks on Freccero and Dante's 'logology.'

36 Bové, *Intellectuals in Power*, 167. Against Bové, it is fair to say that Vico and Dante were invariably coupled in Auerbach's mind, from very early on. 'Auerbach was a life-long student of Vico,' as René Wellek notes in his *A History of Modern Criticism: 1750–1950*, VII, *German, Russian, and Eastern European Criticism, 1900–1950* (New Haven, Conn.: Yale University Press, 1991) 129. In general, Wellek's picture supplies a corrective to Bové's, presenting Auerbach's commitment to an aesthetic historicism as more or less constant from the 1920s on.

37 Auerbach, *Literary Language and Its Public in Late Latin Antiquity in the Middle Ages* (New York: Pantheon, 1965) 314, in a section entitled 'The Western Public and Its Language.' In his Introduction (p. 6) Auerbach writes darkly of the crisis: 'European civilization is approaching the term of its existence; its history as a distinct entity would seem to be at an end, for already it is beginning to be engulfed in another, more comprehensive unity.' While in one way the book is presented as simply filling a chronological gap in *Mimesis*, it could also be taken as seeking the very unity it affirms – and appealing to its readers for help (24).

38 Paolo Valesio's Foreword to *Scenes from the Drama of European Literature* criticizes the 'idolatry of Dante' found in 'Dantean' or 'apologetic' criticism, to which he thinks Auerbach tends. But he is equally critical of that 'Dantesque' or philological criticism that focuses on the text and ignores the theological context or reference. His own approach is at once 'rhetorical' in method and 'Kierkegaardian' in temper, alert to risk and problematics. He accordingly prefers the essay on St Francis to the one on *figura*, on the grounds that it shows Auerbach struggling to align figural logic with Dante's text – a St Francis who is allegorical rather than realistic. He is close to the later Freccero, as discussed below. See also Gabriel Josipovici's *The World and the Book: A Study of Modern Fiction* (London: Macmillan, 1971), which brings out the enactment of language, contrasting Dante's vision of the whole with the modern novelist's entrapment within the labyrinth. More sceptical in temper is Nuttall – for example, in his recent *Openings* – at once decrying 'endlessly fissiperous semesiologies' that hide the peculiar merging of sign and reality in Dante while pointing out that anyway it is all a mere projection in Dante's poetic imagination. He and Freccero quote Charles Singleton: 'The fiction of the Comedy is that it is not fiction.'

In the long tradition of American Dantean criticism we find the well-known Hegelian W.T. Harris, whose *The Spiritual Sense of Dante's Divina Commedia* (Boston: Houghton Mifflin, 1889) nevertheless does not draw at all on Hegel, seeing the poem solely as allegorical of human sinfulness.

39 Freccero, *Dante: The Poetics of Conversion* (Cambridge, Mass.: Harvard University Press, 1986), x.
40 *Purgatorio* 24, 53–4: 'I'mi son un che, quando/Amor mi spira, noto, e a quel modo/ ch'e'ditta dentro vo significando' (I am one who, when Love inspires me, takes note, and goes setting it forth after the fashion which he dictates within me) he declares, referring to the opening verse of *La vita nuova*.
41 Novalis had already used the term: for example, the 46th of his 'Logological Fragments': 'Poetry dissolves alien existence into one's own.' In A. Leslie Willsar, ed., *German Romantic Criticism* (New York: Continuum, 1982), 70.
42 Freccero, *Dante*, 104.
43 Ibid., 108.
44 Ibid., 258–71.
45 Ibid., 271.
46 Nuttall, *Openings*, 68.
47 1928: translated by John Osborne as *The Origin of German Tragic Drama* (London: NLB, 1977), especially 159–235, 'Allegory and *Trauerspiel*.' Benjamin's later thinking remains under the aegis of allegory: see the chapters devoted to him in Bahti, *Allegories of History*, 183–290.
48 It would be fascinating to compare northern allegory and emblematics with what Svetlana Alpers dubs 'the art of describing' (rather than narrating, in symbolic mode). The new art history confronts the old, which had sought to repot its roots in Renaissance humanism or Christian iconography. Benjamin and Alpers both see northern art as a response to a reified world.
49 Yet Winckelmann himself was aware of his own belatedness. See my entry on him in the *Encyclopaedia of Aesthetics* (to appear with Routledge c. 1996).
50 See my 'Hegel and Creuzer, or, Did Hegel Believe in Myth?' in David Kolb, ed., *New Perspectives in Hegel's Philosophy of Religion* (Albany: SUNY Press, 1992), 59–80.
51 On this reduction to figure see my 'Remarks on "Humanus heisst der Heilige"' in *Hegel-Studien*, 17 (1982), 214–25, as well as 'The Semiotics of Hegel' in *Clio*, 11 no. 4 (1982), 415–30. See also Bahti, *Allegories of History*, 124 ff., on the 'mournful anthropomorphism' of Hegel's classical Ideal.
52 De Man, 'Genesis and Genealogy in Nietzsche's *Birth of Tragedy*,' *Diacritics*, 2 no. 4 (1972), 44–53; reprinted in his *Allegories of Reading: Figural Language in Rousseau, Nietzsche, Rilke, and Proust* (New Haven, Conn.: Yale University Press, 1979), 81.

53 See A.C. Danto, *Analytical Philosophy of History* (Cambridge: Cambridge University Press, 1968), now in *Narration and Knowledge* (New York: Columbia University Press, 1985), especially chap. 8.
54 As Hegel once put it: 'The real joke is that things are what they are.' Bishop Butler wouldn't have got the joke, we can be sure.
55 Cf. Linda Nochlin's 'Courbet's Real Allegory: Rereading "The Painter's Studio,"' in Sarah Faunce and Linda Nochlin, eds., *Courbet Reconsidered* (Brooklyn: Brooklyn Museum, 1988), 17–41, for example, at 21. Following a discussion of recent interpretations, which finally seem to have got to the bottom of the picture's meaning, Nochlin remarks: 'The search for meaning is apparently exhausted: there is nothing left to discover. We have come to the end of interpretation.' She continues: 'Having written this, I immediately feel a twinge of annoyance; indeed a surge of rebellion ...' – and not just against this procedure, but also against art history, as an allegory of such allegory. She proceeds, via a consideration of Benjamin in particular, to offer a 'reading as a woman,' and finally to ask how such a meaning might fit into the discipline of art history.
56 *Anatomy of Criticism: Four Polemical Essays* (Princeton, NJ: Princeton University Press, 1957), 89.
57 *Critical Inquiry,* 8 no. 4 (1982), 761–75; further citations in text.
58 Peter Szondi, *Poetik und Geschichtsphilosophie I: Hegels Lehre von der Dichtung* (Frankfurt: Suhrkamp, 1974) 390f.
59 Sec. 20, Remark, p. 51, in *The Encyclopaedia Logic* (3rd ed. 1830), trans. T.F. Geraets, W.A. Suchting, and H.S. Harris (Indianapolis: Hackett, 1991). Cf. *The Phenomenology of Spirit* (Oxford: Oxford University Press, 1977), notably the section on Sense-Certainty (62 ff.), but also 'the language of flattery' (308ff.), and the asseverations of Conscience and the language of the Beautiful Soul (395ff.). At issue here is the community of 'I' and 'We.'
60 1982: now in *The Resistance to Theory* (Minneapolis: University of Minnesota Press, 1986), 3–20.
61 See his 'The Problem of Kant,' a brilliant but typically succinct statement in response to Robert Pippin, in the *Bulletin of the Hegel Society of Great Britain*, 19 (1989) 18–27.
62 Shakespeare, *Henry IV*, 1, ii/i, 53.

PART THREE: RELIGION

6

The Identity of the Human and the Divine in the Logic of Speculative Philosophy

JEFF MITSCHERLING

Four years after Hegel's death, Ferdinand Christian Baur called attention to the features that Hegel drew from the gnostic speculation of the second century in the construction of his philosophical system.[1] Baur argued that 'in the entire history of philosophical and theological speculation, nothing is more related and analogous to gnosticism as the newest [Hegel's] philosophy of religion.'[2] One might expect that Baur's testimony would exert considerable influence on subsequent interpretation of Hegel, but until quite recently what Emil Fackenheim modestly names 'the religious dimension of Hegel's thought'[3] has been played down, when not overlooked entirely. And Baur's reading of Hegel, when attended to at all, has been pushed aside in favour of what we might appropriately label a more 'orthodox Christian'[4] interpretation.[5] Yet as Gerald Hanratty remarks: 'Although the disagreement which emerged among Hegel's earliest disciples has persisted, commentators have recently focused attention again on the affinities between his speculation and the Gnostic systems of the second century and have thus contributed to a clearer appreciation of the nature and scope of the Hegelian synthesis.'[6]

Without an appreciation of the essential role played by the religious, particularly the gnostic, elements in Hegel's thought, the interpreter will at best regard the Hegelian system as an incomparably impressive philosophical curiosity, of value primarily as the masterful yet somewhat quaint record of a great mind gone astray. And this holds good not only for Hegel's explicitly 'religious' analyses but for his thought as a whole – for his science of logic, as an example, no less than for his lectures on the philosophy of religion. Failing to grasp the religious dimension of the logic, we might be persuaded to agree with Charles Taylor when, remarking on the task of the *Logic* to show 'by pure conceptual argument' the conceptually necessary structure of the real, he writes: 'This may sound mad to ordinary consciousness and indeed to most philosophers.'[7] Yet

Taylor is only partly correct in maintaining that '[i]n fact Hegel starts [his transcendental logic] with "being" the category of "simple immediacy" [*WL*, 54], because it seems the emptiest and poorest; it thus presupposes nothing but that there is thought of reality.'[8]

While this is true, it is by no means the whole story. It is precisely the 'emptiness' of the category of Being taken in isolation that initiates the transition to further categories, and Hegel's systematic account of this transition is but the logical expression of the emanation from the divine Logos – God as the One, as empty unity in identity – spoken of by the earliest Christian gnostics and the Neoplatonists,[9] as well as by such later 'gnostic' thinkers as Meister Eckhart (c. 1260–1327) and Jakob Böhme (1575–1624). Hegel's lengthy discussions of the difficulties encountered in attempting to decide on 'the beginning' of any proper inquiry address the problematic theological reflections of the first sentence of John's prologue, and it is not by mere coincidence that already in the second and third sections (85–6) of the *Encyclopaedia*'s 'First Sub-Division of Logic' we find discussion of the religious substitution of 'God' for 'Being.'

Hanratty, after surveying the history of gnostic thought from the days of Joachim of Fiore (1145–1202) to those of Hegel and his contemporaries Fichte and Schelling (whose 'attempts to construct a comprehensive religious philosophy were invariably marked by chiliastic, mystical and theosophic ideas'[10]), concludes his study of 'Hegel and the Gnostic Tradition' with the remark: 'Since Hegel aimed to elaborate a synthesis which would incorporate the ideals of the Enlightenment and of Romanticism, it was inevitable that his speculation would bear the imprint of the broad spectrum of Gnostic influences which he inherited from these sources.'[11] Perhaps the clearest example of this 'imprint' is to be found in Hegel's view of the relation between the human and the divine, and it is precisely his view of this relation that can provide us with a direction in our search for a deeper understanding of the connection between Hegel's philosophy of religion and his system of speculative philosophy as a whole.

It is necessary that we begin with a clarification of the gnostic view of this relation and the manner in which it was transformed in the thought of Eckhart and Böhme. We can then turn to its appropriation and logical reformulation in the presentation of Hegel's system in the *Encyclopaedia*. We find this view recalled by Hegel in the early sections of chapter 7 of the *Encyclopaedia*'s 'Logic' I mentioned above and see it echoed in the concluding passages of the *Encyclopaedia*, where Hegel invokes Aristotle's discussion of the divine, which prefigures the speculation of the gnostics, 'the philosophizing Christians.'[12] As we see below, the concern with the explication of the identity between the human and the divine is central to the structure of the logic of speculative philosophy.

Gnosticism, 'The Alexandrian Philosophy,' Eckhart, and Böhme

The term 'gnosticism' is often employed rather loosely to speak of any variety of religious thinking that tends to be mystical in nature. As such, it is confused with the term 'gnosis,' which refers to the 'knowledge of the divine mysteries reserved for an élite.'[13] As used here, in its more precise, narrow sense, it refers to the systems of Christian Gnosticism that originated in the second century. The 'working hypothesis' proposed by the Messina Colloquium on the Origins of Gnosticism offers a concise characterization of these systems:

> I. The Gnosticism of the Second Century sects involves a coherent series of characteristics that can be summarized in the idea of a divine spark in man, deriving from the divine realm, fallen into this world of fate, birth and death, and needing to be awakened by the divine counterpart of the self in order to be finally reintegrated. Compared with other conceptions of a 'devolution' of the divine, this idea is based ontologically on the conception of a downward movement of the divine whose periphery (often called Sophia or Ennoia) had to submit to the fate of entering into a crisis and producing – even if only indirectly – this world, upon which it cannot turn its back, since it is necessary for it to receive the *pneuma* – a dualistic conception on a monistic background, expressed in a double movement of devolution and reintegration.
>
> II. The type of *gnosis* involved in Gnosticism is conditioned by the ontological, theological and anthropological foundations indicated above. Not every *gnosis* is Gnosticism, but only that which involves in this perspective the idea of the divine consubstantiality of the spark that is in need of being awakened and reintegrated. This *gnosis* of Gnosticism involves the divine identity of the *knower* (the Gnostic), the *known* (the divine substance of one's transcendent self), and the *means by which one knows* (*gnosis* as an implicit divine faculty is to be awakened and actualized. This *gnosis* is a revelation-tradition of a different type from the Biblical and Islamic revelation-tradition).

Basic to gnostic thought is the identity of the human and the divine, an identity both recognized through and achieved by the very activity of its being known. We must not overlook this third, active element of gnosis – 'the means by which one knows.' It is precisely the addition of this element as an essential aspect of the identity of the human and the divine that marks the philosophical advance of gnosticism beyond the historically earlier statements of this identity and thus permits Hegel to regard the gnostics as not merely Christians but as Christians who engaged in philosophical speculation. As we see below, for Hegel the concept (*Begriff*) assumes an activity quite similar to this gnostic 'means by which one knows' – an activity in which the human knower recognizes his or her identity with the divine known.

The gnostics did more than utter statements of human–divine identity: they attempted to explicate their statements by employing them in the construction of religious-philosophical systems cloaked in mythological garb. Many of these systems strike us today as laughably bizarre. Indeed, there were already those among the ancients who found them so. Tertullian, for example, commented on the cosmologies of the Valentinian gnostics:

> Beginning with Ennius, the Roman poet, he simply spoke of the 'spacious saloons [*coenacula*] of heaven,' – either on account of their elevated site, or because in Homer he had read about Jupiter banqueting therein. As for [our] heretics, however, it is marvelous what storeys upon storeys, and what heights upon heights, they have hung up, raised, [and] spread out as a dwelling for each several god of theirs. Even our Creator has had arranged for Him the saloons of Ennius in the fashion of private rooms, with chamber piled upon chamber, and assigned to each god by just as many staircases as there were heresies. The universe, [in fact], has been turned into 'rooms to let.' Such stories of the heavens you would imagine to be detached tenements in some happy isle of the blessed, I know not where. There the god even of the Valentinians has his dwelling in the attics.[14]

Certainly Hegel does not hesitate to criticize the gnostics for this mythological mode of presentation. To the extent that they were compelled to employ the representational thought of myth, they fell short of their mark. Yet the inner drive towards the truth was clearly present in their endeavours. As Hegel remarks in his *Lectures on the Philosophy of Religion*: 'Speaking generally, we see in these [gnostic] attempts to grasp the Idea of the Three-in-One, the reality which characterises Western thought refined away into an intellectual world through the influence of Eastern idealism. These are, to be sure, only first attempts resulting in what were merely paltry and fantastic conceptions. Still we can see in them at least the struggle of Spirit to reach truth, and this deserves recognition.'[15]

Hegel specifies more clearly the nature of 'the Idea of the Three-in-One' in his *Lectures on the History of Philosophy*: 'To them [the Cabalistic philosophy and the Gnostic theology] also the First is the abstract, the unknown, the nameless; the Second is the unveiling, the concrete, which goes forth into emanation. But there is also to be found in some degree the return to unity, especially among Christian philosophers: and this return, which is accepted as the Third, belongs to the λόγος; so with Philo Wisdom, the teacher, the high priest, was that which in the contemplation of God leads back the Third to the First.'[16]

The 'struggle of Spirit to reach truth,' the effort not only to return from the Third to the First but dialectically to comprehend the three moments in unity, remained unsuccessful in gnostic thought, and the gnostic tradition itself was finally suppressed beyond any hope of easy return by the end of the fourth century. Yet behind this effort lay 'a profound necessity of reason, namely, the determination and comprehension of what is absolute as the concrete.'[17] And this same necessity of reason came to dictate ever more clearly the character of subsequent thought, which next finds its philosophical voice in the Alexandrian Neoplatonists, and which continues to whisper in the religious undertones of a secret, esoteric tradition of gnosticism until it again gains philosophical legitimacy in the idealist systems of the nineteenth century.

Hegel regarded 'the Alexandrian philosophy' as the highest development of philosophical thought in antiquity. There the dialectical power of Neoplatonic thought impelled what had previously remained purely abstract principles towards their concretion in the philosophical Idea: 'To this higher culture there more especially belongs the deeper principle that absolute essence must be apprehended as self-consciousness, that its very essence is to be self-consciousness, and that it is therefore in the individual consciousness. This is not to be understood as signifying that God is a spirit who is outside of the world and outside self-consciousness, as is often said, but as indicating that His existence as self-conscious spirit is really self-consciousness itself.'[18]

Hegel has perhaps gone too far in claiming that Neoplatonism did not view God as standing 'outside of the world.' It was precisely there that Neoplatonism conceded a point to the Christians while at the same time undercutting their view of the nature of divine hypostasis. The Neoplatonists and the Christians could happily agree that (infinite) God was separate from His (finite) creation, but from this the Neoplatonists drew consequences that the Christians could not accept. For the Neoplatonists, God, as the One, abided apart from the *logos* (or *nous*) and the world soul, both operating in the realm of created being. For the Christians, however, the divine persons had to be present in God – God, as unity, must preserve within Himself the hypostatic process. Hegel interpreted this 'Alexandrian philosophy' to be in agreement with Christianity regarding God's revelation of Himself in and for subjectivity: not only is He not external to individual consciousness, He is self-consciousness itself.

But again, even Neoplatonic thought proved incapable of fulfilling the demands of the necessity of reason. And after the decline of Alexandrian philosophy following the Arab conquest of the city in 642, the philosophical achievements of the Neoplatonists were for the most part lost sight of with the advent of scholastic philosophy.[19] While there clearly exist Neoplatonic elements in scholastic philosophy – as, for example, in the thought of Erigena – Neoplatonic thought was not again to exercise any thoroughgoing influence on the construction of a philosophical 'system' until Eckhart. In Eckhart's metaphysical speculation, Neoplatonic thought came again to be linked with the 'gnostic' view of the relation between the human and the divine, which Eckhart captures in his conception of the divine 'spark' (*Fünklein*) resting in the human soul. As we see below, already in Eckhart we find the attempt to express this relation by means of a dialectic, but one bound by the dualism of being and intellect, uncreated essence and created existence – the two inseparable aspects of God. It is not until Böhme that the gnostic 'Three-in-One' is recalled in a mode of thinking that, on the verge of blossoming into dialectical expression, finally promises success.

While Eckhart and Böhme are often regarded as 'mystics' – and just as often dismissed as obscure and unintelligible on that count – such a disparaging view is wrong-headed. Gordon Leff's general description of the religious thought of Eckhart indicates the error of regarding him as exclusively or primarily a mystic. It also bears on our point regarding the presence of gnostic elements in the thought of Hegel:

> The significance of Meister Eckhart ... goes beyond the strict limits of mysticism. A German Dominican ... he brought to a new level the combination of scholasticism and Neoplatonism which his confrères Albert the Great and Dietrich of Freiburg had already begun. He thus straddled the paths of speculative theology and mysticism ... His metaphysics formed the basis of his mysticism; his mysticism was the response to his metaphysics. The one points to the nature of God and creation; the other the means by which men must act in order to grasp the truth and so attain unity with God. If this makes Eckhart's mysticism speculative, it also makes it metaphysical, as opposed to affective. The soul remains for him the object rather than the subject; he treats it as one essence in a world of essences rather than the focus of individual experience. In this he was much closer to the Neoplatonist tradition of Plotinus and Proclus than of the western mystics.'[20]

To the extent that Eckhart belongs to this tradition, Hegel would have found in his thought no significant advance over that of the 'Alexandrian philosophers' Plotinus and Proclus. But there is more to Eckhart's thought than this. Two points are relevant to our purpose here. First, as noted above, Eckhart recalls the gnostic view of the relation between the human and the divine when he speaks of the existence in the human soul of a divine spark. Leff distinguishes Eckhart from earlier mystics by noting 'the hypostatic nature of the union': 'The *Fünklein* or *Etwas* was an image of God himself; it was a light or spark, not a faculty ... He compared the *Fünklein* ... to the uncreated spark in angels, enabling them to seize God directly. As such it directly radiated God's image as he was in himself; it was not therefore part of the soul's being but its life of reason through which a man became God's son.' This mention of the 'life of reason' indicates the second point here to be observed. For Eckhart, the relation between the human and the divine is actualized only after an initial process of turning inward, away from being and towards the realm of the non-being of intellect. Here Eckhart makes a bold advance beyond both traditional Christian thought and its Neoplatonic predecessors, and he does so precisely by combining them in an ingenious synthesis, according to which God can be looked at in two ways – either as in Himself (in His own nature or essence) or as creator. Considered in His own nature, God is being; as creator, He is intellect. Whether we regard God as in Himself or as creator, we must employ our intellect at the first stage of the attempt to come to know God: we must begin by turning away from the world of created being and looking inward by means of the intellect. This emphasis on the intellect sets Eckhart apart from the mainstream Christian tradition, which maintained, following Augustine, that the (infinite) human will enjoyed primacy over the (finite) human intellect.[21] For Eckhart, the human intellect emanates directly from the divine intellect – it is itself the mark of human divinity.[22] Yet this Neoplatonic tendency of Eckhart's thought was tempered by his insistence that, in whichever of the two ways we may choose to consider God, we must always discover that God is not entirely cut off from His creation, but that all creation and all thought take place in and through God. The second stage of the journey towards knowledge of God entails movement beyond intellectual abstraction from the world of created being to a higher form of knowing, by means of which we are enabled to discover the principles of created being, the nature of created being as conceived by God – the *rationes* that belong to God's essence and through which He has brought forth created being. These divine *rationes* dwell in the deepest region of the human soul, and it is at this unfathomable depth that Eckhart locates the identity of the human and the divine. To descend to this depth the self must abandon its attachment to itself; it must alienate itself from itself in the denial of its very being.

It is to this feature of Eckhart's thought that Hegel alludes when he speaks of 'the innermost depths of the divine Essence,'[23] and his brief mention of Eckhart is suggestive of the advance in philosophical thought that Hegel attributed to him: 'The older theologians had the most thorough grasp of this divine depth, while among the Protestants of the present day, whose entire resources consist of criticism and history, philosophy and science have been wholly neglected. Meister Eckhardt, a Dominican monk, in speaking of this innermost element, says, in one of his sermons, among other things, the following: "The eye with which God sees me is the eye with which I see Him; my eye and His eye are one. By a righteous standard I am weighed in God, and God in me. If God were not, I would not be; if I were not, then He were not. It is, however, not needful to know this, for there are things which are easily misunderstood and which can only be thoroughly understood in thought."'

The language of the last sentence is significant: 'Dies ist jedoch nicht not zu wissen, denn es sind Dinge, die leicht mißverstanden werden und die nur im Begriff erfaßt werden können.' Hegel appears to have appreciated Eckhart's endeavour to move beyond both sensuous imagery and representational thinking in his effort to grasp, in the *Begriff*, the true content of religion. Yet Eckhart proved incapable of systematic explication of this content, and just as his God was ineffable, so was his grasp of the truth fleeting and elusive. In his insistence that the unity of the human and divine can be grasped only after the individual's attachment to the self (*Ich-Bindung*) has been dissolved, after the self has become thoroughly alienated from the self beyond any possibility of reconciliation, he cuts off precisely that route that alone would make possible the enduring philosophical comprehension of the unity that he seeks. The self can engage fully in the divine thought only at the cost of its very being. Here, once again, we find expressed the recognition of the opposition of thought and being with which the earliest Greek philosophers had already to contend, and it will prove to be the task of modern philosophy and religion to overcome this simple opposition.[24]

It was Jakob Böhme who achieved the next decisive step towards comprehension of the identity of the human and the divine in a thought that is both religious and philosophical – though it is not properly philosophical in form, as Hegel does not tire of reminding us. As with Eckhart, Hegel sees Böhme too as hard at work plumbing those 'utmost depths of divine essence.'[25] In concluding his survey of Böhme's thought in his *Lectures on the History of Philosophy*, Hegel writes that Böhme's most profound thoughts are '(α) the generating of Light as the Son of God from qualities, through the most living dialectic; (β) God's diremption of Himself.'[26] Regarding the former, Hegel earlier quoted from Böhme's *Von wahrer Gelassenheit* (chap. ii sec. 9, 10, p. 1673): 'There is an eternal *Contrarium* between darkness and light; neither comprehends the other and neither is the other, and yet there is but one essence or substance, though separated by pain; it is likewise so with the will, and yet there is no separable essence. One single principle is divided in this way, that one is in the other as a nothing which yet exists; but it is not manifest in the property of that thing in which it is.'[27]

What Hegel regarded as of particular value in this passage is seen in his comment immediately following the quotation: 'By anguish is expressed that which we know as the absolute negativity – that is the self-conscious, self-experienced, the self-relating negativity which is therefore absolute affirmation. All Böhme's efforts were directed towards this point; the principle of the Notion is living in him, only he cannot express it in the form of thought.' With this absolute affirmation, his acknowledgment of the absolute identity of difference, Böhme recalls the self from its self-alienation in the thought of Eckhart. The second 'profound thought' that Hegel attributed to Böhme – God's diremption of Himself – is found in the latter's representation of God 'not as the empty unity, but as this self-separating unity of absolute opposites.'[28] Hegel explains that, for Böhme, 'God as the simple absolute existence is not God absolutely'; nothing can be known of this God. What we do know of God is precisely that which is different from His simple, absolute existence, 'but this "different" is itself contained in God as the perception and knowledge of God.'[29] By way of illustrating Böhme's position, Hegel quotes a passage from *Von göttlicher Beschaulichkeit* (chap. i. secs. 8–10, p. 1739) that might almost have been written by Hegel himself: 'Without adversity life would have no sensibility nor will nor efficacy, neither understanding nor science. Had the hidden God who is one solitary existence and will not of His own will brought Himself out of Himself, out of the eternal knowledge in the *Temperamento*, into divisibility of will, and introduced this same element of divisibility into an inclusiveness [Identity][30] so as to constitute it a natural and creaturely life, and had this element of separation in life not come into warfare, how was the will of God which is only one to be revealed to Himself? How could a knowledge of itself be present in a solitary will?'

It is the course of this movement of God out of Himself in the bringing of divisibility (*Schiedlichkeit*) into 'a natural and creaturely life' that Hegel follows in his philosophy of nature. The *Zusatz* to sec. 247 of the *Philosophy of Nature* begins by stating the very question that we just saw Böhme answer: 'If God is all-sufficient and lacks nothing, why does He disclose Himself in a sheer Other of Himself? The divine Idea is just this: to disclose itself, to posit this Other outside itself and to take it back again into itself, in order to be subjectivity and Spirit. The Philosophy of Nature itself belongs to this path of return, for it is that which overcomes [*aufhebt*] the division between Nature and Spirit and assures to Spirit the knowledge [*die Erkenntnis*] of its essence in Nature.'[31]

According to Böhme's scheme, we appear not to proceed beyond the initial movement of God out of Himself into the realm of nature. Hegel adds to this account the third moment of the philosophy of nature, thereby contributing that conceptual element which alone renders possible the return of God to Himself. It is chiefly with Böhme's contribution of this account of 'God's diremption from

Himself' in mind that Hegel writes that the principle of the *Begriff* is to be found in Böhme, and it is the latter's inability to move beyond sensuous imagery and religious representation that prohibits him from being able to express this *Begriff* in the form of philosophical thought.

Hegel's criticism of religious thought is directed at the entire history of its development. Throughout this history, religious thinkers may have claimed to understand what they were talking about, but they were never able to grasp the truth of what they were saying. The gnostics, the earliest Christian philosophers, journeyed a good way in this direction, and the Neoplatonists of Alexandria travelled roughly the same distance along a slightly different route. But their paths were rudely blocked by the advent of the entirely non-philosophical thought of Scholasticism, which denied the very internal reason that ought to have motivated it and guided its argumentation. Eckhart, borrowing elements from both the gnostic and the Neoplatonic traditions, acknowledged this internal reason, the power of the *Begriff*, but his metaphysical, mystical expression of this reason gave little more than a dim inkling of the true nature of the 'divine spark' within. Böhme's thought also was driven by the *Begriff*, and it reached almost as far as that decisive moment at which the concept comprehends the return of that which has alienated itself from itself – but his thought suffered from the limitations dictated by the sensuous, imagistic language from which the noble 'cobbler of Lusatia'[32] was unable to extricate himself.[33]

Hegel's advance over all these thinkers – his movement beyond both the preceding history of religious thought and the 'traditional' theology of his own day – consists precisely in his development of the philosophical language necessary for the task of expressing the truth of religion. This is the language of the concept, which first enables philosophical thought to grasp religious truth and comprehend the identity of the human and the divine.[34]

The Logic of Speculative Philosophy

Given all that I have said above, it may seem strange to assert at this point that we must be careful not to overemphasize the religious dimension of Hegel's speculative philosophy. But such caution is necessary in order that we not be led to confuse his philosophy of religion with the 'Theology of Reason' that arose in late antiquity – a confusion that in turn might easily lead us to conclude that Hegel's religious thought in fact finds itself 'in the same condition of opposition to the content of religion.'[35] At the same time, however, we must never lose sight of Hegel's repeated assertion that religion and philosophy have the same subject matter – 'namely what is absolutely true – God inasmuch as he is absolute, in and for himself, and man in his relation to him.'[36] It is Hegel's task to demonstrate how this relationship, which must always fall short of adequate expression in religious thought and discourse, can be grasped in the concept of the dialectical thinking of philosophy. There are three central issues to explore in this regard: the inadequacy of religious imagery and representational thought; the nature and power of the concept; and the identity of human and divine as the true subject matter of religion and philosophy.

The content of religious consciousness finds its first expression in the form of religious image, myth, or symbol. This form is that of the picture (*Bild*), which 'derives its content from the sphere of sense, and presents it in the immediate mode of its existence, in its singularity, and in the arbitrariness of its sensuous manifestation.'[37] As the picture remains bound to the sensuous and singular, it remains too limited and limiting a mode of expression for religious consciousness, the true content of which must seek expression in universal form. It discovers this form in the representation (*Vorstellung*), which raises the picture 'up into the form of Universality, of thought, so that the one fundamental characteristic, which constitutes the essence of the object, is held fast [*festgehalten wird*], and is present before the mind which thus forms the representation.'[38] Yet the form of representational thinking remains bound to the sensuous in that its very existence depends on its having arisen as an explicit denial of the claims of the sensuous.

Thus representational thinking, in its struggle to free itself from the sensuous and attain the determinateness proper to the true content of religious consciousness, finds itself caught between the sensuous and philosophical thought. As a result, the concept that impels philosophical thinking cannot find expression in religious representational consciousness, and the sort of argumentation we find in even the highest form of religious discourse – in the Theology of Reason – proves inadequate to the task of expressing the true content of religion. It is a sign of the inescapable frustration of religious consciousness that the Protestant theology of Hegel's day had reached a point at which, as he says, its 'entire resources consist of criticism and history': it remained trapped in the demonstration of its own inadequacy to move beyond its sensuous content. Movement becomes possible only in and through the dialectical expression of the concept in philosophical thinking.

The word 'concept' is not employed consistently in the same sense throughout Hegel's works. Despite the variation in its precise meaning, however, the word '*Begriff*' appears never to have lost for Hegel its basic etymological sense of 'holding together,' of 'grasping' two or more elements in a unity. (The Latin term from which the English derives enjoys a similar sense by virtue of its etymology.) The *Begriff* consists in the activity of grasping mentally, of holding together or comprehending in thought, two distinct entities, be these the subject and predicate terms of a single proposition[39] or, as in the case of philosophical comprehension of the contradictory character of religious thought, the immediate singularity of the picture and the mediated universality of the representation. When Hegel speaks of the concept he is not speaking of some sort of mental entity that resides in the intellect like a goldfish in a bowl. The concept rather is what links together into a unified, 'comprehensive' whole opposing or contradictory expressions of consciousness – or, more precisely, it is this activity of comprehending itself.[40]

It is in philosophical thinking alone that this conceptual comprehension of contradictions finds expression, and its full expression is first achieved only in the speculative dialectic of philosophical idealism. Coloured by the Neoplatonic, gnostic tenor of the age, Hegel's entire system revolves around the fundamental religious insight into the divine nature of creation. The self-revelatory activity of Absolute Spirit comprehended in philosophical thought is nothing other than the absolute manifestation of the same activity engaged in on a personal level by the individual thinker, whose self-revelation consists in the recognition of the identity of the human and the divine. The philosophical expression of this recognition, as a *philosophical* expression, must move beyond reliance on religious representation in order to achieve conceptual comprehension.

This comprehensive expression begins, in Hegel's fully elaborated system of philosophical idealism as presented in the *Encyclopaedia*, with the exposition of the self-movement of thought in the form of the Logical Idea. More precisely, it commences with the analysis of the first subdivision of logic, the Doctrine of Being, in chapter 7. Hegel's discussion of the 'metaphysical definitions of God' in the second paragraph (sec. 85) of this chapter is not simply a criticism of previous philosophical and religious thought, it is an indication of the essentially religious direction of his entire system. In the language of Hegel's system, the category of being is the philosophical equivalent of previous metaphysical conceptions (and religious representations) of God, and just as God is the divine origin from which creation emanates, so is the category of being, as the originary moment of the *logos*, the source from which subsequent logical categories emerge: 'Being itself and the special sub-categories of it which follow, as well as those of logic in general, may be looked upon as definitions of the Absolute, or metaphysical definitions of God ... For a metaphysical definition of God is the expression of His nature in thoughts as such: and logic embraces all thoughts so long as they continue in the thought-form.'[41]

In his exposition of the development of the Logical Idea, Hegel has given systematic expression to the truth that the Neoplatonic *logos*-philosophers of Alexandria were incapable of grasping. Hegel's thought is guided by the same insight, the same religious truth, that inspired the earlier philosophers and the author of the prologue to John's gospel, the most 'philosophical' text of the New Testament. In Hegel's philosophical idealism we find the first systematic, logical elaboration of the creative activity of the divine *logos*, which previous thinkers – most notably, the gnostics and the Neoplatonists – had attempted to comprehend. It is the speculative dimension of the dialectical logic of his philosophical idealism that grants Hegel this success where his predecessors had failed. And it is in precisely this moment of speculation that the recognition of the identity of the human and the divine is achieved. In the absence of the other elements of the system, the logical category of being is indeed 'the emptiest and poorest': the abstractions of logic have no meaning without their natural and spiritual manifestations. And in the absence of the created realms of nature and human spirituality, the metaphysical, religious abstraction called 'God' is equally without meaning.

In Hegel's system, this abstraction receives its necessary complements, and the recognition of this completion, as a philosophical achievement, occurs in the acknowledgment of the identity of human and divine: the *logos* made flesh and self-conscious spirit. This recognition is itself the divine, which, as Hegel stresses in the concluding paragraph of the *Encyclopaedia* (sec. 577), is itself an activity: 'The self-judging of the Idea into its two appearances ... characterizes both as its (the self-knowing reason's) manifestations: and in it there is a unification of the two aspects: – it is the nature of the fact, the notion, which causes the movement and development, yet this same movement is equally the action of cognition. The eternal Idea, in full fruition of its essence, eternally sets itself to work, engenders and enjoys itself as absolute Mind.'[42]

Hegel follows this paragraph, concluding the *Encyclopaedia*, with a quotation from Aristotle's *Metaphysics* (1072b18–30) that points again to the religious direction of Hegel's system as a whole:

> And thinking in itself deals with that which is best in itself, and that which is thinking in the fullest sense with that which is best in the fullest sense. And thought thinks on itself because it shares the nature of the object of thought; for it becomes an object of thought in coming into contact with and thinking its objects, so that thought and object of thought are the same. For that which is *capable* of receiving the object of thought, i.e. the essence, is thought. But it is *active* when it *possesses* this object. Therefore the possession rather than the receptivity is the divine element which thought seems to contain, and the act of contemplation is what is most pleasant and best. If, then, God is always in that good state in which we sometimes are, this compels our wonder; and if in a better this compels it yet more. And God *is* in a better state. And life also belongs to God; for the actuality of thought is life, and God is that actuality; and God's self-dependent actuality is life most good and eternal. We say

therefore that God is a living being, eternal, most good, so that life and duration continuous and eternal belong to God; for this *is* God.

And it is this divine activity, the divine *as* activity, which the speculative dialectical logic of Hegel's philosophical idealism has captured in its explication of philosophical thinking. Only to philosophical thinking is the truth of religion and philosophy accessible, for it is precisely in such thinking that this truth is first actualized as the recognition of the identity of the human and the divine, an identity that consists in the activity of philosophical thinking itself.

Concluding Remarks on Hegel's 'Gnostic' Christianity

It has long been a favourite pastime among commentators, especially those in the English-speaking tradition, to question Hegel's claim that he was a Christian. As recently as 1974, we find Stanley Rosen, for example, maintaining that Hegel 'submits Christianity to an interpretation so rationalistic as to evoke the often overpowering conviction that we are once more in the presence of the pride of philosophers. I note here only that Hegel takes sin, in conjunction with the story of Eden, to refer to incompleteness qua absence of rational knowledge, and that according to him, man is immortal only in knowing eternity by conceptual thinking ... As a teacher of mine once remarked, if Hegel was a Christian, he belonged to a sect of which he was the only member.'[43]

The examination above of Hegel's gnostic and Neoplatonic heritage, as incomplete and sketchy as it is, should suffice to dispel such doubts as those voiced by Rosen's teacher. By Hegel's day, the ideals of the Reformation and Enlightenment had already presented a devastating challenge to the tradition of orthodox Christianity, the 'truth' of which had consequently been called into serious question. In an ironic twist of historical fate, Hegel found himself in the role of the new Christian apologist, defending the Christian faith by elaborating a system that stressed the 'heretical' gnostic notion of the identity of the human and the divine. This view is in opposition to the orthodox emphasis on the radical separation of God and the individual person, a separation that is most clearly reflected in the Catholic insistence on the sacramental mediation of the priest. The importance of the sacraments, in conjunction with the various outward forms of Christian worship, is not denied by Hegel. Yet, consistent with the gnostic and Neoplatonic emphasis on the divine nature of the individual, Hegel affirms the priority of the inward movement of faith: 'The expression "worship" is usually taken merely in the limited sense in which it is understood to mean only outward public acts, and the inward action of the heart does not get so much prominence. We, however, shall conceive of worship as that action which includes both inwardness and outward manifestation, and which in fact produces restoration of unity with the Absolute, and in so doing is also essentially an inward conversion of the spirit and soul. Thus Christian worship does not only include the sacraments and the acts and duties pertaining to the Church, but it also includes the so-called "way of salvation" as a matter of absolutely inward history, and as a series of actions on the part of the inner life – in fact, a movement which goes forward in the soul, and has its right place there.'[44]

That this defence of the Christian faith takes philosophical form might strike some as peculiar, yet such a form is entirely in keeping with the spirit of the gnostics, the earliest 'philosophizing Christians.' And it is by virtue of Hegel's ability so masterfully to reshape and refine this form into that of philosophical idealism that the Christian thinker of today is compelled to come to grips with his thought. Theologians and philosophers, Christian and non-Christian alike, have always grappled with the central problem of the nature of the relation that exists between the human and the divine. This relationship provides the content of divine revelation, and it is divine revelation, in one form or another, that provides the fundamental truth and the starting point for all religions. It was precisely this revelation that Hegel attempted to capture in his philosophical expression of the gnostic insight into the identity of the human and the divine. The degree to which Hegel's attempt was successful can be measured accurately only by the reader who acknowledges the essentially spiritual character of his thought and is capable not only of reading Hegel as a Christian thinker but of recognizing him as the first philosopher to have systematically elaborated the truth of religion in philosophical form.

Notes

1 *Die christliche Gnosis oder die christliche Religionsphilosophie in ihrer geschichtlichen Entwicklung*, first pub. Tübingen, 1835 (Darmstadt: Wissenschaftliche Buchgesellscaft, 1967).
2 Ibid., 24.
3 Emil Fackenheim's *The Religious Dimension of Hegel's Thought* (Chicago: University of Chicago Press, 1967) demonstrated to contemporary scholars the interpretive error they unavoidably commit in overlooking or undervaluing the role of Christianity in Hegel's system. Unfortunately, Fackenheim's account describes the manner in which Hegel reconciles modern Christianity with modern secular society – Fackenheim, that is to say, falls into the camp of those who adhere to the 'orthodox Christian' view of Hegel's religious thought.
4 I follow Elaine Pagels's use of the terms 'orthodox' and 'gnostic,' in *The Gnostic*

Gospels (New York: Random House, 1979). Just as the orthodox Christians succeeded in suppressing the gnostic movement, so has the reading of Hegel as orthodox Christian triumphed at the expense of the acknowledgment of gnostic elements in his thought.

5 This may be in part a mark of the influence of Karl Rosenkranz's *Georg Wilhelm Friedrich Hegels Leben* (Berlin, 1844), which appears to have regarded such an affiliation with the (gnostic) systems of late antiquity as detracting from the value of Hegel's own rigorously logical thinking. He writes, for example: 'Es gibt keine schiefere und seichtere Vorstellung von Hegel's Philosophie, als die, welche nur *Kritik* oder nur *Logik* darin sieht, etwa noch mit dem Zusatz, daß Hegel's Logik freilich nicht die eines gesunden Verstandes, sondern, da sie mit der Metaphysik sich identificire und den Begriff für das Schöpferische erkläre, die einer höchst abenteuerlichen, überspannten Neuplatonik sei, welche sogar speculative Theologie zu sein sich anmaaße. Hegel's System ist vielmehr Philosophie des *Geistes* in dem Sinn, daß bei ihm der Begriff des Geistes allein auch den der Natur und der Idee als logischer erst *möglich* macht' (Darmstadt: Wissenschaftliche Buchgesellschaft, 1963, 100).

6 Gerald Hanratty, 'Hegel and the Gnostic Tradition: I,' *Philosophical Studies*, 30 (spring 1984), 25. ('Hegel and the Gnostic Tradition: II' appears in ibid., 31 [1986-7], 301-25.) Hanratty notes (45 n 7): 'Georges M M Cottier has categorised Hegel's system as "Une Gnose christologique": see his *L'athéisme du jeune marx: ses origines Hegéliennes* (Paris, 1969) 20-30. Eric Voegelin has likewise focused on the Gnostic characteristics of Hegel's speculation: see his *Science, Politics and Gnosticism* (Chicago, 1968) 40-44, 67-80. Martin Buber has also distinguished between the fundamental religious attitudes of *gnosis* and *devotio* ... and from Buber's perspective, Hegel's system would obviously constitute a *gnosis* ... Cf. *The Origin and Meaning of Hasidism* (New York, 1960), 243-244.' See also the PhD dissertation of Raymond Rosenkranz: 'Hegel's Soteriology: A Historical Perspective' (University of Guelph, 1985).

7 Charles Taylor, *Hegel* (Cambridge: Cambridge University Press, 1975), 225.

8 Ibid., 227. Hegel states essentially just this in sec. 86 of the *Encyclopaedia*'s Logic.

9 Speaking of the philosophy of Plotinus, Hegel writes: 'The first, the absolute, the basis, is here, as with Philo, pure Being, the unchangeable, which is the basis and the cause of all Being that appears, whose potentiality is not apart from its actuality, but is absolute actuality in itself.' *Lectures on the History of Philosophy*, trans. E.S. Haldane and Frances H. Simson, first pub. 1894 (London: Routledge & Kegan Paul Ltd, 1963) II, 413.

10 Hanratty, 'Hegel,' 322. Hanratty notes (325 n 125): 'On Schelling's dependence on the Joachimite traditions, see [Henri] De Lubac [*La Posterité spirituelle de Joachim de Fiore*, tome 1 (Paris, 1978)], 378-393. For an account of the influence of the

mystical and theosophic traditions of Württemberg, see [Robert] Schneider [*Schellings und Hegel's schwäbische Geistahnen* (Würzburg, 1938)] *passim.*'
11 Hanratty, 'Hegel,' 323.
12 The expression is Hegel's: 'den philosophierenden Christen, vornehmlich den Gnostikern.' *Vorlesungen über die Philosophie der Religion* (Frankfurt am Main: Suhrkamp Taschenbuch Verlag, 1986), II, 247.
13 This quotation and the following 'working hypothesis' are from the 'Proposal for a Terminological and Conceptual Agreement with Regard to the Theme of the [Messina] Colloquium' on the Origins of Gnosticism (1966), xxvi–xxvii.
14 Tertullian, *Adversus Valentinianus*, VII ('The first eight emanations, or Aoens, called the Ogdoad, are the fountain of all the others. Their names and descent recorded.'), trans. Peter Holmes, in *The Writings of Quintus Sept. Flor. Tertullianus*, II (Edinburgh: T. & T. Clark, 1870), 128. (This passage from Tertullian is referred to also by Pagels, *The Gnostic Gospels*, xxxi.)
15 *Lectures on the Philosophy of Religion*, trans. E.B. Speirs and J. Burdon Sanderson, first pub. 1895 (New York: Humanities Press Inc., 1962), III, 30 (*Vorlesungen über die Philosophie der Religion*, II, 238).
16 *Lectures on the History of Philosophy*, II, 394.
17 Ibid., II, 399. (Hegel is speaking here of Valentinian gnosticism.)
18 Ibid., II, 401–2.
19 Hegel says of scholastic thought that 'it is not a philosophy': 'Scholasticism is not a fixed doctrine like Platonism or Scepticism, but a very indefinite name which comprehends the philosophic endeavours of Christendom for the greater part of a thousand years.' Ibid., III, 38.
20 Gordon Leff, *Heresy in the Later Middle Ages* (New York: Barnes & Noble, Inc., 1967), I, pp. 260–1.
21 Eckhart writes: 'Ich aber sage, dass die Vernunft edler ist als der Wille.' J. Quint, *Meister Eckehart: Deutsche Predigten und Traktate* (Munich 1955), cited in Leff, *Heresy*, 284 n 2.
22 Hegel is in agreement: 'Reason is the divine element in man.' *Introduction to the Lectures on the History of Philosophy*, trans. T.M. Knox and A.V. Miller (Oxford: Clarendon Press, 1985), 91.
23 This quotation and the passage following are from *Lectures on the Philosophy of Religion*, I, 217–8.
24 'This highest severance is the opposition between Thought and Being, the comprehending of whose unity from this time forward constitutes the interest of all philosophies.' *Lectures on the History of Philosophy*, III, 160.
25 Ibid., 206.
26 Ibid., 216.
27 Ibid., 197.

28 Ibid., 198.
29 This quotation and passage following are from ibid., 203.
30 Hegel's insertion.
31 *Philosophy of Nature*, trans. A.V. Miller (Oxford: Clarendon Press, 1970), 14.
32 So Hegel refers to him in *Lectures on the History of Philosophy*, III, 188.
33 As we read in Rosenkranz's *Hegels Leben*, Hegel drew attention to the shortcomings of the language of religious discourse, including that of Böhme, in an introductory lecture for a course (probably that which he offered on 'the whole science of philosophy') in winter 1804–5. See Karl Rosenkranz, *Georg Wilhelm Friedrich Hegels Leben*, first pub. Berlin, 1844 (Darmstadt: Wissenschaftliche Buchgesellschaft, 1963), 181–5, and translated in H.S. Harris and T.M. Knox, trans. and eds., *System of Ethical Life and First Philosophy of Spirit* (Albany: SUNY Press, 1979), 256–9.

As Harris explains, in *Hegel's Development II: Night Thoughts (Jena 1801–1806)*(Oxford: Clarendon Press, 1983), 398–9: 'Religion uses ordinary language too, but it does so in a dangerous way. Hegel takes Boehme's speculation as a paradigm case here, and couples it with "the Oriental attempt to present the Idea." These are both "a *dark half-way-house* between feeling and *scientific knowledge*, a speculative feeling or the Idea, which cannot free itself from imagination and feeling and yet is no longer just imagination and feeling." [Harris's note: 'Rosenkranz, p. 182 (Harris and Knox, p. 257). Here and in the following passages the words are Hegel's own.'] But Boehme's mysticism is "more sorrowful" because it recognizes the inevitability of its own failure to be scientific: "It steps into the depths of the essence with common *sensuous ideas* (*Vorstellungen*) and fights to make itself master of it and bring it before consciousness. But the essence will not let itself be grasped in the form of a common sensuous idea. Any representation of this kind that it is grasped in is *inadequate*. It is only made to fit the essence by *violence*, and must equally violently be torn [away from it]; it presents only the battle of an inward [essence], that is fermenting within itself, and cannot advance into the clear light of day, feels its incapacity with sorrow, and rolls about in fits and convulsions that can come to no proper issue." [*Harris's note*: "Rosenkranz, pp. 182–3 (Harris and Knox, p. 257)."] The attack on Boehme's language (and on the language of religion generally) should be read in the light of the contention that "the truth *should* display itself to us in religion." [Rosenkranz, p. 182; Harris and Knox, p. 256.] Hegel's criticism is thus quite consistent with his evident desire to show that the older alchemical tradition of Paracelsus (and probably Boehme himself) contained symbolic expressions of important speculative truths. The language is attacked as a *veil*. Boehme is at least half-way to the truth. Philosophy ("the concept") as its own mediator, will remove the veil.'
34 It was its failure properly to articulate precisely this relation of identity that constituted Hegel's chief target in his attack on traditional theology. As Walker

The Identity of the Human and the Divine 161

points out in chapter 9, below: 'The feeling of absolute dependence that in Hegel's eyes typically characterized the relation between God and the individual believer in traditional theology is nothing but the subjective manifestation of positivity within consciousness. Such an attitude of dependence, on the theoretical and practical side alike, depends itself on denial of any community of nature or intrinsic identity between the rational individual and the supposed "object" of his belief: the faith located exclusively in another who is regarded as qualitatively unlike ourselves in every way and infinitely remote from us undermines moral autonomy and destroys man's faith in *himself*.' As Walker correctly observes: 'The true model for man's relation to the divine is to be found in the idea of a participative identity that does not destroy the independence or spontaneity of the human spirit, and Hegel uses both the Stoic image of the "Funken Gottes," which he had employed so frequently in Bern, and the neo-Spinozan picture of the individual as "eine Modifikation" (F 304), which he adopts in Frankfurt, to mark his repudiation of the traditional theology of creaturely dependence and its correlative conception of God as "lord."'

35 *Lectures on the Philosophy of Religion*, 30. This is precisely the confusion that runs through the work of 'the right-wing Hegelians who see speculative philosophy as another name for theology,' mentioned by John Burbidge in his Foreword to this volume.
36 *Introduction to the Lectures on the History of Philosophy*, 124.
37 This and the quotation immediately following are from *Lectures on the Philosophy of Religion*, I, 142. 'To present' here translates *darstellen*. The contrast between this immediate, sensuous form of religious consciousness and the higher, mediated form of 'representational' thinking is thus linguistically indicated by the term 'to represent,' *vorstellen*.
38 The translators render *Vorstellung* as 'idea,' with a lower case 'i.' I have here substituted 'representation' for 'idea.'
39 As in Kant's discussion of the function of unity in judgment in the Metaphysical Deduction of the *Critique of Pure Reason*. The analytic unity exhibited in a judgment is identical with the concept articulated in the judgment, and it is this concept that provides the rule for the formulation of the judgment – the particular form of the relation of the subject-representation to the predicate-representation.
40 So, for example, Hegel can write that 'the Philosophy of Nature is a comprehending (*begreifend*) treatment' (*Philosophy of Nature*, sec. 246).
41 *The Logic of Hegel*, trans. William Wallace, first pub. 1873 (London: Oxford University Press, 1963), 156.
42 *Hegel's Philosophy of Mind*, trans. William Wallace (London: Oxford University Press, 1971), 314–15.
43 Stanley Rosen, *G.W.F. Hegel* (New Haven, Conn.: Yale University Press, 1974), 10.
44 *Lectures on the Philosophy of Religion*, I, 67.

7

The Final Name of God

DAVID KOLB

Hegel's system aims at thought's encompassing self-relation. There are many ways of interpreting just what Hegel is trying to achieve in that self-relation and what kind of closure, if any, it demands. It is also difficult to be sure how Hegel intends that self-relation to include the myriad details of the world. In this chapter I look at two models of how that self-relation might come to grips with the detail of the history of religions. I argue that Hegel prefers the stronger of the two models, but that there are serious difficulties in implementing it.[1]

It seems clear from Hegel's various methodological remarks that he is working to complete the metaphysical tradition's aim of grounding and presence and that he works within the Kantian notion of reason as the faculty of totality. In that Kantian vein, Hegel argues that a relation of thought to itself is required as condition of the possibility of conscious experience and practice.[2]

Interpreters disagree about what degree of closure Hegel believes is demanded in order to achieve thought's self-relation. I have argued elsewhere that there are at least two aspects: the logic is to encompass all categorial determinations by which any other to thought could be conceived, and the logic is to involve categories describing its own self-referential structure. Hegel's closure is in the interconnection between these two: the system is complete because its self-referential structure necessarily includes the categories that encompass otherness.[3] If the logic is in principle complete, then the grammar of thought is known as such, and the system affirms that it possesses the categories to do justice to any other.[4] There is nothing untouched by thought, though some things are touched only by their being put in their place as necessarily contingent detail that thought cannot penetrate.

But the world must, for logical reasons, contain more than logic. How does the system deal with the detail of history and life? How does it deal with the history and variety of religions? Religion is a special case. It is one of the historical phenomena that Hegel studies, but it is also one of the ways in which spirit finally comes to know itself as encompassing all otherness. Since religion is a form of absolute spirit, the systematic demand for self-relationship and completeness will be more stringent in the case of religion than in nature or politics. Hegel demands that there be a final religion and a developmental story that demonstrates that finality. I argue that such a story cannot be written.

The Need for Completeness in Logic and Religion

Hegel would say that the only way to appreciate the necessity of the system is to follow its development. Here I only point out a connection that Hegel makes between the claim to self-relation and the need for completeness.

Hegel argues in the *Phenomenology of Spirit* that knowledge, conscious experience, and action ultimately require as their condition of possibility full self-relation. The philosophical system activates that self-relation. But the self-consciousness of spirit achieved through the system has to be complete. It cannot itself be a theoretical knowledge that stands off from the world across some gulf that is outside the system's own self-relation. There cannot be some duality that locates the self-presence of spirit to itself but is not overcome in spirit's self-relation. The final epistemological and ontological condition of the meaning of being is self-presence; it makes no sense to speak of a partial self-presence as somehow ultimate (as Hegel thinks was done by Kant and even Fichte).

In the Logic there can be no final, bad infinity, no endless sequence of as-yet-unknown categories, since this would prohibit full self-relation. If the self-relation to be achieved in the Logic included some infinite task of self-discovery involving endless categorial novelty, either the self-relation would fail, or it would move to a higher level.[5] Any supposed endless sequence of categories would mean that spirit was moving towards a state of comprehension that was not yet actual. And the distance from that state would express a duality, *one* side of which was spirit.[6] Yet if spirit possessed at least a sketch of this ideal future state, the endless sequence of novel categories would then be encompassed within a higher-level self-relation that in its own way included a set of final categories. In this volume, John Burbidge (Foreword) and George di Giovanni (chapter 10) make the Logic into a higher-level self-relation and a similar position can be found in Robert Pippin's book cited above (note 2). Burbidge would not characterize his position as involving a final set of logical categories, but he does regard the logic's method as final, and so provides a kind of higher-level closure.[7]

How does all this affect religion? What is religion's situation with regard to self-relation and closure? Hegel's general definition of religion is that it is the relation of the subjective consciousness to God, who is spirit. 'In the philosophy of religion we have the absolute for our object, not only in the form of thought, but also in its manifestation as of the absolute.'[8] Taken speculatively (in Hegel's special sense of that word), religion is spirit that is conscious of its own essence, its own be-ing (*Wesen*). Spirit is not abstract subjectivity; it is concrete by being for itself as including its other. Religion actualizes spirit's self-relation.

In the Absolute Idea that concludes the Logic, finite determinations are taken up into comprehensive unity. Thought achieves self-relation by thinking all finite categorial determinations of objects as held within the moving, self-referential unity of the Idea. That final category includes a structured recapitulation of the prior sequence, now thought as the subordinate moments of the final unity. By enacting in thought the dialectical process that includes the major categorial determinations of any being, the Logic shows how they all can be contained in the unity of pure thought knowing itself.

But this achievement remains in the medium of pure thought. It is not yet exhibited to spirit self-consciously as an overcoming in the media of otherness – space and time. So the encompassing of otherness has not yet really been performed for spirit. That is, spirit is not yet actually itself, since its being is to exhibit its being to itself. For that there must be actual otherness and an actual comprehensive return from otherness to inclusive unity.

The historical religions record the changing degrees to which this overarching action and purpose are 'revealed' to different communities. Studying these religions, the philosopher can see how the particular distinctions and determinations constitutive of the various religious traditions are arranged into a developmental process that leads to the full revelation of spirit's self-relation with itself through nature and society. To use the Aristotelian language of the closing words of the *Encyclopedia*, the philosopher can study history as an *entelechia*, a process with a goal; but at that goal the philosopher discovers that history is an *energeia*, an action that has its goal within itself, and is the eternal coming to itself of spirit.[9] This is closure, *für sich*.

There is an analogue here to Hegel's famous claim that philosophy is its own age comprehended in thought. Religion also expresses its age. However, it is only in the modern age that we are in a position to affirm that philosophy and religion express the spirit of their times. The principle that each religion expresses the spirit of its time must be the result of self-consciousness about the structure of the process of having religions at all. That self-consciousness is a modern achievement. It is our comprehensive philosophy and final religion that allow us to affirm that philosophy and religion express their time. In affirming this, our own philosophy and religion express our special time in a way that was not achieved before.[10]

Self-Relation and Historical Detail

Hegel is careful to distinguish between categories, which tell us what it is to be this or that kind of being, and empirical concepts, which fill in the details about the various kinds of being.[11] Logic is to provide an essential skeleton for the world, but the details are purely contingent. Such contingency is itself a categorically necessary feature of any world. When the categories appear in time and space – the media of otherness – they must appear embodied in detail that can be understood only through contingent, empirical generalizations. For instance, the number and anatomical details of animal species are contingent, but the general hierarchy from matter through organisms to consciousness is, for Hegel, essential and necessary.

There is some trouble, however, in determining just what is to count as essential structure and what as contingent detail. Likewise it is difficult to determine what aspects of the historical record should be highlighted in the developmental story of spirit's self-return. As we see below, it is not easy to decide which aspects of the historical religions should be taken as the keys to their places in a developmental sequence.

It is also difficult to ascertain to what degree the finality of the logical categories limits future history. Since forms of life take their unity from logical categories, if the logic is complete then on some level no new shapes of life are to be possible. But that level could be quite general; Hegel certainly seems to believe that new nations and peoples will continually arise and have their conflicts, though their political arrangements will tend towards the rationally complete constitution that he sees developing in modern times. No one nation is final.

But does this mean that there can also be a continual series of new religions? On the contrary, Hegel believes that in some sense we have achieved the final religion. Undoubtedly he expects that there will be new religious details, but they will not represent basic improvements on Christianity's set of representations of the absolute.

Representations and Their Key

Here we need to pause and consider how religion structures the awareness that it offers the community. In religion we are filled with the absolute and know ourselves as so filled. In worship and in action we relate the absolute to ourselves as subjects and we 'enjoy' that unity.[12]

The unity is not a blank feeling of closeness; it has content that is provided by 'representations' (*Vorstellungen*). These are necessary as the objective side of what is, subjectively, immediate faith and belief (Lectures on the Philopsophy of Religion, 1827 [hereafter LPR] 144). Faith occurs when the representations and feelings connect immediately with our sense of ourselves as individuals. We need faith if our self-awareness is to be directly affected.[13] But we need content if religious experience is to be more than that inarticulate self-feeling that Hegel condemned in contemporary theologians. In his thinking about religion, one of Hegel's main targets was the claim that we cannot know God but can only intuit or feel him (Schleiermacher and pietism). Hegel's treatment of representation is often taken as criticizing religion for dealing with pictures instead of concepts, but in his eyes he was defending cognitive content in religion against those who would make faith into dog-like feeling.

Hegel lists three sorts of religious representations. The most common are pictures; the examples that he gives are interpreted as involving analogy, simile, and allegory. They constitute a wide category – for instance, the notion that God has a son, the story of the Fall, and the images of the tree of knowledge and of the wrath of God. Actual historical events can also be used as representations, especially the person of Jesus (LPR 147). Finally, non-sensible events can be representations – for example, the relation between God and the world, or creation represented as a special act from which the world arises. Though creation can be a theoretical concept, it is not truly philosophical; it remains a representation because the coherence of the sides (God and world) is not seen as necessary; instead we get a picture of a special external relation between separate entities.[14] In this sense representations at times overlap with what Hegel calls concepts of the understanding. In theology (and in understanding) the concepts used to describe God and his relations are affirmed alongside each other, free and independent in their identity and meaning, with a contingent relation to one another that lacks speculative unification.

Thus representation is not just pictural; it can involve concepts, but treated as discrete items like images. The form of representation is that things are related simply to themselves, as if independent (LPR 149 n 85). This isolated determinacy (LPR 152) contrasts with the form of thought, which is an inner manifold that embraces connection, contradiction, and necessity (LPR 154).

For Hegel, the content of representations can ultimately be separated from their form (LPR 145). In so doing we can get beyond the separations and isolations inherent in the form of representation. How is this done? Hegel employs the traditional hermeneutic gesture of distinguishing outer and inner; there is some inner content that can be freed from its outer presentation. The inner makes itself manifest because there is a key for interpreting religious representations. That key is provided in advance by the philosophical system – in particular, by the logic.[15]

> The Bible is for Christians the basis ... which strikes a chord within them, and gives

firmness to their convictions. Beyond this, however, human beings, since they are able to think, do not remain in the immediacy of assent and testimony, but also indulge in thoughts, in deliberations, in considerations concerning this immediate witness ... But just as soon as religion is no longer simply the reading and repetition of passages, as soon as what is called ... interpretation begins ... certain presuppositions are made with regard to this content, and with these one enters into the process of interpretation ... The interpretation of the Bible exhibits its content, however, in the form of a particular age; the interpretation of a thousand years ago was wholly different from that of today ... So everything depends on whether this content [the presupposed forms of thought and propositions that we bring to the reading] is true ... If [theology] uses these forms [of thought] haphazardly, because one has presuppositions and prejudices, the result is something contingent and arbitrary. [What is pertinent here] can only be forms that are genuine and logically developed in terms of necessity. But the investigation of these forms of thought falls to philosophy alone. (LPR 399–402)[16]

The forms of thought developed by necessity are not for Hegel a clue taken from outside. The logic has already taught us that its categories are the essential structure of thought and spirit.[17]

The Final Religion

One effect of the philosophical interpretation of religious representations will be, as Hegel says, to 'reduce the infinite names of God to a restricted set' (LPR 153). This happens in philosophy, but does it also occur in religion? Do we arrive at a final religion with privileged names and representations for God?

There is no final species of plant, no perfect arrangement of the continents, no culminating number of legs for animals. Why not say that religious representations are another instance of empirical detail that is noted but judged contingent by the system? Why not have one set of logical categories, but an endless series of new religious representations? Hegel does largely treat the Hindu gods this way: he discards detail that is not important as long as we understand the conceptual point, which has to do with the multiplicity of gods and the unity of Brahman. For the most part, what particular representations and gods show up in the Indian multiplicity does not seem philosophically significant to him (though he finds the Trimurti a foreshadowing of the trinity). Why not treat all religions this way? Even if the philosophical self-relation of spirit achieves a final stage, could that not have many different religious self-representations?

For Hegel, religion is not a contingent social phenomenon. It is absolute spirit coming to itself. Spirit cannot come to itself across an infinite series of logical categories; there must be a self-related grasp of its own structure. Still, we might imagine that the logic could provide a key for interpreting an indefinite series of religious representations. It would be a step back from or above religion, which could then vary contingently. John Burbidge argues for a position similar to this in his Foreword to this volume. I want to argue that such a stance is not Hegel's intention, though it is in fact the best that he can achieve with the history of religion.

Religion, as well as philosophy, is the being-for-itself of spirit. If there were an indefinite series of religious representations juxtaposed to a completed logic of categories, then any particular religious representation would become inessential to spirit's self-relation, since it could change without affecting that self-relation in any essential way. But religion is a revelation of spirit's nature to itself; its representations have the same content as philosophy. If there is closure in philosophy, there should be at least some limitation on the variation of religious representations.

Religious representations include concepts as well as pictures and images. The theological concepts used in the doctrines of the trinity and the incarnation are, in Hegel's sense of the term, representations. What they represent is the speculative coming together of universal, particular, and individual, the self-relation of the absolute through otherness, and the presentation of spirit's nature to itself in the community. These speculative motions are themselves represented; they are not merely a logical key for interpreting indefinitely many religious representations.

We might imagine that many particular figures other than Christ could be interpreted as dying and rising again in the community and as manifesting the union of the moments of the absolute idea. But any religion that did represent these speculative truths would have to be structurally similar to Christianity.[18] By analogy, these other representations would be variations on the final religion in a way similar to how Hegel sees the constitutions of the various European states as variations on a final, rational constitution.[19]

Hegel's conclusion is even stronger. Hegel finds that in the modern age institutions have become self-aware of their own structure and operation. Democratic governance is politics become self-aware. Art comes to recognize that its traditional function is ended. Philosophy completes itself as it comes to recognize its own motions and history. When spirit comes to itself, religion as such should also become self-aware.

That is what Hegel claims. Christianity is not just a better religion; it is religion as such become self-aware of its own nature. The very concept of religion (its function as the living, concrete unity of god and finite subjectivity, as the reconciliation through absolute unity of absolute opposites without denying either one) has become the content of Christian representations (the trinity and the incarnation: God is become finite and takes on death but rises to spiritual unity in the community). The doctrines of the trinity and incarnation are not replaceable. Christianity is not just another religion; its representations are religion knowing itself for what it is.

The Need for a Developmental Story

If it is the final religion, how does Christianity deal with earlier forms of religion? Any religion, in accord with its nature, represents its relation to other religions. The guiding structure of religious representation is separateness and independence. In this mode, religions exist side by side and can be judged by the criteria of representation and understanding. So religions represent their own individual histories as the replacement of inadequate gods by a fuller revelation.

Each religion has its own way of representing this. Hinduism, for example, uses its basic conceptual structure (the indefinite one with indifferently many determinate manifestations) to encompass other religions within its own fold. A monotheistic religion such as Judaism or Islam uses its basic representations (single subjectivity) to represent its relation to history in more jealous and possessive terms. Christianity can measure others by the incarnation and the trinity, representing other religions as deficient aspects of this full revelation of inner multiplicity in the absolute. The former, incomplete revelations are harmonized in the paradoxical representations available to Christianity. Thus Christianity can understand itself as the final reconciliation of the partial doctrines in other religions.

However, philosophy thinks the history of religion according to the concept and absolute idea. It unites what representation keeps separate, and it denies the independence of the historical religions; what Christianity represents as a replacement it knows as self-development.

Spirit has its own actualization and self-grasp for its purpose. This ultimate encompassing being-for-itself can have no goal outside itself. Nor can it leave anything outside itself; everything must be touched or accounted for, even if only by being consigned to the space of those things that do not need a philosophical account.

But spirit's past forms are not contingent details, they are the record of spirit's self-return, and since spirit is the revelation of its own self-return to itself, the core features of its past forms have to be exhibited as having an inner necessity that correlates with the stages of spirit's externalization and self-return. The successive earlier forms will be encompassed within the final form. By traversing its history as a record of its own necessary movement towards itself, spirit becomes itself. Hegel is committed to a strong story of developmental culmination in religion.

We could, however, imagine a weaker relation of philosophy to the history of religion. It was suggested above: philosophical understanding might see each religion as embodying structures of spirit but not demand a final religion or a story leading to a culmination. Philosophy might step back from the particular religions and use the logical key to interpret their representations. There would be no incorporation of earlier forms, only a vision that placed them – not in a developmental narrative but in relation to the general, logical preconditions that make possible any religion.

Hegel demands the stronger model. It is essential that, in its self-return, spirit catch up and redeem the particularities of finite spirit and not just surpass them by a step back into their conditions of possibility. It is this inclusive closure that helps establish the absoluteness of absolute spirit.

Difficulties with the Developmental Story

In the stronger model the developmental story redeems the earlier forms of religion by seeing them as stages leading to the final religion. This demands an ascending series of essential types of religion, each of which has room for varying contingent detail. In his lectures Hegel attempts such a story.

However, this task turns out to be extraordinarily difficult. Religions are many-faceted phenomena; it is not obvious what is the essence of each religion, or whether there is anything essential about the bricolage of practices, representations, and doctrines in the historical religions. Further, religions are not just objects; they are modes of self-consciousness. So the analyst has to take into account what they say about themselves, and they say many different things. Amid all this, how does the philosopher pick what is to be the essential nature of each religion? Presumably he attempts to correlate essential representations with stages discussed in the Logic. But which representations and which stages? Faced with the internal multiplicity of religions, Hegel waffled in his analyses of various religions and their place in the developmental story.[20]

In this regard the varying positions of Greek, Roman, and Jewish religions are especially significant. As Louis Dupré points out, Hegel is unable to decide which logical pattern he should use to order their relations.[21] The deep problem here is that the axes around which one might order a developmental sequence are not parallel to one another. If you order the religions according to the ascending universal unity of the godhead you get an ambiguous order (monotheistic Jews over polytheistic Greeks and Romans, but also universalistic Romans over particularistic Jews and Greeks); the axis of deepening subjectivity and interiority gives another ordering (ethical Jews over externalist Romans), while detachment from nature into spirit gives a third (poetic Greeks over Jewish minutiae of daily life), and so on. According to the system these axes should be parallel, but in actual religious history they are not.

So we are forced to wonder: is there a right way to assemble religions into a developmental story? Given the way the Logic has developed its enclosure of particularity, and the essentialism involved in that claim, for Hegel there should be a right way, but he has not found it. He keeps trying, despite the difficulty of deciding on the essence of historical forms, not to mention the problems of making all this fit into a dialectical pattern of determinate negation.

Do we really need a single axis and a single teleology? Think perhaps of the multiple ways Ricoeur discusses for narrative to emplot events.[22] Unfortunately, that won't do for Hegel's self-comprehension as outlined in the Logic. It is crucial that spirit be able to posit its own motion as 'the content of the finite' (LPR 412). Otherwise a foreign purpose is being categorized, not pure being-for-itself. For Hegel, that was a flaw in the determinate historical religions. The final religion and philosophy should do better.

But it looks as if, for religion, the weaker model may be the best that philosophy can do: to present a formal self-awareness of the nature of spirit, while on the empirical level there is endless detail that does not get picked up into a unified teleology. Spirit's self-return would then be at best a step back from any religion to the (a?) concept behind it, not a step along a sequence of religions to a culminating self-consciousness in a final religion. The names of God would remain infinite.

It might seem that with this interpretation we have arrived at a form of 'open' Hegelianism. But because the axes of evaluation are not parallel, the step-back model cannot provide a hierarchical ordering of religions. At best it gives a move from any content to its categorial structure and conditions of possibility; this does not allow any necessary connections between different contents. This lack of connection in turn casts doubt on the applicability of determinate negation, without which it would be difficult to call any position Hegelian, open or closed.

This interpretation could have some far-reaching implications. If religions, at least, are organized with only typology and geography but no unique axial history, could that suggest that worldly history and the state might also lose their teleological finality? The situation is quite different for such institutional structures than for religious representations, but the cases might turn out to be more similar than Hegel expects. If there were no teleological story of development to be told concerning religion and these other areas of particularity, and yet the logic remained self-enclosing and complete, what would happen to the fit between logic and world? Would it become optional or pragmatic which categories fit which collections? Of course, if the logic itself became a multiply connected affair with many axes, then pure self-return would be threatened. Following such considerations, many critics today substitute spatial for temporal metaphors, so we get dissemination instead of development.

But even if chastened, Hegel's questions still remain. Who are the We that know all this? What kind of self-criticism and self-knowledge is involved here? Can it be institutionalized and made common property? In such discussion all the sins and splits of modernity come home to roost, splits that Hegel can still help us avoid making into our own absolutes.

Notes

1 This chapter has benefited from helpful comments an earlier version received when presented at the Department of Religious Studies at Brown University.
2 For a discussion of Hegel's connection to Kantian self-relation, cf. Robert Pippin, *Hegel's Idealism* (New York: Cambridge University Press, 1989).
3 See my 'What Is Open and What Is Closed in the Philosophy of Hegel,' *Philosophical Topics*, 19 no. 2 (fall 1991), 29–50, and *The Critique of Pure Modernity: Hegel, Heidegger and After* (Chicago: University of Chicago Press, 1987).
4 Hegel speaks of 'the entire course [of the science of logic], in which all possible shapes of a given content and of objects came up for consideration.' (*Science of Logic* 12:237/826; references are to the *Gesammelte Werke* volume and page and to the page in the Miller translation: *Gesammelte Werke*, ed. Rheinisch-Westfaelischen Akademie der Wissenschaften (Hamburg: Felix Meiner, 1968 on); *Science of Logic*, trans. A.V. Miller (New York: Humanities Press, 1967).
5 Also, since we are speaking of categories that are the essential determinations of what it means to be, if there were uncomprehended categories in endless novelty, the source of their determination (their being) would remain mysterious, and thought would not yet be self-determining in its relation to itself.
6 In such a case, there would be built in to the basic epistemological and ontological 'action' a gap between its concept and its actualization. But (in an argument reminiscent of Aristotle's for the primacy of actuality over potentiality) Hegel would deny that it could be possible for such to be the case on the primal level. Correspondingly, post-structuralist attacks on Hegel and on metaphysics generally can be seen as a reaffirmation of the primacy of potentiality, though more in pre-Socratic than Megarian terms.
7 A similar position can be found in Pippin, *Hegel's Idealism*. John Burbidge would not characterize his position as involving a final set of logical categories, but he does regard the logic's method as final and so provides a kind of higher-level closure

around the categories that describe that method. Either the future logical novelty is not foreseen, in which case thought's self-relation is not complete or truthful, or it is foreseen, and the 'place' of that novelty is described by a set of categories that are in effect the final categories of thought.

In a note to his Foreword to this book, Burbidge employs some of his final categories when he distinguishes formal from real possibility. (See my discussion of his position in 'What Is Open and What Is Closed.') Burbidge argues that for Hegel possibility is derived from actuality, so that the novel to-be-created categories are not yet 'possible.' (This stance raises the problem mentioned in note 5 above.) As I read him, Hegel is much more Aristotelian than Peircean about the primacy of actuality, and the completion of the system is more akin to the self-transparency and completeness of 'thought thinking itself' in Aristotle (which is quoted at the close of Hegel's *Encyclopaedia*). Nor is this an undue emphasis on the Kantian influence of the first Critique, as Burbidge charges, since the aim of complete architectonic and system runs all through Kant's works, and Kant claims that it is only by its self-established and self-referential completeness that the transcendental philosophy is proved correct. I would grant that there are aspects of the third Critique that threaten to undermine Kant's project, but the same is true of Hegel. It seems to me best to interpret Hegel according to his own, programmatic assertions and then show how these may not succeed. Otherwise we run the risk of reading back current favourite ideas into Hegel, which can ultimately reduce our confrontation with novelty and our need to question ourselves.

8 The quotation is from the Lasson edition of *Begriff der Religion* (Hamburg: Meiner, 1966), 32. Cf. also Hegel's comments in the same edition that spirit that does not appear is not (33). Spirit must be the encompassing negative of all finite forms, and appear as such to itself. References to the one-volume English translation of the 1827 lectures on the philosophy of religion – *Lectures on the Philosophy of Religion*, ed. Peter C. Hodgson (Berkeley: University of California Press, 1988) – are abbreviated LPR.

9 I owe this way of putting the point to a remark of Mark Okrent in conversation.

10 Earlier philosophies and religions comprehended their own time in thought, but only because they articulated the leading principles or categories of their ages; they did not describe themselves as doing so, nor recapitulate the self-knowing circle that understands its own nature. Their self-conception was different from what philosophers can do now, and the new self-conception is the new self-relation.

11 For example, in the Logic he insists: 'Philosophy must know how to distinguish what is according to its nature a self-external matter (*Stoff*); in such a case the progress (*Fortgang*) of the concept occurs only in an external manner, and its moments can exist only in the proper form of externality ... It is an essential requirement when philosophizing about real objects to distinguish those spheres to

which a specific form of the concept belongs (i.e., is present as existence), so as not to confuse through Ideas the peculiar nature of what is external and contingent, and have the incommensurability of the matter distort the Ideas and make them merely formal' (*Science of Logic* 21:203/212).

12. Religion is spirit that realizes (actualizes) itself in our consciousness (LPR 104; cf. the discussion of the necessity of religion in 132 n 47 and the discussion of explicit consummation on 191).

13. Hegel argues that 'only by means of this faith that reconciliation is accomplished with certainty and in and for itself is the subject able and indeed in a position to posit itself in this unity.' But he also insists on the necessity of content and doctrine as the mediation that goes beyond the immediacy of faith (LPR 474f).

14. Creation is a representation rather than a philosophical concept because it talks of one being making another separate being, as opposed to the speculative truth finding objectivity and being in the concept. Similarly, most other concepts used in theology are representations; Hegel speaks frequently about the way the attributes of God are kept separate from one another (cf. LPR 421).

15. This hermeneutical relation is one-sided. Cf. Peter Hodgson's introductory discussion in his translation of the *Lectures on the Philosophy of Religion* about the logic as hermeneutic key (LPR 12, 14).

16. Cf. also the remarks on history and theology (LPR 472) and the claim (98 n 59) that only with closure of the logic as a guide can one move freely among the determinations of the world of actuality.

17. John Burbidge argues in note 13 to chapter 8, below, that the relation, as presented in the *Phenomenology* and the *Encyclopaedia*, is different, that religion 'provides a necessary condition for absolute knowing or philosophy – it justifies the truth claims of the logic.' However, even if one grants the claim that religion is a necessary condition, it does not follow that the relation is one of justification (nor is it clear that the logic makes 'truth claims' in any straightforward sense). There are several senses in which religion is seen as necessary for the full self-return of spirit and for the historical development of absolute knowing, but, given Hegel's insistence on the independence of pure thought, their relation is not one of one fact or activity (religion) justifying another (pure thought). Nor are they the same activity, as I argue in this chapter. And in their dialectical relation it is logic that has the primacy in its fuller self-relation.

18. John Burbidge's candidates for new religious representations maintain such structural similarity to Christianity. Cf. his presidential address to the Hegel Society of America, 'Is Hegel a Christian?' in David Kolb, ed., *New Perspectives on Hegel's Philosophy of Religion* (Albany: SUNY Press, 1992).

19. This raises, of course, the issue of the uniqueness of Christ, which Henry Harris has explored. Cf. John Burbidge's contribution to this volume (chapter 8) for a position

on this issue that seems to me to allow too many kinds of individuals to play the Christ-role, because it defines that which must be incarnated too loosely as 'a framework for life in a community ... the way the world really is – its ultimate determinate character ... [that] sets the standard for action and behaviour.' Burbidge seems to confuse a trinitarian description of the method of incarnation with the incarnation of the trinity itself. But the uniqueness of Christian religion for Hegel is that the concept of religion and the speculative trinitarian unities are themselves represented, not merely that they provide a framework for representing whatever framework or values are deemed ultimate.

20 The various versions of the developmental story are summarized by Peter Hodgson (LPR 498–9); they are discussed in Walter Jaeschke, 'Zur Logik der bestimmten Religion,' in *Hegels Logik der Philosophie*, ed. Dieter Henrich and Rolf-Peter Horstmann (Stuttgart: Klett-Cotta, 1984), 172–88. Cf. also Jaeschke's *Reason in Religion: The Foundations of Hegel's Philosophy of Religion*, trans. Peter C. Hodgson and Michael Stewart (Berkeley: University of California Press, 1990), 230ff, and Louis Dupré, 'Transitions and Tensions in Hegel's Treatment of Determinate Religion,' in David Kolb, ed., *New Perspectives on Hegel's Philosophy of Religion* (Albany: SUNY Press, 1992), 81–92.

21 'Until the final series of lectures delivered in the year of his death (1831) he kept changing the order and, more significantly, the principle of classification ... Which one was religiously superior? The free form but internal necessity of the Greeks, or God's sovereign freedom, subject to no formal necessity yet dominating life with divine commands? ... The succession of particular religions follows a pattern of increasing internalization and universalization. Those two principles do not always follow an identical development, however, as Hegel's continuing hesitation about the place of the Jewish religion – internal but not universal – indicates.' Dupré, 'Transitions,' 83–91.

22 Paul Ricoeur, *Time and Narrative* (Chicago: University of Chicago Press, 1984). Religious representation remains recalcitrant because Hegel has conceived the nature of religious images and representations too simply.

8

Hegel's Open Future

JOHN W. BURBIDGE

If John Marco Allegro's thesis in *The Sacred Mushroom and the Cross* were true, would it destroy Hegel's philosophy? This question, originally posed by H.S. Harris, is a difficult one to answer.[1] Allegro claimed, after having investigated some of the Dead Sea Scrolls, that the person Jesus of Nazareth, who figures in the Gospels, did not really exist. Instead 'Jesus' was the code name for a hallucinogenic mushroom that generated certain kinds of 'religious' experiences.

While not endorsing Allegro's thesis, Harris says that the outcome of the debate over its truth would have no effect on Hegel's philosophy of religion, or his philosophy generally. All that Hegel really needs is St. Paul, and Paul's experience on the Damascus road. Paul believes that there was a historical Jesus in the past, even though he has never seen him. And it is that belief that is built into his religious feeling and religious practice. Though Harris admits that Hegel probably did believe that there was an historical Jesus, he adds that this personal conviction is not an essential constituent of his philosophical system.[2]

The advantage of this interpretation lies in the fact that one can be a Hegelian without having to be a Christian in any conventional sense of the word. As a result, the Hegelian philosophy is not a closed theory, tied to a particular socio-historical context, but is open to contingency and novelty as time proceeds.

When first posed with Harris's question, I took a contrary position. While in the *Phenomenology* all that Hegel appeals to is the belief that there was an historical individual in the past who was both God and man, evidence from the *Encyclopaedia* pointed in another direction. That evidence I have already discussed elsewhere,[3] but it is perhaps useful to review its argument here, focusing on the point in question.

In the eight short paragraphs in the *Encyclopaedia* on revealed religion, Hegel makes explicit the rational structure involved.[4]

The trinity before creation is a universal that particularizes itself into contraries. Because that difference is none the less internal to its own activity, it is balanced by an integrating relation that 'negates the negation.' This singular[5] relation is thus not opposed to an abstract universal but is rather one moment within the universal's self-determination.

A full contradiction between radical singularity and abstract universality results when the difference introduced by particularity is not internal but external. In creation, the two particularized extremes are not reintegrated but simply conjoined by judgment. Qualitatively creation's relation to God takes both affirmative and negative forms, with the two kinds of judgment quite indifferent to each other. When finite spirits reflect on themselves in an infinite judgment, they fall away from that simple relation. As a totality of collected diversity they stand as the correlate to God's comprehensive universality. So the conjunction assumes the garment of quantitative judgment. Yet the two sides are related: God is the categorical essence as well as the necessary condition of the world. The relation becomes fully explicit when God and creation become disjunctive alternatives that exhaust all possibilities – when creation sets itself up as explicitly not-God in the fall. The relation that unites the two into a disjunction starts out as a mere possibility, becomes actual, and, once actual, cannot be undone and thus is necessary. In other words, the Christian doctrines of creation and fall embody the full range of propositional forms.

In the logic, syllogisms mediate necessary judgments. In a similar way, the paragraphs on reconciliation describe mediations that establish a necessary relation. Following the pattern of the first (or categorical) syllogism, a singular that as God-man unites both sides of the disjunction shows itself to be particular by passing through death and thereby becomes universal.

In response, individual men and women reflect on their own particularity, identifying it not only as that which separates them from God but also as that which brought about the demise of the singular God-man. This singular reflection, however, is the means by which each particular comes to participate in transcendent universality. This whole response of faith incarnates the structure of induction and arguments from analogy: the second syllogism of reflective inference.

In the third, disjunctive, syllogism, the universal spirit within the comprehensive community particularizes its members as agents who act and thereby differentiate themselves from the whole, yet at the same time it identifies those same members as singulars who integrate the universal with particular differences.

This review of the logical structure described in the eight paragraphs from the *Encyclopaedia*[6] provides some background for my response to Harris. St Paul's experience on the Damascus road is that formalized in the second syllogism – in which a singular reflects on its own particularity. It presupposes the first syllogism, in which the singular God-man dies and thereby becomes universal. Therefore it must have this story from the past as a condition for its religious experience.[7] It seems to me, however, that the whole dynamic would be dissipated were that story a fiction. The seriousness of existential anxiety is lost once the account that triggers its agony is seen to be a fable. The anxiety is no longer a moment of profound insight into the ultimate constitution of the universe, but rather a peculiar aberration of an unhealthy mind.

So the first syllogism, if it is to be a constituent in the total picture, must have the same status in reality that the rest have. While the reality of the fall does not require an historical Adam and Eve, since the disjunctive opposition is realized in the actions of most (if not all) finite spirits, we cannot as easily appeal to myth and metaphor in this case. For the key initiating moment is a singular individual, and the mediating transition is a particular death. This is not an action that is representative of reality more generally. It is specific and distinctive. As an object of reference it can be indexically indicated. The singular must have been actual to have really died; and that death is the necessary condition for the actual, universal presence of the spiritual Christ.[8]

These, then, are my reasons for disagreeing with Harris's thesis concerning the sacred mushroom. Nevertheless there is a paradox in my position. I agree with Harris that Hegel's philosophy is open to contingency. It is not closed and complete, allowing only instantiations of the truth discovered in principle. On the contrary, the absolute method of knowledge involves continually taking account of the partiality in whatever has already been achieved, anticipating something else, whatever it be, that will expose how partial it is, yet being able to incorporate that novelty into a comprehensive perspective that is thereby altered and transformed.[9]

Why do I believe the system to be open? This conclusion has become inescapable from my analysis of Hegel's logic. Any system that purports to be complete affirms that there is nothing beyond. There is an absolute barrier over which it cannot go. Yet Hegel shows that such a barrier demarcates the finite. As soon as a limit has been identified there is an obligation to go beyond it; indeed we can only know that it is a barrier because we have already tried to go beyond. That means, however, that we have in principle already at least thought beyond the limit, so that the finite is not the last word. There is something else. Anything that purports to be complete has already in principle moved beyond that completeness.

This logic of finitude repeats itself throughout the logic. The true infinite that becomes fully self-contained as being-on-its-own-account (*Fürsichsein*) repels other beings, and we have no longer a unit but a plurality of such units.

This is an early stage of the logic. When Hegel comes to the end – to the absolute idea – he identifies the method that is the implicit life of the whole process, and the result is no different. The method involves a dividing into opposites and an identifying of contraries – analysis and synthesis. These two moves are reciprocal; each implies and presupposes the other. That reciprocity is its determinate character, defining its limits. But thought presses further. What about a realm where the two are not complementary but simply diverse, externally related? What about a realm where non-rational contingencies disrupt and confound rational neatness? Since that realm is (or would be?) not itself logical, it cannot be described in the language of pure thought. Yet thought can be open to it and can expect that – once its determinations have occurred – they can become the constituents of an explanatory theory that sets them within a rational context. That context, to be sure, will be conditioned by those contingent determinations, and hence novel, but it will none the less be comprehensible and hence able to rely on logical categories and processes.[10]

That logical point, developed by Hegel in the last few paragraphs of the *Science of Logic*, fits with what he does at the end of the *Encyclopaedia*. The last three of the six paragraphs devoted to Philosophy describe three syllogisms. While Hegel omitted them from the 1827 edition,[11] he reintroduced them three years later without altering significantly the previous section. He does amend his introductory clause, however; it is no longer the same as that used in 1817.

He starts by saying: 'It is this appearance which *next* gives the ground for *further development*' (my italics). 'Appearance' refers to elements of immediacy and unjustified assumption that are taken up into the simple necessity of the logic. This dissolution of contingency in the world of nature and history constitutes philosophy's task. Yet Hegel does not suggest (as he had in 1817) that it is thereby complete. For the appearance continues and 'grounds further development' – a development that moves through a pattern of three syllogisms: immediate transitions, posited syntheses, and disjoined explanations. Since the development is going beyond what has already been achieved, the pattern by itself cannot specify in advance what will appear as immediate, or what positings will be required.

Both the *Logic* and the final edition of the *Encyclopaedia* thus provide strong evidence that Hegel's system is not closed, but open. This conclusion, however, confronts me with a dilemma. On the one hand, as Harris has argued, if Hegel's philosophy is genuinely open to the future, then Jesus as God-man is not historically necessary. History moves on, and cultures decline. The Germanic culture, nourished by the Christian religion, will itself pass away. Its religion will become more superficial and irrelevant. And in due course another society will emerge that has its own distinctive faith and ultimate commitment. While the experience of an existential dark night may still be a component of religious feeling,[12] it will have a distinctive character, determined by the new doctrine that has become orthodox. The incarnation, however, would be as relevant to that culture as the Delphic oracle is to ours.

On the other hand, if the individual God-man is a necessary component of Hegel's philosophy, then that system cannot be completely open to the future. If that story must be believed to initiate the other two syllogisms, then it conditions the kind of reconciliation they achieve. And any subsequent events must somehow simply instantiate that determinate pattern. There will be nothing genuinely new.

One might seek to avoid the dilemma by arguing that the necessity of the incarnation may well be true of Hegel's understanding of religion but that it does not affect his philosophy. Such an objection fails to take account of the role of Hegel's paragraphs on revealed religion. They immediately precede the final six paragraphs of the *Encyclopaedia* on philosophy. These latter do not introduce any new content to the philosophical discussion. They simply identify the logical form of everything that preceded – a form that explicitly constitutes reality as a whole only in the paragraphs on revealed religion. Abstracted from its content, that form becomes the basis and inherent pattern for all philosophical knowledge. If the incarnation is necessary in revealed religion, it is equally so in philosophy.[13] Hence the system must, in some final sense, be closed to contingent novelty.[14]

The dilemma appears inescapable. It is not simply a problem with my interpretation – a contradiction that could be used to reduce it to absurdity. Rather, it is a paradox inherent in Hegel's philosophy itself. How can he possibly grasp both horns? How can Hegel both require that the God-man's death be an historical event and maintain a philosophy open to the future?

Even Hegel, however, does not rest content with paradoxes. Any radical contradiction goes aground or collapses. We have to investigate its ground: why both sides are required and whether they can be united in a single claim. The contradiction has emerged because its two sides have been expressed in abstract terms. To say *simply* 'the future is open,' for example, allows the future to be totally indeterminate, with possibilities whose range is limited only by the constraint of internal consistency.[15] But the future will not be abstract. It will be a future that comes to be out of the present and the past. The transition from present to future involves things becoming other than they were. Change and alteration introduce differences. Differences are novel, however, only when they are not at all similar to what has preceded. That is to say, they are not just other; they introduce a contrast: the new is in some way antithetical to the old. The new is established as new only by an act of comparison. So the difference is balanced by continuity, albeit a continuity that is in no way simple identity. In recognition of the new as new, new and old are held together in a reflective synthesis.

Hegel's Open Future 181

This synthetic move of reflection has a significant implication. Not only does it highlight the contrast; it also discovers that the old was one-sided and partial, that its limitation and finitude in some sense required the transition to something else, that the new complements what was lacking, or at least not present, in the old. If the old can now be seen to require in some sense the new, the new can be recognized as new only because of its relation to the old. In other words, the new is parasitic on the partiality of the old. In this way the pattern of mutual conditioning becomes integrated into a comprehensive explanation that comes to understand the new world order and why it has turned out to be what it is.

The novel is not general and indeterminate. It is always something particular, setting itself against what is already there. So it never replaces completely what precedes it but instead becomes a new component in a more comprehensive reality. That reality itself will become past; in due course time will introduce further particular novelties that will alter and at times transform the way the world functions. Yet no novelty, however radical, will be absolute. And no transient present, however obsolete, will become totally irrelevant.

How does this logic of novelty relate to Hegel's claims about the Christian religion and about Jesus in particular? The first thing to notice is that it instantiates the logical pattern of conceiving, judging, and inferring. A comprehensive present is conceived: its moments are rendered particular and distinct, yet related in an integrated singular. The novel breaks this integration apart into a judgment. The new is particular, radically opposed to the old; it shows that the present's singularity is opposed to its supposed, now abstract universality. The two are simply the extremes of a process of transition. Comparisons and syntheses, however, begin to identify the mediating relations by which they are integrated – the three syllogistic patterns: particular transitions from singular to universal; individual syntheses that recognize how particulars complement and condition each other as parts of a totality; and a universal comprehension that explains both how the moments are diverse and particularized and how they are integrated yet singular.

The movement into the new has then already been described in the final three paragraphs of the *Encyclopaedia*. It is this common pattern that makes it possible for reflective thought and social structures to bridge the gap between the old and the new – to establish a continuity despite even the most radical difference. It is the very logic that Hegel found instantiated in the Christian religion, with its doctrines of the trinity, creation and fall, atonement, justification, and sanctification; the logic that required the incarnation to be true of the world. Thus the appearance of the new reconfirms Hegel's appeal to the historical God-man.

The second thing to notice is that the past is never simply abandoned. Once the novel has been reintegrated with the old, both sides play a constitutive role in the result. History develops; it does not haphazardly skip to unrelated stages. In this particular case, the singular, actual incarnation cannot easily be relativized, for it realizes most completely a moment in the logical pattern that recurs in all sorts of combinations and permutations throughout the natural, personal, and social world. The union of universal and particular happens in a singular individual that does not recur; it is actual and not simply a permanent possibility; its experience of radical finitude in death marked the transition to universal presence; and this was an act not of some partial moment of reality but of the ultimate ground of all existence – God, in religious terms, and absolute spirit, in the language of philosophy. Throughout Hegel's lectures on history, art, religion, and philosophy this religious doctrine, with its 'scandal of particularity,' stands apart from the reported incarnations of Vishnu in the Hindu tradition, or the actual incarnations of Buddha in the succession of Dalai Lamas.[16] It takes seriously both historical actuality and radical singularity.

However, when we move beyond Christendom – the world in which the incarnation is the constitutive religious doctrine – what happens to that doctrine? At this point we leave behind Hegel's guiding hand and venture on our own. But we are not left to pure speculation. For a hundred and sixty years have intervened, and we can look back on a number of events that were unexpected and unanticipated in 1831. We can spot novelties that did in fact emerge, and we can ask how they would fit into Hegel's philosophical perspective.

Let us consider simply the question of religion. The nineteenth century continued the Enlightenment challenge to 'superstition.' Strauss and the higher criticism challenged the divinity of the historical Jesus. Comte and positivism moved away from grand explanations to scientific correlations and humanist religion. Marx and communism reacted against the mirage of religion in promoting a humane utopia by way of revolution. Darwin and biology undermined the authority of Christian scriptures by showing how species were not created out of nothing but were part of an ongoing continuum. Henry Ford and capitalist technology made God a redundant hypothesis in a world that could be manipulated and controlled to meet human ends. And John Stuart Mill and liberal tolerance extended the dominant culture into Asia, Africa, and the Americas, relativizing the ultimate claims of traditional religions wherever they were found.

There have been counter-movements. The fundamentalism of the twentieth century descended from evangelical revivals in the nineteenth. Despite the liberal surrender of Christ's uniqueness, the missionary movement took Christianity to the ends of the earth, stimulating indigenous churches that have developed their own spirituality. Neo-orthodoxy has affirmed the divine initiative. Yet even these movements have become part of a culture that is inherently pluralistic. No dominant religious paradigm characterizes the present age. While such a pluralistic society emerged in the heady days of the Roman Empire, never before has it been so all-pervasive and so integrated with a humanism that can find hope, if at all, only in human initiatives. From the perspective of Hegel's day, this is a new world order.

This new world order has, however, generated its own reactions: people and societies who appeal back to the traditions of the past not to reinstate what has gone but to integrate past and present into a more comprehensive perspective. For the new world is seen to be itself partial and incomplete just to the extent that it has reacted against and rejected what was old. The ecological movement in North America finds balance in the Native American respect for nature. Offended by the crass brutality of modern culture, Islam is reaffirming the transcendent, all-encompassing will of God. Threatened with total annihilation, Judaism has reaffirmed its covenanted responsibility to survive and be faithful to its past. Lost in a world without meaning, people both East and West have learned through meditation to overcome frustrations and desires and find inner peace. Oppressed by the inhumanity of the capitalist economy, Christians of Latin America have discovered the liberation involved when God becomes incarnate in human life. And what is called 'fundamentalism' of whatever sort affirms that there is a transcendent reality to which we must conform and which offers fulfilment in a world that has lost itself in the endless quest for means. Each one of these appeals to tradition is a synthesis. The past has not simply been revived. The new has had as much influence in moulding and directing what has appeared as the old. Modern pluralism has been fruitful and multiplied.

The challenge to the uniqueness of the incarnation is evident. To be sure, its relevance has been reaffirmed by many in our world. But that is now only one voice among many. If Hegel's system is genuinely open to what has in fact occurred, how can it maintain the historicity of the God-man?

Let us recall what was evident in Hegel's claim. We have been told that in the past there was an individual who integrated the divine and the human – the transcendent and the mundane. This individual passed away – but in passing away allowed that unity to become universal – a possibility that could be appropriated and become the basis of community.

When we look around us, we find that Christianity is not unique in that kind of claim. Wilfred Cantwell Smith[17] has pointed out that the counterpart to Jesus in Islam is not Muhammad but the Koran. Here is a singular text, recited in mundane sounds, that is at the same time the divine will of Allah. That initial unity, recited by Muhammad to his scribes, passed away but has thereby become universal. In a similar way, Judaism appeals to a historical individual – the moment of the covenant between Israel and the Lord at Sinai, an agreement that united the divine and the human. It is no longer yet has thereby become general. And in more recent days Jews have experienced the sense of a horrible unity of transcendence and immanence in the Holocaust, an ecstatic unity in the founding of Israel: two moments that, albeit past, now define what it means to be a Jew.

Modern studies in comparative religion have shown that the particular pattern of a unique historical individual that passes away and becomes universal is not peculiar to Christianity but characterizes other traditions as well. Is it universal and comprehensive? At first sight it would seem not to be so. Hinduism, for example, talks of a number of incarnations, many of them mythic. While Buddhism may recount the initiating stories of Gautama, the Mahayana tradition sees no need to rely on the past as a condition for achieving enlightenment. And modern secularism has dismissed transcendence entirely.

Let us, however, look more closely. What is the function of God and transcendence in religion? They explain why the world is the way it is; they tell us which actions will be ultimately successful and which self-defeating; and so they set the standards against which human behaviour is measured. Actions that fit the nature of ultimate reality are fulfilling; those that work against it are frustrating.

Not only religions talk that language. Capitalists are convinced not only that *the world is so ordered* that the industrious thrive and the slothful perish, but also that society should be ordered according to the same principles. Marxists identify a dialectic that works *implacably* through history, radicalizing class conflict to the point of revolution, at which time a new society emerges. Humanists appeal to the deepest roots of *human nature* that all people share, urging us to bring them up to the light. Liberals are so convinced that indifferent tolerance is *ultimate* that they are intolerant of intolerance.

Wherever we advance a framework for life in a community we appeal to the way the world really is – its ultimate, determinate character. That sets the standard for action and behaviour. Our explanation of the world is the way we integrate individual actions and people into a community. This stance is common not only to the religions of the West and of the East, but also to the new secular ideologies. For all of their secularism, they make claims that have a religious character.

But there is something more. An ultimate explanation is simply an idea, a way of thinking about the world. To make it convincing we need some evidence that at some specific place and time – at some individual, historical moment – it has functioned unambiguously. In other words, there needs to be some individual that is both transcendent and mundane.

Marx could point back to Iroquois culture as a classless community and to the

English Civil War and French Revolution as class-based revolutions. Hinduism and Buddhism have their impact not because of quasi-mythical stories but because there have been Bodhisattvas and saints – perhaps only one, perhaps several – who have in fact achieved, or almost achieved, enlightenment. Capitalists point to the success of the American way of life.

In these stories of unique events, ultimate explanations become credible as bases for action, because they have become incarnate in historical singulars, where the universal has been integrated with the particular. Yet in every case they have passed away and shown themselves to be finite. The world as a whole is not what it ought to be. The achievement is past ... and future. It is no longer; yet it is implicit in whatever will be. That is why we strive – why we constantly appeal to an explanation to justify our actions and our convictions. The world as it is is ambiguous. The ambiguity is dissipated by the transcendent/mundane individual who has passed away.

To universalize its achievement, we must abandon the distractions of the world – the features of its ambiguity that lead us astray – and enter into communities whose rituals re-enact the universal achievement.

In sum, I am arguing that, for all that we have gone beyond Hegel, and for all the novelty in the different, ultimate explanations of the way things are, the logical pattern he identified in the chapter on revealed religion remains. Indeed, since Christianity is there described in the abstract vocabulary of philosophy, that description is not necessarily limited to a single, Christian, example. It is potentially a universal phenomenon that a singular, historical incarnation passes away and becomes universal.[18] So Jesus is now only one among many – the Koran; the founding of Israel; Sri Aurobindo; the Jacobin revolution (or the Paris commune); nature's struggle for survival; the traditional Ojibwa hunter, smoking a peace pipe over the bear he has just killed; Freud's therapies; ... Each has become the focus of stories, because in each all the transcendent and ultimate have become actual.

Not all of them will turn out to be genuine. While Hinduism and Buddhism have survived from the ancient world, the cults of Apollo and Thor, of the ancient Mayans and the palaeolithic cave-painters of Lascaux, have vanished.[19] At the present time it is impossible to identify those current ultimate perspectives that are sufficiently based in the actual world to justify their perpetuity.[20]

Yet when we look at the major religious traditions of the world we are faced with at least five that have survived over many centuries and through radical social change: Hinduism in all its variety, Buddhism, Judaism, Christianity, and Islam.[21] In light both of the resurgence of these traditions in the twentieth century and of the renewed discovery that all embody the rational structure of an individual passing over to universality, it would be presumptuous to affirm that all plurality will be overcome. Each one of the traditions has a distinctive claim about ultimate reality, conditioned by the determinate character of the historical individual who unambiguously integrated the transcendent and the mundane. They are not, and cannot be made to be, species of a single, abstract genus.

If this analysis of the contemporary situation is fair, then we have something genuinely novel: a plurality of historical individuals, diverse in character, each one of which unambiguously unites transcendent universality with mundane particularity. The stories about these individuals generate profound religious feelings by which particular people come to share in that unity, now universally available; and cultic practice integrates them into a comprehensive community. But there are now several communities, each distinctively determined by its own originating history. It is not just the story of the sacred mushroom that will be perverse, but also the kinds of explanation that reduce Muhammad's reception of Gabriel's message to hallucination or Gautama's search for enlightenment to a form of the Oedipus complex.[22]

Such plurality has always been present. Novel is the fact that it now is the religious dimension of a single, more comprehensive social reality that is gradually acquiring its own political institutions. While there is as yet no universal state, the diversity of international corporations has evoked political structures to regulate their activity and redress inequality.

In Hegel's language, objective spirit, while still comprehensive, has become more internally diverse. It incorporates a diversity of ultimate religious commitments, none of which has priority, each of which is distinctive – in tension, if not in actual conflict – with the others. Jesus as the historical God-man is still critically significant because his individuality is an expression of spirit – of a singular, complete, self-conscious life. Now, however, his claim is one among many, and no longer unique.

We cannot anticipate what kind of resolution will emerge when future generations learn how to integrate this diversity. Some have already started to trace the ways in which the several traditions have mutually conditioned each other.[23] The different character of the initiating individuals will ensure that the plurality will remain; the fact that each one is the incarnation of what is ultimately significant will mean that it cannot take second place to any other; the fact that they embody the all-pervasive logical pattern suggests that they have some level of legitimacy; yet the fact that they are diverse within a single social order cannot be the final word. They must learn to interrelate in some way; even if they continue to compete and differ, they will also cooperate and learn from each other.

This, then, is my suggestion as to how Hegel, at least to the present day, could retain both openness to the future and commitment to an historical incarnation. I cannot establish that the two will continue to hold for ever. After all, if the future is genuinely open, we cannot predict what will actually occur. Nevertheless, the structure of openness involves the three-fold pattern of mediation – Hegel's three syllogisms. So that will continue. In addition, this pattern as constitutive of the universe was first made manifest in the doctrine of the incarnation; so Christianity will never lose its historical primacy. It will continue to be critical even as it becomes relativized within more comprehensive perspectives.

My speculative venture into a post-Hegelian Hegelianism has one further, interesting implication. The model proposed was a diversity of ultimate perspectives coexisting within a single social order. That in itself is novel, unanticipated in Hegel's system. This novelty, however, suggests that the logic itself needs to be revised – it requires 'elaboration in detail.'[24] In the logic of essence, the discussion of difference now leads to diversity, which slips into bipolar opposition before becoming contradiction. Now the move through diversity may have to be radicalized by the introduction of plurality – an indefinite multiplicity of contraries that leads into an explosion of mutually repelling moments before it collapses into its ground. The nature of such a multi-valued logic boggles the mind, both in terms of its logical description and in terms of how it will be grounded back into the fabric of existence. Yet such a logic will not be unfaithful to Hegel – and would make it manifest that reason too must be genuinely open to the future.

The answer to Harris's question concerning the sacred mushroom has led us into the prospect of an indeterminate and challenging future. As we face it, however, our action will be rooted in the conviction that what is ultimate has become unambiguously united with the mundane in a past, historical individual. For this justifies our confidence that the future will not be incomprehensible.

Notes

1 This question was put to me by Harris at my oral defence of my doctoral dissertation.
2 What is in question is not the historical existence of a particular human, Jesus of Nazareth, but the stronger claim that this particular person was a unity of the universal and the particular – in religious language, that he was both God and man.
3 See 'The Syllogisms of Revealed Religion, or the Reasonableness of Christianity,' in *Owl of Minerva*, 18 no. 1 (1986) 29–42; reprinted in my *Hegel on Logic and Religion* (Albany: SUNY Press, 1992), 131–40.
4 This is introduced into the second edition of 1827.
5 Throughout this chapter I use 'singular' and 'individual' interchangeably, depending on the context. Both are legitimate translations of Hegel's '*Einzelheit.*'
6 Paragraghs 564–71. This is a developed form of the argument that I used in response to Harris's challenge at the time of the defence.
7 Up to this point Harris does not disagree.

8 Compare here Hegel's comments about the incarnations of Vishnu in the Indian religious tradition, which lack the radical singularity that the Christian tradition affirms.
9 David Kolb, in chapter 7, argues that Hegel's system is closed because there can be 'no endless sequence of yet unknown categorical possibilities.' His argument appears plausible because of an ambiguity in the term 'possible.' If 'possible' means something that is not internally self-contradictory, then there are lots and lots of such possibilities that have not been thought of. But to talk of possibilities that are 'unknown' implies that they have some kind of ontological status prior to their becoming either actual or known. In that sense of 'possibility' the genuinely novel is not possible before it is actual. Its possibility emerges only from its actuality, not vice versa. Hegel in his *Logic* derives possibility from actuality. (See my 'The Necessity of Contingency' in *Art and Logic in Hegel's Philosophy* (Atlantic Highlands, NJ: Humanities Press, 1980), 201–18, reprinted in *Hegel on Logic and Religion*, 39–51. In this, he is to be distinguished from Aristotle or Schelling. So the genuinely novel will never be a categorial possibility at present unknown.
10 In other words, logic can expect the unexpected. The paradox in that statement is dissolved when we realize that the first 'expect' talks of formal or logical possibility, while the second talks of real possibility. See above, note 9.
11 That is the same edition in which he makes it explicit that revealed religion incarnates rational judgments and syllogisms.
12 An interesting example of this phenomenon in a non-religious context can be found in John Stuart Mill's *Autobiography*. His spiritual crisis has many parallels with the mystic experience of the death of God. For the latter see my 'Is Hegel a Christian?' in D. Kolb, ed., *New Perspectives on Hegel's Philosophy of Religion* (Albany: SUNY Press, 1992), 93–108; reprinted in *Hegel on Logic and Religion*, 141–53.
13 In note 14 to chapter 7, above, David Kolb says that Hegel's logic provides a one-sided hermeneutic key to the philosophy of religion. When one considers only Hegel's lectures, such a conclusion may appear justified, but in both the *Phenomenology of Spirit* and the *Encyclopaedia* it is revealed religion that provides a necessary condition for absolute knowing or philosophy – it justifies the truth claims of the logic.

Hence it is incorrect to see the logic simply in Kantian terms as the condition for the possibility of experience (as is currently fashionable). A better parallel is Peirce's concern to discover the logic inherent in all lived action. Hegel, like Peirce, sees knowing and acting as complementary disjuncts of a single, rational discipline. If one is going to refer to Kant to understand the *Logic*, it must be to the Kant of all three critiques, not just the *Critique of Pure Reason*.
14 This is, for example, the position taken by Stephen Houlgate. See his 'World History

as the Progress of Consciousness: An Interpretation of Hegel's Philosophy of History,' *Owl of Minerva*, 22 no. 1 (1990), 79–80.
15 The qualification 'internal' is relevant. Because at this point each possibility is considered in the abstract, there is as yet no synthesis through which inconsistent combinations of possibilities can be identified.
16 Whether or not this accurately represents Tibetan Buddhism, it is at least the way Hegel viewed it in 1827.
17 'Some Similarities and Differences between Christianity and Islam,' in Kritzeck and Winder, *The World of Islam* (New York, 1959).
18 I developed this thesis that the first premise for coherent and meaningful action in the world involves an individual that integrates universal and particular in chapter 6 of *Being and Will* (New York: Paulist Press, 1977), 62–76: 'First Premises.' While I there applied the argument explicitly to the plurality of religious traditions, I had in mind the extension of the claim to secular ideologies as well.
19 Though remnants of those cults may certainly remain in current religious practice.
20 It is tempting to think that the ones that vanish will be those that have arbitrarily abstracted an historical event or individual, idealizing it to make it fit the theory, rather than allowing it to be, warts and all. But such a charge is dangerous, since it is clear that many of the stories of Jesus and Gautama, the Koran and the covenant, have been embroidered to reflect the piety of later generations. Once we discover that an individual that was supposed to be an unambiguous incarnation of ultimate truth is in fact ambiguous, it loses its authority.
21 There are, of course, many minor traditions that are equally resilient. The Parsees and the renewed discovery of Native spirituality in North America are two that come to mind.
22 Freud, in *Civilization and Its Discontents*, suggests that it is a primordial wish to return to the womb.
23 See, for example, Wilfred Cantwell Smith, *Towards a World Theology: Faith and the Comparative History of Religion* (London: Macmillan Press, 1981).
24 Preface to the *Science of Logic*, trans. A.V. Miller (New York: Humanities Press, 1967), 54.

9

Hegel's Encounter with the Christian Tradition, or How Theological Are Hegel's Early Theological Writings?

NICHOLAS WALKER

I am probably not the only reader of Hegel who, attempting to penetrate the forbidding edifice of the mature system and reconstruct the animating purpose of his philosophy, has sought illumination in the apparently more accessible earlier writings. Of course it is only in our century that the so-called early theological writings, as Hermana Nohl entitled them in 1907, have become such a privileged object of ardent debate and painstaking research.[1] During the last century these writings were certainly known to the earlier students of Hegel's development such as Rudolf Haym and Karl Rosenkranz, but it was not until Wilhelm Dilthey began his research into the genesis of Hegel's thought that any serious attempt was made to edit and publish the early manuscripts.[2] In a sense they were rediscovered, like Marx's similarly neglected 1844 'Economic and Philosophical Manuscripts,' when they were needed, when a genuine grasp of the intellectual and cultural context in which they arose could no longer be taken for granted and Hegel's intellectual world had become alien to ours, when Hegel himself had become almost 'a dead dog,' as Marx once put it, echoing Hegel's own reference to Lessing's earlier remark about Spinoza.[3] If it is true, as Hegel claimed, that the true is the whole and that the truth of the whole is the essentially self-developing result that gathers up into itself all the stages through which it has passed (*Theorie Werkausgabe* [TWA] 3, 13, and 24), then it is not unreasonable to believe that examination of the evolution of Hegel's thought could cast considerable light on its ultimate purpose and character. And since his philosophy clearly did not spring fully armed, Athena-like, from the brows of its creator, few today would deny that Nohl's publication of Hegel's so-called early theological writings in 1907 represented a crucial watershed in the understanding and critical reception of Hegel's philosophy.[4]

But why 'so-called' theological writings? Partly because Nohl's title is arguably tendentious in suggesting an overall interpretive scheme for a group of extremely heterogeneous, if internally connected, writings that cover historical, political, economic, ethical, and philosophical, as well as traditionally theological and religious, issues.[5] At the same time Nohl's controversial title names the problematic space for the question that I have taken for my title here: how theological are Hegel's theological writings? In modern times the key to the elusive secret of Hegel has increasingly been sought in the early manuscripts. J.H. Stirling wrote a book famous in its time (1865) with the imposing title *The Secret of Hegel, Being the System in Origin, Principle, Form and Matter* (2nd ed., Edinburgh: Oliver and Boyd, 1898; reprint Bristol: Theommes, 1990). It was inevitably pointed out that the author had succeeded admirably in keeping the secret to himself. Yet Stirling clearly set up the terms of the problem when he trenchantly stated that 'the secret origin and constitution' of Hegel's philosophy could be found precisely in God and further that Hegel had good claim to be regarded as *the* philosophical interpreter and justifier of the substance of historical Christianity and all its principal doctrines – an Aquinas for Protestantism, in fact. And Karl Barth, who was notoriously ambivalent about Hegel, famously asked why Hegel did not become the angelic doctor for modern Protestant thought. We should also attempt to understand why Hegel actually failed to become the philosophical defender of the faith. Franz Rosenzweig saw the attempted reconciliation of faith and reason, of religion and philosophy, as the very nerve of Hegel's thought but also identified its deeply problematic character when he described Hegel as a 'heretic within the church.'[6]

Many of the immediate members of the Hegelian school thought quite otherwise of course, and we know what one fiery spirit among them thought of Hegel's secret. If for Hegel philosophy represented the 'truth' of religion, so for Ludwig Feuerbach it is now anthropology that is the demystified 'truth' of theology (in the radical sense that chemistry is the truth of alchemy or astronomy of astrology). In *The Essence of Christianity* (1841) he wrote that he was only betraying 'the secret of the Christian religion itself' by radicalizing Hegel's admittedly inconclusive project and going beyond the half-way house of Hegel's speculative reconciliation of faith and reason. The key question is whether this inconclusiveness is a fault to be eliminated in one direction or the other, in terms of theism or atheism, or whether it might not be fundamentally constitutive of what Hegel wishes to say (in which case 'intrinsic ambivalence' rather than 'inconclusiveness' would be a more appropriate label). Feuerbach sometimes claimed – superficially enough, we might think – that religion consisted in the belief in 'ghosts.' Hegel's absolute religion was pre-eminently one of 'Geist,' and Stirling claimed that Hegel's mature philosophy of religion was nothing but a restatement of the traditional Christian conception of the Holy Spirit, or the 'Holy Ghost,' as we used to say. How then does it stand with Hegel's 'spirit' in the struggle between theism and atheism, and what would a true interpretation of religion in the spirit of Hegel be like?

But to return to the 'conflict of interpretations' with respect to Hegel. For obvious reasons Heinrich Heine has not been taken very seriously by conservative interpreters of Hegel's philosophy, as if wit and insight were incompatible bedfellows. Heine may not have been a penetrating speculative mind, but many of his stories, apocryphal or not, have a genuinely Hegelian ring to them. In a remark subsequently repeated by Kierkegaard, Heine satirized the proverbial obscurity of German philosophers: 'On his deathbed Hegel is supposed to have said 'only one man has understood me, and even he has not."' Perhaps we ought to try and extract the truth moment from Heine's exaggerations when he also claimed that Hegel composed 'the music of atheism in such abstruse signs that no one should be able to understand them.'[7] In the context of this hermeneutic problem, it is instructive to examine the first major text of Hegel where he articulates an account of the essence of Christianity and attempts philosophically to exploit the concept of spirit itself.

The most natural starting point for a discussion of Hegel's essay on the spirit of Christianity is the preliminary section, which Nohl edited as a subdivision under the title 'The Spirit of Judaism.' These pages represent a kind of *Gegenbild* to Hegel's construction of the original significance of Christian teaching. As the very anti-type of true religion, Hegel's picture of Judaism is a direct extension of his Bern reflections on heteronomous faith and the essence of positivity. The extreme distortion of authentic religion and the complete misunderstanding of the proper relationship of man to the divine, which are all that Judaism represents in Hegel's eyes at this time, here reveal by way of negation the salient characteristics of Hegel's ideal-typical form of religious union. When we read these pages we cannot fail to sense that we are moving in a new and distinctly 'Hegelian' atmosphere, even though the writing here clearly betrays the direct influence of Hölderlin's language. It is as if the exposure to Hölderlin's thought and the immediate impact of renewed personal contact have helped to liberate Hegel's thinking into its own essence, as it were. The characteristically pithy and trenchant style of Hegel's earlier writings on positivity is gradually tempered by a much more flexible 'poetic' quality, and Dilthey described this piece as the most beautiful Hegel ever wrote.

Here for the first time we sense a developing, dynamic interpretation of a wide range of human experience. Hegel's descriptive method can be called broadly phenomenological, aiming at depicting a concrete, socio-historical shape of consciousness: figures and types that embody some characteristic posture towards reality and a corresponding mode in which reality is disclosed, an internal correlation of subjective and objective moments in the ongoing process of experience.[8] The presentation in this essay of so many different forms of union thus prefigures the procedure of the *Phenomenology*, which consists in running through the whole circle of experience with all its inadequate way-stations and defective forms of subject–object relation until the subject learns to recognize itself fully. The basic thought behind Hegel's account of religious experience in this context is: as man's God is, so is he.[9] In respect of Judaism, Hegel merely extends his account in the 'Life of Jesus' and 'The Positivity of the Christian Religion,' where he had already depicted the Jewish consciousness as the exemplary case of the alienated spirit in bondage to an alien law.

The unsparingly harsh characterization of Judaism and the correspondingly unflattering portrait of the Jewish people in Hegel's writing at this time are certainly disturbing and make uncomfortable reading, but they need to be firmly placed in the context of his earlier, guiding concern with the internal link between religious positivity and political domination. It was obvious from Hegel's Bern manuscripts that his picture of Judaism was only an extension of Kant's demeaning view of this religion as the very type of fetishistic *Afterdienst* – as Kant liked to put it with Lutheran frankness – a cult of purely external, statutory observance.[10] But it was also clear that for Hegel the case of orthodox Christianity was even worse than that of Judaism, to the extent that the latter went beyond the performance of legalistic ritual and actually attempted to regulate our innermost thoughts and feelings, producing chronic guilt and self-contempt in the process. In a sense, Hegel merely interpreted traditional Christianity as a continuation of Judaism by other means, as an intensification of central features of the Judaic tradition.

Hegel's original analysis of the Jewish background – as one in which men had lost all sense of their moral dignity and the innate spark of absolute autonomy had been all but extinguished – was motivated by his awareness of the affinity between his own age and the time of Jesus. Hegel saw himself placed in an analogous situation with Jesus, who had also attempted to preach the gospel of moral self-determination in a culture where righteousness was supposedly held to consist in passive obedience to external commandments. Hegel's task lay in vindicating the claims of the absolute of pure practical reason (which is what God is according to the 'Life of Jesus') against the absolutism of despotic political authority legitimated by the doctrine of human depravity and worthlessness (*Briefe*, I, 24–5). The religiously inculcated spirit of total dependence naturally holds men in thrall to a patriarchal political system. This heteronomous relation is reproduced on the theological plane by the doctrine that posits the absolute difference between God and human nature and denies man any share in the divine. The relationship between God and man accordingly comes to be conceived on the model of master and slave. The ideological consequences of this view on the political level are obvious (and an appreciation of this essential connection between man's conception of his relation to God and his understanding of political authority remained with Hegel throughout his life and finds expression in his mature thought in his attitude to Roman Catholicism).

Hegel pursues the ultimate origin of this understanding of the divine–human relationship back into the Judaic sources of Christianity. But of course what Hegel is interested in principally is the wholly contemporary problem of the orthodox religious heritage, still very much at work in the European political present. In this respect Hegel's violent polemic against the Judaic spirit, patently unjust as it is, represents more than a reflection of the endemically anti-semitic bias of the Christian tradition, for it also constitutes a direct assault on that tradition as he understood it (and here he follows the example of the deists of the Enlightenment, as well as Kant).[11] The structural similarities between Judaic and orthodox Christian culture were grounded for Hegel in the fact that the former represents the not-yet of civic and religious freedom, while the latter documents the no-longer of freedom after the demise of the Greek city-state and the Roman republic.

The situation of the moral teacher Jesus among his people is exactly analogous to that of the *Volkserzieher* that Hegel originally aspired to be among his own contemporaries. Hegel draws an explicit parallel between the two epochs since his own time is also characterized by 'a yearning, a sighing after a purer and freer condition' ('Frühscriften,' or F, in TWA, 269). The *Volkserzieher* – the educator of the people – shares the principal aim of Jesus, one 'who wished to restore man in all his wholeness' (F 324). The religion against which the messenger of the new gospel struggles duly reflects all the 'alienated' features that Hegel had identified in the essay on positivity as the defining characteristics of contemporary Christian orthodoxy. However, the way in which Hegel characterizes the alternative form of religious relationship, in direct contrast to the perverted and alienated form, also emphatically reveals the inadequacy of anything resembling Kant's or Fichte's *Vernunftreligion* for even remotely fulfilling the second ideal criterion for a true *Volksreligion* that Hegel had long since laid down (namely, the requirement in the 'Tübingen Fragment' that 'imagination, heart and sensibility be not sent empty away' [F 33]).

The powerful, latent tensions within Hegel's original project emerge as soon as he goes beyond his own 'hermeneutics of suspicion,' beyond the negative function of exposing heteronomy and unmasking superstition. The stark contrast with Kant and Fichte is underlined by Hegel's appeal to a union of the ethical-political and the aesthetic dimensions. Both the continuity with the earlier analysis of positivity and a new readiness to criticize Kant explicitly are revealed when he says: 'What more profound truth is there for slaves than that they have a master? ... Truth is something free and open, something that we neither control, nor let ourselves be controlled by ... Something upon which we are dependent cannot have the form of truth; for truth is beauty' (F 288). Kant is gradually drawn within the sphere of Hegel's critique of the Judaic spirit by virtue of one of the most striking characteristics of his ethical and religious thought: the sublime unrepresentability to sense of the moral law in all its majesty and the deliberate extrusion of the aesthetic moment from the realm of true religion.

But the most significant feature of the Frankfurt manuscripts (collectively entitled 'The Spirit of Christianity and its Fate' by Nohl) lies in the centrality of the concept of 'Spirit' itself. These writings assume crucial importance in the story of Hegel's intellectual development in so far as his mature thought can legitimately be considered a philosophy of spirit par excellence.[12] In his first great published work and indispensable introduction to the final system, Hegel evokes the definition of the absolute in terms of spirit as 'the most sublime concept which belongs to our most recent times and to its religion' (TWA 3, 28). And it certainly cannot be said of either Fichte's radical moral philosophy of the self-positing ego or of Schelling's neo-Spinozan monistic metaphysics (however much both thinkers undeniably contributed to the conceptual formulation of Hegel's thought in the subsequent Jena period, 1800–1806) that the social and essentially intersubjective reality of spirit provides the key concept for the ultimate philosophical interpretation of experience. Since for the mature Hegel 'Spirit is properly the first name of God,'[13] and it is by means of the idea of spirit that Hegel attempts the speculative recuperation, or *Aufhebung*, of Christianity through philosophy, it is rewarding to look more closely at Hegel's first extended discussion of 'spirit' and identify the distinctive features of his approach in Frankfurt.

The text on which Hegel's philosophical interpretation of the gospel in 'The Spirit of Christianity' is preached is John 4:24: 'God is a spirit, and those who pray to him, must pray to him in the spirit and in truth' (F 382), and it is remarkable how much of Hegel's exegesis of the text remains essentially unchanged in the course of his subsequent development. In spite of the critical examination of the 'fate' of the Christian religion with which these papers are also concerned, the analysis of the incarnation and the true nature of faith in Christ clearly reveals the basic pattern of Hegel's later philosophy of religion in embryo.[14] To see this we must only be more attentive to what Hegel does with his sources here and not allow ourselves to be misled by some of the broad terminological distinctions in his writing that do undergo significant change after 1800.[15]

However, the first thing that strikes the reader about Hegel's reflections here is the clear evidence of continuity with the radical polemic conducted in the Bern writings against the exaltation of the personal authority of Jesus and the concomitant concentration on his 'name' rather than on his 'virtue,' as Hegel put it, in echo of Lessing (F 85–6). We should note Hegel's marked antipathy towards the language of 'dependence' that this appeal to authority inevitably implied (for Hegel's attitude to *Anhänglicheit* and *Abhängigkeit* see F 119–20 or F 179). The feeling of 'absolute dependence' – a phrase destined to become famous in theology during Hegel's time – typified in Hegel's eyes the relationship between man and God in traditional religion and represented nothing but the subjective manifestation of positivity within the sphere of consciousness.

Such an attitude of dependence, on the theoretical and practical sides alike, itself depends on denial of any community of nature or intrinsic identity between the rational individual and the supposed 'object' of belief. Faith directed exclusively towards another, who is regarded as qualitatively unlike ourselves in every respect and infinitely remote from us, undermines moral autonomy and destroys man's faith in himself.[16] And Hegel continues to pursue just this problem in the more extended interpretation of the relation between Jesus and the disciples in the Frankfurt papers.

Hegel's difficulties with the religious orthodoxy of his time should be recognized as the central problem that it is – one that arises inevitably from the fundamental distinction between positive/revealed religion and natural/rational religion necessarily drawn in one way or another by thinkers such as Lessing and Kant. If one were to avoid the traditional neo-Lutheran argument to the necessity of faith and the need of grace from the innate weakness of reason and impotence of the will, then acceptance of the 'revealed' truth of Christian teaching (whether by the original believer from the mouth of the founder or by the contemporary believer on the basis of the revealed word of scripture) must be reinterpreted as an expression of spontaneous assent, freely given. Such assent cannot represent purely passive reception of or submission to the 'deliverances' of revealed doctrine as something externally laid down from without' (i.e., as positive), 'as something subsisting outside of us, as something given' (F 189).[17]

For Hegel any relation other than one of active recognition or spontaneous acknowledgment 'in spirit and truth' can only serve to encourage the spirit of tutelage that is ineluctably involved in dependence on an alien authority. If the assent is not autonomous, we cannot possibly avoid the old theological logic of saving grace and all the other, associated doctrines that represent such an offence to reason on any Kantian-type Enlightenment account of morality.[18] We should not regard Hegel's attitude to the problem of saving grace and his unsympathetic approach to traditional theological dogmas simply as an expression of a limited, rationalistic sensibility on his part. Hegel's problem here is only a special case of that posed by the authoritative status of all revealed religion: the truth of revelation cannot be imposed on us externally, since we must first be able to receive or recognize it, just as we must already be in a position to accept grace, if and when it is proffered.

This problem underlay the whole of Hegel's revised version of Christ's teaching in 'The Life of Jesus.' It was a direct consequence of his bold identification of divinity with the law of practical reason in that work that God could no longer be meaningfully conceived as a personal being at all (a consequence that Schelling was prepared to draw very early on, as his correspondence with Hegel shows – *Briefe*, I, 21–2). The real focus of Hegel's interest in the 'Life' was the idea of the enlivening spirit of God in us, as his appeal to the imagery of the vine (John 15:1 ff.) clearly revealed. There Jesus addresses his disciples: 'As the shoots of a vine, which bear fruit from their nourishment upon it, and now that they are removed from it bring their burden to ripeness through their *own* living power ... You have grown into the independence ... into the freedom of your *own* will, and you shall bear fruit through the power of your *own* virtue, if the spirit of love, the power which inspires you and me alike, is one and the same' (Nohl, ed., *Hegels Theologische Jugendschriften*, or N, 126; my emphasis).

Hegel stresses, in contrast to his text, the continuing independent life of the 'branches' even after they have been separated from their original source of life in the tree.[19] Hegel had pointedly concluded his gospel account within the limits of reason alone by excluding any reference to the central mystery of the historical gospel: the supposed fact of the resurrection, which the young theological student had once dutifully echoed Storr in calling 'the coping stone of the Christian faith (Hoftmeister, *Dokumente zu Hegels Entwicklung*, or Dok., 182). With his decision to provide a rational *Auslegung der Schrift* in the Kantian manner, Hegel rigorously eliminated every possible vestige of the 'miraculous,' for he had long held this to be one of the most potent sources of 'positivity.'

In 'The Spirit of Christianity' Hegel draws together all the threads of his previous analyses, reworks the central themes, and begins to integrate them more organically with one another. For the first time he considers the resurrection in a more constructive manner and attempts to bring this 'miracle' into an intimate connection with his interpretation of the immediate relationship between Jesus and his disciples before his death and of the pentecostal descent of the spirit after it. Hegel now begins to understand that he will have to think these different moments together as so many aspects of or phases of a single process. All of his reflections come now to focus on John's treatment of the incarnation, comprehended by Hegel not as a discrete supernatural act, a miraculous incursion into the order of nature, but as the inauguration of a potentially universal historical process, a humanization of the divine, in which the transcendent God of monarchial tradition dies and is resurrected exclusively in and as the community of believers united in the spirit. The key to the 'secret of Hegel' is surely to be found here in his deepening meditations on what his friend Hölderlin later evoked as the secret mystery of the vine in his great poem dedicated to the commemoration of the fourth evangelist.[20]

In Hegel's 'Life of Jesus' we can already see the crucial significance of the emerging idea of 'recognition' beneath the more obvious Kantian appearance of the work. The implicit Platonic conception of knowledge – as a participative mode of experience possible only on the presupposition of an original, shared identity of life – explains why in the present essay Hegel can determine 'faith' as an imperfect, transitional stage on the way to 'knowledge.' Careful examination of Hegel's remarks on the christological problem and particularly of his treatment of the relationship of Jesus and his disciples reveals the seeds of the later, notorious subordination of faith to reason and the *Aufhebung* of religion into philosophy. This is not immediately apparent, since Hegel begins his discussion of the nature of true faith by contrasting *Erkenntnis* with *Glauben*, but it soon transpires that by 'knowledge' here Hegel understands a rationalistic and reflective mode of thinking that abstractly separates out the moments of a concrete, unified experience (it anticipates a salient characteristic of what *Verstand*, as opposed to *Vernunft* signifies in his mature thought). Hegel writes: 'The relationship of Jesus to God, as that of a son to a father, could be grasped in terms of either knowledge or faith, according to whether man posits the divine *completely outside of himself* or not' (F 380; my emphasis).[21] And he proceeds to identify this kind of 'knowledge' as one that fruitlessly attempts to put together what it has torn asunder and to unite the incommensurable.

Hegel suggests that those who deny the community of divine and human natures in Christ are more consequent in their reasoning (doubtless thinking here of the Arian challenge to early Christian doctrine) than those who posit the absolute difference of the human and the divine and nevertheless try to combine them in an incomprehensible unity (as, for example, in the Nicaean formulation of consubstantiality). Those who insist on the total qualitative difference of the human and divine natures 'elevate the understanding, absolute separation, the act of killing, to the highest character of the spirit' (F 380). This approach is stylized by Hegel as the 'Judaic principle,' which expresses only 'opposition in relation to the divine, the consciousness of an impassable gulf between human and divine being' (F 381). But of course this is the central principle of positive Christianity too, as Hegel had laboured at length to show in his Bern writings.[22]

In his poem 'Menschenbeifall' of 1788 Hölderlin had written: 'The slave honours only the violent; / In the divine those alone believe who share in it themselves'; and these lines capture the spirit of Hegel's reflections in this part of the essay. What I have called the Platonic model of knowledge as participative recognition structures the whole argument of Hegel's text, for, in accordance with the ancient principle of affinity that like alone knows like, 'spirit alone recognizes spirit' (F 381). Hegel here gives us a first statement of the 'speculative' relation of reciprocal self-recognition that he had sporadically suggested in his earlier writings. Already straining language to express his thinking, Hegel writes: 'The mountain and the eye which beholds it are subject and object, but between man and God, between spirit and spirit, this gulf of objectivity is not present; the one is only one and another to the other insofar as it recognizes the other' (F 381).[23] It can be seen from this passage just how concrete the source of Hegel's apparently abstract 'epistemological' philosophical concerns is. It is difficult to translate Hegel's use of the term *Erkennen*, either now or later, without overintellectualizing what he is trying to say. From now on in his writing the verb *Erkennen* always signifies much more than 'cognition' or 'knowledge' as ordinarily understood, since there are many contexts where it is not strictly distinguishable from *Anerkennen*. The emphasis is on the active process of recognition and acknowledgment, and of course the word already carries the biblical overtones of sexual 'knowledge' (the fragment on love is an important precedent for this development – F 244–50). Throughout the present text Hegel avoids the substantive *Erkenntnis* (except to indicate an inferior mode of purely factual or intellectual knowledge, as above) in favour of the verbal form, which hints strongly at mutual recognition.

It is principally because Hegel is so anxious to preserve the moment of equality and avoid any implication of hierarchy or subordination that he obviously feels it necessary to qualify the traditional image of the relation between God and Jesus as that of father and son. Like his friend Hölderlin, he constantly fears lest a patriarchal conception distort the real meaning of this relation: 'The relationship of Jesus as Son to his Father is a child-like relationship since the Son feels himself to be one in essence and in the spirit with the Father who lives in him, and it bears no resemblance to that childish relationship in which man would like to put himself with the rich lord and master of the world, whose life man feels to be utterly *alien* to his own, and with whom his only connection is through *donated* things, through the crumbs which fall from His rich table' (F 381; my emphasis).

The true model for man's relationship to the divine is to be found rather in the idea of participative identity, which does not destroy the independence or spontaneity of the human spirit. The Stoic image of the 'scintilla dei,' '*der Funken Gottes*,' which he had employed so frequently in Bern and the neo-Spinozan conception of the individual as '*eine Modifikation*' (F 304) increasingly adopted in his Frankfurt writings both mark Hegel's emphatic repudiation of the traditional theology of creaturely dependence, with its correlative conception of God as Lord or 'Herr' (and this is also the source of Hegel's later polemic against Schleiermacher's fundamental appeal to the 'feeling of absolute dependence').

It is because, in the last analysis, man spontaneously draws the truth out of himself as an innate and therefore inalienable possession that he can and must transcend the state of tutelage. In a significant passage from his 'Life of Jesus' Hegel had claimed that 'the dignity of man' was grounded in his capacity 'to draw forth and produce (*schöpfen*) out of himself the concept of the Godhead as well as the knowledge of His will' (N 88). The strength of Hegel's commitment to this absolute sense of moral autonomy explains his hostility to any other notion of creation (*Schöpfung*). There are innumerable passages that reveal Hegel's allergic response to all creationist theology: in positive religion, he tells us, 'God's rights against us and our obligation of obedience towards Him now rest upon the fact that He is our mighty Lord (*Herr*) and commander (*Gebieter*), and we His creatures (*Geschöpfe*) and subjects (*Untertanen*)' (F 191), and he specifically singles out the characteristically Kantian locution 'vernünftiges Geschöpf' for harsh criticism, stigmatizing it as a strange turn of phrase ('eine sonderbare Zusammenstellung') (F 325).

Again in the so-called *Systemprogramm* we read that the mutual positing of the world and the free self-conscious self is 'the only true and conceivable creation out of nothing' (F 234). In this connection it becomes easier to understand why Hegel was so interested in excerpting passages from German mystical authors in the mid-1790s even though there is nothing remotely 'mystical' in the usual sense about Hegel's own concerns (either now or even much later). Rosenkranz reports that Hegel collected quotations from the writings of Tauler and Eckhart (Ros. 102) from contemporary journals. But one of the excerpts printed by Nohl gives a fair indication, I think, of the spirit in which Hegel approached these texts and reveals the polemic against orthodox creationist theology particularly clearly: 'There is something uncreated and uncreatable within our souls, and that is the reasonable part in us' (Meister Eckhart, in N 367).

A number of critics and commentators have depicted Hegel's development in Frankfurt especially as a radical turn from the apparently more rationalistic concerns of the Bern period, his most overtly 'Kantian' phase, towards a more subjective, emotive, and supposedly irrational interest in 'life,' 'love,' 'fate,' and so forth. It is true that in Frankfurt Hegel resorts more frequently to the idiom of *Geheimnis* and indeed on more than one occasion employs the description *mystisch* to characterize the nature of life and love, but I do not think that the seeds of his later dialectical rationalism are difficult to detect even here. Hegel appeals to such formulations because they provide a paradoxical 'dialectical' schema more appropriate for the expression of experience than the purely analytic procedures of what he already sometimes designates as the operation of the understanding (*Verstand*).

Comparison with Kant illuminates the two men's quite different conception of the scope and function of philosophical thought. The original founding gesture of Hegel's thought as a whole, and of his philosophy of religion in particular, is his claim to comprehend the 'mysteries' of faith and to render even the most mysterious aspects of human experience ultimately intelligible. It is obvious, by contrast, that the fundamental theological moment of Kant's thought emerges most clearly whenever reason (our essentially finite, human, and non-intuitive reason, as he never fails to stress) comes up against its own limits. This is where for Kant, and in an analogous sense for Wittgenstein and Heidegger too, the mysterious announces itself in its unmasterability. The ultimate ground of finite being remains inaccessible to rational articulation and inscrutable to theoretical reason. For Kant therefore, as for Augustine, we can be said to comprehend God only in not comprehending him, to find him only in not finding him, in agreement with the tradition of negative theology. So too in the sphere of moral philosophy, for Kant we know only the mysterious 'fact' of our freedom but nothing of the real nature of the rational will, of which we can comprehend only the incomprehensibility, as he says. In addition to the unfathomable mysteries of the last questions of death and immortality (where we are ineluctably led to 'the brink of an abyss'), Kant never tires of emphasizing the 'inscrutable' (*das Unerforschliche*) in the domain of theoretical knowledge as well: like the hidden essence of gravity, natural philosophy, or the apparently teleological character of organic life, which no Newton will ever be in a position to explain.

Hegel, in contrast, strives from the first to articulate a whole that is in principle knowable and thus to banish all reference to an ultimately inaccessible 'in itself' or noumenal realm beyond the reach of possible experience. To do so requires a quite different account of 'experience' and the bold claim to appropriate without loss or residue the burden of 'revealed' religion and all its mysteries.[24] In Hegel's ambitious project what was least knowable for the critical philosophy (above all, the free subject of theoretical and practical reason, as against the 'objects' of phenomenal experience) becomes the paradigm of all explanation, and the experience of embodied spiritual self-consciousness becomes the light in terms of which everything else is proleptically interpreted.

Hegel's recuperation of Christian 'revelation' is perhaps the decisive legitimating step in the whole enterprise. Hegel worships 'in spirit and truth' before the altar of a known rather than an unknown God, and whether we regard his philosophical interpretation of historical Christianity as an expression of hubris or of humility, as a tendentious or an authentic rational hermeneutic of faith, depends on our own response to the 'revelation' that Hegel claims conceptually to redeem. For Hegel the self-articulating movement of philosophy is always already to be grasped as an intrinsic and necessary moment of the religious life itself rather than as an external reflection on a supposedly unanalysable, brute given. In the Frankfurt papers Hegel presents an explicit account of the progressive self-overcoming of the external position of faith, which (mis)takes its object as an alien essence, and of its transformation into the self-certifying witness of the spirit (Lessing's 'proof of the spirit and its power').[25]

So faith is initially grasped not as sheer ignorance but as a presentiment, a stage of intermediate comprehension, characterized by an imperfect consciousness of the identity of the believer with the 'object' of his or her belief. The possibility of spiritual advance rests on the implicit community of terms involved in the relation, though this is something that must first be raised to consciousness: 'This belief in something actual is a cognition of some object or other, something limited; and just as an object is something other than God, so too this cognition differs from belief in the divine' (F 382). Underlying the radical implications for the christological question, Hegel continues: 'Belief in something divine is only possible if there is something divine within the believer, if it *finds itself*, recovers its *own* nature in that in which it believes, even if it is not conscious that what it has found were its *own* nature' (F 382; my emphasis).

The looming 'sublation' of religion clearly announces itself in Hegel's claim that this state of implicit identity on the part of consciousness represents an 'intermediate condition between the darkness, the remoteness of the divine ... and a wholly divine life of its own, a state of confidence in itself.' The disciples find themselves in the temporary imperfect state of believing 'upon' Jesus, rather than 'in' themselves (the benighted state of tutelage prior to sun-clear enlightenment). They believe through him on God in so far as they depend on him as a master – in so far, that is, as they insist on positing a qualitative difference between his spirit and their own. Thus the faith of the disciples remains 'a presentiment, the recognition of the divine and the yearning for union with it, the desire for the same life [as the divine] ... but this is not yet the strength of the divine itself ... The belief in the divine stems from the divinity of their own nature; only the modification of divinity can (*erkennen*) recognize the divine' (F 382).[26]

The emphasis on community of essence here, far from eliminating the moment of individual subjectivity or spontaneity, is intended, I suggest, to safeguard it: 'For in each and every human being there is light and life ... He or she is not merely illuminated by a light, like a dark body which merely reflects an alien gleam ... On the contrary his or her own combustible substance is set alight and constitutes a flame on its own account' (F 382). This aboriginal identity with the divine cannot be externally imparted, cannot be 'learned' from without, and the true model for understanding what *erkennen* means here is once again the Platonic one of spiritual *anamnesis* (at least, once it has been divested of its 'mythical' form).

The fundamental *agon* between reason and revelation, the ancient variance between philosophy and religion, has surely already been resolved in favour of the former. Henceforth Hegel will make Anselm's confession ('credo ut intelligam') his own in a radical manner, and philosophy will claim to 'comprehend' the truth of the latter in the literal sense of embracing and encompassing it. Hegel later reminds us that Plato conceived the practice of philosophy as participation in the divine, and he endorses that lofty conception without reservation. Philosophy ceases to be the handmaiden of theology and becomes once more the queen of the sciences (TWA 2, 287) and constitutes the true *Gottesdienst* itself. It seems that we shall ultimately have to put off 'faith' for Hegelian 'knowledge.'

Hegel has discovered how to employ the language of *Offenbarung* without subscribing to a positive concept of revelation (the difference between the two forms, or rather stages, in the true comprehension of revelation are marked in Hegel's mature philosophy of religion by the distinction between *offenbare Religion* and *geoffenbarte Religion*). When Simon Peter finally recognizes Jesus as the Son of God, Jesus says that his Father in heaven has 'revealed' this to him: 'It did not require a revelation merely for knowledge of the divine nature; a large part of Christendom learns about this kind of knowledge.' And echoing all his early enthusiasm for Lessing, Hegel continues: 'Conclusions drawn from miracles are administered to children to prove that Jesus really is God; but this learning, this reception of belief cannot be called a divine revelation' (F 383). But Peter's confession eventually showed itself only as faith when confronted with the departure of the Master: 'A belief that had certainly felt the presence of the divine, but was not yet a fulfillment of his whole being in and through the divine, not yet the receiving of the Holy Spirit' (F 383).

This faith must transcend itself inasmuch as it is 'merely the first stage of the relationship with Jesus, which in its true fulfillment is represented as so intimate that his friends are one with him' (F 384). Hegel insists that Jesus had to depart from them and disappear as a concrete, sensible presence if the disciples were to advance beyond the stage of faith: 'As long as he still lived amongst them, they remained only believers ... Jesus was ... an individual focus upon whom they depended; they did not yet possess an independent life of their own; the spirit of Jesus ruled them; but after his disappearance even this objectivity, this partition between themselves and God fell away' (F 384). Hegel emphasizes that Jesus did everything possible to discourage this dependence and that he claimed no decisive ontological pre-eminence for himself: 'There can be no thought of a difference between the essence of Jesus and those who believed in him, in whom the belief in him had become something living, in whom the divine exists ... So it was that Jesus decisively declared himself against [the principle of exclusive] personality, against any individuality of his own essence that would be opposed to his friends (against the idea of a personal God), the ground of which essence would be an absolute particularity of his being over against theirs' (F 385 and 387).

This is why we could say that in a strictly terminological sense Hegel's religious position in the Frankfurt manuscripts is already one of principled a-theism, a position that he was never to change. In Hegel's later thought there is certainly a deepening appreciation of the speculative possibilities of the Christian tradition, an act of hermeneutic retrieval, but there is no 'return to orthodoxy' or 'rehabilitation of positivity.' All the elements that the young Hegel found objectionable about 'positive' faith remain anathema to him, and his recuperation of the tradition in terms of speculative pneumatology is far removed from traditional apologetics, and he never had any doubt that faith is properly assessed and autonomously legitimated by philosophy alone as the ultimate court of appeal.

We can see from this discussion that Dilthey's influential description of Hegel's Frankfurt thought as a form of 'mystical pantheism' is more misleading than illuminating. It certainly underlines Hegel's evident distance from an orthodox conception of a transcendent, personal deity – from traditional theism – but it overstates the supposedly mystical character of his analysis. Hegel rejects the traditional emphasis on the personal God not because he wishes to submerge the believer in an impersonal sea of life but because he wants us to reconceive the divine life as spirit (and in Hegel *das Leben Gottes* and *der Geist Gottes* must be read both as a subjective and an objective genitive), as an interpersonal, intersubjectively experienced reality that cannot be located exclusively in one authoritative or privileged individual. Hegel's real interest here, and the one that points most suggestively forward to his later philosophy of religion, is the proper interpretation of the Holy Spirit in relation to the incarnation. It is the Holy Spirit that bridges 'the distance between faith and its consummation,' for it is only 'after the disappearance of his [Christ's] individual being that their dependency upon him could cease, and their own spirit, or [sic] the divine spirit could exist within themselves' (F 388). To gather in Christ's 'name' is simply to share in his spirit and nothing more, as Hegel's translation of Matthew 10:41 makes clear: 'Where two or three are united in my spirit ... in the respect in which being and eternal life is in me, in which I am, I am in your midst, and so too is my spirit' (F 387).[26]

Notes

1 In what follows I refer mainly to the *Theorie Werkausgabe* (or TWA), in Hegel, *Werke* (Frankfurt: Suhrkamp Verlag, 1970–1), of Hegel's writings on account of its accessibility, and particularly to volume I, containing the 'Frühschriften' (F), because the long-awaited second volume of the Meiner critical edition (to contain 'Der Geist des Christentums und sein Schicksal') has still not appeared. I refer to, as N, Hermann Nohl, ed., *Hegels Theologische Jugendschriften* (Tübingen: Mohr, 1907) only when his edition contains material not reprinted in F (mainly 'Das Leben Jesu'). Other abbreviations in the text are Ros., for K. Rosenkranz, *Hegels Leben* (Berlin: Dunkler und Humblot, 1844; reprint Darmstadt: Wissenschaftliche Buchhandlung, 1971); Dok., for J. Hoffmeister, *Dokumente zu Hegels Entwicklung* (Stuttgart: Kohlhammer, 1936); GW, for G.W.F. Hegel, *Gesammelte Werke*; Br., for G.W.F. Hegel, *Briefe*; and GSA, for F. Hölderlin, *Grosse Stuttgarter Ausgabe*, in *Sämtliche Werke*, ed. F. Beissner and A. Beck (Stuttgart: Kohlhammer, 1946–85). All the translations from the German are my own.

2 When I mention the 'young' or 'early' Hegel in what follows I refer to Hegel up to 1801 when he went to join Schelling in Jena. Some have followed Merleau-Ponty and Lukács in speaking of the young Hegel with reference to the *Phenomenology*, though he was already more than 'half way on the road of our life' when he embarked on his journey of discovery. Yet it is a great merit of such readings that they do not attempt to cut the concerns of Hegel's first great published book adrift from those that animated all of his earlier work.

3 Compare Wilhelm Windelband's remark at end of the last century concerning the *Phenomenology*: 'The generation of those capable of understanding the riches of this work is dying out and it is to be feared that in all too short a time no-one will be adequate to the task.' H.S. Harris has identified this problem as one of the principal reasons for his undertaking to trace the evolution of Hegel's thought in the context of the cultural situation that shaped it and to which it was itself conceived as a practical response; 'The Use and Abuse of Hegel,' in *Contemporary Trends in Philosophy* (1976), 223–38, especially 225–6).

4 This is far less true of the anglophone literature, which has traditionally been more interested in the *Logic* and the *Encyclopaedia* and rather distrustful of the *Phenomenology*, let alone the earlier material. J.N. Findlay claimed that Hegel's thought did effectively spring into existence in this way as 'a dateless and inexplicable product of genius, not led up to quite understandably by the past of philosophy or by Hegel's own past,' and he consequently paid scant attention to the evolution of Hegel's thought; *Hegel: A Re-examination* (London: Allen and Unwin, 1958), 33.

Stanley Rosen, in his masterly and austere account of Hegel's thought, considers the early writings juvenile and overstates the reasonable case that it is 'inappropriate to base the study of a philosopher's ripe teaching on impressions garnered from the study of fragments by a boy scarcely out of his teens'; *Hegel: An Introduction to the Science of Wisdom* (New Haven, Conn.: Yale University Press, 1974), 3.

Apart from the fact that Hegel was nearer thirty than twenty when he wrote the material discussed here, it would not be inappropriate to examine the contributions of a teenager if the writer turned out to be a Hegel or a Schelling. As for religion, there is arguably much in Hegel's earlier work to support Rosen's, in certain respects quasi-Kojèvian, interpretation of the mature philosophy. However, the marked distrust and ambivalence towards Hegel's early works often shown by the best 'theologically' inclined interpreters, such as Quentin Lauer and Emil Fackenheim, is intelligible and well-grounded, as I hope to indicate here.

5 This would be even more obvious if Hegel's early manuscripts on Stewart's political economy and Kant's moral writings had survived. Thus we can better understand how Karl Rosenkranz, who probably had more of the original manuscripts before him than anyone since, was already impressed by the universality of Hegel's range and noted it as 'a fundamental characteristic of Hegel's nature that he continually developed his systematic thought in a gradual and all-rounded manner' (Ros. xv).

6 See K. Barth, *Protestant Thought in the Nineteenth Century* (London: SCM Press, 1972), 384, and F. Rosenzweig, *Der Stern der Erlösung* (Frankfurt, 1921), reprint Frankfurt: Suhrkamp, 1990, 7–12.

7 H. Heine, *Zur Geschichte der Religion und Philosophie in Deutschland* (Leipzig, 1970), 152. K.H. Ilting has strongly developed the thesis of an 'esoteric' as opposed to an 'exoteric' Hegel with respect to the Berlin period in the introduction to volume IV (pp. 45–66) of his edition of the *Vorlesungen über Rechtsphilosophie*. See also J. D'Hondt, *Hegel en son temps* (Paris, 1968).

8 See J.D. Collins, *The Emergence of Modern Philosophy of Religion* (New Haven, Conn.: Yale University Press, 1967), 223–4: 'Like Pascal before him and Kierkegaard in his own wake, he delights in working out different religious and anti-religious viewpoints from within, developing each one in its internal logic to the point where it comes into open conflict with the others, and then searching after a fresh position. These intensely developed explorations of the varieties of religious belief and disbelief provide Hegel with a concrete instance of the essentially dialectical character of all human activity.'

9 In Bern, Hegel had described the positive, alienated conception of the divine as an inverted image of man and his age, a 'Spiegel' and 'Bild seiner Zeit' (F 210). In this connection H. Busche, *Das Leben der Lebendigen*, Hegel-Studien, Beiheft 31 (Bonn: Bouvier Verlag, 1987), 192, quotes Goethe's lines: 'Was der Mensch als Gott verehrt, / Is sein eigenes Innere herausgekehrt.'

10 For Kant, Judaism hardly qualified as a religion at all, and he could see nothing in

its 'mechanischen Cultus' but the very 'Inbegriff bloss statuarischer Gesetze.' Kant also refers to the 'Sklavensinn' of the Jews and notoriously ascribed any signs of intellectual life among them to the external influence of Greek culture.

11 Politically speaking there is nothing remotely anti-semitic about Hegel's position. He rejects the idea of racial or cultural exclusivity and insists on equal civil rights and the principle of religious toleration (which was one of the main themes of the 'Positivitätsschrift'). There is nothing romantic or 'German-Christian' about Hegel's mature political thought either, as compared with so-called liberals such as Fries. See the excellent discussion of this issue in S. Avineri, *Hegel's Theory of the Modern State* (Cambridge: Cambridge University Press, 1972), 119–21 and 169. See Hegel, *Die Philosophie des Rechts*, secs. 209 and 270 – TWA, VI, 361l, 421 and 425, in particular).

12 See Nicolai Hartmann's judgment: 'Amongst the thinkers of the modern age it is Hegel who is the philosopher of spirit'; *Die Philosophie des deutschen Idealismus*, first pub. Berlin 1929 (Berlin, 1974), II, 243.

13 H.S. Harris, *Hegel's Development II: Night Thoughts (Jena 1801–1806)* (Oxford: Clarendon Press, 1983), 163.

14 As anyone can see who turns from a close reading of the central sections of 'Der Geist des Christentums' concerned with the incarnation (F 336–97, for example) to the penultimate chapter of the *Phenomenology*, 'Revealed Religion' (TWA 3, 552–74). These incredibly dense pages reproduce Hegel's argument in the Frankfurt manuscripts more closely than almost anything else he had written during the Jena period. M. Westphal, *History and Truth in Hegel's Phenomenology* (Atlantic Highlands, NJ: Humanitas Press, 1979), reveals the links between Hegel's early manuscripts and his first major work, the subject of which is in a sense nothing but the 'humanization [incarnation] of the divine essence' (TWA 3, 552).

15 As H.S. Harris has pointed out in connection with the apparent reversal of status in relation to the respective roles of 'religion' and 'philosophy' after 1800. *Hegel's Development: Toward the Sunlight (1770–1801)* (Oxford: Clarendon Press, 1972), 390–9. See also F. Chiereghin, *Dialettica del assoluto e ontologia della soggetività in Hegel* (Trento: Verifiche, 1980), 42–6.

16 Concerning the moral system of positive faith, Hegel had declared: 'The foundation upon which it is built is not a fact of our own spirit, a proposition that could have been developed from out of our consciousness, but represents [merely] something learned [from without]' (F 179) – an obvious echo of Lessing's conviction that divine revelation cannot in principle teach us anything that could not ultimately be drawn forth in the course of time by reason from experience itself.

17 For Hegel's acute sensitivity to passive reception and his distrust of external 'learning,' compare F 111, F 123, F 179, and F 224. The significant remarks on St

Anthony of Padua in the last two of these passage clearly reveal the 'transcendental' dimension of his problem concerning the conditions of the possibility of the reception of revelation in the first place.

18 I do not mean to imply that Kant's philosophy of religion can be read simply as a typical expression of the Enlightenment (for in some decisive respects we could almost claim the reverse), but as far as the autonomous grounding of morality is concerned, Kant's rejection of any special revelation is absolute. However, though he allows no heteronomous determination of the content of morality by the claims of revelation, Kant is characteristically very concerned to 'save' some of the doctrinal mysteries in his own original and complexly qualified manner (apart from the idea of original sin and radical evil, he is particularly interested in discovering rational 'practical' sense in the doctrines of grace and even in the difficult sayings of faith concerning God's 'hardening' of the sinner's heart despite their apparently predestinarian implications).

19 Chiereghin claims that the Bern writings already imply 'the death of God even if not in an explicitly declared form' in Hegel (*Dialettica del assoluto*, 28–30). It is probably less misleading to say that what we witness here is 'the death of faith based upon authority and the initiation of the age of independent spirit ... With the sacrificial death of Jesus the last authority has extinguished itself in order that this immortal death in the hearts of men should eliminate all belief in something alien and simultaneously arouse the autarchic life of reason in them'; Busche, *Das Leben der Lebendigen*, 104 and 119).

    This aspect of Hegel's thought is directly relevant to Hölderlin's contemporary work on the 'Empedokles' project, which is similarly inspired by the pathos of autonomy; see especially the 'Testament' of Empedocles in GSA, 62ff. In the 'Life,' Hegel's Jesus underlined the necessity that he depart from his followers and denies the qualitative difference between them and himself in a passage that looks back to his Tübingen sermons (Dok. 175ff.) and forward to the 'Spirit of Christianity' (F 385ff.): 'Be not cast down that I am parted from you – honour the spirit which dwells within you, hearken to its uncorrupted voice; thus although our persons are separate and divided from one another, yet our living essence is one' (N 125). Hegel himself tells us the nature of the God that does indeed die and is not resurrected: namely, the transcendent God of traditional theism, 'the abstract pure essence' or 'the abstraction of the divine essence,' as Hegel describes it in the *Phenomenology* (TWA 3, 560 and 571).

20 See the first version of Hölderlin's 'Patmos' hymn (GSA II, 167):

> The storm-bearer loved the simplicity
> Of his disciple, the watchful man
> Who closely saw the face of the God
> As they sat together at the evening meal

Before the mystery of the vine;
And in greatness of soul, with calm foreboding,
The Lord pronounced his death and ultimate love.

Compare this to Hegel's reference to the text of John in the preparatory notes for 'The Spirit of Christianity,' where he is speaking of the disciples in relation to Jesus: 'They too are one with him, an actual transubstantiation, an actual indwelling of the Father in the Son and of the Son in his followers – these all considered not as substances, simply separated from one another and united only under a universal concept, but rather as a vine and its shoots; a single living life of the divinity is within them' (F 304). And again in the main body of the text: 'The living union of Jesus [with his disciples] is shown forth most clearly in his final discourse words in John: they in him and he in them; together they are one; he is the vine, they the shoots; the same nature in the parts, one and the same life that is in the whole. It is this fulfilled state (*Vollendung*) of his friends which Jesus asks of his Father, and it is this he promises for them after he his departure from their midst' (F 384).

21 According to the essay on positivity, the essence of self-alienated, positive Christianity lay in positing the divine as an object outside the self, as a being belonging 'to a world alien (*fremd*) to ourselves ... in whose realm we have no share, where we can achieve nothing for ourselves through our own activity, but where we can only hope to gain entrance through begging or superstition' – a world where 'man himself is a non-ego and his divinity another non-ego' (F 212). Similarly, everything admirable in human nature is regarded 'as the work of a being which exists outside of us, in whom we share nothing, which is remote from us and with whom we have nothing in common' (F 210). Compare the ringing declaration in the 'Systemprogramm'; 'Absolute freedom of all spirits who bear the intellectual world within themselves and should seek neither God nor immortality *outside themselves*' (F 235).

22 With reference to St Anthony of Padua, Hegel remarks that men can respond to the truth of the gospel only because of a native capacity within themselves, not 'through something given completely independently of themselves, through support from above' (special revelation or grace) (F 224). But the Christian religion 'becomes glaringly positive when human nature is utterly separated from the divine, when no mediation between them is permitted, except exclusively through *one* individual, when on the contrary all human consciousness of the good and of the divine is debased until it is stupefied and annihilated in a faith which believes in something utterly alien and overpowering' (F 224–5).

23 Compare Hegel's remarks in the Tübingen Fragment (F 30): 'Love which ... finds itself in other human beings or rather, forgetful of itself, puts itself forth from out of its own existence and lives, feels and acts as it were in others.' Karl Rosenkranz, the first commentator to look through Hegel's early papers for the preparation of his

biography, was immediately struck by this passage: '[Hegel] found a dialectical character in the movement of love, which passes over from itself into something other than itself and finds itself at home in the other, only to return again to itself in order to externalize itself once more' (Ros. 46). In this connection we should remember the literal, etymological significance of the word 'speculation.' Similarly, in the preparatory studies for the essay on positivity: 'Why do we not recognize in virtuous human beings, that they are not only flesh of our flesh, bone of our bone, but feel with moral sympathy that this is spirit of our spirit, power of our power?' (F 96). Also the Frankfurt fragments: 'Love can only transpire towards our equals, towards the mirror, the echo of our being ... Religion is one with love. The beloved is not opposed over against us, he is one with our being: we see only ourselves in him, and yet again he is not ourselves; a miracle that we cannot grasp ... True union, authentic love only transpires amongst living beings who are equal in power ... In love life finds itself again as a duplication of itself, and as a unification of itself' (F 243, 244, and 245).

For similar imagery with reference to this exemplary 'speculative' relation in the Jena period cf. the 'Differenzschrift' (TWA 2, 19) and the 'System of Ethical Life.' The most condensed mature statement of the speculative movement of self-recognition, which clearly reveals the connection with Hegel's earliest reflections on the dialectic of love, can be found in the *Phenomenology* (TWA 3, 145 and sec. 436) and the addition in the *Encyclopaedia* (TWA 10, 226–7).

24 Hegel's attitude to the hidden mysteries of faith and the nature of revealed religion is made very clear at the end of the 1805–6 Jena philosophy of spirit: 'But the absolute religion is that depth which has emerged into the light ... true religion insofar as the absolute being is spirit, manifest religion without mystery, for God is the self, God is man' (GW, 8, 282). In the *Phenomenology*: 'The mystical is not the concealedness of mystery or unknowing, but consists rather in the self knowing itself one with the [divine] essence which is thus made manifest' and the reference to the transformation of 'the mystery of bread and wine' into the higher, self-disclosing 'mystery of flesh and blood' (TWA 3, 526–7).

25 Expressing it in the language of the rationalist tradition, which reproduces the original Platonic distinction between 'doxa' and 'episteme,' we could say that we are still confined to the intermediate realm of 'confused knowledge,' which must be further developed towards ultimate self-transparency. In the *Phenomenology* *Vorstellung* stands to *Begriff* as doxa to episteme, as presentiment (*Ahnung*) to fulfillment (*Vollendung*') (TWA 3, 573). Faith is not yet 'fulfilled' until it has moved beyond the 'objectivity' that characterizes the 'form of representation' (560). Faith as consciousness still harbours the tendency to seek the risen one in the grave, for in its essential dependency it only recognizes 'this objective individual, but not itself, as spirit' (556). For spirit at the stage of consciousness as opposed to self-

consciousness, the divine still appears to it as if 'revealed by an alien being, and in this the thought of spirit it does not recognize itself' (560), since the self-revelation of God to spirit is not yet grasped as the revelation by spirit of itself but is reified instead as 'the act of an alien benefaction' (573).

26 See the first appearance of 'absolute spirit' as such in the *Phenomenology*, which seems inspired by the same text: 'The word of reconciliation is the spirit actually present ... a reciprocal recognition which is absolute spirit ... the God manifest amongst those who know themselves as pure knowledge' (TWA 3, 493 and 494). Hegel says further that 'God is attainable only in pure speculative knowing, and he exists only in that knowledge, and he is simply that knowledge itself, for he is spirit.' One is reminded of Bernard Bosanquet's remark that the most difficult thing to learn is to accept that great thinkers sometimes mean precisely what they say. H.S. Harris points out that, either by accident or by design, in one of his earliest excerpts Hegel altered references to 'God's spirit' and 'our spirit' in his source text to read simply 'the spirit' (*Toward the Sunlight [1770–1801]*), 25.

10

'Wie aus der Pistole':
Fries and Hegel on Faith and Knowledge

GEORGE DI GIOVANNI

[The] goal [of Hegel's philosophy] is to bring the kingdom of the spirit down to earth ... and raise the quest itself into wisdom, by making it terminate in knowledge (Spirit's knowledge of itself) rather than in faith.

Hegel turned the speculative tradition of Christian panentheism into a properly critical philosophy – i.e. one in which 'God' has *no* transcendent status whatever, being only the *Gestalt* in which the transcendental structure of experience appears as a *whole*.

H.S. Harris, *Hegel's Development II: Night Thoughts (Jena 1801–1806)*[1]

I

Much has been said about Kant's strategy of making room for faith while subjecting its claims to the controls and limits of reason.[2] This reaction is understandable, for the strategy had undoubtedly been an imaginative and appealing way of harmonizing the Enlightenment's otherwise-divided loyalties to faith and reason. And it also was to set the stage for much of the nineteenth century's reflection on the same duality. Yet the importance of Kant's work should not blind us to the fact that, though the outline of his strategy was already clearly visible in the first edition of the *Critique of Pure Reason* (1781), its possibilities were vividly brought home to the general public only in the course of the controversy over Lessing's alleged Spinozism occasioned by the publication of Jacobi's *Letters to Mendelssohn on Spinoza* (1785).[3] Reinhold was the first to appeal to Kant's new critique of reason as a medium for reconciling the otherwise-intractable opposition between philosophers and believers evidenced by Jacobi's book.[4] The controversy influenced Kant himself and also had its effect on Fichte. Most important for our purposes, however, is the fact that the psychological turn that philosophy took in Germany at the beginning of the nineteenth century was to be the work of individuals who were, like Schleiermacher, Bouterweck, and Fries, either Jacobi's disciples or his sympathizers. This psychological revolution – if I may call it so – had major consequences for the nineteenth-century debate on the relationship of reason to faith. However philosophically significant Kant's compromise between faith and reason, it was eventually hijacked, so to speak, reformulated, and passed on to later generations, by Jacobi and his group.

This is not the place to discuss the philosophy of Friedrich Heinrich Jacobi or relate the history of Kant's reception in the nineteenth century. My intention is rather to clarify Hegel's position on the relationship of faith to reason by contrasting it with that of Jakob Friedrich Fries (1773–1843), a contemporary of Hegel's and a Jacobi sympathizer. To this end I concentrate on Fries's doctrine of faith. How, and why, this doctrine was eventually to provide a direct link between Kant and the nineteenth century, which bypassed Hegel, can be seen by first considering its historical and conceptual context.[5]

Though Kant had severely restricted the scope of reason in determining the truth about things as they presumably are in themselves, he had still granted as much autonomy to it, as an activity of the human mind, as any rationalistic system could require. Reason, according to Kant, is a law-generating faculty. At such, it determines a priori, through its ideal representations, the shape of what counts for us as the real world. Of course, in Kant's scheme of things the possibility is left open that reason's ideal constructs, however subjectively necessary, might bear no relation to the order of things in themselves and are therefore mere tools of self-delusion. Kant had, however, held this possibility in check by identifying two points in experience where the works of reason can be tested against transcendent reality.

First, at the theoretical level of experience, reason's ideal constructs must be shown to be relevant to the work of the understanding. The special function of this faculty of the mind is to determine a priori, on the basis of the mind's subjective requirements, not just how things must be conceived, but how they must actually appear to us in sense experience. To be sure, sense appearances are valid only for us. They none the less bear a relation to independent reality, in virtue of which they significantly limit the range of what we can accept as real even if only for us. Kant's claim in this respect was a very strong one, and his contemporaries did not fail to notice it. They understood that the aim of the *Critique of Pure Reason* had been not to abolish metaphysics but to re-establish it on a new basis. Kant had sought to establish a priori the principles of a science of nature.[6]

Second, at the practical level, when reason legislates, it does so autonomously

– with the implicit certainty that, in formulating a law, it establishes the order of a world that exists in itself. Reason acts in its full capacity as reason precisely when it determines how things ought to be – not just as they happen or appear to be. Here the reality test for reason's activities is its very commitment to create a world according to its own laws. When reason acts, it spontaneously considers itself as giving rise to effects on the side of things in themselves. Of course, because of the limitations of sense experience, it can have no direct intuition of these effects. Yet its commitment to a rational world – its sense of duty – is an integral dimension of its activity and, as such, an existentially undeniable fact. This same commitment, according to Kant, also causes us to believe in the reality of the conditions – to wit, an omnipotent God and an immortal soul – in virtue of which we can at least hope to see the work of reason eventually realized even in the world of appearances. In this way, by informing faith with moral motives and thereby bringing it under the control of reason in general, Kant thought to have preserved the substance of traditional religious belief while respecting the claims of rationality.

Kant's strategy was indeed formidable. Its most striking feature, when looked at globally, is the pivotal role of reason, considered as an autonomous source of activity. And this is a feature that could well go lost in the format of the *Critique of Pure Reason*, in which Kant gave at least the impression of assuming a multiplicity of faculties of the mind, without making explicit how, in the overall scheme, the work of each was a function of rationality. Reinhold could not be blamed therefore when, in his attempt to make Kant more intelligible and hence acceptable, he tried to systematize the *Critique* on the basis of a single principle and chose the 'faculty of representation' as this principle.[7] To represent is an idealizing activity, and fundamentally a function of reason.

Reinhold's project, however, suffered from many shortcomings, and it made even more obvious the weak point of Kant's strategy, thereby rendering it all the more vulnerable to attack in the sceptical *Ænesidemus*, which was soon to come.[8] It became clear from the success of the attack that Kant had not demonstrated to the satisfaction of his contemporaries that the categories of the understanding are found realized, even when schematized, in the senses. The most that he had done was to exhibit their determinations at the level of imagined experience. He had not foreclosed the possibility that in sensation we are only immediately aware of a stream of purely rhapsodic events, or that the orderly sequence of events, which are the object of our sciences and which we presume to be appearances of the thing in itself, is in fact an imagined construct that we superimpose on the sensations for strictly subjective purposes.

This meant that reason could not rely on the understanding to test through its medium, as Kant required, the existential relevance of its ideas. And if reason had no such test for its theoretical constructs, its moral ones became just as suspect. If, theoretically speaking, reason can deal only with a world of make-believe order, why should anyone suppose that anyone's commitment to live by it is more than just a gesture – an empty intention, perfectly adequate for a life of make-believe but in no way sufficient as incentive for real action? All the talk about duty may be only a mask to cover the natural and unconscious causes that in fact move us to action.

In brief, all that Kant had done was to give a brilliant account of the assumptions about ourselves and the world at large which, as a matter of fact, we make in science and in morality. He had not, however, demonstrated their validity, and to this extent he had not gone further than any sceptic. Kant could have tried of course to validate reason's ideas by claiming that they are the expression of a faith in freedom, God, and the immortality of the soul, which, as a matter of fact, we all share and which provides (again, as a matter of fact) the fundamental motive of our actions. But in that case he would have still not exceeded what any sceptic would also grant. Reason wold not be containing faith (as Kant wished), but, on the contrary, it would be contained by it.

The strategy of Fichte's early *Wissenschaftslehre* (as Fichte renamed 'philosophy') was intended to meet precisely this objection against Kant.[9] Fichte began with the recognition that the autonomy of reason is the centre-piece of Kant's philosophy and that, if the latter had to be reconstructed systematically, its architectonic must depend on precisely the idea of such autonomy. But, to be consistent with this idea, the *Wissenschaftslehre*'s relation to its object had to be a special one. Like Reinhold's theory of representation, Fichte's new science had to be a product of reflection: its aim was the 'representation of representation.' It could not, however, simply discover its object through some sort of internal inspection (as in Reinhold), because, to the extent that its object was indeed so discovered, it was just a 'thing' and not the freely performed act that any expression of reason *ex hypothesi* is. In order to be faithful to its intended object, therefore, the *Wissenschaftslehre* had to do both: generate its object (*ex nihilo*, as it were) and reflect on it. Thus the Fichtean philosopher had to consider his decision to engage in the project of the *Wissenschaftslehre* as itself an expression of freedom – indeed, its highest possible expression, because it is not bound to any end except its own fruition – and the *Wissenschaftslehre* itself as the reflective attempt to objectify it. The *Wissenschaftslehre* is at once spontaneous performance and reflective awareness of this performance – or, more precisely, the product of freedom's spontaneously undertaken resolve to know itself as freedom. Purely speculative reason is born of this attempt.

Fichte's new science therefore was a highly personal affair. It depended on the free choice of individuals to engage in it for its very object – in other words, not just extrinsically, as every science must inasmuch as it is a human activity, but in order to understand itself. It formally presupposed a certain moral commitment and the implicit certainty – which its task was to justify by defining the conditions of its possibility – that that commitment could be realized.

Fichte cannot therefore be altogether blamed if he thought of himself – unwisely perhaps – as philosophizing in the spirit of Jacobi. In his *Letters on Spinoza*,[10] Jacobi had attacked the Berlin philosophers on the ground that their science was nothing but the product of empty abstraction; for the sake of their compulsive need for order and unity of experience, they had mistaken conditions of reflection for conditions of existence, thought for being, and had sacrificed individuality, freedom of choice, and everything that counts most in human existence, to the altar of universal explanation. And here was Fichte, who, on the contrary, made science formally depend on individual commitment to a moral existence, and the purpose of all reflection to articulate what had to be an unshakeable faith in freedom implicit in all experience. On the face of it, Jacobi could not have asked for more.

Fichte thought equally that he had met the sceptical attack by Ænesidemus on Kant. Like Kant, and even more so, Fichte was saying that every judgment of experience entails a 'posit,' a certain decision as to what counts for us as 'reality.' Ænesidemus had not denied this thesis of Kant's but had concluded from it that the objectivity of every conceptual determination – notably, that of Kant's *a priori* principles – must therefore remain always open to question. Fichte's reply now was that Ænesidemus's conclusion follows only if 'being,' and not 'freedom,' were the ground of objectivity. The *Wissenschaftslehre*, however, establishes not what things are, but what they ought to be. Nature must therefore ultimately remain for it, and for us, only a speculative idea, because for us nature can only be in itself what it ought to be for us, in order that we may live as free individuals before it.[11] And the fact that it does not actually appear in experience as conforming to that idea is not as important as that we none the less act with respect of it in terms of the idea. Indeed, we should not expect ever to find our idea of nature realized in experience, for if we did it would mean that our freedom has become a 'thing,' that it is no longer freedom, and that we have therefore lapsed from our moral stand point. Fichte had made an asset of Kant's inability, on which Ænesidemus had capitalized, to effect in a judgment of perception (*Wahrnehmen*) his desired transition (*Übergang*) from reflection to immediacy, from category of the understanding to sensation.

Jacobi of course would have nothing of Fichte's gestures in his direction. What he advocated was a form of empirical realism à la Thomas Reid (to whom he referred),[12] based on immediate awareness of our freedom, and of things outside us.[13] He called this awareness, which fosters knowledge dependent on historical and empirical observation, 'faith,' since it defies demonstration.[14] It had nothing to do with Fichte's 'moral faith' or with his 'intuition of freedom.' And Jacobi made this point most incisively in his famous open letter to Fichte (1799),[15] at the height of the 'Atheism dispute.' Already adumbrated in that letter is the criticism against speculative thought, which, whether it came from Kierkegaard, Marx, or Nietzsche, was to become standard in the nineteenth century – namely, reflective thought is an essentially self-deceptive activity, for its conclusions are self-validating and therefore hide the real causes that actually motivate it. Jacobi made his point, relying, as usual, more on metaphor and intuition than on argument. Fries was soon to repeat it, however, in systematic form.

II

Unlike Jacobi, who had strong pietistic leanings but had learned his philosophy at the feet of the French *philosophes* in Geneva,[16] Fries received his formation in the schools of the Moravian Brethern in Niesky and Barby.[17] He was prevented from proceeding with his theological training because of his aversion to the quietism of the brethern. He thereupon pursued secular studies, first in Leipzig, and then at Jena, where he attended Fichte's lectures. He conceived the basic ideas of his philsophy during this first sojourn at Jena in 1797–8 but expanded them into a system only during a second stay in 1801–5, which coincided with Hegel's presence there. His position, which, as we see below, suffers from internal inconsistency, can be summed up as follows.

Because of the many ambiguities in the *Critique*, Kant had led his followers (notably Reinhold and Fichte) into two errors, which he had very probably incurred himself. The first was to think that we know that sensations are the effects of things in themselves and that sense experiences are therefore the appearances of these things.[18] The second was to think that through the categories we can determine a priori the constitutive principles of a science of nature.[19] Because of these errors, Kant had made his whole critical theory vulnerable to the sceptical attack of Ænesidemus, with which Fries could not but sympathize.[20]

Fries countered these two alleged errors with two claims.[21] First, sensations are strictly mental events; hence, to the extent that they reveal anything, they are only appearances of the mind. This claim was enshrined by Fries in a distinction that he claimed to have been the first to define – namely, between what he called empirical truth and transcendental truth.[22] Empirical truth depends on the accuracy of the observations that we perform on the mind in order to establish its content (including the sensations that we find in it). Inasmuch as this truth entails comparison at all, such activity must limit itself to the mind – it must be performed between two or more reflective accounts of the mind's content, and its only aim can be to determine which of these accounts, on the basis of direct observation, is the most faithful to the facts of consciousness. Transcendental truth, on the contrary, entails by definition a comparison between the mind and things as they presumably are in themselves. In fact, however, we are limited in experience to the mind.[23] And since therefore every comparison between the latter and external reality must at the end turn out to be only a comparison between one conception of that reality and another – both subjective – any existential commitment regarding it must ultimately be done on faith. In today's debate between phenomenalists and neo-realists or physicalists, Fries would squarely line himself on the side of the phenomenalists.

The second claim accompanied a criticism directed against both Hume and Kant. Kant had unfortunately followed Hume in uncritically accepting the classical prejudice that science must be based on demonstrable principles.[24] But whereas Hume had therefore denied that science, in the strict traditional sense, is possible, the prejudice had led Kant to the misguided attempt to prove a priori that the categories apply to sense experience. He had tried to generate a set of allegedly synthetic, yet a priori, principles of the science of nature. The attempt had been a dismal failure[25] – an outcome that could have been predicted, because, contrary to past prejudice, true science can be based only on simple and discursively undemonstrable observations. The function of 'critique' can therefore be not to provide the constitutive principles of science but rather to establish the method to be pursued in obtaining adequate observations and in joining them together into a body of scientific knowledge. As Fries never tired of repeating, 'The only essential element of Kantian philosophy is its critical method.'[26]

Presupposed by the two claims was the assumption, explicitly made by Fries, that all knowledge ultimately rests on intuition.[27] According to Fries, Kant had realized that much, as his insistence on the need to find a sensible content for the categories of the understanding demonstated. But Kant had again fallen victim to long-standing prejudices – specifically, in this case, to the habit of conceiving the senses, the understanding, and reason as if they were totally heterogeneous parts of the mind. The result had been that, within the mind, he had unduly restricted intuition to the senses and had then found it impossible to relate intuition significantly to the conceptions of the other two faculties.[28] Fries claimed that, on the contrary, the mind is essentially reason, and reason is essentially a faculty of reflection – a power of at once intuitively perceiving itself and expressing itself in a representation.[29] Neither intuition nor reflection could possibly be independent activities, because, as Kant had recognized, an intuition that is not reflectively aware of itself would be nothing for us, and a reflection that is not the representation of something already in our grasp would be just an empty gesture.[30]

Now, according to Fries, reason reflectively perceives itself at one level of experience as aroused (*erregt*) to activity by certain events that we, considering them in abstraction, call 'sensations' (*Empfindungen*). This (again, according to Fries) is a matter of fact, and so too is the circumstance that, on the one hand, these sensations occur as scattered events apparently unrelated to one another and, on the other hand, reason naturally tends (because of its reflective nature) to conceive its objects as unities. Accordingly, reason equally perceives itself as engaged in the activity of synthesizing sensations in accordance with rules of order, which it also establishes reflectively. It is one reason that reflectively perceives itself both as aroused to reflection by sensations and as reflecting on its consciousness of these sensations. Yet the two – reason's reflective unity, and the manifold of sensations – must remain irreducibly distant from one another, because of the spatio-temporal character of sensations (their 'mathematical form'), which renders them by nature incapable of complete determination. Reason's perfect unity must therefore remain only an 'idea,' and its principles only heuristic rules of synthesis, never constitutive laws of nature.[31]

Here we come to Fries's most characteristic thesis, certainly the one most influential in the nineteenth century. According to Fries, Kant had defined the understanding's rules – its categories – in their most abstract form possible, where they form a system of mutually supporting propositions, but at the price of their amounting to no more than a formal syntax. If Kant had succeeded in demonstrating that this syntax applies to the world of sensations as well, he would have realized his dream of a new science of nature based on *a priori* principles. But he had accomplished no such feat. His talk about apodictic science had only obfuscated the one important fact about the understanding's categories – whatever binding power these categories have over the mind results from the fact that they are highly abstract, reflective, expressions of laws that govern the mind as a natural entity and that the mind itself can intuitively establish through rational reflection. It follows that all science is some form or other of psychology, for it everywhere consists of a reflective inventory of the intuitively grasped content of the mind. And philosophy is *scientia prima* only because it discovers and defines the natural laws according to which the mind spontaneously organizes its contect. Philosophy is psychology *tout court*, or, better still, anthropology.[32] In 1828 Fries titled the second edition of his major work – originally published in 1807 as *Neue Kritik der Vernunft* – *Neue oder anthropologische Kritik der Vernunft*.

Appealing to the authority of an early, pre-critical essay of Kant's, the method that Fries prescribed for philosophy was regressive analysis and exposition of the content of the mind.[33] Philosophy cannot and should not try to imitate the apodictic method of mathematics, which, according to Fries, constitutes a special case, since it can test its ideal constructs against the intuitions of space and time.[34] Rather, philosophy must proceed by resolving the mind's content into ever-simpler elements, which it then methodically reassembles into progressively larger and more coherent totalities. To be sure, this analysis depends on the abstractions that reason periodically performs on the content of sense experience to determine what will count for it as an original element. Such repeated abstractions also establish the principles that guide reason in its further analyses and subsequent reconstructions. And, since every abstraction always entails an element of arbitrariness (for abstraction is contingent on what reason happens to focus on at any given time), philosophical demonstrations are always open to revision. They all are, to some extent at least, artificial (*künstlich*) productions.

None the less, within the limits of an avowedly ongoing process of analysis and reconstruction, philosophical reflection can determine an area of acceptable truth through the reciprocal processes of ever enlarging the scope of its methodical reconstructions (thereby bringing them ever closer to a full representation of everyday experience) and justifying the principles that it uses as guide in this process through the results that it obtains.[35] This method, according to Fries, naturally leads to 'critique,' or to the reflective abstration of the rules that govern all experience. Such a 'critique' ought to precede (again, according to Fries) all scientific investigation. Under no circumstance, however, can philosophy ever provide a proof (*Beweis*) for either its theories or its principles. It only justifies them by way of exposition (*Aufweisung*) or *Deduktion* – this last, a term that Fries obviously uses according to its Latin root of 'leading' the mind, presumably in a process of discovery.[36]

It follows from the idea of experience implicit in Fries's analysis of the philosophical method that that of the particular sciences cannot substantially differ from it. The sciences cannot pretend to offer apodicitc knowledge. Nor can they rely on induction or generalization. This is another empiricist myth that Fries was eager to explode.[37] No less than philosophy, the sciences must proceed, contrary to both rationalist and empiricist claims, by way of abstractive reflection on the content of sense experience. And, since all abstraction entails an element of arbitrariness, it also follows that they too, no less than philosophy, are artificial products, contingent on individual circumstances. 'For [science] is in general only a product of men's culture,'[38] as Fries says. Accordingly, Fries distinguishes between the historical certainty attained in virtue of direct observation of the sense data, and the certainty attained by way of reflective systematization in the form of theoretical totalities of the same data. The one certainty is objectively grounded; the other, subjectively. The two differ in kind, not just by degree. Neither can therefore either replace or approximate the other.[39] Science itself operates on the strength of the two, translating into subjectively based theories the experiential data of which it is objectively certain through direct observation.

Here is, however, where we meet the inconsistency in Fries's position alluded to above. For one would expect that, since the distinction between sensation and conceptualization, or between observation and reflection, must itself be the artificial product of an abstractive reflection, the two – historical observation and reflective theory – must be only ideal limits. One would expect Fries to claim that, in actual fact, there is no reflection that does not feed on intuition, and no intuition that is not directed to its object by reflection – or, again, that every sensation, even one that to us appears as the simplest, already entails a historically reformable judgment about its object, or is already theory laden, and that every reflective act, no less than any natural object, is itself open to historical reformation.

In fact, however, Fries never makes any clear statement to this effect.[40] On the contrary, despite his insistence on the unity of the mind, his concern is to stress the irreducible difference between observation and theory, as if there could be an area of historically ascertained facts immune to theoretical doubt (because immediately accompanied by consciousness) and an area of reflectively achieved order that is not to be disrupted by historical discovery (because exhaustively defined through self-observation).[41] Fries gives at least the impression of believing that philosophy (when turned psychology) can yield through the art of self-observation that very exhaustive inventory of the mind's content that Kant had hoped for.[42] But of course, just because Fries has restricted empirical truth to an examination of the mind, he cannot very well draw any clear-cut distinction between 'consciousness' and 'self-consciousness,' or between a supposed immediate datum and a product of reflection. Even within the confines of empirical truth as defined by him, Fries, no less than Kant, is still vulnerable to sceptical attack.

III

Fries did not perhaps appreciate his vulnerability because he thought that he had dealt with scepticism at a completely different level of reflection. There was another side to Fries's theory – the most important, so far as he was concerned – which showed that he had learned not only from Hume and Ænesidemus but from Reid and Jacobi as well. 'Transcendental truth' retains for Fries a positive meaning, because, as he claims, the fundamental intention that motivates all our judgments is to express reality as it is in itself. Though we can never justify such judgments except in terms of what is present in the mind to us, in cognition we still have the implicit certainty that, in saying something about reality for us, we also express something about reality in itself.[43] In other words, the fundamental assumption underlying all experiences, even the most primitive, is that all our objects are (or ought to be) appearances (*Erscheinungen*) of a transcendent thing in itself. That we make this assumption – indeed, that we even cannot escape making it – is, according to Fries, a fact of experience and an object of internal intuition.[44] No human being can deny the fact – hence, no philosopher should. The most that philosophy can accomplish is to justify it reflectively, just as we justify any fundamental fact of the mind and thereby raise it to the status of theoretical principle.[45]

It follows that the true tension within experience is not between what exists only for us (and hence lacks ultimate standing in being) and what exists in itself, but between the finitude of our representations and the infinite object that we constantly try to perceive through them.[46] And this tension would be a mere play-acting – nothing to motivate the movement of experience effectively – if, everywhere in our experiences, we were not actually in contact with the infinite object we seek to comprehend. According to Fries, in experience reality actually manifests itself to us as it is in itself, albeit in a way consistent with the limits of our subjectivity.[47]

This was a strong claim to make, much stronger than anything that could be found in Kant. Yet Fries also did not say that we know anything determinate about reality per se.[48] In this respect he followed Kant and went even further than he by explicitly denying that we can prove (*beweisen*) that the objects of experience are appearances of the supposed 'thing in itself.' Fries chided Reinhold, and to a certain extent Kant himself, for having attempted precisely such a proof, thereby placing themselves in the impossible situation of comparing two terms, one of which (the thing in itself) escapes us altogether.[49] So far as Fries was concerned, we can never escape the limits of our subjectivity. And there is no point in appealing, as Fichte had done, to a presumed 'intellectual intuition,' for any such intuition, if there were one, would be nothing to us unless first conceptualized and, to this extent, subjected to the limits of the mind.[50]

Fries's full position thus included two apparently contradictory claims. On the one hand, the 'thing in itself' cannot be to us just an empty point of reference – the mere product of abstraction and inference. Its presence in experience, as it is in itself, must be, on the contrary, something real to us. On the other hand, this presence cannot be the object of an intuition, as is the case with empirical objects. It must therefore somehow be the object of a judgment, however primordial and spontaneous. In other words, the circumstance that all our objects are the appearances of a transcendent and absolute reality, though not itself the object of an inference, must none the less constitute an object of interpretation and hence entail reflection.

But – we may ask – how can the 'thing in itself' both be really present to us in experience yet not be the object of either intuition or inference? Fries's full answer is that we are aware of that presence because of reason's awareness of its own transcendence with respect to the objects of sense intuition. In virtue of this awareness, reason is immediately convinced that it belongs to a higher realm of existence – one not subject to the contingencies of space and time – and, on the basis of this conviction, it spontaneously judges all objects of experience to be finite, though genuine, appearances of a transcendent reality. This judgment has objective form, in the sense that, however spontaneous, it still conforms to the rules of reflectivity. Yet, since it is based on feeling and therefore lacks the determination of what normally counts as scientific or historical knowledge, it does not yield cognition proper. We must say therefore that it is an expression of faith. This faith is such a primordial, such an immediate state of mind, that we require a deliberate reflection to bring it to explicit consciousness.[51] None the less, that we have this faith, and that this is an essential element of the mind's economy, are facts open to empirical inspection and hence the object of scientific knowledge.[52]

Closely connected with the state of mind called 'faith' is the phenomenon of feeling (which is not to be confused with sensation).[53] The faculty of feeling lies precisely in reason's ability to reflect at will and to pass judgment immediately, without going through any process of inference. It is a function of reason's spontaneity.[54] Accordingly, Fries speaks of a 'feeling for truth,' a 'self-trust,' which guides reason in its immediate judgments, especially in moral matters.[55] Fries's theory of feeling is an intricate one, and we need not dwell on it here. According to Fries, however, we become reflectively aware of the nature of faith and of its role in experience only on recognizing the failure of empirical cognition ever to apprehend as such the real object (namely, reality itself) towards which reason is in fact always directed.[56] The objects of faith are reflectively expressed in negative form, precisely as what surpasses the limitations of experience. In this way we form such purely negative ideas as that of the Infinite, or of the Good per se, or of the Sublime.

On this point of doctrine, Fries closely followed Kant's *Critique of Judgment*. Yet Fries, unlike Kant, insisted that, though the ideas in which we express our faith are even more an artificial product of reflection and abstraction than any of the concepts of science, and though their content cannot ever be instantiated in experience, they do have cognitive value.[57] This is so not only because these ideas provide points of reference for the mind by which the latter can orient itself in its search for empirical truth, but because we, in entertaining them, discover possibilities in us and in our world that we would otherwise miss. There is more for Fries than just a lack of opposition between faith and reason. The two are positively related, for faith is the matrix on which reason feeds and within which it evolves its science.

Fries thus identifies, intertwined with empirical cognition (*Wissen*) and faith in objective reality (*Glaube*), a third kind of mental phenomenon, which he characterizes as 'intimation' (*Ahndung*). Intimation is the feeling that, in the presence of natural objects, we are actually in contact with realities that transcend the whole of nature.[58] Intimation is what fuels the arts, religion, and morality; it, more than anything else in the mind, is subject to the arbitrariness of individual creation. Yet it should not be mistaken for *Schwärmerei*, for, unlike the unruly divinizing of a religious fanatic, genuine intimation can and must know its limits.[59] Like the many human activities that it animates, it has a social dimension. It can therefore be educated along with the society whose growth it fosters. Fries's social theory (which, again, we need not consider here) is closely connected with his doctrine on faith and his theory of the arts.

IV

Fries established friendly relations with Jacobi only after moving to Heidelberg, soon after his departure from Jena in 1805. Jacobi appreciated Fries's estimate of the power of reason and quickly began to rely on his system for an expression of his own views.[60] Fries, for his part, could with justice feel that he finally had given philosophical form to Jacobi's intuitions regarding the nature of true knowledge. He had satisfied Jacobi's realism; he had granted that all cognition is fundamentally intuitive and historical; he had done justice to Jacobi's early insistence that true reason must be a form of sensibility;[61] most of all, he had made good Jacobi's contention that scientific knowledge is the product of an abstractive *Wiederbewußtsein*. The only point that he had not conceded was that reflection is essentially falsifying. On the contrary, by identifying its proper function within the life of the mind, Fries could claim that he had finally established the basis for an integral connection between reflection and concrete experience (which includes faith).

The ultimate criticism that Fries was then able to raise against all his predecessors was precisely that they all had allowed theory to be divorced from actual, ordinary experience.[62] The objection echoed Ænesidemus's original objection against Kant and Reinhold – that they had been guilty of 'formalism': they had forced a web of empty logical forms onto the otherwise-rich content of real experience.[63] Jacobi himself was not immune to this criticism, because he, by unduly denigrating reason, had finally had to settle for an impossible dualism – a faith to all appearances blind, on the one side, and a pagan reflection, on the other. Fries did not mince words in pressing this objection against his friend. But the main culprits in matters of formalism had been Kant and Fichte. Both had allowed the connection between reflective system and actual experience to remain accidental, and for both, according to Fries, the cause of the lapse had been the same failure to appreciate the dependence of reflection on faith.[64]

As Fries explained, in Kant's system, belief in freedom, God, and the immortality of the soul is postulated only for the sake of resolving a difficulty inherent in the system itself – namely, the need to synthesize formal with final causality in moral theory. It follows that one cannot recognize Kant's faith, let alone share it, unless one has already accepted his system. And since the latter, like all products of reflection, is ultimately a limited and an artificial product, so too must be the faith postulated on its basis.[65] True faith, in contrast, pervades experience essentially. It is not just called for by reflection but is presupposed by it as its starting point.[66]

Fichte seemed immune to this line of criticism, for, at least in his more popular writings, he had put faith in absolute freedom at the head of the system.[67] But nothing could be further from the truth. Fichte's faith was itself the product of the abstraction that had made his system possible and had been inserted by Fichte at its head only ex post facto, for systematic reasons. Fichte, according to Fries, had actually been guilty of a grave error of reflection. He had based his whole system on a supposed fundamental opposition between 'I' and 'not-I,' or between 'subject' and 'object,' whereas in actual experience any such opposition is always limited by contextual determinations and is never in principle impossible to resolve.[68] The terms of Fichte's opposition, and the opposition itself, are themselves phenomenal objects. Far from yielding a privileged point of view from which to reconstruct the whole of experience, they depend for their meaning on experience itself.[69] That Fichte should have thought otherwise, and that he should have excogitated an 'absolute I' a priori, could be the result only of his fixation with apodictic science – hardly a universal ground on which to justify a theory of faith.

We know that Fries conceived his program of reinterpreting Kant psychologically, in purely naturalistic terms, during his first stay at Jena, while attending Fichte's lectures.[70] Whereas Fichte, to remedy the weakness in Kant's critical program which Ænesidemus had attacked, was in those lectures reinterpreting the program in purely idealistic terms, Fries moved in the opposite direction by reducing critique itself to the status of empirical inquiry. While listening to Fichte, Fries had methodically turned him upside-down – which is exactly what the nineteenth century fancied it had done to Hegel. Fries's opposition to Fichte, moreover, like much of nineteenth-century polemic against speculative thought, carried strong moral overtones. Fichte's anti-naturalism was especially distasteful to Fries, because, more than any other theory, it diverted attention from the true psychological forces that motivate and govern all our thinking.[71] Fichte had mistaken for substance what in fact is only a phenomenon of nature. In essence, this was Fries's systematic justification of Jacobi's animosity against idealism in general and Fichte's in particular.

Fries himself was of course motivated by religious considerations.[72] His confidence in nature was based on the belief that in it we find God immediately and that, unless we apprehend Him there in faith, no amount of reflection will ever grasp Him for us. It is a matter of historical record, however, that later philosophers, who equally relied on nature for truth, found there only quite different and much darker forces. Yet, conceptually speaking, Fries needed the certainty that the Absolute is with us in order to avoid the complete relativism that his theory of empirical truth, if divorced from the possibility of 'transcendental truth,' would entail. And he needed it as well to fend off the objection, which could be raised against his whole theory of rationality from the side of those less inclined to find reason everywhere at work in the universe, that that theory is itself, no less than Fichte's, a form of self-deception. On his own assumptions, Fries could not counter this objection except empirically, by showing that we in fact need to believe in God. And here is precisely where he was open to attack, for that we must believe in God and in ultimate truth, however much we enshrine this claim in theory, can be obvious only to someone who already believes in God and in Truth – God only knows for what reason.

Fries did not see – so far as I know – this quandary into which he could be forced. If he had, he might have been less unsympathetic to the new idealism that Schelling was advocating at the time of Fries's second stay at Jena. Schelling too was then claiming that the Absolute must be with us from the beginning and that its presence must be sought immediately in nature. Schelling moreover had given up Fichte's standpoint of the 'I' and had replaced Fichte's supposed fundamental opposition in experience between the 'I' and the 'not-I' with the opposition between 'finite' and 'infinite,' which Fries also favoured. Fries did not fail to acknowledge the agreement or to borrow from Schelling's language.[73] Yet he found Schelling, too, wanting, mostly because of his unwarranted postulation of an intellectual intuition that allegedly allows us to apprehend the Absolute in us and in nature as if all at once.[74] On the basis of this intuition, Schelling could claim that we have a positive knowledge of the Absolute, whereas Fries insisted that we have no such thing.[75] The Absolute (or God) is to be sought in faith, through toiling at particular objects of experience while knowing all along that what we really seek in this process – truth – escapes the concept and must be celebrated instead in ritual and myth-making. Reflective conceptualization is no doubt important to this process, but, according to Fries, where the Absolute is at issue, reflection must restrict itself to the labour of the negative. It can express the Absolute only as 'the negation of a negation' (Fries's expression) – as that which must transcend the negation implicit in every limit.[76] This kind of negative reflective conceptualization, though significant, cannot amount, according to Fries, to determinate knowledge.

One can indeed be sympathetic to Fries's refusal to accept Schelling's more romantic effusions concerning the Absolute.[77] Yet, to the extent that Fries denied any positive knowledge of truth per se, to that extent he had to concede that his faith in it is as much a mere phenomenon as any other faith, and just as open as any of them to the charge that it is the product of a self-serving assumption. But then Fries could not escape the same accusation of formalism that he had made against Kant and Fichte, and this was his dilemma. Though nowhere does Hegel mention Fries by name in the *Phenomenology of Spirit*, he must no doubt have had him in mind when in the Preface he made it a point of claiming that the negation of a determinate negation does yield (contrary to Fries, we may gloss) a determinate result.[78]

V

Fries worked out his anthropological critique in full and, for practical purposes, in definitive form only during his second stay at Jena. That was the period when he and Hegel worked side by side, so to speak.[79] At the time Fries did not clearly distinguish Hegel from Schelling but simply assumed that Hegel was a follower of his more famous collaborator. Yet Fries and Hegel's intellectual developments seemed to be running parallel courses – witness the remarkable similarity of themes in the works that the two either published or (in the case of Hegel) at least intended to publish. From Fries we have an essay on Reinhold, Fichte, and Schelling (1803),[80] a treatise on the Philosophy of Law (1803),[81] another essay on the subject of Knowledge, Faith, and Intimation (1805),[82] and, finally, his great opus, the *New Critique of Reason* (1807); from Hegel, a critical essay on the Difference between Fichte's and Schelling's Philosophy with reference to Reinhold (1801),[83] an essay on Faith and Knowledge (1802),[84] another on Natural Law,[85] a series of unpublished fragments of philosophical systems that include a System of Ethical Life (1802–3)[86] and lectures on the Philosophy of Spirit (1803–4; 1805–6),[87] and, finally, the *Phenomenology of Spirit* (1807), which, like Fries's *New Critique of Reason*, is a kind of anatomy (or, perhaps better, vivisection) of the mind. Fries and Hegel did not share philosophical points of view but certainly had philosophical interests in common.

When read with Fries in mind, the Preface and the Introduction of the *Phenomenology* give the impression that they methodically repeat Fries's main theses, but in order to turn them against him. The *Phenomenology* is based on the assumption that absolute knowledge is with us from the beginning; were it not so, no amount of ratiocination would bring it within our grasp. And we must be immediately aware of its presence in us before we can even begin to try to express it reflectively.[88] Accordingly, science is historically conditioned at least in so far as certainty about its truth always chronologically precedes any objective determination of it.[89] But, however immediately present to us, the Absolute is not the object of an 'intellectual' intuition; for knowledge is only as great as its expression, and hence awareness of the Absolute must be expressed reflectively before it can have any significance for us.[90] The attempt at this expression is the moving force of experience.

All these are theses that Hegel shares with Fries. In addition, though there is no talk in Fries of a 'bacchanalian revel' in which every particular determination of truth collapses and is replaced by another as soon as it emerges,[91] yet, for him just as much as for Hegel, experience is a process of transcending every object attained in space and time in favour of yet another. In this movement, the surpassed object is each time reflectively reduced to the status of just a partial expression of the truth. The movement itself is the effort at expressing the Whole in which alone, for Hegel as well as for Fries, truth as such consists. We are immediately aware of this truth throughout the process; in this sense, we believe in it from the beginning. But, just to voice our belief in it without demonstrating *in concreto* the difference that the belief makes to our perception of particular objects – without, in other words, subjecting the belief to the labour of the negative – would be to indulge, for Fries as well as for Hegel, in empty formalism.[92]

Another crucial thesis that Hegel and Fries share is that we cannot do science of being without at the same time doing science of mind. And the mind in question cannot be an a priori construct, as in Fichte, but must be phenomenal mind itself. Hence there is no need to import into our search for truth any criterion external to experience, for phenomenal mind carries its own standards of truth. For Hegel, this meant that phenomenal mind is already applying these standards as it draws a distinction between its own 'self' and its 'object' and thereby passes judgment on what counts for it as true in itself. In our critical reflection, we need only observe how the distinction undergoes modifications at the hand of phenomenal mind itself under pressure from the difficulties that the latter encounters when trying to abide, in actual experience, by its own implicit criteria of truth, and its notion of objectivity thus evolves.[93] Though the *Phenomenology* is not an anthropology in Fries's empirical sense, it is the science of the historical development that self-consciousness undergoes because of its reflective activity: this is an object that the *Phenomenology* shares with Fries's *New Critique*.

Yet the similarities between Fries and Hegel end here. From the need to conceive truth phenomenally, Hegel derived the very thesis that we expected from Fries but never found in him – namely, that 'immediacy' and 'reflection' are relative terms: there is nothing in actual experience that counts as immediate in one context that cannot also be taken in another as being the result of reflection, and we separate the two through abstraction only at the risk of never being able to bring them back together. Hegel's *Phenomenology* is the detailed and methodical elaboration, across the whole range of possible experience, of precisely this thesis. Thus Hegel extended even to what Fries called 'transcendental truth' the claim that Fries, at best, would have accepted only for 'empirical truth' – namely, that Truth is to be conceived (in the image that Hegel borrowed from Lessing) not as a 'ready made coin,'[94] but as a self-making process which, in becoming for itself, also becomes for us and, in becoming for us, also becomes for itself.[95] What is more, just because there is no opposition in principle between reflection and immediacy, and we implicitly know from the beginning that whatever we grasp reflectively is an appearance of the Absolute in us, Hegel concluded that a complete system of experience is possible and, through it, also knowledge of – not just faith in – the Absolute. On the basis of the inherent relativity of experience, Hegel argued for the possibility of systematic knowledge, where Fries argued for the need to accept the possibility of truth itself on faith. In the *Phenomenology* Hegel saw himself as preparing the way for the very apodictic conceptualization of reality that Kant and Fichte had thought they could attain only under the modality of the 'ought to be,' and Jacobi and Fries, who did not like this modal restriction, had instead rejected altogether as neither possible nor desirable.

From Fries's point of view, Hegel's conclusion would have defied every standard of good sense. Hegel would in effect be saying that he had exhaustively comprehended history and had knowledge not just of what the Absolute is in itself, though only for us, but of what it is for itself as well. '*Pure self-recognition in absolute otherness, this Aether as such*, is the ground and soil of Science or *knowledge in general.*'[96] This is how Hegel defined in the *Phenomenology* the possibility of knowledge. And it seemed that he now claimed to have recognized himself in the Absolute (the absolute 'other'), as if he had managed to transcend his own consciousness and to place himself on God's side of things, whence to behold the whole of creation according to God's own point of view.[97] On the face of it, Hegel's system comprehended the trinitarian life of God, and the created universe as part of that life. It not only reiterated traditional theological doctrines: it presented them as fully rationalized. Seen in this way, Hegel appeared indeed to be the ultimate Christian theologian, who had finally transformed theology entirely into philosophy. And this is how Hegel was actually to be seen in the nineteenth century, by friends and foes alike.

But is this what Hegel was really up to, or had he rather so altered the terms of the issue of faith versus knowledge as to make the kind of objection that Fries could raise against him altogether unintelligible? Here is where the significance of H.S. Harris's recent work becomes apparent.[98] For Harris has definitively shown that the young Hegel eventually adopted a position of radical immanence and that he finally found his way to a complete and consistent articulation of this position in the Jena years. The mature Hegel meant by the 'Absolute' only a special form (*Gestalt*) of experience. When stated on the basis of this assumption, Fries's theses (on Hegel's lips) acquire an entirely new meaning. Fries, no less than Kant or Fichte, still assumed that, abstracted from our relation to it, the 'thing-in-itself' – or, in more idealistic language, the 'Absolute' – transcends experience absolutely. Whether one therefore denies knowledge of it altogether (Kant), or makes it the object of an intellectual intuition (Fichte) or of some sort of feeling (Fries himself), one must yet claim that, to the extent that one refers to it for any reason whatsoever, one subjects it to a determinate reflection and conceives it therefore only as it is for us rather than as it is in itself. However much Fries might have decried Kant and Fichte's posited dichotomy between immediacy and reflection, in this one aspect of experience – its relation to the Absolute – he had retained that dichotomy untouched. Or, in other words, when Fries says that 'truth' is to some extent always an artificial product, his claim applies to 'empirical truth' unqualifiedly and to 'transcendental truth' only according to our expressions of it. Truth per se is all there from the beginning: our unshakeable belief in it rescues our empirical knowledge from scepticism and relativism. On Hegel's lips the same claim applies to truth as such, for Hegel was now defining the Absolute itself in terms of experience. For him to say that one can have absolute knowledge did not *ipso facto* mean that one has transcended the limits of experience.

But how could Hegel make this claim seriously – without thereby reducing the particular objects of experience to a mere deceptive 'show' (*Schein*) of the one true reality that is the Absolute – yet retain enough of the traditional meaning of the latter to avoid sliding into pure relativism? The answer is that Hegel capitalized on the connection of 'immediacy' to 'reflection' that Fries needed to assert but had ultimately failed to understand. 'Immediacy,' according to Hegel, is a function of 'reflectivity' and as such inseparable from it. Only inasmuch as, through reflection, we gain in experience mental distance from the many things on which we are dependent because of circumstance of birth and upbringing do our previous relations to these things begin to appear contingent. Only then do the things themselves appear to us in their 'immediacy' – what they actually are or may be becomes for us an issue yet to be settled and, perhaps, never to be definitely so. Rather than being just bound to them by the circumstances of place and time, we begin to play with their possibilities (Harris's image),[99] just as we do in speculation and, indeed, in every scientific endeavour. At that point, of course, there is no bound of experience that is not for us open to challenge, in principle at least. Here is where relativism and scepticism raise their ugly heads. But theirs is in fact no threat at all; that the limits of experience, as reflectively expressed, are always reformable is a truth available to us only because, through reflection, we have attained in experience a universal standpoint. Everything in experience is relative, except the reflective activity of reason itself. And that is what Hegel now meant by the Absolute.

Kant and Fichte had already implied as much by basing their systems on the idea of reason's autonomy. But, because of their belief (itself a residue of dogmatic metaphysics) that truth *per se* is, or ought to be, independent of our expression of it, they had reflectively conceived reason's own reflection in purely formal terms, thereby divorcing it from the immediacy of actual experience. In this way Kant had made himself vulnerable to Ænesidemus's charge of formalism, and Fichte, with his strange claim that 'nature' ought only to be an idea, to Jacobi's attacks and to the less-charitable lampooning of a Jean-Paul (another of Jacobi's adepts).[100] In fact, Fichte and Fries had both been equally right and wrong. Fries had been right in claiming that reason is a natural activity. We know this much at least because, however much control we might gain over nature and our body in particular through the use of reason, we have no say over its origin. We discover ourselves reasoning just as, at some point, we discover ourselves eating or loving. But Fichte too had been right, for through reason we do not simply represent reality but apprehend it as well. We do not just know it, in other words: we also know that we know it and are therefore capable of positing the conditions of this very knowledge as the point of reference in terms of which to systematize and interpret experience. The crucial characteristic of reason is that it posits itself at the centre of its own activities. Whatever unity nature might (or might not) have on its own, independently of reason's activities, in the latter it finally achieves at least the possibility of a complete unity. In this sense – namely, inasmuch as reason is still part of nature yet introduces reflection into it – nature can be said to transcend itself through reason. Fichte and Fries had therefore both been right: system and systematization always entail an element of artificiality, for they are our doing and hence presuppose a positing on our part. But both had also been wrong – Fichte, because he had conceived this positing as the work of a would-be absolute freedom intent on retrieving through reflection its pre-conscious origin (the *Wissenschaftslehre* is like a pre-temporal history of the self), and Fries, because he had totally subjected the positing to the accidents of history and culture. Hence, whereas Fichte's system, though allegedly absolute, required an added moral commitment to connect it with actual experience, Fries's had to fall back on immediate faith in a transcendent truth in order to avoid relativism.

The truth, according to Hegel, is quite different. The physical sciences and history are indeed, as Fries's empiricism required, open-ended and ever-reformable enterprises. But their many aspects, and their many stages of evolution, are all held together by the very idea of rationality on which they all are at least implicitly based (even when that is being denied). Reason itself, through its very work of reflection, gives testimony to the idea's actuality, hence to its possibility. And there will be periods of history when humanity tries to demonstrate how much our idea of nature and of society (without either of which our very humanity would not be possible) depends on it. Hegel's system is one such attempt, in which the objects of both the physical and the moral sciences are summed up (in the Philosophy of Nature and the Philosophy of Spirit) as reflections of reason's self-reflection. And this self-reflection is further objectified (in the Logic) in terms of the categories that reason itself generates in the process of defining itself, and which it then projects into the world at large as sign-posts to guide it in its contemplation of things. It is possible that Hegel thought his summing up to be definitive for all times, though it is more likely that he would have recognized that every culture interested in its own rationality would have to repeat the project for itself and according to its own peculiar historical circumstances. What is important, however, is the sense in which any such summing up, if successful, would indeed be definitive. And that is because it would give expression to reason's awareness of itself as the self-contained, self-limiting form of activity that provides in experience the place where to stand and, from it, look at nature (including our human one) for whatever it happens to be.[101]

VI

There is a passage in the Preface to the *Phenomenology of Spirit* where Hegel gives a preview of the process that knowledge must go through before it becomes genuine science. The process cannot be what is commonly understood by 'an initiation ... into Science'; nor can it be the 'foundation of Science.' 'Least of all,' Hegel continues, 'will it be like the rapturous enthusiasm which, like a shot from a pistol, begins straight away with absolute knowledge, and makes short work of other standpoints by declaring that it takes no notice of them.'[102] It is of course idle to speculate whether in this passage Hegel was taxing with 'enthusiasm' any particular individual, or who any such individual might be. Any of the many contemporaries of Hegel's who were given to pietism could, in his mind, fit the bill. Yet the accusation of trying to attain to the Absolute all at once was one that Fries had been making against Schelling at Jena, and it is at least tempting to believe that Hegel could not avoid including his former colleague Fries as the target of this polemical passage. Whatever the merits of Schelling's new idealism (which does not concern us here), Hegel was meeting Fries's criticism by turning it against him.

It is easy to understand why Fries's neo-Kantianism should have been attractive to the nineteenth century. It was like a manifesto of liberal thought. It made room for a potentially infinite variety of individual beliefs independent of scientific knowledge, yet it tested the validity of both the beliefs and the knowledge by measuring them against each other – the beliefs, in terms of whether they provided the right emotional tone conducive to the pursuit of knowledge; the sciences, inasmuch as they succeeded in systematizing experiences according to the subjective requirements of feelings and emotions. And the balance between the two could be struck in ways that differed according to personal, cultural, and historical circumstances. Regardless of differences of place, time, and individual temperaments, poets could go on creating their myths, and the scientists excogitating their theories, each side abiding by different requirements, yet secretly in collusion. Pitted against this rich and dynamic picture of the progress of experience, Hegel's system, his Logic in particular, could appear, to generations of philosophers immediately following, as a conceited play of empty abstractions.

Yet it was the nineteenth century that also brought home to consciousness how much the feelings and beliefs on which Fries put so much trust can be the functions, even at their apparent noblest, of irrational, subconscious forces of nature, and how little reason can do, when exclusively bent on what Fries called 'empirical truth,' to counteract the charge that, far from providing a check on these forces, it itself is an instrument of their secret designs. To any such charge Fries's reason cannot respond without admitting that it is acting on the basis of a particular belief and under the guide of a particular theoretical construct. And this amounts to admitting the possibility that rationality in general is simply a form of legitimizing relations already established on a purely natural level, and that any particular argument used to counter the charge is itself a way of either buttressing or subverting the ascendancy of an established power. Short of capitulating to historicism and scepticism (which Fries definitely did not want), this admission is fatal to Fries's 'anthropological critique.' And the failure is due to the fact that Fries's theorizing, by its own principles, must be a highly particularized activity. As such, it remains external to the beliefs or other sundry facts of consciousness that it is to bring to reflective conceptualization; it 'falls immediately by their side,' as Hegel would put it, despite Fries's intention to keep reflection and immediacy together. As understood by Fries, reflection necessarily comes on the scene ex post facto, when a certain mental universe has already been established, as just one more ingredient of that universe. It might indeed serve to make an orderly inventory of its content, but, since it does not transcend it, it cannot genuinely criticize it. The very 'concreteness' of Fries's reflection that ought to have saved it from the dreaded formalism of Kant and Fichte makes it vulnerable to it.

By contrast, the abstractness and emptiness of Hegelian thought, as the latter would appear to Fries, turn out to be its strength instead. This is not to say that Hegel's system is not the product of a historical consciousness. The *Phenomenology* is the record of an individual consciousness's journey across its past, intended to attain, on the strenght of the self-knowledge thereby achieved, to the universal standpoint of pure science. This work of self-enlightenment is one that every individual mind (if not every age) must redo for itself. But the difference in this case is the special relation that reflection bears to its own subject matter. For reflection does not now merely re-present supposed facts of consciousness that it happens to discover; it is not *Wiederbewußtsein* in Jacobi's or Fries's sense. It rather considers these facts as *facta* (in Fichte's sense, but without his anti-naturalism) – as the products of consciousness's previous attempts at transcending its particular historical position by means of reflection, in order to comprehend it. And it considers itself as the last of these attempts – one that takes the attempt itself for its object. Moving from one stage of reflection to another, which is higher and hence more abstractive, does not therefore mean, as it must in Fries's empirical science, formulating ever more general laws of mental behaviour. These laws would gain in extension only at the price of losing in content, until they amounted to no more than a formal syntax. It means rather overcoming at each stage one more historical inhibition in the discovery of the limits of consciousness. Of course, nature presides over its origin, and it might well be that consciousness was implicated at the beginning, and ever shall be, in some form of power struggle – be it a contest for prestige between fathers and sons, males and females, or what have you. But the assumption of Hegel's *Phenomenology* is that a nature which through reflection knows itself to be just nature, or a power struggle that knows itself to be just that, cannot remain the same. And to know at the end, as we learn in the *Phenomenology*, that reflection does make a difference will itself make a yet-greater difference. The *Phenomenology* is abstract and formal only in the sense that it is only an instrument of self-knowledge, critique pure and simple. The 'negation of negation' that it performs at each of the stages of its recovery of consciousness's past, and as a total work, yields indeed a determinate product – namely, a new self-awareness, which, potentially at least, has universal significance.

In the final analysis, the differences in the relation of faith to knowledge according to Fries and to Hegel coincide with those between the 'anthropological critique' of the one and the 'phenomenology' of the other. Fries simply discovers his faith as a surd of mental life – something that someone less inclined to pietistic feelings than Fries might well consider a neurotic trait. For Hegel, faith is not just an object of reflection but itself a reflective activity from the beginning. It is essentially a faith seeking knowledge of itself and of its beliefs. It is none other than reason itself, in other words. And if we contrast it with knowledge, we do so only because, at some stage in the development of humanity's awareness of itself, and in some quarters of humanity, it still does not know itself explicitly as reason.

Notes

I am indebted to my research assistant, Hans-Jakob Wilhelm, for help in assembling materials for this paper.

1 (Oxford: Clarendon Press, 1983), 569, 570.
2 Cf. Immanuel Kant, *Kritik der reinen Vernunft* (Riga: Hartknoch, 1787), Bxxx.
3 *Über die Lehre des Spinoza in Briefen an den Herrn Moses Mendelssohn* (Breslau: Löwe, 1785).
4 For the first years of the Kant reception, see my 'The First Twenty Years of Critique: The Spinoza Connection,' in Paul Guyer, ed., *The Cambridge Companion to Kant* (Cambridge: Cambridge University Press, 1992), 417–48, especially sections III and IV. The relevant references here are C.L. Reinhold's 'Briefe über die kantische Philosophie,' which appeared in *Der Teutsche Merkur* between August 1786 and September 1787, and Jenisch's letter to Kant of 14 May 1787, in *Kant-Briefwechsel* (Berlin: Berlin Royal Academy) (Academy Ed.), X, 462.
5 For the relevant literature on which the following sketch is based, cf. my 'The First Twenty Years' and my *The Facts of Consciousness*, in *Between Kant and Hegel: Texts in the Development of Post-Kantian Idealism*, trans. and notes by G. di Giovanni and H.S. Harris (Albany, NY: SUNY, 1985), 3–50. My only intention here is to introduce the figures and the issues of Fries's immediate conceptual world.
6 *Kritik der reinen Vernunft* (1781), Axx–xxi, and (1787), Bxxxvi–xxxvii. Kant followed up with his most concerted effort to establish a priori the first laws of physics in his *Metaphysische Anfangsgründe der Naturwissenschaften* (1786). He certainly did not see himself, nor was he seen by his contemporaries, as just an 'epistemologist' (to use a modern term).

7 In *Versuch einer neuen Theorie des menschlichen Vorstelungsvermögen* (Prague and Jena: Widtmann & Mauke, 1789).
8 Anon. [Gottlieb Ernst Schulze], *Ænesidemus, oder über die Fundamente der von Herrn Prof. Reinhold in Jena gelieferten Elementar-Philosophie* (N.p.:n.p., 1792). The name of its eponymous main character is derived from that of an ancient sceptic.
9 Fichte's first public adumbrations of his strategy came in his review of *Ænesidemus*, in *Allgemeine Litteratur-Zeitung* (11 and 12 Feb., nos. 47–9, 1794).
10 *Über die Lehre des Spinoza in Briefen an den Herrn Moses Mendelssohn* (Breslau: Löwe, 1785). For how Fichte saw himself with resepct to Jacobi, cf. my 'From Jacobi's Philosophical Novel to Fichte's Idealism: Some Comments on the 1798–99 "Atheism Dispute,"' *Journal of the History of Philosophy*, 27(1989), 75–100.
11 One of Fichte's most striking statements to this effect is to be found in *The Vocation of Man* (*Die Bestimmung des Menschen*, 1800): 'Nature must gradually be resolved into a condition in which her regular action may be calculated and safely relied upon, and her power bear a fixed and definite relation to that which is destined to govern it – that of Man.' 'Thus shall Nature ever become more and more intelligible and transparent, even in her most secret depths; human power, enlightened and armed by human invention, shall rule over her without difficulty, and the conquest, once made, shall be peacefully maintained.' Trans. William Smith, ed. R.M. Chisholm, Library of Liberal Arts (New York: Bobbs-Merrill, 1956), 103, 104.
12 *Woldemar* (Königsberg: Nicolovius, 1796), Part I, p. 80. Letter of Jacobi to Johann Neeb, 18 Oct. 1814, *Friedrich Heinrich Jacobi's auserlesener Briefwechsel*, 2 vols, ed. F. Roth (Leipzig: Fleischer, 1825–7), No. 351, II, 445.
13 'Individuality is a fundamental concept; individuality is the root of intelligence and of all knowledge; without individuality there is no substantiality, and without substantiality there is absolutely nothing. '*Ichkeit*' ... is a bare non-thought ... I make a great leap and say: Just as for Fichte all is *subjectivity*, so all is for me objectivity' Letter to Jean-Paul of 16 Feb. 1800, *Aus F.H. Jacobi's Nachlaß*, ed. R. Zoeppritz (Leipzig: Engelmann, 1869), No. 71, pp. 238–9.
14 Jacobi, *David Hume über den Glauben, oder Idealismus und Realismus. Ein Gespräch* (Breslau: Löwe, 1787), 26; English translation: F.H. Jacobi, *The Main Philosophical Writings and the Novel 'Allwill,'* trans. and ed. George di Giovanni (Montreal: McGill–Queen's University Press, 1994), 266 (henceforth referred to as *Jacobi's Writings*). Reid is mentioned in this context.
15 *Jacobi an Fichte* (Hamburg: Perthes, 1799), included in *Jacobi's Writings*.
16 Cf. Jacobi's account of his introduction to philosophy in Jacobi, *David Hume*, 11ff. in *Jacobi's Writings*, 261.
17 Cf. *Neue deutsche Biographie*, V, article on Fries, 608–9.
18 *Reinhold, Fichte und Schelling*, 24 (1803), 103, 455–6. Unless otherwise indicated, I

cite Fries's works by volume and pagination of *Jakob Friedrich Fries, Sämmtliche Werke*, ed. G. König and L. Geldsetzer (Aalen: Scientia Verlag, 1967–9). The text of this early work of Fries's is here reproduced according to the second edition (1824). Though I am concerned with Fries's Jena years, I feel free to cite from later editions because Fries's position as canonized in those years, and his relation to idealism, did not undergo significant subsequent changes.

19 *Reinhold, Fichte, und Schelling*, XXIV, 305. *Neue oder anthropologische Kritik der Vernunft* (henceforth cited as *Neue Kritik*), IV, 45. This is the 1828 edition of Fries's major work, originally published in 1807 as *Neue Kritk der Vernunft*. According to the editors of the *Sämmtliche Schriften*, Fries wrote down the three volumes of this work in one year after taking up his position at Heidelberg. But he had been preparing for it uninterruptedly during the previous twelve years. The second edition was left practically unaltered, except for some major changes in the Introduction. Cf. IV, 3–4.
20 Cf. *Reinhold, Fichte und Schelling*, XXIV, 466–7.
21 Whether Kant and Fichte had been guilty of the first of the two errors diagnosed by Fries is debatable. Reinhold, for his part, had certainly incurred both.
22 *Reinhold, Fichte und Schelling*, XXIV, 466–7; *Neue Kritik*, IV, 408–11.
23 *Neue Kritik*, IV, 411.
24 Ibid., 55–6, 416.
25 Witness Ænesidemus, Fries could have said.
26 *Reinhold, Fichte und Schelling*, XXIV, 310.
27 *Wissen, Glaube und Ahnden*, 1805 (Göttingen: Vandenhoeck & Ruprecht, 1905), 74–5.
28 *Neue Kritik*, IV, 94. Witness Ænesidemus's criticism, Fries could again have said.
29 'I claim, to the contrary, that the distinction between intuition and concept only relates to the subjective validity of knowledge, only to two different ways in which we become conscious in reason of the being of our knowledge – namely, whether through inner sense (as intuition) or through reflection (by means of concepts). We must therefore rise above this separation of intuition and concept up to the *immediate totality of our knowledge*, which stands above both, before we can speak of the objective validity of this knowledge' (my translation). *Selbstrezension der Neuen Kritik der Vernunft* (1808), IV, 10. *Reinhold, Fichte und Schelling*, XXIX, 173–4, 346. *Neue Kritik*, IV, 94. See Heinrich Kampmann, *Jacobi und Fries. Ein Beitrag zur Lehre von der zweifachen Erkenntnis* (Münster: Westfälische Vereinsdruckerie, 1913), 24.
30 *Reinhold, Fichte und Schelling*, XXIV, 181–2; cf. Kant, *Kritik der reinen Venunft*, B75.
31 *Reinhold, Fichte und Schelling*, XXIV, 302–7, 346–7.
32 Ibid., 312, cf. also 325ff. (the whole section is relevant); *Neue Kritik*, IV, 45, 95–6.

33 Kant, *Untersuchung über die Deutlichkeit der Grundsätze in der natürlichen Theologie und Moral* (1763); cf. *Reinhold, Fichte und Schelling*, XXIV, 384.
34 Cf. *Reinhold, Fichte und Schelling*, XXIV, 383. Apparently, Fries took these intuitions to be intuitively apprehended facts of mental life.
35 On Fries's regressive analytical method, cf. *Reinhold, Fichte und Schelling*, XXIV, 382–94; *Selbstrezension*, IV, 14.
36 *Reinhold, Fichte und Schelling*, XXIV, 391.
37 Ibid., 463–4.
38 Ibid., 369.
39 Ibid., 374, 376ff.
40 On the contrary, Fries seems to say that 'sensation' carries with it an immediate consciousness of itself – a sort of 'immediate reflection' (my expression) – which can then become the object of the deliberate reflection of science. Thus: 'In [intuition] we immediately cognize the presence of an object, and we then become again immediately conscious of this cognition of ours, we need no reflection to discover them [i.e., the object and the cognition] in us' (*Glauben, Wissen und Ahnden*, 121). But how can Fries deny the possibility that this original self-consciousness does not already entail a decision as to the nature of the object supposedly present in intuition – i.e., that the object of intuition already is a *künstlich* product?
41 Cf. *Reinhold, Fichte und Schelling*, the distinction between *Anschauung* and *Reflexion* (XXIX, 374): 'Intuition is the immediate cognition or cognitive representation of an object: we are in turn conscious that we have this cognition or cognitive representation, or are capable in turn of knowing it, just as immediately. In general I call reflection, on the contrary, the activity of the understanding or of reason whereby our knowledge attains concepts, judgements, conclusions and the systematic form of science; it is, therefore, that activity of the understanding whose laws are prescribed by Logic ... Through reflection we only become once more conscious of a knowledge which otherwise already belongs to reason immediately.' The connection between 'intuition' and 'reflection' seems here to be totally external.
42 Cf. Kant, *Kritik der Reinen Vernunft*, Axx; *Reinhold, Fichte und Schelling*, XXIV, 385.
43 Cf. *Wissen, Glauben und Ahnden*, 54; *Selbstrezension*, IV, 18; *Neue Kritik*, IV, 122–3.
44 *Wissen, Glauben und Ahnden*, 54–5.
45 Cf. *Neue Kritik*, IV, 122–3; cf. also a somewhat later work of Fries, in which he defended Jacobi against Schelling: *Von deutscher Philosophie, Art und Kunst* (Heidelberg: Mohr und Zimmer, 1812), 48–9.
46 *Neue Kritik*, IV, 122; *Wissen, Glauben und Ahnden*, 4.
47 *Neue Kritik*, XXIV, 468–9; *Wissen, Glauben und Ahnden*, 54; *Fichte's und*

Schelling's neueste Lehren von Gott und der Welt (Heidelberg: Mohr und Zimmer), 605–6.
48 *Neue Kritik*, IV, 122.
49 *Reinhold, Fichte und Schelling*, XXIV, 327–8, 455–6, 466; *Neue Kritik*, IV, 55.
50 *Reinhold, Fichte und Schelling*, XXIV, 137, 140, 346; *Wissen, Glauben und Ahnden*, 57–8; *Neuesten Lehren von Gott und der Welt*, 609.
51 For Fries on 'faith,' see especially *Glauben, Wissen und Ahnden*, 121–3, 129ff.
52 *Von deutscher Philosophie, Art und Kunst*, 47–9.
53 Fries accused the English empiricists, especially the opponents of Hume, of having mistakenly taken 'feeling' to be a 'finer sense.' *Neue Kritik*, IV, 469–70.
54 Cf.: 'Hence the faculty of feeling is in no way sense or sensation; it is rather arbitrary reflection (as opposed to mediated inference) in its immediate activity.' *Neue Kritik*, IV, 471.
55 Ibid., 470–1, 472, 475.
56 Ibid., 122; *Glauben, Wissen und Ahnden*, 121–3.
57 *Von deutscher Philosophie, Art und Kunst*, 51–3.
58 *Wissen, Glauben und Ahndung*, 60: 'Intimation ... is based on the conviction that finite being is the appearance of eternal being, that eternal being itself appears to us in nature.' See also 74, 173–6.
59 In fact, Fries thinks that by showing 'intimation' to be a natural function of every reason he can put an end to all mysticism: '[W]e show that the secret inner light enlightens indeed each and every one, but each only in the aesthetic ideas of the beauty and sublimity of nature; that we cannot however make use of these ideas, in some sort of poetic transport, for the purpose of prophesy or of some other knowledge of the eternal; but that we must here rather restrict ourselves solely to the unutterable feeling.' *Wissen, Glauben und Ahnden*, 178–9.
60 Witness the many references in the footnotes to Fries's works in the Preface to Jacobi's *David Hume*. This Preface was added to the 1815 edition of the *David Hume*; see *Werke*, ed. J.F. Köppen and C.J.F. Roth, II (Leipzig: Gerhard Fleischer, 1815). The text of the Preface is included in *Jacobi's Writings*.
61 Cf. Jacobi, *David Hume* (1787), 123–35, in *Jacobi's Writings*, 298–304. Jacobi modified this passage somewhat in the 1815 edition (cf. 219–21, and footnote to 221; *Werke*, II, in *Jacobi's Writings*, 298–9, footnote).
62 Cf. *Von deutscher Philosophie, Art und Kunst*, 34–7.
63 *Ænesidemus*, 386–8.
64 *Von deutscher Philosophie, Art und Kunst*, 34.
65 *Reinhold, Fichte und Schelling*, XXIV, 348; cf. *Wissen, Glauben und Ahnden*, 156.
66 *Reinhold, Fichte und Schelling*, XXIV, 349–50; cf. *Neue Kritik*, IV, 57.
67 Cf. *Reinhold, Fichte und Schelling*, Introduction, XXIV, 53–5.
68 Cf. ibid., 175–6.

69 Ibid., 282–3.
70 Cf. *Sämmtliche Schriften*, editors's note, IV, 3–4.
71 Cf. *Reinhold, Fichte und Schelling*, XXIV, 281; *Neueste Lehren von Gott und der Welt*, 20–1, 55.
72 *Neue Kritik*, IV, 122: 'For me the final goal of the critique of reason is the justification of these ideas of faith and their recognition in the religious-aesthetic view of the world.'
73 Cf., inter alia, *Reinhold, Fichte und Schelling*, XXIV, 283, 289.
74 Ibid., 295.
75 Ibid., 298–9.
76 Ibid., 299, 300; *Glauben, Wissen und Ahnden*, 122–3.
77 Cf. *Neueste Lehren von Gott und der Welt*, 36ff., 41–2, 56–7, 49ff., 79–80.
78 G.W.F. Hegel, *System der Wissenschaft: Erster Theil, Die Phänomenologie des Geistes* (Bamberg and Whrzburg: Goebhardt, 1807), 11–12.
79 I am not interested here in Fries's later, totally negative treatment of Hegel, in *Nichtigkeit der Hegelschen Dialektik* (Heidelberg: Oßwald, 1828), or in Hegel's later, dismissive, treatment of Fries, in *Wissenschaft der Logik: Erster Band, Die objektive Logik* (Nürnberg: Schrag, 1812), xvii note. *Enzyklopädie der philosophischen Wissenschaften im Grundrisse*, 2nd ed. (Heidelberg: Oßwald, 1827): I take it that paragraph 66 implicitly refers to Fries; Hegel notes that supposedly immediate facts of consciousness are in fact the result of a long process of mediation.
80 *Reinhold, Fichte und Schelling*.
81 *Philosophische Rechtslehre und Kritik aller positiven Gesetzgebung ...* (Jena: Mauke, 1803).
82 *Wissen, Glauben und Ahnden*.
83 *Differenz des Ficthe'schen und Schelling'schen Systems der Philosophie in Beziehung auf Reinhold's Beyträge* (Jena: Seidler, 1801).
84 'Glauben und Wissen, oder die Reflexionphilosophie der Subjectivität, in der Vollständigkeit ihrer Formen, als kantische, jacobische, und fichtische Philosophie,' *Kritische Journal der Philosophie*, 2 no. 2(1802), 3–189.
85 'Über die wissenschaftliche Behandlungsarten des Naturrechts,' ibid., 3–88, 2 no. 3 (1803), 1–34.
86 The title is not Hegel's; edited by G. Lasson (Leipzig: Verlag, 1913).
87 Ed. Trede, Horstmann, Düsing, and Kimmerle, in Vols. VI and VII of *G.W.F. Hegel: Gesammelte Werke* (Hamburg: Meiner, 1975, 1976).
88 Cf. *Phänomenologie*, 6.
89 Ibid., 7–8.
90 Ibid., xii.
91 Ibid., lvi.

92 Ibid., 9.
93 Ibid., 15–18.
94 Ibid., xlv (cf. Lessing, *Nathan der Weise*, 1779, act III, scene 6).
95 Cf. *Phänomenologie*, xlii–xliii.
96 Ibid., xxix–xxx.
97 'Let [Hegel] teach the fools who wish to follow him how to raise themselves to the divine view of things [*göttlichen Weltanschauung*] or even how to understand it!' *Neueste Lehren von Gott und der Welt*, 46.
98 I am referring to the two volumes of Harris's *Hegel's Development: Toward the Sunlight (1770–1801)* (Oxford: Clarendon Press, 1972), and *Night Thoughts (Jena 1801–1806)* (Oxford: Clarendon Press, 1983).
99 *Night Thoughts (Jena 1801–1806)*, 563. In what follows I am not trying, nor would I be able in the present context, to demonstrate my thesis about Hegel. I am simply stating what I have learned from Harris's reading of Hegel.
100 Cf. his satirical *Clavis Fichtiana* (1800). In private Jacobi could be just as harsh with Fichte. Regarding Fichte's *Die Bestimmung des Menschen*, which he had found comic throughout when not outright boring, Jacobi wrote to Jean-Paul: 'And philosophy is done with trumpets and cymbals, to the accompaniment of the sound of every bell, and the organ bellows with all the stops full open.' Letter to Jean-Paul of 13 Feb. 1800, *Aus F.H. Jacobi's Nachlaß*, No. 70, p. 235.
101 'Give me a place where to stand [and I shall move the earth].' Hamann quoted this saying of Archimedes' to Jacobi, and Jacobi inscribed it in the frontispiece of his *Doctrine of Spinoza*. Hamann made it clear that his 'place' was God's *logos*; for Hegel, it is the 'concept.' Hamann's Letter to Jacobi of 14 Nov. 1784, *Hamann-Briefwechsel*, ed. A. Henkel, 7 vols. (Wiesbaden and Frankfurt/Main: Insel, 1955–79), V, No. 782, pp. 265–6.
102 *Phänomenologie*, xxxii.

PART FOUR:
PHILOSOPHY

11

Der Unterschied zwischen 'Differenz' und 'Unterschied': A Re-evaluation of Hegel's *Differenzschrift*

SUSAN-JUDITH HOFFMANN

Among his English-speaking readers, Hegel's intention in his essay on the *Differenz des Fichte'schen und Schelling'schen Systems der Philosophie*[1] has been misconstrued as a result of the translation of the title of the essay as *The Difference between Fichte's and Schelling's Systems of Philosophy*. It was in the *Differenzschrift* that Hegel attempted to save Fichte and Schelling from the same sort of misinterpretation that much of his own work, including this early and seminal essay, has suffered at the hands of hasty commentators. In this chapter I seek to defend Hegel against such comment. I argue that, contrary to the current, standard interpretations of the *Differenzschrift*[2] Hegel's intention was not primarily to announce the break between Fichte and Schelling's systems of philosophy but rather to show that the telic advance of philosophy can arise only when there is a recognized need for 'new' forms of philosophy to emerge in an organic way from such 'old' ones as those of Fichte and Schelling. Hegel refers to this process as 'system-differentiation,' and the main import of the essay lies neither in the announcement of a breach between Fichte and Schelling nor in his well-focused criticism of his predecessors, but rather in his formulation of the history of philosophy in terms of a radically new teleological framework.

Rather than attempting to do away with past philosophical systems by criticizing them from perspectives outside their proper context, thereby degrading the science of philosophy into a futile game of lifeless intellectual puzzles, the task of the philosopher is, according to Hegel, to 'gain a clear awareness' of previous philosophies by distinguishing the spirit from the letter – that is, by examining them within their own historical and teleological context and by working out, from within their own parameters, whatever internal contradictions they may entail. Such, as Hegel saw it, was his task in the *Differenzschrift*, and we would do well to approach his essay in the same spirit.

In what follows, I begin by suggesting that Hegel consciously chose *Differenz* instead of *Unterschied* and that this choice has significant implications for the interpretation of the *Differenzshrift*. I next examine the manner in which the terms *Differenz* and *Unterschied* are employed in the *Encyclopaedia* and in the *Lectures on the History of Philosophy*. I suggest that the fact that Hegel sometimes uses *Differenz* as a subsequent *Aufhebung* of *Unterschied* proves illuminating for an interpretation of the *Differenzschrift*. I then briefly summarize Hegel's understanding of the transition from the reflective, critical philosophy of Fichte to the 'authentic' – that is, speculative – philosophy of Schelling and himself. Finally, I discuss how Hegel's position develops out of the philosophies of Fichte and Schelling and to what extent we may speak of his 'original' contribution to the history of philosophy in this early and seminal work.

Differenz and *Unterschied*

The difficulty involved in translating *Differenz* into English without losing the particular connotations that Hegel intended is obvious. Nevertheless, such a problem warrants explanation in a translator's preface.[3] Why did Hegel choose *Differenz* rather than *Unterschied*? We have to take a closer look at the German terms.[4] *Unterschied* usually means difference in the sense of a clear distinction – the sort of distinction we recognize between an acorn and a dog. Philosophy as a science, according to Hegel, cannot advance when there is a fundamental *Unterschied* between philosophies. Were philosophers to attempt to change the course of philosophy by decree, and destroy the old philosophies in their eagerness to erect their own 'new' philosophies, they would, in effect, be trying to put a dog in the place of an acorn, when what they really need is an oak tree.

This self-defeating perspective on the history of philosophy hopes that new philosophies will render the old ones not only obsolete but entirely irrelevant, thereby excluding the possibility of dialectical relation between various forms of philosophy. Such an approach to philosophy presupposes that philosophy is a kind of technical skill at which one can be clever. 'Each new invention presupposes acquaintance with the turns [of skill] already in use and with the purposes they serve; but after all the improvements made so far, the principal task remains. Reinhold evidently seems to think of this task as the finding of a universally valid an ultimate turn of skill such that the work completes itself automatically for anyone who can get acquainted with it ... The preceding philosophical systems would at all times be nothing but practice studies for the big brains.'[5]

According to Hegel, a history of severed and different (*unterschiedliche*) philosophies is an 'externally reflective' tale of 'accidental vicissitudes of the human spirit and senseless opinions.'[6] *Differenzierung* in philosophy, in contrast, is the process and result of 'internally reflective' philosophy – that is, of one eternal Reason, which presents itself in a manifold of forms that differ, or grow out of, and away from, one another: 'Reason that is directed towards itself and comes to recognize itself, produces a true philosophy and solves for itself the problem which, like its solution, is at all times the same. In philosophy, Reason comes to know itself and deals only with itself so that its whole work and activity are grounded in itself, and with respect to the inner essence of philosophy there are neither predecessors nor successors.'[7]

Differenz can mean difference is the sense of distinction but also in the sense of a divergence (*Abweichung*); it implies a movement of branching out, of growth within the same essential structure.[8] The absence of a definite article before *Differenz* in the title of Hegel's essay calls attention to this sense of divergence.[9] Every state of *Differenz* is a divergence from an original, or 'originary,' state, and it is in this sense that 'new' philosophies 'diverge' and 'differ' from older philosophies: the new ones emerge organically from the old.[10] *Differenz* between two systems points reflectively back to an impulse (*Trieb*) that drives one system into another from a common ground – a common *Geist* that initiates and sustains the dialectic between two philosophical systems. This impulse, which Hegel refers to as the 'seething urge,' originates in the natural necessity to take shape in the form of a system, an urge that at the same time battles against this necessity by denying the very possibility of enduring shape. The 'impulse' corresponds to the 'need of the times' – the *Zeitgeist*.

A differentiation (*Differenzierung*) between systems in philosophy thus indicates that while they differ in form their essential aim remains the same. Philosophy appears in a manifold of forms, but the diversity of philosophical systems is the progressive growth or *Differenz* of one Reason, of one common ground. The *Wörterbuch des Philosophischen Begriffe* defines *Differenz* as a difference that is opposed to 'sameness,' as an 'apartness.' It defines *Differenzierung* as the development of new characteristics by means of which one can identify various stages of a unified process. The stages are distinct (*unterschiedlich*) in that they are not the same, but they are all part of a unified, organic process.[11] Thus *Differenzierung* indicates coming into being of new distinguishing characteristics or features (*Merkmale*), and these, according to Hegel, are determined by the need of the times. Philosophy carries with it its own verdict – namely, the inner telic drive that guides its progress. The time had come for system, and for *system differentiation*. The notion of system differentiation is the very core of Hegel's *Differenzschrift* and his radically new contribution to our understanding of the history of philosophy. It is the need for such system differentiation – the need of philosophy (*Bedürfniss der Philosophie*) – that drives us from Kant through Fichte through Schelling to Hegel. As Harris and Cerf point out in their translation of *Differenzschrift* (hereafter HC – see note 2 for details), 89 n 7, 'the need of philosophy' for Hegel, means both 'the need (at this time) for philosophy, *and* what philosophy needs (at this time).'

A brief look at the manner in which Hegel uses the terms *Differenz* and *Unterschied* in his later works points back to the *Differenzschrift* in an illuminating way. While it would be folly to deny that Hegel uses the terms inconsistently and at times interchangeably, there is sufficient consistency to lend support to the claim that Hegel's choice of *Differenz* in the title of his essay of 1801 is not insignificant. After the essay of 1801, Hegel employs the term *Differenz* in the strict technical sense discussed above in *The Philosophy of Right*, the *Logic* of the *Encyclopaedia*, *The Philosophy of Nature*, the *Lectures on the Philosophy of Religion* (vol. II), and the *Lectures on the History of Philosophy* (vol. III). Even a cursory reading of the relevant passages of these texts suggests that the appearance of the term in the title of Hegel's essay is indeed significant: in each of these texts, the term appears to bear the connotations described above. It is in the *Encyclopaedia*, both in the *Logic* and in the *Philosophy of Nature*, and in the *Lectures on the History of Philosophy* that Hegel addresses the notion of *Differenz* most directly, and we can here profit from a careful examination of the texts.

'Differenz' in the Encyclopaedia

Hegel's Absolute can be illustrated in terms of a syllogism, the distinct terms of which are fully intelligible only in their relatedness. Together the terms form a reasoned whole in which each term mediates the connection of the others. These terms are Idea, Nature, and Spirit. The analysis of the Absolute Idea in the Logic is aptly summarized by Findlay as follows: 'The absolute Idea is the abstracted notion of absoluteness, i.e., of the return to self in and through otherness, and it contains within itself all that leads up to such a consummation: the "descriptive" surface categories of the Doctrine of Being, with their coverage of mere quality and quantity, the "explanatory" categories of the Doctrine of Essence, with their reference of everything to everything *else* for explanation which in its turn refers back to the point of origin, and the 'self-explanatory' or absolutist categories of the Doctrine of the Notion, where all is a commerce of self with self. and a development of self into self, until we end up with the self-explanatory teleological conceptions of Life, Cognition, and Practice, and of the practical-theoretical Absolute Idea.'[12]

The dialectical relationship of the 'categories of thought' – Being and Nothing, Quality and Quantity, Identity and Difference, Whole and Part, Universal and Individual, and so on – is discussed in order to demonstrate that none of these terms is fully intelligible when taken as isolated, distinct entities and that it is only when they are correlated with their 'other' that one can make sense of them. Only when the relation between the categories has been fully grasped can we speak of having achieved a properly rational mode of thinking.[13]

Hegel explains that thought develops in three stages – (a) the Abstract side, or that of understanding; (b) the Dialectical, or that of negative reason; and (c) the Speculative, or that of positive reason. In the Abstract stage the understanding tries to keep the categories of thought distinct, and fixed. But the categories cannot be kept distinct, and these finite determinations are self-sublated (*sich aufheben*) and transformed into the other. Finally, Reason apprehends the unity of the determinations in their opposition – the affirmation that is embodied in their disintegration and their transition. Clearly, for Hegel, to think rationally is to move beyond *Unterschiede*, which are externally and artificially imposed on things by the understanding, and to see reality in its various manifestations as organic and dialectically interrelated. Here his use of *Differenz* is consistent with its use in the *Differenzschrift*. However, whereas in the *Differenzschrift* Hegel is referring to the difference between systems of philosophy, here he is discussing the differentiated unity of the Absolute Idea. In the Logic, the many differentiations of this unity are the chain of categories, which follow a necessary, dialectical process in order to reach the Absolute Idea. And this process involves the sublation (*Aufhebung*) of distinctions (*Unterschiede*).

The term *Differenz* first appears in section 85 in the discussion of The Doctrine of Being: 'Being itself and the special sub-categories of it which follow, as well as those of logic in general, may be looked upon as definitions of the Absolute, or metaphysical definitions of God: at least the first and third category in every triad may, – the first, where the thought-form of the triad is formulated in its simplicity, and the third, being the return from differentiation [*Differenz*] to a simple self-reference ... The second sub-category in each triad, where the grade of thought is in its differentiation, gives, on the other hand, a definition of the finite.'[14]

Differenz is next used is in the second part of the *Encyclopaedia* – the *Philosophy of Nature*. According to Hegel, Nature is the Idea self-externalized, lost is its externality, its otherness, and having as purpose a progressive casting away of self-externalization in the journey towards Spirit itself, which Nature eventually becomes. Nature's aim is to achieve a self-independent unity – a unity that can be properly fulfilled only in Spirit.

Hegel's philosophical interpretation of Nature falls into the usual triad – here, of Mechanics, Physics, and Organics – and discloses the eventual victory of unity over mutual externality. In the Mechanics Hegel introduces us to Space, Time, Motion, and the distribution of Matter. He explains that the dynamics of attraction and repulsion account for the logical differentiation and reintegration which, when unified, become the Absolute. Having attended to the quantitative aspects of matter, Hegel proceeds, in the Physics, to a study of the qualitative dimensions of Matter. The first part of the Physics concerns the universal qualities of physical being, and the second examines the specific qualities of being that differentiate various sorts of matter. The third and final section deals with the reintegration of the various species of physical bodies.

In the second part, 'The Physics of Total Individuality,' Hegel moves from an account of the spatial determination of bodies (Shape), through the relation between the properties of bodies and the elements (Particularization of the Individual Body), to the chemical process that occurs between bodies (The Chemical Process). In the discussion of the properties of bodies Hegel offers an analysis of colour, of the relation of fire, air, and water to physical bodies, and of electricity. Hegel held that electricity can be explained as the attempt of bodies to overcome their difference (*Differenz*). The relevant passage is as follows: 'In the mechanical sphere, bodies manifest their self in an ideal movement, in the *internal* oscillation of sound; but now, in their reciprocal *physical* tension, they manifest their *real* – although still only abstractly real – selfhood as their *light*, but as a light that is pregnant with difference (*differentes*): this is the electrical relation.' Electricity explains how 'physically individualized bodies, as the totality of their properties, behave toward one another': 'While to our senses, these separate properties fall apart from each other, the individual body is their unifying bond; precisely as our conception of things recombines them into a unity. Now this individual totality stands in a relationship, and it is this relationship which we must consider from this standpoint. But as developed totality, body is a differentiated (*differente*) totality; and this difference (*Differenz*) in remaining a totality, is only difference (*Differenz*) as such, which therefore necessarily requires two terms mutually related' (323).

'Differenz' in the Lectures on the History of Philosophy

I conclude my discussion of Hegel's use of *Differenz* with a cursory look at a section of Hegel's *Lectures on the History of Philosophy*. It is here that Hegel's use of the term most clearly provides support for my contention that he distinguished between *Differenz* and *Unterschied* and that this distinction anticipated the systematic enterprise brought to fruition in his subsequent works.

In the passage in question, Hegel is engaged in a critical exposition of Schelling's Absolute – 'the night in which all cows are black.' The central problem with the Absolute is its apparent inability to explain the construction of the finite. If the Absolute contained diversity and negations, then it would not be a genuine Absolute, yet it must have content, for it can exist as Identity only if it

Der Unterschied zwischen 'Differenz' und 'Unterschied' 251

is identity of something. The content of the Absolute, Schelling claims, consists of disparate elements that are quantitatively different (marked by *Differenz*): 'Between Subject and Object nothing else but quantitative difference (*Differenz*) is possible.' For no qualitative difference (*Differenz*) regarding these two is possible.'[15]

For Schelling, quantitative difference is the basis of all finitude – every determined 'power' or 'potency' of the Absolute marks a quantitative difference of subject and object. However, Hegel remarks, this merely quantitative difference is not enough to render the Absolute concrete or self-developing. The difference (*Differenz*) between subject and object must be understood as a qualitative one, as a distinction (*Unterschied*) that is sublated. Hegel seems to think that when Schelling speaks of quantitative *Differenz* he means quantitative *Verscheidenheit*, which is not the true difference (*Unterschied*) that is needed at this point. Schelling needs to show how the qualitative *Differenzierung* of the Absolute is the result of the sublation of distinctions (*Unterschiede*). In a move that hearkens back to the *Differenzschrift*, Hegel criticizes the opening developments of Schelling's dialectic for failing to show how the Absolute is self-particularizing or self-differentiating.

The 'Unterschied' between Externally Reflective Philosophy and Internally (Speculative) Reflective Philosophy

In the *Differenzschrift*, Hegel explains that in order to appreciate the development of contemporary philosophy, it is necessary to understand the two sides of the philosophy of Fichte, who serves as a transition figure between reflective, critical philosophy and authentic speculative philosophy. Hegel characterizes the tension between the two sides of Fichte's philosophy as follows:

> There are two sides to Fichte's system. On the one hand it has established the pure concept of Reason and of speculation and so has made philosophy possible. On the other hand, it has equated Reason with pure consciousness and raised Reason as apprehended in a finite shape to the status of a principle. That these two sides should be distinguished (*unterscheiden*) must be shown to be an inner necessity of the problem itself (*die Sache selbst*), even though the external occasion for making the distinctions is a need of the time and is now provided by a bit of contemporary flotsam in time's stream, namely Reinhold's *Contributions* ... In these *Contributions* the aspect of authentic speculation and hence of philosophy in Fichte's system is overlooked; and so is the aspect of Schelling's system which distinguishes (*unterscheidet*) it from Fichte's – the distinction being that in the philosophy of nature Schelling sets the Subject-Object beside the subjective Subject-Object and presents both as united in something higher than the subject.[16]

The external occasion for making this distinction, as Hegel writes, is not only a 'need of the times,' but is also provided by Reinhold's *Contributions*, in which he 'overlooks' the authentic philosophizing in Fichte's system. Hegel writes:

> An age which has so many philosophical systems lying behind it in its past must apparently arrive at the same indifference which life acquires after it has tried all forms. The urge toward totality continues to express itself, but only as an urge toward completeness of information. Individuality becomes fossilized and no longer ventures out into life. Through the variety of what he has, the individual tries to procure the illusion of being what he is not. He refuses living participation demanded by science, transforming it into mere information, keeping it at a distance and in purely objective shape. Deaf to all demands that he should raise himself to universality, he maintains himself imperturbably in his self-willed particularity. If indifference of this sort escalates into curiosity, it may believe nothing to be more vital than giving a name to a newly developed philosophy, expressing dominion over it by finding a name for it ... In this way philosophy is transposed to the plane of information. Information is concerned with alien objects. In the philosophical knowledge that is only erudition, the inward totality does not bestir itself, and neutrality retains its perfect freedom from commitment.[17]

Science (philosophy) demands 'living participation' in order to fulfil the 'urge toward totality.' The perennial character of authentic philosophy, which demands a living interest, is contrasted with the stolid indifference of the historical empiricist's approach to philosophy, which regards all philosophical perspectives as purely idiosyncratic. The historical empiricist dismisses philosophies of the past as failures, or as mere relics. Such an attitude, Hegel writes, can only arrest the growth of philosophy and its internally reflective history – the 'inward totality does not bestir itself.'[18] According to Reinhold, Hegel writes, the history of philosophy is a handy source of information that philosophers may use in order to avoid past 'mistakes.' Philosophies of the past are useful in so far as they introduce helpful techniques for thinking about the world.

However, as Hegel observes, 'the project of such an investigation presupposes an image of philosophy as a kind of handicraft, something that can be improved by newly invented turns of skill.'[19] If philosophy were indeed 'a lifeless product of alien ingenuity' it would have the same kind of 'perfectibility of which mechanical arts are capable.'[20] Yet it is the pursuit of 'newly invented turns of skill' or 'technical knacks' that severs Reason from the forms it takes in history and reduces the history of philosophy to a series of defunct philosophies, each one distinct (*unterschiedlich*) from the others, with no common inner essence or purpose to bind them together.

Der Unterschied zwischen 'Differenz' und 'Unterschied' 253

If we study the particular forms that various philosophies have taken in the past, we can recognize patterns emerging that correspond to the inner shape of life itself. By remembering that the history of philosophy is the coming to be of the Absolute, which appears in the form of one Reason, we are able to detect the Spirit that arises through the different forms of philosophy. If we adopt Hegel's systematic-teleological point of view, we can understand what Hegel means by an 'urge to totality': by looking beyond the appearances of Reason we see that every philosophy is complete within itself, and all are teleologically oriented by the Absolute as it discloses itself in the process of history. Reason does not annul or reject the deficient forms of philosophy, rather it grows away from them. In its struggle for freedom, Reason strives towards the Absolute by 'outgrowing' the particular form of philosophy in which it finds itself embodied.

If a philosophical system has failed, it has done so because the time had not yet come for Spirit to be in-and-for-itself. The particular form that Reason assumes at a given moment in history is merely the appearance of Reason not yet on a level with the totality of Reason – the Absolute. 'If we look more closely at the particular form worn by a philosophy we see that it arises, on the one hand, from the living originality of the spirit whose work and spontaneity have reestablished and shaped the harmony that has been rent; on the other hand, from the particular form of the dichotomy (*die Entzweiung*) from which the system emerges.'[21] By attending 'more closely,' we can recognize the distinction (*Unterschied*) between the form that a particular philosophy assumes and Spirit itself. Moreover, we can see that philosophy emerges and flourishes in response to the fragmentation and disharmony of a particular time.

Philosophy flourishes, Hegel writes, when the world is in the process of decline, and the task of philosophy, which is to strive for the Absolute by overcoming the dichotomy (*Entzweiung, Unterschied*) in knowledge, is determined by the 'needs of the times': 'When the might of union vanishes from the life of men and the antitheses lose their living connection and reciprocity and gain independence, the need of philosophy arises.'[22] Philosophy responds to the fragmentation and disharmony by 'growing,' by bringing life into the fossilized form of philosophy, which is crippling the telic advance of science (philosophy). The history of philosophy consists in nothing more than the telic progress of the one authentic philosophy – speculative philosophy.

The 'Differenz' between Externally Reflective Philosophy and Speculative Philosophy

In the *Differenzschrift*, Hegel announces that the time has come for systematic philosophy, which would give new vitality and movement to the entire history of philosophy and comprehend and unify the history of philosophy in an organic manner. To approach the formulation of such a systematic philosophy or system of science, Hegel proposes to show how Reason 'grows away' from reflective philosophy towards speculative philosophy.

It must be pointed out that 'reflection' has a different meaning for Hegel that it does for Kant and Fichte. Kant, in 'The Amphiboly of Concepts of Reflection' (KrV A261/B317), defines transcendental reflection as follows: 'The act by which I confront the comparison of representations with the cognitive faculty to which it belongs, and by means of which I distinguish whether it is as belonging to the pure understanding or to sensible intuition that they are to be compared with one another, I call *transcendental reflection*.' For Kant, reflection entails the ability to distinguish the sphere of sensibility from that of understanding, and so it cannot be assigned simply to one sphere or the other. Neither is it identified with Reason, for Reason is a faculty that seeks unity, not differentiation or diversity. For Fichte, reflection is the means (or activity) whereby consciousness reflects on its own activity. In the reflection of the action of the Ego on itself, there exists a fundamental opposition between the reflecting Ego and the part of the Ego that is reflected on.

For Hegel, refection mediates between finite oppositions of the understanding and the infinite activities of (speculative) Reason. The distinction between 'reflective philosophy' and 'speculative philosophy' is well explained by Cerf: 'Reflective philosophy that has not yet come to be the true conception of philosophy, philosophy that is not really philosophy – inauthentic philosophy over against authentic philosophy which is, and cannot but be speculative. In terms of Kantian faculties reflective philosophy is philosophy of the intellect (*der Verstand*) and speculative philosophy is philosophy of Reason (*die Vernunft*), but of a Reason which has been allowed to trespass on territory Kant believed to be inaccessible to finite man.'[23] It is typical of reflective philosophy, Cerf writes, that it relies on arguments, proofs, and the whole apparatus of logic and that it sticks to the natural sciences as the source of the only reliable knowledge of nature. Speculative philosophy is philosophy that 'has finally come into its own truth'; it expresses its holistic vision of the whole of God, nature, and self-consciousness in a systematic, organic form. Speculative philosophy is able to unite God, nature, and self-consciousness.

Fichte's system is, for Hegel, the mediating element by means of which Reason takes its first speculative steps. It was Fichte, according to Hegel, who turned Kant's deduction of the categories into a genuine science of knowledge. Kant began with an empty 'Ego' as the subject of transcendental apperception, hence he could not account for the relationship between the categories and the unity of self-consciousness.[24] However, Fichte did try to deduce the categories from the unity of self-consciousness, or from Ego = Ego. Furthermore, in the construction of his system of idealism, Fichte developed a method that made a profound impression on the young Hegel and which Hegel himself adopted and refined. Fichte's science of knowledge consists of a series of mental acts of the Ego (which the philosopher observes), as well as acts that are themselves the observations of the philosopher. What impressed Hegel so deeply about this 'double series' is the self-generating nature of the first series.[25] Fichte explained that the Ego-Subject of introspection was constituted in and through the very act of introspection. Hegel embraces Fichte's method as genuinely speculative and adopts it in his own system.[26] In the *Phenomenology of Spirit*, for example, the progress of the concept, which corresponds to Fichte's 'first series,' consists of the development of successive forms of consciousness, which eventually metamorphose into the standpoint of the philosopher.

At this point, one might be inclined to ask: 'If Fichte's philosophy was genuinely speculative, then in what way did Schelling's system constitute an advance over it?' Fichte's philosophy presents a genuinely speculative theory of the Ego, which shows how the Ego produces a world. However, Fichte's system does not successfully demonstrate that the world is the real world of the Ego, and hence it fails in its speculative goal. Though Fichte hoped to overcome the oppositions between the Ego and the world, between phenomena and noumena, or between the Ego and the non-Ego, by 'subjectivizing' the non-Ego, he ended up conceding that the world of phenomena is all we can know. Fichte concludes his system with 'Ego *ought* to be equal to Ego' rather than Ego = Ego. For Hegel, Fichte's mere 'ought' was not good enough for the science of knowledge. The system, if it is indeed authentic speculation, must conclude with the principle of identity – that is, Ego = Ego. Fichte's philosophy remains only partially speculative.[27]

Despite the shortcomings of Fichte's system, his foundation of the principle of identity – that is, 'intellectual intuition' – which is pure thinking in itself (I = I, where the 'I' is the identity of subject and object), points to the path we must follow if philosophy is to advance as a science. It was Schelling who elaborated the system in this direction. The task of the transcendental philosopher, according to Schelling, is to 'start with the subjective, as the first and absolute, and to let the objective arise from it.' Schelling must show how both the self becomes a world, the 'subjective Subject-Object,' and how the world becomes a self, the 'objective Subject-Object.' Schelling attempts to fulfil his double task by beginning with the 'point of indifference' – the transcendental intuition of the self positing itself as other in order to attain self-consciousness. The 'point of indifference,' which Hegel calls the 'vanishing point,' constitutes the moment where finite consciousness annihilates itself by recognizing its own antinomic character.

Schelling's 'point of indifference' is clearly indebted to Fichte's notion of the self-positing Ego, but Schelling successfully posits both Subject and Object in the Absolute and hence is able to posit the identity of Object and Subject: 'The principle of identity is the absolute principle of Schelling's system as a *whole*. Philosophy and system coincide. Identity does not lose itself in the parts, still less in the result.'[28]

Hegel is concerned to show that Fichte and Schelling's philosophies are part of one system, In the title of the *Differenzschrift* 'des ... Systems' is singular; Hegel is attempting to show that Schelling's system grew out of, and is part of, Fichte's system. According to Lukács, it was Friedrich Engels who was the first to stress Hegel's role in bringing to the public domain the extent to which Schelling's philosophy had gone beyond Fichte's: 'Only this is certain, that it was Hegel who made Schelling aware of how far he had, without realizing it, gone beyond Fichte.'[29] But what is most important is the way in which Hegel went about this – by means of a radically new teleological framework of the history of philosophy, which showed how Fichte's system was internally deficient because it did not adequately reflect the need of the times. The pervasiveness of Schelling's system, Hegel claimed, is inevitable, since it expresses a stage of the community that has already manifested itself.[30]

The task at hand is to examine the difference (*Differenz*) between reflective and speculative philosophy from a systematic-teleological perspective. In judging philosophical systems, one must distinguish the philosophy (or philosophizing) from the system and clarify Hegel's view of the relation between 'philosophy' and 'philosophical system' (or 'system of science'). Once this relation has been understood it will become clear that the fundamental need from which philosophy arises is crucial for Hegel and that it is this teleological perspective that Hegel wants us to understand – the transition from reflective to speculative philosophy. Authentic philosophizing must embody the connection of the finite to the infinite Absolute and must be able to produce a totality of knowing, a *system of science*: 'For true philosophizing on the other hand, even though it may be incoherent, the posited and its opposites disappear because it does not simply put them into contact with other finite things, but connects them with the Absolute and so suspends things. Since the finite things are manifold, the connection of the finite to the Absolute is a manifold. Hence, philosophizing must aim to posit this manifold as internally connected, and there necessarily arises a need to produce a totality of knowing, a system of science.'[31] Fichte's philosophy is an example of a system in which authentic philosophizing fails to express itself completely: 'If the fundamental need has not achieved perfect embodiment in the system, it has elevated to the Absolute something that is conditioned and exists only as an opposite, then as a system it becomes dogmatism.'[32]

Der Unterschied zwischen 'Differenz' und 'Unterschied'   257

But we must be careful not to misinterpret Hegel here. It must be understood that 'if the fundamental need has not achieved perfect embodiment in the system,' then the philosophy fails as a system, but only as a system. The fundamental need – that is, speculation – remains at the heart of philosophizing: 'The speculation at the basis of the system demands the suspension of opposites,' even though 'the system itself does not suspend them.'[33] Hegel is not intent on explaining where Fichte went wrong as much as he is interested in preserving the authentic speculation struggling to express itself in Fichte's system. His intention is not to destroy Fichte's philosophy in favour of Schelling's. When the conflicts and dichotomies in philosophy reach a decisive level of polarity in history itself, Reason suspends the conflicts and instills movement into the telic advance of philosophy as science. In the *Differenzierung* occurring between reflective philosophy (Kant and Fichte) and speculative philosophy (Schelling and Hegel), Reason had 'exhausted' reflective philosophy by taking it through its paces. While reflective philosophy is dying a natural death, the seed of speculative philosophy has already begun to germinate, ensuring that Reason will continue to progress towards its goal of self-realization. Philosophy embodies its own verdict.

An objection could be raised against my claim here – namely, that Hegel specifically points out at the end of the section entitled *Contemporary Philosophy* that he is concerned primarily with Fichte's philosophy as a system rather than as authentic philosophizing: 'It will become clear from what has been said that we are concerned in this presentation with Fichte's philosophy as a system and not as authentic philosophizing. As a philosophy it is the most thorough and profound speculation, all the more remarkable because at the time when it appeared even the Kantian philosophy had proven unable to awaken Reason to the lost concept of genuine speculation.'[34] Does this not show, one might object, that Hegel is concerned more with the difference (*Unterschied*) between *systems* rather than with the difference (*Differenz*) between philosophies?

In order to address this objection, it must be recalled that for Hegel the systematic character of philosophy arose necessarily out of the problems of the time. Hegel thought of his age as a time when the disintegration of culture had reached a climactic point, which called for a new harmony, in the form of a systematic philosophy. The needs of the time determined the particular form that philosophy had to take. Because the systematic character of philosophy emerged from the concrete, historical situation of the times, Hegel was anxious that philosophy's nature be properly understood. The understanding of the systematic nature of philosophy is inseparable from the understanding of the historical-teleological framework that Hegel introduces in the *Differenzschrift*. The distinctions (*Unterschiede*) between the two systems must be understood as part of the natural progress of authentic philosophizing – the *Differenz* between (or among) philosophies over time. In short, Hegel is of course interested in the stems themselves, not in order to point out how they are different (*Unterschiedlich*) but rather to show how it is that one system grows out of the other.

There has been much debate about the extent to which Hegel was sympathetic to Schelling and the degree to which one can speak of Hegel's 'original' contribution to the objective idealism at the time of the *Differenzschrift*. James Stirling, in *The Secret of Hegel*, claims that Hegel 'cunningly' identified his philosophical platform with that of Schelling in order to secure Schelling's support. However, Lukács, in *The Young Hegel*, writes that Hegel genuinely identified his own thought with that of Schelling, though not without reservations: 'Hegel makes no attempt to subject Schelling's philosophy to scrutiny and there is not even a hint of criticism. The most that can be claimed is that the modern reader who is already familiar with the differences between Hegel and Schelling can see that in a number of places Hegel imputes to Schelling a tendency which seems to fit in better with his own thought than that of Schelling.'[35]

Other Hegel scholars, such as Surber and Harris, have made a somewhat more forceful case for the young Hegel's original contribution at the time of the *Differenzschrift*. In his thorough and definitive statement in *Hegel's Development II: Night Thoughts (Jena 1801–1806)*, Harris writes: 'There are, I think, three principal novelties in the "philosophy of philosophy" that Hegel propounds at the beginning of the *Difference* essay. Two of them are direct developments of his Frankfurt position; the third is the consequence of those developments. There is no doubt that Hegel's coming into Schelling's orbit was the crucial stimulus for the two developments. But neither of them was at all like anything in Schelling's own philosophical development; and the consequence was a new conception of philosophy as "speculative" which influenced Schelling's own thought rather more directly than he influenced it.'[36]

In the *Differenzschrift* Hegel formulates an entirely new, systematic teleological framework that fully comprehends and unifies the history of philosophy in a systematic manner. Hegel understood the fragmentation and disunity of the philosophies of the day as a reflection of the fragmented state of the times, and his 'speculative revolution' in philosophy was a metaphysical expression of the working out of the internal problems of the culture in which he lived. As Lukács observes: 'The defeat of subjective idealism at the hands of objective idealism is not merely the narrow parochial concern of a few philosophers but the intellectual apex of a great socio-historical transformation.'[37] This is precisely what constitutes Hegel's profound and original insight in the *Differenzschrift*: his comprehensive grasp of the historical problems of his day and his ability to relate them to developments in philosophy. It is in the *Differenzschrift* that the seed of Hegel's life's work is to be found.[38]

Notes

1 The full title of the essay is *Differenz des Fichte'schen und Schelling'schen Systems der Philosophie in Beziehung auf Reinhold's Beytrage zur leichtern übersicht des Zustands der Philosophie zu Anfang des Neunzehnten Jahrhunderts, 1stes Heft*; hereinafter cited as *Differenzschrift*.

2 In *Hegel: Reinterpretation, Texts and Commentary* (London: Weidenfeld & Nicolson, 1966), Walter Kaufmann recognizes that Hegel was concerned to examine the systematic character of philosophy. However, he fails to notice that Hegel was interested primarily in how Schelling's philosophy grew out of Fichte's, rather than in the differences (distinctions) between them: 'On the second and more important level, Hegel considered it his first task in philosophy to absorb and fully understand Fichte and Schelling. Schelling had not yet broken with Fichte, whose foremost disciple he was held to be. Hegel articulated the difference between their respective philosophies' (72).

Similarly, Robert Solomon, in *The Spirit of Hegel* (Oxford: Oxford University Press, 1983), writes that the *Differenzschrift* announces the break between Fichte and Schelling: 'The essay was prompted by, and was superficially a response to, an article by Reinhold, who had now become an ardent critic of the new idealism of Fichte and Schelling. Thus the two-fold purpose of Hegel's article was to defend the idealist movement against Reinhold and to distinguish the philosophies of Fichte and Schelling, which, according to Reinhold, Hegel had conflated and confused. In fact, the largest part of the essay is a critique of Fichte's philosophy and a demonstration that Schelling's system was not only different but very much an improvement on Fichte' (107-8).

It is misleading to describe an essay that introduces a radical new approach to philosophy simply as a defence of the idealist movement. Furthermore, Solomon maintains that Hegel had no intention of unravelling the internal variations in Fichte and Schelling's systems of philosophy in the *Differenzschrift*: 'Of the Differenz-essay, Hegel insisted that it was an "external" treatment of the two philosophers, an examination from the outside in which they were weighed and compared, but without any attempt to get 'inside' and see where they would lead. This is what Hegel would do some five years later, in the Phenomenology, when he would add his own system to the history of German Idealism as a synthesis and improvement upon both of them' (109). It is clear from the above passage that Solomon's reading of Hegel lacks any appreciation for Hegel's vision of philosophy at the time of the *Differenzschrift*.

Harris and Cerf, in their otherwise-excellent translation (HC) of the *Differenzschrift* – *The Difference between Fichte's and Schelling's System of Philosophy* (Albany: State University of New York Press, 1977) – fail to explain the implications of the word *Differenz*. The translator's preface states that Cerf detected in the essay 'speculative insouciance and even simple carelessness, the latter no doubt due to the extraordinary speed with which Hegel wrote the essays.' It is difficult to estimate how careless Hegel was in the writing of the essay itself. However, a strong case can be made that he chose his words with great care when he wrote the title of the work.

At least one other author shares my concern over the implications of the term *Differenz*. Gary Percesepe, in 'Telos in Hegel's *Differenz des Fichte'schen un Schelling'schen Systems der Philosophie*,' *Philosophy Research Archives*, 10, (March 1985), points out that the use of *Differenz* must not go unnoticed.

3 Even Walter Cerf, a native German speaker, fails to recognize the effect that Hegel's use of *Differenz* in the title has for interpretation of the text as a whole.

4 Percesepe makes the same point in 'Telos': 'The question is: Why did Hegel choose to employ this term when he had a perfectly good word available, i.e., *Unterschied*? The answer is not unimportant and harbors within it hermeneutic possibilities' (395).

5 Ibid., 86–7.

6 Ibid., 114.

7 Ibid., 87.

8 The metaphor of growth/*differenz* arises throughout Hegel's writings, most notably in the *Phenomenology of Spirit*. For example, in A.V. Miller's translation (Oxford: Oxford University Press, 1977): 'The more conventional opinion ... does not comprehend the diversity of philosophical systems as the progressive unfolding of truth, but rather sees in it simple disagreements. The bud disappears in the bursting forth of the blossom, and one might say that the former is refuted by the latter; similarly, when the fruit appears, the blossom is shown to be a false manifestation of the plant, and the fruit now emerges as the truth of it instead. These forms are not just distinguished from one another, they also supplant one another as mutually incompatible. Yet at the same time their fluid nature makes them moments of an organic unity in which they do not only conflict, but in which each is as necessary as the other; and this mutual necessity alone constitutes the life of the whole' (Preface, p. 3). 'Spirit in its formation matures slowly and quietly into its new shape, dissolving bit by bit the structure of the previous world ... The gradual crumbling ... is cut short by a sunburst which ... illuminates the new world. It [the new world] comes on the scene for the first time in its immediacy or its Notion. Just as little as a building is finished when its foundation has been laid, so little is the achieved Notion of the whole the whole itself. When we wish to see an oak with its massive trunk and spreading branches and foliage, we are not content to be shown an acorn instead' (Preface, pp. 6–7).

9 In HC it was the publisher who inserted the definite article. Since Hegel had not used a definite article, Harris had intended to render the title without it, but at the

publisher's insistence he relented, since he felt at the time that he did not have a strong argument for leaving it out.
10 Percesepe ('Telos') offers an enlightening explanation of *Differenz* in terms of biology: 'Every difference (differentiation) which *is* in fact a difference is necessarily tied to the emergence of new forms. This is true whether we speak of biology or of philosophy. Biologists recognize an early stage in the strict differentiation of cells, when cells split off from one another, forming, in their turn, blood cells, neural cells, muscle cells, etc. Following this early differentiation there follows a developmental stage, where the biologist discerns further structuring in the process, such that various organs begin to form out of the partially differentiated cells' (396).
11 Hoffmeister's *Wörterbuch* defines *differenz* as follows: '**Differenz** (gr. *diaphora*, lat. *differentia*), der Unterschied, die Verschiedenheit; in der Logik ein aus dem beziehenden Denen entspringender Begriff, dessen korrelat Gleichheit ist ... **Differenzierung**, die Feststellung der Unterschiede, bes. der feineren; in der Entwicklungslehre die Entstehung neuer Merkmale, durch die gleichartige Wesen sich bei der Fortentwicklung voneinander unterscheiden.' Johannes Hoffmeister, *Wörterbuch des Philosophischen Begriffe* (Hamburg: 1955), 167.
12 *Hegel's Philosophy of Nature*, trans. A.V. Miller, with foreword by J.N. Findlay (Oxford: Clarendon Press, 1970), xii.
13 When Hegel speaks of a rational mode of thinking, his view of reason both differs from, and is a critique of, Kant's distinction between reason and understanding. Hegel acknowledges his debt to Kant but insists that, contrary to Kant's claims, reason is endowed with the power to attain knowledge of ultimate reality. Hence reason is superior to understanding, since understanding remains limited, given that the categories with which it understands the world are one-sided and finite. In the *Logic* Hegel writes: 'Kant was the first definitely to signalise the distinction between Reason and Understanding. The object of the former, as he applied the term, was the infinite and unconditioned, of the latter the finite and conditioned. Kant did valuable service when he enforced the finite character of the cognitions of the understanding founded merely upon experience, and stamped their contents with the name of appearance. But his mistake was to stop at the purely negative point of view, and to limit the unconditionality of Reason to an abstract self-sameness without any shade of distinction. It degrades Reason to a finite and conditioned thing.' *The Logic of Hegel*, trans. William Wallace (Oxford: Oxford University Press, 1963), 92–3.

It is the task of reason to dissolve and progress beyond the static categories of the understanding: 'The metaphysic of understanding is dogmatic, because it maintains half-truths in their isolation: whereas the idealism of speculative philosophy carries out the principle of totality and shows that it can reach beyond the inadequate formularies of abstract thought. Thus idealism would say: – The soul is neither finite

only, nor infinite only; it is really the one just as much as the other, and in that way neither the one nor the other. In other words, such formularies in their isolation are inadmissible, and only come to account as formative elements in larger notion ... We show more obstinacy in dealing with the categories of the understanding. These are terms we believe to be somewhat firmer – or even absolutely firm and fast. We look upon them as separated from each other by an infinite chasm, so that opposite categories can never get at each other. It is the battle of Reason to break up the rigidity to which the understanding has reduced everything.' Ibid., 67.
14 Ibid., 156–7.
15 *Gesammelte Werke*, Band 20 (Frankfurt: Suhrkamp, 1986), 440, my translation.
16 HC, 82. Harris and Cerf point out that Hegel is playing here with Reinhold's use of 'Übersicht,' which can mean both 'overview' and 'oversight.' 'In his "Contributions to an *Overview*" Reinhold manages to *overlook* the most important points' (HC, 82).
17 Ibid., 85.
18 Ibid., 85
19 Ibid., 86.
20 Ibid., 86.
21 Ibid., 89.
22 Ibid., 91.
23 Ibid., xvii.
24 In the *Lectures on the History of Philosophy*, trans. E.S. Haldane and Frances H. Simson, 1st pub. 1894, London: Routledge and Kegan Paul, 1963, III, Hegel writes: 'Kant [thus] accepts the categories in an empiric way, without thinking of developing of necessity these differences from unity' (439).
25 Hegel writes: 'What [the science of knowledge] makes into the object of its thinking is not a dead concept which would only behave passively toward the investigation of it, and which is made into something only because the science of knowledge thinks about it. Rather, it is living and active, generating cognitions out of itself by its own activity so that the philosophers need merely observe it. His business in the matter is nothing more than starting the animate object upon a course of purposive activity, watching its activity, conceiving it and comprehending it as one.' *Science of Knowledge (Wissenschaftslehre), the First and Second Introductions*, ed. and trans. Peter Heath and John Lach (New York: Appleton Century Crofts, 1970), 30.
26 In the *Science of Logic* Hegel writes that philosophy cannot employ the method of subordinate sciences such as mathematics: 'Rather it can only be *the nature of the content, setting itself in motion*, which provides the subject matter of philosophical cognition. It is this content's own reflection which then posits and originates the specific character (*Bestimmung*) of philosophy.' (*Science of Logic*, trans. W.H. Johnston and L.G. Struthers (New York: Macmillan, 1929), 36.
27 It has often been pointed out that Hegel misinterpreted Fichte. Though Fichte made

several attempts to reformulate the principles of the *Science of Knowledge*, Hegel persisted in basing his critiques on early versions. Helmut Girndt, in *Die Differenz des Fichteschen und Hegelschen Systems in der Hegelschen 'Differenzschrift'* (Bonn, 1965), attempts to rescue Fichte from Hegel's criticisms by undertaking a rebuttal of Hegel's speculative position from the point of view of the *Science of Knowledge*. In *Hegel's Fichtekritik und die Wissenschaftslehre von 1801* (München: Karl Alber, 1970), Ludwig Siep argues that the 1804 version of the *Science of Knowledge* provided valuable emendations that ought to have addressed Hegel's concerns but that Hegel chose to ignore them and continued to rely on the 1794 edition as the authoritative and complete formulation of Fichte's position. More recently, Reinhard Lauth, in 'Hegels Speculative Position in seiner "Differenz des Fichteschen und Schellingschen Systems der Philosophie" im Lichte der Wissenschaftslehre,' *Kant Studien*, 72 (1981), 430–61, undertakes a critical analysis of Hegel's arguments from the point of view of the *Science of Knowledge*, relying only on Fichte's texts before and including those of 1801. He argues that Hegel's idealism lacks any scientific foundation and cannot meet the epistemological requirements of Fichte's *Science of Knowledge*.

28 HC, 155.
29 Lukács, *The Young Hegel*, trans. R. Livingstone (London: Merlin Press, 1975), 241.
30 Percesepe offers an enlightening account of Hegel's role in the 'breach' between Fichte and Schelling: 'The crucial matter them, is that Hegel wants to *elevate* the conflict between Fichte ... and Schelling, so as to raise the conflict between subjective and objective idealism to a decisive polarity *in history itself* ... In order to accomplish this, Hegel need a high-powered method of criticism which will not merely offer abstract objections to a system but will follow the system's dialectical unfolding, demonstrating concretely how a deficient system *carries within itself* the seeds of its own destruction. This approach to the criticism of the history of philosophy is attempted quite consciously for the first time in the pages of the *Differenzschrift*' ('Telos,' 401).
31 HC, 113.
32 Ibid., 114.
33 Ibid., 117.
34 Ibid., 117–18.
35 James Stirling, *The Secret of Hegel* (Edinburgh: Oliver & Boyd, 1908), 662–3; Lukács, *The Young Hegel*, 252.
36 *Differenzschrift*, trans. Jere Surber, ii; H.S. Harris, *Hegel's Development II: Night Thoughts (Jena 1801–1806)* (Oxford: Clarendon Press, 1983), 140.
37 Lukács, *The Young Hegel*, 261.
38 I wish to express my gratitude to Henry Harris for his criticisms of an earlier draft of this paper.

12

Dialectic as Counterpoint: On Philosophical Self-Measure in Plato and Hegel

JAMES CROOKS

> Hegel's philosophy is a four-part fugue, because the three parts of the 'system' lead back to what is outwardly presented as the 'prelude.' It does this because its goal is to bring the kingdom of the spirit down to earth, to bring philosophy down out of the clouds, and to raise the quest itself into wisdom, by making it terminate in knowledge (Spirit's knowledge of itself) rather than in faith.[1]

The final chapter of H.S. Harris's *Night Thoughts (Jena 1801–1806)* is mounted handsomely in a series of counterpoint metaphors.[2] Coming as they do at the end of a substantial study, their reference is primarily programmatic. Harris employs them to express what he takes to be essential to the Hegelian project viewed at the most comprehensive level of internal analysis.

It seems to me, however, that these metaphors – especially that of the fugue – are also useful for exploring questions about the status of Hegel's philosophy which extend beyond strictly programmatic interests. For instance, the idea of a philosophical counterpoint could act as an effective standard for comparing Hegel's speculative dialectic with the multiple procedures of dialectic's first great advocate, Plato. Then again, some workable concept of the difference between the ancient and modern forms of dialectic could cast more light on the notoriously difficult problem of the relation between Hegel's thought and the modern world, in which philosophy on the European continent became entangled less than a generation after Hegel's death and that persists, unresolved, in the age of post-modernity.

In what follows, I pursue these matters taking Harris's metaphors not only as an impetus but as a challenge. It is my hope, in reflecting on counterpoint and dialectic, to grasp adequately that and why Hegel's philosophy is a fugue – and why the form of the fugue remains central in post-Hegelian thought.

It has occurred to me that the readership of philosophy would be better served if scholars and commentators were constrained to begin their researches as Spinoza began the *Ethics* – with a bald statement of the axioms upon which their work as a whole could be said to rest. Were I to proceed in this way I would here acknowledge at least three. First, the purpose of any account, of any *logos*, is measure. Second, the measure proper to the *logos* of philosophy has always been taken to include a self-measure. Third, philosophical self-measure may be of two kinds – immanent or transcendent. The first two items I treat as uncontroversial: all accounts (*logoi*), whatever their nature, aim at bringing some matter into view (at describing its dimensions), and the philosophical *logos* has always counted its own reflective activities among the matters that it seeks to describe. The third item, however, requires some provisional explaining. I am concerned there to propose the distinction that prompts my own experiment with Harris's counterpoint metaphors – a distinction with which some readers might well take issue. What might be said, briefly, in advance of commentary on specific texts and by way of preparation?

As far back as Aristotle and Plato, philosophy is concerned with itself, determined to measure itself, in two radically different ways. It assesses its form or structure as a body of argument, as a theoretical discourse – it takes as its own the study of logic and methodology. It also sometimes concerns itself with what we might call its supra-theoretical essence or constitutional activity – what Goethe indicates, with the incomparable economy of the poet, by having Faust translate *logos* as 'deed' (*That*).[3] The difference between these modes of measure is spanned adequately, I think, in the distinction between immanence and transcendence suggested in my third axiom. In logic or methodology, theoretical discourse takes account of itself. It polices itself from within, attempting to counter and neutralize the various structural obscurities that hamper use of natural language. By contrast, those thinkers out to account for the essence of the theoretical – for the 'deed' that stands behind proposition and argument, or, to put a recurrent prejudice bluntly, conceals itself within such things – must devise ways of penetrating the theoretical, of negotiating its limit, of going beyond it in order to disclose its supra-theoretical foundation.

It is not my purpose, in the reflections that follow, to justify this second measure (the transcendent) or to assert its superiority over the first (the immanent or logical/ methodological). I argue only that Plato and Hegel have more or less constant recourse to it, that both Plato's deployment of irony, or of the inspired speech of divine madness, or of dramatic situation, and, in a different way, Hegel's determination to philosophize systematically represent attempts to articulate what is constitutive in the theoretical by playing that discourse against other modes of speech. In terms of our impetus from Harris's *Night Thoughts*, they compose a kind of philosophical counterpoint – theoretical discourse contra the supra-theoretical. But now how is this counterpoint worked out in Plato's text and in Hegel's? What emerges, taking those workings as a frame of reference, on the question of dialectic – the obvious methodological link?

My response begins with a look at three of Plato's dialogues – the *Charmides*, the *Phaedrus*, and the *Parmenides*. Each contains a distinct supra-theoretical voice, each of these voices is contrasted or combined with theoretical discourse in a different way, and each of these contrasts or combinations illuminates some portion of Plato's dialectical procedure. The larger purpose of this reading, however, is to lay out something like a compendium of contrapuntal strategies – a rough map of transcendental or contrapuntal self-measure – useful both for distinguishing modern dialectic from that of the ancients and for speculating on Hegel's significance in the project of modern philosophical measure.

To the *Charmides* first. The conversation there concerns *sophrosyne* (itself a species of self-measure). In it, Socrates, Charmides, and Critias consider a number of possible definitions for this virtue with the expressed intention of grasping it theoretically. This consideration, taken as a whole, conforms to a pattern common to other *elenchtic* dialogues.[4] Under close interrogation, each of the proposed definitions is brought to the encounter of its limit, made to collapse, so that as the discussion draws to a close, there is a recognition, shared by the interlocutors, that the theoretical inquiry has failed.

As a final gesture, Socrates acknowledges this failure. He gives expression to the fact that the search for a theory of *sophrosyne* has become entrapped on all sides in contradiction. But the mode of his expression itself effectively undermines and opposes the failure it acknowledges. And it does so by playing theoretical discourse as a whole against a discourse whose sole function is to disclose the 'deed' which constitutes the essence of the *logos* and which is enacted in theoretical inquiry regardless of its success or failure.

For the sake of easy reference, I cite the speech in question together with the rejoinders of Charmides and Critias, which are helpful for interpreting it:

> I think indeed that there is a mistake, and that I am a bad inquirer, for wisdom or temperance I believe to be really a great good. And happy are you, Charmides, if you possess it. Wherefore examine yourself, and see whether you have this gift and can do without the charm, for if you can, I would rather advise you to regard me simply as a fool who is never able to reason out anything, and to rest assured that the more wise and temperate you are, the happier you will be.
>
> Charmides said, I am sure that I do not know, Socrates, whether I have or have not this gift of wisdom and temperance, for how can I know whether I have a thing, of

which even you and Critias are, as you say, unable to discover the nature? Yet I do not quite believe you, and I am sure Socrates, that I do need the charm, and as far as I am concerned, I shall be willing to be charmed by you daily, until you say that I have had enough.

Very good, Charmides, said Critias. If you do this I shall have a proof of your temperance – that is, if you allow yourself to be charmed by Socrates, and never desert him in things great or small.[5]

Let us treat this text, in the spirit of our experiment, as a bit of contrapuntal thinking (a texture), isolating its voices or discourses and examining their relation. I said above that in the speech here reproduced Socrates acknowledges theoretical failure. The acknowledgment in and of itself belongs to the foregoing inquiry. It is its end or limit. One of the voices of this text, the most obvious, is that of theory. But Socrates is also speaking ironically here. He apologizes for being 'a bad inquirer.' Yet even the reader with no wider experience of Plato's writings knows that the contradictions that punctuate his attempt at defining *sophrosyne* are not the accidents of an incompetent but the productions of a skilled dialectician. He suggests that Charmides might well forego his 'charm' (a Thracian cure for headaches to be given in combination with a 'curing of the soul').[6] Yet in the context of the work as a whole, it is clear that the genuine 'charm' of Socrates is nothing but dialectical investigation – the abandonment of which he would never recommend in earnest.

In both instances, irony has the same function. It points us away from the acknowledged theoretical failure – determined as it is by the absense of a result, a definition – and back to the process or activity, the 'deed,' of inquiry itself. And it sets before the interlocutors the possibility that it is just this 'deed,' this supra-theoretical engagement for which the failure in question is ultimately of no consequence, that constitutes what is essential in the words that have passed between them.

In the *Charmides*, the supra-theoretical discourse that Plato plays against that of theory is ironic, and in the moment of decision the relation that holds between these voices or discourses is one of inversion, reversal, or opposition. The condition for the possibility of this opposition is laid down by the failure of the theoretical inquiry into *sophrosyne*, by the encounter of contradiction. Its purpose is to disclose the essence of the *logos* and to submit the entire discussion to its measure.

We find further support for this kind of reading in the interpretation of Socrates' apology, which Plato himself puts in the mouths of Charmides and Critias. In spite of Socrates' failure to produce a definition of *sophrosyne*, Charmides declares himself willing to be 'charmed' daily by dialectical inquiry – something he could do only by fastening on the possibility of its supra-theoretical justification disclosed in the discourse of irony. Critias takes this declaration as evidence that Charmides is already in possession of the virtue they have been seeking – a conclusion that he could draw only by granting as inseparable the self-measure that is *sophrosyne* and the self-measure enacted through Socratic inquiry.

This glance at the *Charmides* provides a frame of reference sufficient for introducing a thesis on ancient dialectic, and so also a main point of contrast between Plato and Hegel. In Plato's philosophy, the mechanism of dialectic is always one moment or aspect of a more fundamental, contrapuntal structure. The dialectical inquiry guides theoretical discourse to its limit (to contradiction) – to the place where we are better disposed to the hearing of other discourses, other voices. On this view, the theoretical inquiry undertaken by Socrates, Charmides, and Critias would be essentially the invocation of the opposition of theory and irony that emerges at the end. Let us note, in anticipation of later discussion, that Hegel's own appraisal of the ancients, and of Plato in particular, passes over this operation precisely because it is determined to grasp all dialectic speculatively in terms of the nullity of limitation as such. From such a standpoint, Plato's method seems to consist only in 'abolishing and refuting limited assertions through themselves' and to result in 'nothingness."[7] Hegel is unwilling to admit the possibility of a limit in philosophical reflection that may be met and transgressed (in irony or some other form of supra-theoretical discourse) but not sublated (*aufgehoben*). The ground of this fundamental difference, together with our own thesis on the relation of dialectic and counterpoint in Plato, may be clarified further in reference to a second text – the *Phaedrus*.

Treating the *Charmides* and the *Phaedrus* in succession, we cannot help but be struck, first of all, by a rather pronounced stylistic difference. The external structure of the earlier work is thoroughly dialectical. The supra-theoretical ironic voice that Plato opposes to theory there is not itself verbal. Like all irony, it resounds in another discourse. In the *Phaedrus*, however, dialectical inquiry is itself subordinated to a second art – that of the rhetorician. Given the many occasions on which Socrates expresses his predisposition to the language of question and answer, this development is itself significant and worthy of question. What is at work in Plato's deployment of rhetoric here? Specifically, what can be made of it from the standpoint of contrapuntal analysis?

The *Phaedrus* concerns itself with the measure of good speaking and writing. It is essentially an extended critical review of a speech by Lysias, a copy of which Phaedrus obtains and reads to Socrates. The composition compares the advantages of lovers and non-lovers in the matter of friendship, coming out firmly against love. Phaedrus is impressed by Lysias's ability to confound customary opinion. He finds his praise of the non-lover both clever and convincing. Socrates, however, holds the work to be both materially and formally deficient – mistaken about the nature of love, but also careless in its definition, needlessly repetitious, and so forth. These points Phaedrus is moved to accept with the proviso that Socrates himself do justice to the matter. After considerable urging, Socrates agrees to this. He offers a pair of speeches on love: one in which the position of Lysias is reformed and presented more effectively, and one in which it is retracted and reversed.

I would like to draw attention, first, to the manner in which Plato frames his words. For this framework discloses the connection between the *Phaedrus*'s deployment of rhetoric and the relation between dialectic and counterpoint that marks Platonic thought generally.

Socrates prefaces his rejoinder to Lysias as follows: 'Come then, ye clear-voiced Muses, whether it be from the nature of your song, or from the musical people of Liguria that ye came to be so styled, "assist the tale I tell" under compulsion by my good friend here, to the end that he may think yet more highly of one dear to him, whom he already accounts a man of wisdom.'[8] About halfway through the speech that ensues, Socrates breaks off, asking Phaedrus if he thinks his words 'divinely inspired.'[9] When Phaedrus agrees that he has been 'vouchsafed a quite unusual eloquence,' Socrates responds: 'Then listen to me in silence. For truly there seems to be a divine presence in this spot, so that you must not be surprised if, as my speech proceeds, I become as one possessed.'[10]

Finally, in transition between his reformation of Lysias's composition (the first speech that he makes) and its outright reversal (the second) – having soured apparently on his experiment with rhetoric, and at the point of taking his leave – Socrates says to Phaedrus: 'At the moment when I was about to cross the river, dear friend, there came to me my familiar divine sign – which always checks me when on the point of doing something or other – and all at once I seemed to hear a voice, forbidding me to leave the spot until I had made atonement for some offense to heaven.'[11]

As with the passage from the *Charmides* cited above, these texts make manifest a discourse above and beyond that of theoretical reason. The Socratic experiment with rhetoric is framed on all sides by references to the Muses, to divine voices and divine possession, and to prayer – the mode of our conversation with God. Thinking now contrapuntally (in terms of these ecstatic voices and modes of discourse) we may interpret the species of self-measure deployed in the *Phaedrus* as the subordination of the theoretical to the daemonic. What Plato sees in the practice of rhetoric is the possibility of a disclosure, a transcendental measure, that belongs specifically to a discourse that is enthusiastic or inspired.

It is easy to see how this second contrapuntal disclosure might parellel the first in structure at least. Like ironic discourse, the daemonic voice speaks always from the limit of ordinary reason. It bodies forth as a kind of possession, a kind of madness. At the same time, however, there is an ambiguity or duplicity in such displacements that we do not meet in the more straightforward opposition of theory and irony. For it is clearly Plato's view that daemonic speech may be authentic or inauthentic and that philosophy must concern itself with mastery of the difference.[12]

We can make clear to ourselves what is at stake here in general terms by looking, as we did with our text from the *Charmides*, at what conditions the appearance of the limit of theoretical discourse. In the early dialogues, Socrates invariably describes this limit dialectically by producing contradictions. There the idea is to surmount the strictly theoretical inquiry in and through its very failure. In the daemonic discourse – authentic or not – something else is at work. To speak of love, or indeed of anything, as one possessed is to subordinate straightforward argumentation at the outset by leaping to its limit and appropriating it directly. The inspired discourse begins with the wilful transgression of the theoretical, with the unapologetic declaration, in word itself or in gesture, that it is madness that speaks. Inasmuch as this is so, the problem of distinguishing the authentic daemonic from the inauthentic is essentially that of determining the circumstances in which such a wilful transgression is justified.

Socrates' reversal of Lysias's position – his great speech in praise of love – provides that determination. From the standpoint of our contrapuntal analysis, the message there appears to be that transgression of the theoretical is justifiable if it is undertaken on behalf of supra-theoretical truth – with a view to disclosing the essence of the *logos* as 'deed.' What Socrates celebrates in the lover's madness is essentially an act of memory or recollection. But recollection, as it is here described, is itself nothing but the essence of thinking. All true lovers are lovers of wisdom, philosophers.[13] If we now ask what in these connections (between love and recollection, between recollection and philosophy) justifies the excesses of the daemonic, we may answer that in praise of love Socrates describes a truth that is itself an act of transgression. In the recollection proper to divine madness we mortals touch a higher dispensation. We take part in the very measure by which we are defined. Such participation transports us beyond the finitude and limitation that marks our world, while at the same time setting us in right relation to it. The genuine power of this fundamental existential contradiction is never disclosed to us by means of the theoretical. On the contrary, we gather it up directly only in a discourse that is itself ecstatic, embodying (and so drawing attention to) our leap into the infinite – the transport that constitutes the essence of thinking. All words of love, all authentically daemonic speeches, are essentially reflexive. What the genuine enthusiast says is compelling and seductive because it makes manifest an engagement or pursuit – a mode of participation in the measure of things – that is itself the highest truth and that no mere argument can reproduce or represent.

What role does the dialectic play in all of this? I suggested above that in Plato's philosophy that mode of inquiry is always one moment or aspect of a more fundamental contrapuntal structure – that it directs our theoretical discourse to its proper limit (contradiction), where we are better disposed to the hearing of other discourses, other voices. In the *Charmides*, this direction takes the form of an extended prelude to the opposition of theory and irony. In the *Phaedrus*, it functions as a kind of recapitulation – consolidation and clarification – of the thesis on the daemonic. How so? Consider: we said that in subordinating the theoretical to the daemonic Plato also makes himself responsible for distinguishing its authentic and inauthentic forms. Now dialectic has no power to establish the authentic daemonic. As a mode of theoretical discourse, it cannot justify or explain discursive leaps. However, it may very well be enlisted for purposes of exposing the inauthentic. And this is precisely what Socrates does in the second part of the dialogue. After his definitive account of love, he and Phaedrus return to the original question of good speaking and writing. Taking the reflexive structure of the authentic daemonic as a point of departure, as a measure, Socrates demonstrates dialectically that rhetoric aimed primarily at anything other than disclosure of the truth is defective and inherently absurd. In this he draws attention both to the foundation of the philosopher's relation to rhetoric (to authentic daemonic discourse) and to what distinguishes this relation from the inauthentic extravagance of lawyers, sophists, and others who seek to divorce the form of their discourse from its content.

It is the subordination of the theoretical that is accomplished in the system of speculative thought. But whereas in the *Phaedrus* the role of dialectic itself is also subordinate and negative, in Hegel's philosophy it is wedded to the direct utterance of transcendent truth, of the *logos* as 'deed.' I have more to say on this difference shortly. In advance, apropos of the relation of Hegel's thought to the modern world in general and to post-Hegelianism in particular, we must sketch a third mode of philosophical counterpoint, presented in Plato's *Parmenides*.

Stylistically, of course, the *Parmenides* differs again from both the *Charmides* and the *Phaedrus*. In it, Plato returns to inquiry by dialectic. But the playful irony of the early works is nowhere to be found. It is replaced by a dense and relentless logical investigation (to which Socrates himself is essentially only witness). This development is connected in turn to the critical/theoretical examination of a new matter – the doctrine of the forms and the Eleatic philosophy of the One on which it may be said to rest. Though presupposed in all of Plato's investigations, the forms are rarely treated directly, and never critically, prior to the works of his maturity. The *Parmenides*, the *Sophist*, and other later dialogues address themselves clearly to another set of questions, a different problematic. To what extent does this new direction represent a continuance of the project of philosophical self-measure that we have attempted to sketch in relation to the other texts? What are we to make of Plato's critical/theoretical examination of his own doctrine from the standpoint of our experiment with counterpoint?

We need no detailed reproduction of Parmenides' critique of the forms or of the assertion of the One in order to respond to these questions. We need only call to mind the dilemma at the centre of Parmenides' critique. This we are given at the end of Parmenides' initial engagement of the young Socrates. After elucidating dialectically some of the logical problems presented by Socratic thinking, he concludes: 'These difficulties and many more besides are inevitably involved in the forms, if these characters of things really exist and one is going to distinguish each form as a thing just by itself. The result is that the hearer is perplexed and inclined either to question their existence, or to contend that, if they do exist, they must certainly be unknowable by our human nature.'[14]

The detailed consideration of the Eleatic One that follows this provisional critique does nothing to resolve these perplexities. On the contrary, they are confirmed in that dialectic at a much deeper level. But that renders all the more remarkable the words of Parmenides that follow those just cited: 'But on the other hand ... if, in view of all these difficulties and others like them, a man refuses to admit that the forms of things exist or to distinguish a definite form in every case, he will have nothing on which to fix his thought, so long as he will not allow that each thing has a character that is always the same, and in so doing he will completely destroy the significance of all discourse. But of that consequence I think you are only too well aware.'[15]

What shall we make of these statements? And of their juxtaposition? Here as before, we are presented with a text in which theoretical discourse is overstepped in the name of the philosophical *logos*. The dilemma that Parmenides sketches above and develops in subsequent dialectic admits of no logical solution. In the end, the form, the One – in short, transcendent truth – shows itself absolutely resistant to definition. At the same time, however, in accordance with what is said at 135c, it must remain the condition for the possibility of definition (indeed, the condition for the possibility of all significant discourse). Thus theoretical discourse as a whole rests either on an unintelligible and indefensible presupposition (in which case philosophy as such becomes impossible) or on a presupposition that may be expressed and justified only in a supra-theoretical discourse. In other words, presuming it to be Plato's intention that philosophy itself endure, we are constrained to hear in the logical/dialectical dilemma of the *Parmenides* an apostrophe to some other voice, some other relation to language.

The apostrophic discourse, as it is deployed here at least, separates transcendent truth from theoretical discourse. It demonstrates the extension of the one beyond the other. In so doing, it implies some further discourse – ironic, daemonic, or possibly something else (I return to this point in a moment). But this implication, grasped as such, is itself supra-theoretical. While Parmenides himself never abandons the rigour of dialectic, the conversation in its entirety is presented as a 'preliminary exercise,'[16] a bit of pedagogy intended to make Socrates reform his own manner of philosophical expression. The text as a whole looks ahead to something else, so that the radical indeterminacy of its own conclusion is effectively the preparation of a more adequate measure.

At this last point, someone with an interest in asserting a more fundamental difference between early and later Plato might argue that the apostrophic measure of the *Parmenides* as described above still represents a departure from earlier works by virtue of its very indeterminacy; while Plato may remain committed to the transcendence of the theoretical in philosophy, he becomes less certain in his mature writings about how this ought to be accomplished and what there is to be gained by it. And our critic could point to the foregoing analysis for support. My claim, in discussion of both ironic and daemonic discourse, is that Plato plays these voices against that of theoretical argumentation in order to disclose the essential 'deed' harboured there. In apostrophe, in contrast, we are apprised only of an absense, a lack, a need.

We should respond to such a person not by arguing this point (it is quite true) but by thinking it in relation to the dramatic context of the *Parmenides*. Specifically, we ought to couple the indeterminacy of the apostrophic discourse with the decisive chronological inversion that functions as its backdrop. The *Parmenides* may well represent a document of Plato's maturity, but it reports an encounter between Socrates and Parmenides in which the former is young and inexperienced in philosophy. Considered dramatically, this encounter comes before those reported in the *Charmides*, the *Phaedrus*, and other earlier texts. With that in view, however, it becomes somewhat more difficult to interpret the separation of transcendent truth from theoretical discourse that marks Parmenides' 'preliminary training' as an apostrophe to one or some number of supra-theoretical discourses that are wholly unspecified.

On the contrary, the whole exercise seems to point us back (or, following the dramatic chronology, ahead) into the heart of the Socratic-Platonic project. It appears to justify dialectically the necessity of something like the opposition of theory and irony, or the subordination of the theoretical to the daemonic, in the pursuit of essential self-measure. Thought contrapuntally, the ponderous dialectic of the *Parmenides* articulates the limit at which Platonic philosophy as a whole turns back on itself, binding itself together in recognition of a single purpose – transcendent self-measure. That rather grand *da capo* is what modernity seeks from the very beginning and, paradoxically, what it ultimately stands to lose.

Like the experiment with counterpoint that provides its occasion, our reading of Plato is ultimately reducible to three basic propositions. First, in addition to the theoretical voice obvious in that thinking we ought to grant at least three supra-theoretical discourses: the ironic, the daemonic, and the apostrophic. Second, each of these additional discourses 'plays against' the theoretical in a different way: the ironic is opposed to it, the daemonic subordinates it, and the apostrophic arises in its separation from transcendent truth. Third, the mechanism of dialectic in Plato (the principal form of theoretical discourse at work in the dialogues) is one moment or aspect of a more fundamental contrapuntal structure intended to disclose what is constitutive for the philosophical *logos* (what we have been calling, in paraphrase of Goethe, the 'deed'). If we turn now to the problem of modern counterpoint, and to the Hegelian philosophy in particular, we see these elements partly abandoned and partly retained. A brief preamble on this relation may be useful.

Modern philosophical counterpoint differs from the ancient first and foremost by virtue of its obsession with a single form – that of the fugue. Harris's recourse to this word in describing the Hegelian program is accordingly compelling in a double sense. It represents effectively both the internal structure of Hegel's project and its continuity with a tradition. How is it that speculative metaphysics (or, indeed, any other thinking) approximates fugal counterpoint?

In music, of course, the basic idea of this form is grasped quite readily. It consists in regarding a subject or theme or motif as the material of its own development. In a musical fugue, all voices sing the same tune in different registers, at different times, tempos, and so forth. The idea is to uncover the possibilities of the subject by posing it against itself, to elicit from it its own measure. In defining provisionally something like a philosophical fugue we may retain this description, terms and all, provided that we think the word 'subject' in the context of metaphysics rather than of melody. The 'subject' of the modern philosophical contrapuntalist, whether it be Kant, Fichte, Schelling, Hegel, or someone more contemporary, is always 'transcendental subjectivity.' The philosophical fugue is determined by whether and to what extent it is possible to play this most fundamental subject against itself – to have it disclose its own truth.

I want to explore the history of that question now, taking the analysis of Plato as a point of departure. Specifically, I would like to use the compendium of contrapuntal strategies that one sees in his text to explicate the development of modern philosophical counterpoint. It seems to me that the specific relations of discourse to which we pointed in the dialogues – opposition, subordination, and separation – recur in the development of the philosophical fugue as modes of the transcendental subject's relation to itself. My return to these modes is guided by two objectives. First, I attempt to bring out the difference between dialectic in its speculative employment and dialectic in Plato, arguing for the centrality of Hegelian thought in modern or fugal philosophical self-measure. Second, I suggest that Hegel's speculative dialectic, in which the contrapuntal thinking of our era celebrates its emancipation from the ancients, simultaneously problematizes modernity itself.

Any attempt to consider seriously the difference between the speculative dialectic and the dialectic of the ancients requires at least a passing nod at a third, intermediary species – that developed by Kant. By Hegel's own account, Kant's dialectical adventures in the *Critique of Pure Reason* constitute an essential moment in the development of the method. The commentary from the *Science of Logic* mentioned above, for example, presents us with the following, rather striking comparison: 'Even the Platonic dialectic, in the *Parmenides* itself and elsewhere even more directly, on the one hand, aims only at abolishing and refuting limited assertions through themselves, and, on the other hand, has for result simply nothingness. Dialectic is commonly regarded as an external, negative activity which does not pertain to the subject matter itself, having its ground in mere conceit as a subjective itch for unsettling and destroying what is fixed and substantial, or at least having for result nothing but the worthlessness of the object dialectically considered. Kant rated dialectic higher – and this is among his greatest merits – for he freed it from the seeming arbitrariness which it possesses from the standpoint of ordinary thought and exhibited it as a necessary function of reason.'[17]

In this recommendation of Kant, Hegel expresses the first of what I take to be his two crucial differences with the ancients on form and logic. He argues that if dialectic is to be accorded its rightful position in the enterprise of modern thinking, it must shed the appearance of 'mere conceit' accorded it by Plato's Socrates and a host of others and reveal itself as a 'necessary function of reason.' The singular accomplishment of the Kantian philosophy, on this view, is its demonstration of that necessity. In contrast to ancient thought, the critical program incorporates limit and contradiction into the positive determination of human subjectivity. It makes possible, for the first time, a thinking in which human reason speaks to *and* about its own limit and so determines itself as a whole. We could put this claim in another way, to make clear the fundamental point of departure for modern dialectic in terms of our own analysis: Kant understands the challenge of transcendent or contrapuntal self-measure (and so of the dialectical inquiry essential to it) to be that of producing a system, the material of which is nothing but the multi-faceted discourse of subjectivity itself.

Speculative dialectic then differs from that of the ancients first by presupposing the concept of rational self-determination – the systematic account of transcendental subjectivity. Inasmuch as Kant is the first to attempt construction of such a system, Hegel owes him a debt. The critical philosophy expresses a condition necessary to further development. Necessary – but obviously not sufficient. If we now go on to ask why Hegel conceives Kantianism to be merely an intermediary step in the development of philosophical self-measure, why he holds consistently to the view that it must be surmounted, we approach the second difference between his thinking and that of the earlier dialecticians. And we come again to the first of the contrapuntal structures that we encountered in the analysis of Plato's text – opposition.

For Hegel, the problem with the philosophy of the *Critiques* is that in it Reason is for ever statically opposed to itself, divided in terms of its theoretical and practical employments. Such an opposition is inadequate to the project of rational self-determination, of modern philosophical self-measure, in two ways. First, it reduces the project of the philosophical system to a kind of ad hoc account of an aggregate of faculties, the inner unity of which must remain unexplained. Second, it keeps dialectic fettered in its traditional, negative role, persisting in the understanding of it as the invocation of a theoretical limit, a nullity, the truth of which can be contacted legitimately only in action (in 'deed').

In this regard especially, we might say that from the Hegelian perspective, Kant is ultimately too much like the Socrates of Plato's *Charmides*, that his liberation of dialectic from the sophistic conventions of irony and wit is undercut by the fact that he still uses it in order to demarcate a fundamental difference. Hegel's argument, as we see below, is that dialectic attains its truly modern, speculative form only when it is no longer limited by differences or oppositions of any kind – even the Kantian opposition of Reason to itself. The speculative dialectic is no longer simply one moment or aspect of a more fundamental measure. It is the very principle of modern, or fugal counterpoint. We can now attempt a more positive description of this principle.

Consider: Kant and Plato use dialectic to *ex*pose theoretical discourse to its own limit (contradiction) and to *op*pose it to supra-theoretical truth. In both cases, the dialectical inquiry is made to serve something more basic: the task of deriving the terms of opposition. At the same time, it remains itself limited (as a mode of inquiry) by the contradictions or theoretical nullities that it brings into view. If this situation is to change, as it must in the project of a truly speculative thought, such nullities must cease to be determinative. The encounter or disclosure of the limit of theoretical discourse, constitutive for traditional dialectic, must extend itself into the act of transgressing that limit. Speculative dialectic must therefore claim for itself the task that Plato assigns to supra-theoretical discourse – disclosure of the concealed essence of the *logos*, of the truth that appears to theoretical inquiry in the form of nullity and contradiction. In terms of the compendium of contrapuntal strategies that we saw at work in Plato's texts, dialectic becomes speculative if and when it refuses to let itself be defined by the static opposition of theoretical and practical Reason – namely, if and when it resolves to give utterance to the continual subordination of theoretical knowledge which is the act, the 'deed,' the being of Reason as a whole.

That something like this act of subordination, this transgression of oppositional limits and terms, belongs to Hegelian thought is obvious even to a casual reader. The more difficult and enduring question is that of how it belongs. Hegel clearly renounces the kind of passage that Plato grants Socrates in the *Phaedrus* (the leaps of divine madness, the discourse of possession). His venture beyond theoretical discourse is driven by dialectic alone. But under what conditions can dialectic negotiate its traditional limit? How does Hegel surmount the 'Transcendental Dialectic,' the *Parmenides*, and other masterworks of the traditional form? This question is addressed definitively in the opening volleys of the *Science of Logic*. At the beginning of that work's first major division, the 'Doctrine of Being,' Hegel tries to show that and how the terms of the most fundamental opposition – that of Being and Nothing – transgress their common limit and pass into each other. In other words, he tries to demonstrate dialectically that what *is* from the very beginning itself essentially transgression and passage. The crucial advance here is made in the short text that falls under the heading 'Becoming.' I cite it in full: 'Pure being and pure nothing are, therefore, the same. What is the truth is neither being nor nothing, but that being – does not pass over but has passed over – into nothing, and nothing into being. But it is equally true that they are not undistinguished from each other, that, on the contrary, they are not the same, that they are absolutely distinct, and yet that they are unseparated and inseparable and that each immediately vanishes in its opposite. Their truth is therefore this movement of the immediate vanishing of the one into the other: becoming, a movement in which both are distinguished, but by a difference which has equally immediately resolved itself.'[18]

If the truth of being itself – and so of all its instances or limited cases – is a movement or becoming in which its very limit is surmounted, then Hegel's speculative dialectic is not only possible, it is necessary. Philosophy is called on to provide the measure of what is. But what *is*, Hegel says (in the most important subclause in all of the *Logic*) 'does not pass over [i.e., out of some prior, stable state] but has passed over.' What *is* is in truth the very transgression represented by speculation. With this granted, the problem of negotiating the limit of traditional dialectic seems to dissolve. If and when the displacement of opposition (the passage of one term into its other) becomes objectively fundamental, as it does at the beginning of the *Logic*, contradiction and nullity show themselves redeemed and integrated into the development of the speculative system.

But there is a difficulty. While we speak (in mounting our contrapuntal sketch) about a new disclosure or manifestation of limit, and of its incorporation into philosophy, what Hegel describes in the passage above is an 'immediate vanishing.' One might suppose, with this in view, that if the reader were given only the first text on 'Becoming' and were questioned on the matters that we have made our concern, he or she would be tempted to argue that Hegel's metaphysical speculation simply reconstitutes a nullity and/or limit external to its discourse in the mutual vanishing of Being and Nothing. What he seems bent on celebrating as a great advance in philosophy and philosophical self-measure – the displacement of the oppositional relation by the speculative act of subordination – is actually the annihilation of significance that Plato's Parmenides warns against. If Being and Nothing simply vanish into each other, all propositions are false and meaningless. There is literally nothing to say.

The logical safeguard against such a reading is implicit in the text cited above. But it is also explicitly formulated by Hegel, later in the same chapter, under the heading 'Sublation of Becoming.' There he writes: 'The resultant equilibrium of coming-to-be and ceasing-to-be (being and nothing grasped in terms of the speculative movement or passage) is in the first place *becoming* itself. Being and nothing are in this unity only as vanishing moments; yet becoming as such *is* only through their disinterestedness. Their vanishing, therefore, is the vanishing of the vanishing itself. Becoming is an unstable unrest which settles into a stable result.'[19] What Hegel describes – in displacing the relation of opposition – as becoming (movement, passage, transgression of limit) is indeed a 'vanishing.' But this vanishing, as the truth of both Being and Nothing, constitutes what is. Becoming is – these words, and no others, are stressed in the statement above. The 'is,' 'isness,' or 'being' is implied in our talk about anything, obviously. But when the object of discourse is fundamental Becoming (as it is throughout Hegel's *Logic*) the talk itself acquires a new significance. That is because pure or immediate Becoming, Becoming as the vanishing of Being into Nothing and Nothing into Being, is decisively altered by the very fact that it is. To be is to endure and stand preserved, to stay on as present. Such presence, however, it itself the cancellation of vanishing. Thus, to say that Becoming is is to say that it endures and is preserved by virtue of the cancellation of its pure or immediate state. Becoming, rightly conceived, is always a double movement, a double negation, a vanishing that is itself vanished in some form of determinate presence, some mode of the synthesis of Being and Nothing. Becoming is, in Hegel's own speculative terminology, *Aufgehoben* ('sublated').

I said above that the speculative dialectic is the very principle of what we are calling modern or fugal counterpoint and that it therefore takes on itself the task that Plato assigns to supra-theoretical discourse – disclosure of the concealed essence of the *logos*. The precise sense of the disclosure may now be grasped in terms of the Hegelian *Aufhebung*. When we say that speculative dialectic reveals the essential in discourse, we mean that it follows and makes manifest the 'deed,' the activity of *Aufhebung*, by virtue of which what the tradition calls alternately the *logos*, being, reason, *Geist*, or transcendental subjectivity itself is constituted. For Hegel, this above all belongs to thinking. Philosophy is nothing but the *fortspinnung* of a single metaphysical 'deed' – the systematic expression of rational self-measure and self-determination. But if that is the case, then from the point of view of our contrapuntal analysis Hegel's is the philosophical discourse of modernity. His speculative metaphysics thoroughly internalizes the play of the transcendental subject against itself. It is indeed a fugue, whether regarded programmatically, as a single movement, or in terms of the multiplicity of its individual moments.

I gave notice above of my intention to argue that Hegel's speculative metaphysics, in which the contrapuntal thinking of our era celebrates its emancipation from the ancients, simultaneously problematizes modern philosophical self-measure. In turning now to this thesis, I have recourse to the discussions of dialectic above. Beyond that, however, or rather in concert with it, we benefit from some specific orientation in the rather complex world of post-Hegelian thought. Towards this end, Fackenheim's study of Hegel and religion is particularly instructive. Its concluding sections open up the entire Hegel/post-Hegel 'problem' to the hermeneutic of discourses that we have attempted to develop. Consider a statement of its principal claim with this in view. In the penultimate chapter of *The Religious Dimension of Hegel's Thought*, we find the following summation: 'What has emerged, then, is Hegel's faith in the modern world, and this is the ultimate condition in life of the possibility of his entire philosophic thought ... It is this last-named faith which in the end is decisive. Only on the assumption of an actual – and, in principle, final – secular-Protestant synthesis in modern life can Hegel venture that final synthesis which is his philosophic thought and yet maintain that it will not end the life which has made it possible.'[20]

In the final analysis, Fackenheim argues that the Hegelian philosophy is viable only as long as we continue to recognize its irreducible religious dimension, only as long as we continue to see and approve in it what is here called the 'secular-Protestant synthesis.' In other words, the subordination of the theoretical (of definition, of proposition and position) that is enacted in speculative dialectic still requires the force of the daemonic and moves to some extent within its element. We see below that what we might call the post-Hegelian conversation – the extended reaction to Hegel in continental philosophy – offers at least negative evidence in support of this view. What Fackenheim says above may be taken, from our contrapuntal perspective, to illuminate rather directly the manner in which modern philosophical self-measure is problematized in its very emancipation from that of the ancients. How so?

The modern concern with transcendental subjectivity, which for Hegel acquires its proper determination in the speculative subordination of theoretical discourse, is also quite clearly a displacement of other voices or discourses. What subjectivity encounters in play against it is always ultimately its own Self. In the thought that describes such a play, accordingly, all differences show themselves to be internal. Limit as such is sublated. This counts as an unprecedented intellectual liberation. Unlike Socrates, who must rest content with borrowing the discourse of gods and muses in moments of divine inspiration, Hegel can lay claim to the legitimate appropriation of the divine Other and its truth. The tale told again and again by the speculative dialectic, by the *Aufhebung*, is that Self and Other are one. But this very synthesis threatens immediately to cancel itself. Lurking in the revelation that the divine is human is the possibility of coming to see that it is only human, of coming to see in modern or speculative self-measure a measureless extension of subjectivity sanctioned by nothing other than its own growth or power.

That this view was taken up after Hegel – by Feuerbach, Marx, Nietzsche, Freud, and their influential contemporary readers – is a historical fact. Our point, following Fackenheim, is that it may be held at bay even within Hegelianism only as long as the discourse of transcendental subjectivity (the speculative system) is conjoined with the attestations of a faith, a way of existing, that still regards the divine as truly Other and which can see on that account that the synthesis of divinity and transcendental subjectivity in speculative metaphysics is not an illegitimate extension of the domain of that subjectivity but an utterance of the holy. Unless the speculative system is itself also imbued with the authority of a daemonic discourse, it may be said to cancel the very measure that it seeks to provide. But that means that in the Hegelian system we have a discourse the success of which requires both the displacement and the retention of the daemonic[21] – a discourse in which the project of philosophical self-measure is perfected only to be put in the charge of an evanescent 'faith in the modern world.' The crisis associated with the predictable default of this faith stands quite naturally at the centre of post-Hegelian thought. It constitutes the final object of our analyses here.

At the outset of our discussion of modern counterpoint we said that the elements of this kind of thinking observed in reflection on Plato would be partly abandoned and partly retained. The basic character of the relation we are positing between the ancient and the modern in this regard ought now to be clear. Our thesis is that modern counterpoint preserves the basic structures or strategies of its Platonic forerunner while replacing its numerous voices with the multi-faceted discourse of transcendental subjectivity. Thus Kant's critical program opposes theoretical Reason to Reason in its practical employment yet does not disclose this relation in the discourse of irony. Hegel's system subordinates theoretical Reason to the movement of speculative dialectic (to the 'deed' of the *Aufhebung*) yet thereby makes problematic the status both of other voices (particularly that of the daemonic) and of transcendent philosophical self-measure as such.

If, with this in mind, we now inquire into the contrapuntal structure of post-Hegelianism, we might reasonably expect to find there something like the separation of theoretical discourse (in both its customary and its sublated speculative forms) and transcendent truth that we sketched above in relation to Plato's *Parmenides* – but without apostrophe. And, I suggest that we do. Post-Hegelianism (which, in view of the central position that we have accorded Hegel in modern metaphysics, means essentially post-modernism) is determined by the attempt to twist free of the discourse of transcendental subjectivity, to separate our thinking from it, without genuine advocacy of anything further or discovery of anything more 'fundamental.'

The basic projects of the most influential and enduring continental thinkers after Hegel – Kierkegaard, Marx, and Nietzsche in the nineteenth century, Heidegger, Foucault, and Derrida in the twentieth – surely bear this out. Their sustained analysis of the problem of totalization (of the oppressive and unlimited expansion of the interests, values, institutions, and/or discourses of some class or gender or school of thought) is quite clearly an expression of the danger associated with interpreting the world, being itself, as an extension of subjectivity which both displaces and retains the Otherness that it requires in order to claim legitimacy. The various species of revolution to which those thinkers are committed, their modes of flight from or transcendence of political and intellectual totalization, all displace some clearly defined collective subject: an explicit act of separation. But while this act is absolutely central to post-Hegelian or post-modern thought (it is as important for post-modernism to free itself of the Hegelian 'One' as it was for Plato to embrace that of the Eleatics), it is never achieved. The post-modern movement of our day, in France and elsewhere, is increasingly occupied with the realization that it is constitutionally bound to the very discourse that it seeks to surmount – its flight from transcendental subjectivity has been, at least hitherto, nothing more than a series of covert reinscriptions.

At this last point, it might be argued by someone with an interest in asserting a more fundamental difference between the metaphysics of Kant and Hegel and the contemporary project of post-modernism, that the call for revolution, whether in the form of a political uprising of the underclass (Marx), an existential revaluation of values (Nietzsche), or something else, is itself an apostrophe, and so the introduction of a voice or discourse that counters that of transcendental subjectivity. However, the object of our contrapuntal analysis here is not so much individual philosophers as it is post-Hegelianism and post-modernism generally.

If, instead of considering Marx or Nietzsche in abstraction, we ask about the manner in which their revolutions have been integrated into the development of the post-modern conversation, it seems to me that we arrive at the operation of reinscription mentioned above. The first volume of Foucault's *Histoire de la sexualité*,[22] for example, makes a convincing case for adopting the view that the Marxist/Freudian discourse of liberation in sexuality is itself (and from the beginning) a function of the very power relations that it claims to subvert. We find a parallel argument in Heidegger's *Nietzsche*,[23] a meditation on the philosophy of power the central claim of which is that Nietzsche unwittingly consummates the very metaphysics of transcendental subjectivity from which he seeks deliverance.

Neither of these studies is concerned with intellectual idiosyncrasy or the failure of personal vision. On the contrary, they are descriptions of the ways in which the post-modern discourse of revolution dissolves into the repetition and entrenchment of totalizing thought, or descriptions of the ways in which totalizing thought plays against itself after Hegel. We need not reflect long or deeply on these descriptions in order to draw their implications for our own experiments with counterpoint. If works such as the *Histoire de la sexualité* and *Nietzsche* may be taken as representative statements of mature post-Hegelianism or post-modernism (and it is certainly my view that they may), then this movement as a whole in no way surmounts the fugal principle of the Hegelian system. It simply understands the 'deed' which lies at the heart of that system and that provides the material of its own development (the *Aufhebung*, the constitutional act of the transcendental subject) as a formula for some form of oppression. We say 'simply' – but this understanding makes all the difference. Within its frame of reference, the repeated subordination of limit celebrated in Hegelian speculation must appear a perpetual deception, as thinking's decisive abrogation of measure – and so, on our reading, of its very nature – for the sake of power.

The project of transcendent philosophical self-measure in post-Hegelian thought remains determined by the fugal structure that Harris attributes to the Hegelian system. But the transcendental subject now finds itself reinscribed (played against itself) in the act of flight and self-alienation. The post-modern fugue is constituted by the dissolution of revolutionary thinking into the discourse of totalization.

The failure of modern measure – made manifest in the difference between Hegel and post-Hegelian thinking but also in the odd proximity of the two (the displacement of other discourses by that of transcendental subjectivity, perfected in speculative metaphysics, seems to be the condition for the possibility of the entanglements of post-modernism) – is still our fundamental problem. We ought therefore to beware taking it lightly. It would not do, for example, on the basis of what we have argued above, to recommend some sort of straightforward return to Hegelianism. I have tried above to bring out a dimension of the problem associated with gaining emancipation from the ancients and their procedures in and through the systematic representation of a self-determining transcendental subject. What would permit us to return to Hegel? Nothing less than restoration of the tenuous connection between systematic metaphysics and daemonic discourse, resurgence of what Fackenheim calls 'faith in the modern world' – a turn of events that seems unlikely at present.

But I am concerned, especially in reflection on the contrapuntal structure of modern and of post-modern thought, with pressing another point. Perhaps the time has come to explore in new ways the traditional question of the *logos* and its nature (specifically, the age-old question of the *logos* as 'deed'). This would require of us something in addition to the discourse of revolution, which is the present coin of continental philosophy. It would require, I think, the sort of distance from that discourse that Plato grants Parmenides with regard to dialectical inquiry in the work that bears his name. There the radical indeterminacy of thought and language – the entanglement of the One and the Many that forms the mirror image of our contemporary predicament – is held at bay by the assurance, given early on, that the entire conversation is preliminary, a kind of training. And the presence of the young Socrates offers the promise of something further, something more satisfying.

We have no Socrates in our midst, unfortunately – no living embodiment of philosophy's future. But we do confront, on a daily basis, a body of thought, a tradition, that may be made animate still in the work of gifted scholars. Attention to such work may yet make it possible to regard even the conundrums of modernity as 'preliminary' – to hear, in the ever-expanding set of variations on the theme of 'revolution and totality,' an apostrophe to other discourses.

Notes

1 H.S. Harris, *Hegel's Development II: Night Thoughts (Jena 1801–1806)* (Oxford: Clarendon Press, 1983), 569.

2 The title of the final chapter (545ff.) is 'Recessional Voluntary, Fugue of the Olympian in Shephard Guise.' Its third subsection bears the title, 'Ricercare a tre voci: The Spiritual substance,' its fourth, 'The Fugue of Thought and Life.'
3 Goethe's *Faust*, lines 1223–37, read as follows:

> Geshreiben steht: 'im Anfang war das Wort!'
> Hier stock ich schon! Wer hilft mir weiter fort?
> Ich kann das Wort so hoch unmoeglich schaetzen,
> Wenn ich vom Geiste recht erleuchtet bin.
> Geschreiben steht: im Anfang war der Sinn.
> Bedenke wohl die erste Zeile,
> Das deine Feder sich nicht uebereile!
> Ist es der Sinn, der alles wirkt und schafft?
> Es sollte stehn: im Anfang war die Kraft!
> Doch, auch indem ich dieses niederschreibe,
> Schon warnt mich was, dass ich dabei nicht bleibe.
> Mir hilft der Geist! Auf einmal seh' ich Rath
> Und schreibe getroft: im Anfang war die That!

4 Discussions of courage, friendship, and piety in the *Laches*, the *Lysis*, and the *Euthyphro* respectively reach the same sort of impasse that the interlocutors of the *Charmides* encounter.
5 Plato, *Collected Dialogues*, ed. Edith Hamilton and Huntington Cairns, *Charmides*, trans. Benjamin Jowett (Princeton, NJ: Princeton University Press, 1961), 122.
6 Ibid., 103.
7 Hegel, *Hegel's Science of Logic*, trans. A.V. Miller (New York: Humanities Press, 1967), 55–6.
8 Plato, *Collected Dialogues*, *Phaedrus*, trans. R. Hackforth (Princeton, NJ: Princeton University Press, 1961), 484–5.
9 Ibid., 486.
10 Ibid., 489.
11 Ibid.
12 See, for example, Plato's critique of poetic discourse in *Republic*, Books II and III. The program of censorship that Socrates advocates there is undertaken clearly on the supposition that enthusiastic or inspired speech – song – has the power to lure us away from the truth, to distract us.
13 Plato, *Collected Dialogues*, 496.
14 Ibid., 929. *Parmenides*, trans. F.M. Cornford, in *Collected Dialogues* (Princeton, NJ: Princeton University Press, 1961).
15 Ibid., 929–30.
16 Ibid., 930.

17 Hegel, *Hegel's Science of Logic*, trans. A.V. Miller (New York: Humanities Press, 1967), 55–6.
18 Ibid., 82–3.
19 Ibid., 106.
20 Fackenheim, *The Religious Dimension in Hegel's Thought* (Chicago: University of Chicago Press, 1967), 212.
21 This double requirement is not satisfied by the Hegelian *Aufhebung*. The daemonic discourse stands for ever opposed to that movement in so far as it preserves the Otherness of the Other.
22 Foucault, *Histoire de la sexualité* (Paris: Éditions Gallimard, 1976).
23 Heidegger, *Nietzsche* (Tübingen: Verlag Guenther Neske, 1961).

13

Hegel's 'Freedom of Self-Consciousness' and Early Modern Epistemology

JOHN RUSSON

> Denn die vernünftige Intelligenz gehört nicht dem einzelnen Subjekt als solchem wie die Begierde an, sondern dem Einzelnen als zugleich in sich Allgemeinen.[1]

H.S. Harris once responded with an expression of amazement to a remark that I made equating solipsism and Cartesianism. He followed this up by stating that for Descartes the truth is the self *qua* universal, rather than the self *qua* singular, and further insisting that I not continue to misrepresent Descartes. This turned out to be one of the most valuable lessons I learned in my graduate studies. It was coupled with another insight from Harris – namely, that the unhappy consciousness, rather than the master and slave, must form our basic model for the completed form of self-consciousness. My attempt to understand the significance of universality in Cartesian rationalism came to mesh precisely with this theme of the primacy of unhappy consciousness.[2]

My study in this chapter is a consideration of this primacy of unhappy consciousness from the point of view of epistemology, and it is in articulating the epistemology of unhappy consciousness that the logic of Cartesian epistemology becomes clear. I ultimately show how it is that this epistemology of unhappy consciousness of which Descartes is such a powerful exponent is equally the basis for Hegelian epistemology – the basis, but not the completed form, for in Hegel this epistemology transforms itself in a way that simultaneously perfects and destroys the Cartesianism from which it arises. Essentially, the Cartesian form of the argument produces a distinction between transcendental and empirical selfhood and a dualism of mind and body. The full development of this argument, however, leads to a conception of reason as self-determining, which will in turn lead us to reject the mind–body dualism of Descartes and to replace it with a dialectical phenomenology of reason as self-embodying. Let me begin this journey by explaining what is behind my reference to 'an epistemology of unhappy consciousness.'

'The Freedom of Self-Consciousness' is the title of the concluding section of chapter 4, 'Self-Consciousness,' in Hegel's *Phenomenology of Spirit*.[3] This section has been variously interpreted in the last few decades. In Kojève's influential *Introduction à la Lecture de Hegel*, the three forms of this freedom of self-consciousness – stoicism, scepticism, and the unhappy consciousness (*das unglückliche Bewußtsein*) – are understood as 'slave ideologies,' unsuccessful strategies by which the slave defers an act of rebellion by instituting some form of intellectual escape from slavery.[4] Harris, in contrast, sees this as history's first entry point in the *Phenomenology*; this line is followed by many interpreters who stress the references to Hellenistic philosophy in 'stoicism' and 'scepticism' or who argue about how well 'the unhappy consciousness' portrays medieval Christendom.[5]

My own approach accords more with work by Burbidge and others who stress the transportability of the *arguments* of these sections.[6] In particular, my analysis would focus on how the forms of the freedom of self-consciousness provide universal and necessary stages in the development of the completed form of self-consciousness, which is achieved in the third stage of unhappy consciousness.[7] My purpose here, however, is not to consider the position of this section in terms of the intrinsic demands of the argument of the *Phenomenology*. Rather, I want to take advantage of the transportability of these forms of self-consciousness to develop an account of how Hegel should be understood as responding to traditional problems in seventeenth- and eighteenth-century epistemology. In particular, I want to bring out how the forms of the 'Freedom of Self-Consciousness' work out epistemologies of rationalism, empiricism, and transcendental idealism and systematize these positions in a way that shows why their characteristic problems emerge and how they should be handled. It is in this sense that my ultimate goal is to show how and why 'the unhapppy consciousness' is the key to Hegel's epistemology.[8]

Stoicism, Scepticism, and Empiricism

One of the most distinctive features of the so-called Scientific Revolution is the assertion that knowledge is something that one can attain on one's own, by one's own efforts. Any one of us evidently can be a scientist, for the essential tools employed in the search for knowledge are our reason and our senses: we need to be able to observe what goes on and to be able to appreciate how what happens happens according to a rational order. This focus on the independence of the mind in the pursuit of scientific knowledge, which we associate with such people as Bacon and Descartes, is equally the focus in 'stoicism' and 'scepticism' in Hegel's *Phenomenology*.

The stoic is the agent who recognizes her own self-containedness. The stoic recognizes that her choices reflect herself and herself alone, in that there is no external force capable of compelling her will to move.[9] Thus any choice that she makes is clearly her choice, her responsibility. Thus whatever she accepts as truth is something for which she is accountable: what she accepts is what she chooses to accept, and thus, just as nothing external can force her will, so no external authority can be invoked to justify her adherence to her beliefs. In particular, whatever she chooses to accept about reality is precisely that: it is precisely how she has chosen to interpret what confronts her, whether what confronts her is scientific data, simple observations, or authoritative opinions.[10]

This then is the double-sided emergence of the scientific initiative: it is both the liberation of self-consciousness from reliance on authority and the responsibility of self-consciousness not to rely on authority. The freedom of self-consciousness is thus just as much a discovery of new power as it is an acceptance of a new limit. Indeed, it is the shifting emphasis on these two sides of this freedom that marks the development through the three forms in Hegel's 'Freedom of Self-Consciousness.' Hegel's category of 'stoicism' marks primarily the primitive recognition of this freedom, and the recognition takes the form of differentiating the sphere of one's choice from the sphere of those things over which one has no control. I cannot, for example, control what goes on in your sphere of choice, or in the sphere of natural causality; the 'insides' of the things I encounter are outside the sphere of my choice, but equally this fact demarcates the sphere of my choice as something independent of the choice of others or of natural causality.[11] Stoicism thus involves an inherently atomistic anthropology, and it is not hard to see how the posited alienation from nature will equally make epistemological scepticism its real outcome.

The best that the stoic can offer as a scientific method is careful observation and rational judgment on that observation. This (empiricism, basically) is no small offer, but in such an immediate and indeterminate form this epistemology can do little to answer serious challenges.[12] The stoic wants to be responsible in taking account of why she believes what she does, but to give a fully rational account of her observations will involve acknowledging that these observations are precisely limited to being her observations, and there is no ground by which she can justify generalizing the particularities of her experience to universal claims about existence in general. What would be required to do so would be for her to be able to claim that her experience is representative, but this she cannot do, since her initial premise was her alienation from the essence of nature and the essence of other selves. In the absence of some claim of an immediate identity between her thought and reality, there is no justification for assuming either that others see things the same way or that nature always shows a typical face. And the claim about an immediate identity of her thought and truth is absent, since

(a) an alienation is initially posited and (b) even if the claim happened to be true, there would again be no way for the stoic to know this or, even if she had some such intimation, to prove this.[13] Thus to take full responsibility for her judgments on her observations, the stoic scientist must admit that she has no science; she must ultimately conclude that science is in principle impossible – she must finally become a sceptic. The experience of the power of singular self-consciousness thus turns into the experience of the limit.

Stoicism begins in an attempt to differentiate that specific kind of reality that one has as a self-conscious self, but this effort itself concludes in the impossibility of making this differentiation, for there is nothing to which one has access from which to make this differentiation. Scepticism is the recognition that all that one encounters has ultimately the same status of being products of one's own powers of choice and judgment: all being is essentially the same, for all that exists for me is my experiences.[14] Hegel's description of the sceptic self as a 'medley of sensuous and intellectual representations' perfectly matches Hume's characterization of the self as a 'bundle of perceptions,' because all there is is experiences – 'ideas and impressions' – and there is no possibility of situating them in a scheme that differentiates the two poles of self and other, themselves at best constructions within experience, and not self-subsistent items to which experience could ever have or justify access.[15] There is thus only one accessible reality, and it does not permit scientific claims about anything beyond itself.

This conception of the essentially stoic self underlies the epistemological debates of early modern philosophy, and the problem of scepticism is its real driving issue. This stoical self with a sceptical epistemology is visible in Locke's empiricism, with its emphasis on recognizing the limits of human knowledge; in Hume's focus on the problems surrounding induction, analogy, and necessary connection; in Descartes's response to sceptical arguments with a self-certain ego that passes judgment on sensation; and in Kant's 'Copernican Revolution,' which limits knowledge to things as they appear rather than to things as they are in themselves. Clearly Hegel's treatment of this dialectic will be pivotal for understanding his relationship to early modern epistemology. Let us look further at Hegel's treatment of scepticism.

Every shape of spirit studied in Hegel's *Phenomenology* plays a double role: it simultaneously marks out a real phenomenon of, and permanent possibility for, human existence and enacts the self-destruction of an inadequate candidate for the status of the absolute nature of spirit. In relation to scepticism, this means that there really are essential experiences of being divided from others and of having no ground for making decisions, but this is not an adequate characterization for the whole reality of human life. A schizophrenic, for example, may live out the exact life of the sceptical self, finding a constant contradiction in every possible decision or action, being unable to stabilize the flux of experience and to have an integrated experience of selfhood. Further, the general demand that one establish that one's perceptions are representative before going on to make universal and necessary claims about the real nature of things is an absolutely legitimate demand and has problems attached to it that make a sceptical response to many claims entirely justified. In these senses, scepticism is not to be overcome, in Hegel or anywhere. As a characterization of the fundamental nature of self-conscious selfhood as such, or of knowing as such, however, it is inadequate, and this is the direction that Hegel's critique takes.

The sceptic self is not a determinate being apart from the appearances but is just the assemblage of these appearances, and this is the claim that the sceptic puts forth as an adequate characterization of the nature of self-conscious selfhood. Yet the sceptic self is a single self that opposes itself to (negates) this flux and multiplicity inasmuch as the sceptic is the single point of view (what Hegel would call the simple power of 'negativity'), for which there is experienced difference and that recognizes the insubstantiality of these determinations of appearance.[16] Even though the immediate 'show' of consciousness is already a product of self-conscious negativity – that is, of perspectival judgment – and even if self-conscious negativity or intentionality must be recognized as the very substance of appearance, one can logically differentiate two negations – one, which is the implicit *pre*-judging that has already operated in providing for the self a world of appearance, and another, which is the explicit judgment that is called on to assent to or dissent from these appearances – within the negativity that is self-consciousness.

The actuality of the sceptic self is the unreconciled relation of these two aspects of selfhood, each of which depends on the other: 'It pronounces an absolute vanishing, but the pronouncement *is*, and this consciousness is the vanishing of what is pronounced.'[17] Arguing that the self is just the flux of appearances presupposes the stasis of the self as the unified power of recognizing that posits the appearances as merely appearance. Arguing that this self-identity is the true determination of sceptical self-consciousness, one must presuppose the presences of those immediate appearings that constitute the consciousness of which this unified self is the agency and orientation and on which it thus depends as on its 'materiality.' Sceptical self-consciousness is in bad faith: it claims both that the self is the static, unitary, self-consistent power of negation (intentionality), which (to use Kantian language) supplies the (negating) form of consciousness, and that the self is a flux of multiple, non–self-subsistent determinations, which supply the (negated) matter of consciousness, without admitting that it is saying two different things. To maintain either claim alone requires maintaining the other in its place: 'Its deeds and its words always belie one another and equally it has itself the doubly contradictory consciousness of unchangeableness and sameness, and of utter contingency and non-identity with itself.'[18]

In epistemological terms, this means that it is not possible simply to deny any ground for knowledge within the sphere of self-conscious selfhood. While it is true that 'the self' is not another datum alongside a set of units of information given without intrinsic connection, it is not true that there is no reality to selfhood as a phenomenon in its own right. Equally, while there is no access to some other object of knowledge outside the sphere of self-conscious experience, it does not thereby follow that knowledge of truth is impossible. What the phenomenology of the sceptic self reveals is that there is a complexity and an intrinsic dynamism within self-consciousness that is itself sufficient to play all the roles in knowledge: experience may well be only the self's experience of itself, but this 'self' is not in immediate and full self-communion, and experience is this self's experience of itself as opaque to itself. Thus the self may itself be the truth or the reality of the objects of experience, but truth, reality, and objectivity are no less true, real, and objective on that account.[19]

The discovery of the two correlative aspects within self-conscious selfhood – the moment of overarching negation, and the determinate moments as negated – reveals that there is as much difference and lack of self-identity within self-consciousness as there is identity. The dynamic of selfhood will simultaneously be the pursuit of self-consciousness and the pursuit of knowledge as such, and it will take the form of the transformation of the immediate identity (and the immediate difference) of these two sides into a fully developed systematic relation. It is 'the unhappy consciousness' that provides the basic character for this completion of self-consciousness and of knowledge.

Unhappy Consciousness and Scientific Rationalism

What primarily characterizes 'unhappy consciousness,' especially in relation to questions of epistemology, is that the unhappy consciousness finds itself compelled to be the being that it is: unhappy consciousness is the experience of necessity *within* the sphere of its own self-conscious selfhood.[20] A stoic epistemology posits the independence of its own rational powers but as an isolation from the world that will ultimately be the intended object of its knowledge. The sceptic epistemology emerges from the recognition that the stoic positing of self-independence as self-isolation precludes any coming to identity with the intended object of knowledge and posits instead the ultimacy that the self deal only with itself. The unhappy consciousness accepts the sceptic claim that there is only the independent world of the self but acknowledges further that this is not an immediately harmonious world and that the alienation that the stoic posited between the knowing subject and the world, its would-be object, is in reality the opacity of the self to itself.

The unbridgeable gap of subject and object posited in stoicism is overcome in the recognition that the self is indeed after itself in cognition, and the meaninglessness of the empty self-identity or of the equally empty absolute differentiation that characterizes the sceptic epistemology is overcome in the recognition that complete self-identity within experience is not immediately present. Unhappy consciousness recognizes a play of identity and difference within self-identity, and this is the foundation of systematic knowledge.

In the *Phenomenology*, Hegel draws his illustrations of the phenomena of unhappy consciousness from the world of religious devotion, for it is here that there is manifest a self-conscious self that distinguishes within itself an apparent self and a real self and recognizes that real self as what guides the self it apparently is. We need not consider these religious images, however, to understand the basic logical relations of this form of self-consciousness, especially as regards their relevance to epistemology.

Unhappy consciousness is logically subsequent to stoicism and scepticism, because it involves the recognition that 'I am myself the substance of my whole experience' or something similar, but within this recognition that the self only ever encounters itself the agent can identify those aspects of experience within which it finds that what it itself does is something it *has* to do. The unhappy consciousness is the self that finds compulsion within itself – that is, who it really is forces it to act in ways that are not under its own immediate control. Unhappy consciousness is thus the self that finds itself subject to an intrinsic necessity.

There are three essential forms of this unhappy consciousness.[21] In the first form, the apparent self posits a real self that makes its decisions for it, and this real self is conceived of as entirely alien to the apparent self: the dualism of inner and outer that characterized the stoic metaphysics is here reintroduced within the sphere of self-conscious selfhood; here, however, both sides of this duality are the self, and the apparent self thus puts itself in the moment of the outside, with the impenetrable, other moment posited as its real, inner self. The first form of unhappy consciousness recognizes itself as essentially the moment of negated consciousness *for* the real, negating self, which is the source of necessity that directs the life of the apparent consciousness, but which does not in turn suffer any influence from the apparent self. The second form of unhappy consciousness still posits this mutual alienation but posits a third term mediating between the two extremes. In terms of the religious images of Hegel's presentation, this is Christ the God-man who mediates humanity to the godhead; in terms of our epistemological story, we would see such a mediating term, for example, in a sensory representation taken as that which we can perceive truly and which can lead us to the truth of our object, though the object is itself not directly perceivable. The second form of unhappy consciousness is the approach to a dynamic of real and apparent selfhood that posits some similar intermediate in the process of the apparent self trying to come to terms with its real identity. This is again a self that wants to identify with its own real, governing selfhood but posits an impenetrability there and looks instead to substitute means, rather as someone claiming to be a Hegelian might, when challenged, refuse to turn to direct explication of Hegel's text to justify her claims and turn instead to commentators. What matters for our account, however, is not these two preliminary forms, which repeat errors characteristic of stoicism and scepticism within this new context, but the third, completed form.

In the third form of unhappy consciousness, the alienation of the real and the apparent self is not the first premise: for the first form, the two are taken as simply separate; for the second form, the absolute isolation which is the implication of this simple separation is recognized, and to overcome the isolation the real and the apparent self are taken to be related indirectly through their respective relations to a common third term. For the third form of unhappy consciousness, the apparent and the real self are already in relation in themselves, and the two terms do not thus stand in a dualistic relationship. It is here that we see the proper appreciation of the two moments of negating and negated selfhood, which we first discovered in the sceptic epistemology, which failed to recognize their difference. Here the apparent self is capable of identification with its real self, indeed, already is identified in principle, and the actualizing of this identification is precisely the overcoming of the opacity within its experience. The apparent self comes to identify with its real self when it explicitly responds to its experience as it finds itself compelled to respond, for here, in allowing itself to be directed by its own intrinsic necessity, its own experience of necessity, it is acting as the representative – as the real appearing – of the real self. From the point of view of our epistemological concerns, the unhappy consciousness is that agent who distinguishes within her experience a set of decisions and choices that are arbitrary and idiosyncratic and a set of decisions to which she is driven by her very nature – by the very demands of self-consciousness as such. The unhappy consciousness knows that it is in the truth when it can show that it is acting in the way it is compelled to act by its nature as self-consciousness, which means when it can show how its judgments are judgments that are demanded universally and necessarily of self-conscious agents. The stoic found freedom in an ability to assent. The unhappy consciousness finds truth in its ability to have its assent compelled. Truth is found in the universal and necessary judgment, for when she makes this judgment the apparent self acts as the legitimate representative of the real self, which means that her judgment is one that she legitimately passes on behalf of any who share in the nature of self-consciousness.

Articulated in this way, unhappy consciousness is clearly the category in which Descartes's rationalism is to be placed. Descartes argues that it is only knowledge derivable on the basis of self-consciousness as rational self-cognition that can count as access to truth, for it is there that any agent *qua* self-consciousness is compelled to assent. Notice that this is like the stoic position in that it is the single agent herself whose own singular selfhood compels the assent, but because it is a compulsion that derives from the very nature of self-consciousness as such, it is a compulsion that will equally affect every self-conscious agent singularly.[22] The fact that it derives from the nature of self-consciousness as such implies its universality; the fact that it is not an external authority of the sort that the stoic self can ignore but compels each agent singularly and intrinsically implies its inescapable necessity. Just by understanding Descartes's arguments, therefore, one is compelled to assent to them.

It is important to see that Descartes is not simply a stoic. It might have seemed initially that 'stoicism, scepticism, and unhappy consciousness' would neatly parallel the trio 'rationalism, empiricism, and idealism,' but the rationalism of Descartes and his seventeenth- and eighteenth-century successors is far more sophisticated than the logic of stoic assent and is itself already closer to the Kantian and Fichtean arguments normally titled 'idealistic.' The key to stoicism was simply the discovery of the self-containedness of the immediate, singular ego; this conception really gives foundation only to a naive empiricism. For Descartes, however, that ego is not the one who apprehends truth: it is only that ego after having gone through the purificatory trials of scepticism in meditation 1, and after having discovered a sphere of compulsion within its experience in meditation 2, that is in a position to know. The Cartesian ego must essentially distinguish what in Kantian language we call a transcendental and an empirical ego, where this transcendental ego is the universal and necessary demands on experience that impinge on each self-conscious agent singularly by virtue of that agent's nature as a self-conscious self. Thus truth for Descartes does not come simply through the immediate efforts of the immediate ego but emerges through the mediating process of the empirical ego coming to identify with the transcendental ego. Let us consider what this means in relation to Descartes's actual argument.

The second meditation in Descartes's *Meditations on First Philosophy* contains the argument that is the foundation for Descartes's response to the universal scepticism developed in the first meditation and, consequently, the foundation for his epistemology. The argument is that any attempt to deny one's own existence is self-refuting, for it enters into an immediate self-contradiction by announcing a conclusion that is at odds with the very enacting of the announcement. To say 'I do not exist' is simultaneously to posit and enact an 'I' – a subject, as agent of awareness for which this putative non-existence is the object, the observation – at the same moment as this very 'I,' this very denying agent, is posited as not existing. The statement is the performance of its own falsehood.[23]

The basic argument is easy enough to follow, but its significance is by no means obvious; I here develop its implications and maintain that its logic is very close to what Descartes says it is. From this position that '"I think" is true every time I utter it' emerge several motions: self-refutation, experienced necessity, universality and necessity in (self-)consciousness, the distinction between mind and body, transcendental and empirical selfhood, the insufficiency of finite selfhood to account for its own infinite ideas, and the impossibility of global scepticism. We must begin in this endeavour to explicate the *cogito* argument by asking, 'Who is the self whose existence has been thus proved?'

The question 'who?' is itself asked by Descartes, and his answer is that it is 'I' as a thinker – as *res cogitans* – that cannot doubt its own existence. The first meditation has established that much of the way in which things immediately appear to me is dubitable, and this is as much true of the identity of things in the world as it is of my own identity. When it is established that, *qua* the agent doing the doubting, my existence cannot be doubted, the 'I' whose existence is proved is not the 'I' that I normally identify as me – I am not, for example, a 'rational animal,' or anything else that has been posited by an imperfect philosophy – but rather the agent defined by the necessary conditions for the possibility of doubt. I specify these conditions below, but let us first note what we have already established, just at a formal level.

We have established a distinction within selfhood between those aspects of selfhood that are necessary and those that are not; as indicated above, the argument of the second meditation works for each and any reader, which means that (i) it is 'personal' – it speaks to each of us in our uniqueness as 'this self,' as 'I' – but (ii) it attaches not to any of the idiosyncracies of the self but only to those features that are universally present in self-conscious selfhood as such. Indeed, feature (i) is just an instance of feature (ii): being individualized is a universal and necessary feature of self-conscious selfhood. The distinction above between the self as it immediately appears to itself and the self whose existence cannot be doubted has become the distinction within the self between the 'I' as idiosyncratic and the 'I' as universal and necessary – that is, between the empirical ego and the transcendental ego. Let us turn to a further characterization of the self whose existence cannot be doubted.

What is the criterion that gives us truth in this *cogito* argument? It is the experience of necessity, or rather the threat of immediate self-contradiction – the experience of the 'necessarily not.' This same criterion for argumentative certainty is invoked at another crucial juncture, this time in the third meditation. It had seemed that the truths of mathematics could be doubted, but in the third meditation we discover that this is not so: it can seem so only for so long as one does not actually think about what one is saying. While it seems to be a logically entertainable idea that an all-powerful god could deceive us even about these things, the content of this idea undermines this formal possibility: 'Yet every time I turn my attention to those very things that I think I perceive with such great clarity, I am so entirely persuaded by these things that I spontaneously burst out with these words: "let him who can deceive me; as long as I think that I am something, he will never bring it about that I am nothing, or one day make it true that I never existed, because it is true now that I am; nor will he ever bring it about that two plus three yield more or less than five, or that similar matters, *in which I can recognize an obvious contradiction*, exist."'[24]

In an arithmetical puzzle, for example, to think the quantity 'two' and simultaneously to think another quantity 'two' is no different than to think the quantity 'four,' and the operation of summation does not add any new material to the added quantities: addition is just the act of synthesis in and by which the two thoughts of quantity are held together in and as a single thought. So to think '$2 + 2 = 5$' is to think '$4 = 5$,' which is to think '$4 = \text{not-}4$' – that is, simultaneously to affirm and deny the identity of the thought of 4. Thus immediately apparent contradiction is the criterion of truth because it is that which the ego cannot resist: its very existence as this ego has implications – its very identity prescribes assent to, and dissent from, certain claims. The key to this Cartesian epistemology is the notion of self-determining self-integrity, which exists as an act of resistance to self-contradiction. Now let us consider this self-identical act of self-affirmation, to see how the autonomy of this self which is structured by universal and necessary truths is equally a self that must not be defined by any bodily involvement.

The very nature of the ego is that it is *in its being experienced as me* that this 'I' has its identity.[25] This is the ego whose existence is proven, for (recall our discussion of the criterion above) the proof comes in the immediate self-contradiction that would be experienced by positing this self's non-existence; therefore whatever extraneous conditions might characterize the existence of the ego do not affect this argument.[26] This is simply an autonomous derivation from the very concept of being self-consciousness, and it is in no way dependent on body unless one can show that body is already necessarily involved in its very concept (which would be the Hegelian tack).[27] But Descartes's argument has aimed to show that body is not involved in the concept of self-consciousness, for he can doubt body without doubting self-consciousness, so, if body is thus external to the concept, it is external to the existence. From here comes the celebrated dualism of mind and body, and its attendant problem – that if mind and body are utterly independent substances, they can have no communication, yet it seems they do communicate. For now, however, that problem need not concern us; we need see only that it follows quite naturally from the argument about self-consciousness that self-consciousness must be autonomous, which means that its external conditions cannot affect it.

We have then a clear picture of the subject of knowledge – the self-conscious, autonomous ego, driven only by a self-determining necessity that resists immediate self-contradiction. This ego is further specified through Descartes's argument.

Descartes's argument about the experience of the changing character of the piece of wax in the second meditation essentially continues the story of the self-determining nature of self-consciousness, arguing that the form that our experience takes is given by intellect. Descartes describes this feature as the claim that 'the human mind is more known than body,' and the argument about the wax serves to establish that 'clear and distinct ideas' – structures of significance that are constitutive of self-conscious experience – function as the innate grounds of meaning.[28] The argument works as follows. A given piece of wax continues to be recognized by me as one and the same piece of wax, despite the transformation of each and every one of its sensible features; indeed, I would recognize the self-same wax through more changes than I can imagine. Consequently, it can be neither sensation nor imagination that is the foundation of the recognized identity of the wax; rather, it must be the mind that approaches its sensation with the predisposition to recognize substantial unities 'stretched out' through spatial and temporal continuities, which are themselves thus features of what must be an innate idea of body. A substantial unity is something that is not seen, but something that is understood. Such an idea of a spatially and temporally continuous substance – a 'body' – is a logically clear idea and a logically distinct idea. It is the foundation of one's determinate experience, while not being itself a content derived from that experience – it is innate, rather than adventitious or factitious. Thus innate ideas are not products of my imagination, but neither are they received from without; they are internal, but I am subject to them, rather than vice versa.

Since I thus find them constitutive of my experience, they are the grounds of truth in experience. These ideas are really of two types. The first is the type that we saw above in the demonstration of the existence of the thinking self, and in the demonstration of mathematical truths – those ideas the denial of which is an immediate self-contradiction; we see another such idea below when we consider the idea of God. A second type, like the idea of body, does not so immediately reveal a contradiction when it is denied but still guarantees truth. Descartes articulates this guarantee in terms of the concept of a God: God is all-good, so he cannot be a deceiver, and therefore he cannot have put us in a position of being forced to believe something if it is not true, and so, if our innate ideas compel us to think a certain way, that must be truth. We do not need this language of God to see the strength of the argument which is entirely contained in the last line. By being ideas to which I am subject, they function as necessarily true for me – I must take them as true of reality, for I have no faculty for challenging them. Here, it is not the content of the idea the denial of which leads to immediate self-contradiction; rather, it is the very form of an innate idea that makes it a literally meaningless proposal for any one of us to claim that we doubt the idea. And notice what this consideration of the innate ideas that structure our experience says about the self: since I am subject to these ideas, they are unaccountable for by me; 'I' am really on the side of empirical ego, always finding that the transcendental ego does me the courtesy of allowing me to make use of it and to identify with it (I say, 'I understand that,' and so on). Thus the 'I' exists and functions in the realm of necessity when I live by reason, which I *qua* finite cannot account for and which 'I' am identical with only in being indiscernible from any other 'I.' It is my universal self, rather than my idiosyncracies, that puts me into the realm of truth.

But here we have just seen the force of Descartes's argument for the existence of God in the third meditation: the determinacy of the ideas that we find in our minds (their objective reality) is not accountable in terms of the substance of our finite consciousness, which is the medium of their appearance (their formal reality). We find ourselves subject to a reality greater than ourselves, which is both the source of our own experience and universally the source of the experience of every self.[29] I want now to consider how this Cartesian conception of selfhood lays the foundation for a scientific epistemology.

The key to differentiating scientific rationalism from simple stoicism is that the latter is built on an essential withdrawal and isolation from 'the nature of things,' whereas the scientific epistemology is geared towards a reconciliation with all reality and is premised on the fundamental identity of the real and the apparent self into which context the argument has been transformed. Science is the attempt to find out why experience had to happen the way it did: the scientist has to see how she has already been compelled, why what appeared to happen had to appear to happen. This comprehension must use the scientist's own necessary method – reason – to see why the world is what it is by necessity – why it is rational. Scientific rationalism is thus the recognition by the apparent ego of the need to identify with its real self by answering the demand to identify its real self – the necessity of self-consciousness in and for itself – with all reality as reason. Thus, whereas the stoic finds herself by differentiating herself from all reality, the rationalist finds herself only in and through identifying her real self with reality *qua* rational. It is in the identification with the rationality of her world that the apparent ego is here able to identify with her real self.

It is the recognition of one's real self in the recognition of the (rational) reality of the other that is thus especially characteristic of an epistemology of unhappy consciousness, and it is because it takes this form that scientific rationalism, or transcendental epistemology in general, must be understood as primarily an actualization of self-consciousness as the third form of unhappy consciousness.[30] Chapter 5 of Hegel's *Phenomenology of Spirit*, 'Reason,' goes on to show that the particular form of this identification of self and world that characterizes such immediate scientific rationalism is inadequate because too abstract, and it is the progressive improvement of this project that is gradually achieved first in the phenomena of 'Spirit,' in which the apparent ego identifies with its real self through enacting a mutual, social recognition in social institutions, and then further in religious communion, and ultimately in the completely self-conscious standpoint of philosophical science called 'absolute knowing.'

Having found in the logic of unhappy consciousness the key that allows us to see simultaneously both the strength of the achievement of early modern rationalism and idealism and the need to go beyond that stages we can look explicitly at how the Hegelian epistemology proper completes this project in dialectical phenomenology, even as it undermines the most cherished belief of this rationalism – the dualism of mind and body.

Dialectical Method, Phenomenology, and the Problem of Induction

These transformations, which institute an epistemology of unhappy consciousness, leave us with the conclusion that in knowing the reality of the other I know the reality of myself and that it is as thus recognized as the reality of the self that the reality of the object is found. I have called Descartes's epistemology one of unhappy consciousness, but, while his transcendental argument operates according to such a logic, it is not clear that Descartes himself realizes this – it is not clear that his philosophy posits itself as a philosophy of unhappy consciousness. Before going on to see how such an epistemology flowers in Hegel, I want to consider how this epistemology of unhappy consciousness comes to recognize itself as such in the German idealism of Kant and Fichte, which effects the transition from Descartes's early modern rationalism to Hegel's absolute idealism.

In Kant, the identity of our selfhood – the transcendental structures of consciousness – with the form of objects is posited; in knowing the forms of objectivity we are equally knowing the truth about subjectivity, but Kant still operates with a dualism of things-as-they-appear and things-as-they-are. For Kant there remains a permanent need to make this distinction, and that from which things-as-they-appear are distinguished remains an otherness that it is necessary to posit, and to posit as necessarily inaccessible (two claims which it seems impossible to endorse at the same time inasmuch as the simple positing of this otherness already amounts to a kind of access to its determinateness).[31] Here a necessary feature of that which exists for the subject is posited as not a product of subjective synthesis, and there is thus an incomplete carrying out of the project of finding out the identity of the self through the other (indeed, through the necessary form in which the other appears).

It is with Fichte that the decisive entry in the real self-conscious epistemology of unhappy consciousness is made, for Fichte systematically argues that the very form of objectivity is itself a function of selfhood. There is no absolutely existing other from which to distinguish self-conscious selfhood, for the very category of otherness is itself to be identified as a player within the dynamic of self-conscious selfhood. (Here we are clearly seeing replayed the moves from stoicism to scepticism to unhappy consciousness *within* the epistemologies of unhappy consciousness of Descartes, Kant, and Fichte.[32]) Thus we see an epistemology of unhappy consciousness recognizing itself as such.

In Fichte's argument that relation to an other is an intrinsic structure of consciousness and cannot be explained by the external input of 'empirical intuitions' we thus see an epistemology of unhappy consciousness. The recognition that otherness is itself a stage in the self-positing of the transcendental ego is representative of the whole move by Fichte to unite Kant's transcendental unity of apperception with Kant's categorical imperative (that is, reason as self-determining) and to see in the 'Category' a dynamic principle from which all the more determinate forms of transcendental subjectivity are generated. We are not left with a transcendental ego and twelve categories but have instead one selfsame process of self-determination and self-differentiation. Thus, if we want to know finally who is the real self, we will find that self by seeing the totality of the determinate categories as the unified expression or self-development of a single animating principle. With this, our story of Hegel's relation to seventeenth- and eighteenth-century epistemology is nearly complete.

The epistemology of unhappy consciousness, as it is developed in Fichte and Hegel, tells us that in looking at what appears, we see its reality when we see it as the integrated totality of determinateness of a self-determining system, and the 'self' of this self-determining is equally our real self. Subjectivity as such – rationality, mind, self-consciousness, or however we want to term it – thus is that which realizes itself as the totality of appearance. The real self, mind as such, is ultimately nothing other than the totality of determinations of that which appears taken in their unity. But this means that all determinations that could count as 'body' are not to be dualistically separated from mind as one substance is separated from another but must be seen as separated only as object is separated from subject in a process of self-othering self-consciousness. No doubt the detailed response to the dualism of mind and body that is typically associated with Descartes needs to be addressed on its own terms and needs to show its self-refutation in the context of a detailed phenomenological observation, but we can see here why in principle the very dualism that allows Descartes to launch his transcendental epistemology of unhappy consciousness is exactly what falls in the culmination of that project.

Various other versions of this dualism still exist in Kant and Fichte, and the detailed phenomenology of the self-development and self-refutation of mind–body dualism would indeed have to develop through these shapes. In Kant, an analogous dualism appears between sensibility and understanding and, more important, between things-as-they-appear and things-as-they-are-in-themselves. In Fichte, it is posited that there should not be such a dualism – alienness as such must be a product of subjectivity – but an ultimate dualism between the self and the other remains in Fichte, in the portrayal of the other as *Anstoss*, as the ultimately underivable 'check' about which we know that it ushers from our 'true self' but never how it can do so.[33] It is because some such dualism is at the core of all the pre-Hegelian idealisms that Hegel's epistemology of unhappy consciousness, while completing the epistemological project of early modern philosophy, simultaneously is its radical rejection and its transformation into something quite new. Having now seen where Hegel stands with respect to early modern epistemology in the forms of simple empiricism, Cartesian scientific rationalism, and critical idealism, I want to end with a brief articulation of what this new stance is that comes with Hegel's completion of unhappy consciousness.

The logical core to the epistemology of unhappy consciousness is the recognition by the empirical ego that it must wait on the transcendental ego to effect the synthesis within experience that will produce knowledge. Once this happens, the empirical ego certainly legitimately says, '*I* know,' indicating that it is really itself who synthesizes, but the enacting of this synthesis is something that happens 'behind its back.' for it is not immediately in control of the motor of its own self-consciousness. In our discussion of Kant and Fichte, we have seen that the form that scientific observation must take, given this epistemology, is to recognize appearances as the appearances of a self-developing system.[34] These two sides of our story neatly coincide.

To see the other as engaged in a process of self-development means to approach the other in the form of asking it how it is a self-determining process. This means to look for how it is what it is by being the expression of a single drive, and to see how this drive precipitates changes in itself through its very enactment. We must ask of the other, 'How are you a self-mover, a self-developer?' To see the object of our experience in this fashion requires us not to bring external criticisms to bear on it, not to start with some positing of the metaphysical ultimacy of this or that kind of relation of subjects and objects, and so on: it is what is appearing to us that is our object, and it must be our object as such an appearing, and our task is to describe how it appears. The epistemology of unhappy consciousness thus prescribes a phenomenological method.

Equally, our wait for synthesis is no different from our looking to the object's own movement: the need to wait means that our idiosyncratic 'empirical' egos cannot do the synthesis on their own, and the goal of watching the other's self-movement means that our empirical egos must not do the synthesis. The two themes thus dovetail perfectly. What we can and must do is look and ask, we must approach the object as those who are waiting for an answer, where the question is 'How are you a self-determining unity?' (And, as those of us who have gone through this process in the *Phenomenology of Spirit* know, it is this fundamental activity of looking for unity that will ultimately be the name of the real self, which is the self-developing source of the whole systematic story of appearance, which means that our very existence as such questioners is the immediate form in which the transcendental ego appears.[35]) We are thus just open projects in search of completion, and we must wait on the object to answer our needs. But whereas in Fichte's system we are necessarily left with an infinitely unfulfilled *Sollen*, Hegel's method does not allow such a specification in advance, for its openness demands an openness to finding closure, and this is where the dialectical phenomenology ends, though this last can be presented only as an undefended, abstract statement until the actual phenomenological viewing finds the object demanding of it that it complete the investigative activity.[36]

In this openness we see that the dialectical phenomenology which enacts an epistemology of unhappy consciousness ultimately returns us to a kind of empiricism. Empiricism is right in its first principle of the necessary singularization of self-conscious egos, and the need to develop all knowledge from this point of view; this is the source of Hegel's demand for a 'ladder to the absolute' in the 'Preface' to the *Phenomenology of Spirit*. The dialectic of the 'Freedom of Self-Consciousness,' however, shows us – and this is played out in the history of early modern epistemology – that this empiricism needs to become science. This science in turn needs to become dialectical phenomenology, or science in

Hegel's sense. This finally is a return to empiricism, but empiricism as *aufgehoben* by way of its own dialectic.

This *aufgehoben* empiricism is no longer a passive empiricism in the manner of Locke but is an active empiricism in the manner of Aristotle.[37] This empiricism is still essentially open, and it is passive in that it waits for the other to give it determinateness, but it is active in its search for this other, which means that this empiricism ask of things, 'How are you a self-unity?' In this new context, the empiricist 'problem of induction' – the core of scepticism – is equally *aufgehoben*, appearing now as the phenomenological observation which must wait on the intrinsic dialectic of the object to enact the synthesis that organizes experience. That is why Hegel's 'Introduction' to the *Phenomenology of Spirit* portrays phenomenology as the new scepticism, as a concrete, rather than an abstract, scepticism, which is not burdened by the dualistic metaphysics of the alien other, because it has returned to scepticism within the context of unhappy consciousness and can now see negation – the characteristic of self-consciousness – as intrinsic to the very being of the object.[38]

Notes

1 Hegel, *Vorlesungen über die Ästhetik* I (= *Werke* XIII) 59, hrsg. v. E. Moldenhauer und K.M. Michel (Frankfurt: Suhrkamp, 1986): 'For rational intelligence does not belong like desire to the simple object as such, but to the single as equally in itself universal.'

2 My understanding of the relation between unhappy consciousness and reason is developed primarily from a reading of *Enzyclopädie der philosophischen Wissenschaften (1830)*, hrsg. F. Nicolin und O. Pöggeler (Hamburg: Felix Meiner, 1959), secs. 436–9.

3 G.W.F. Hegel, *Phänomenologie des Geistes*, hrsg. v. Wessels und Clairmont (Felix Meiner, 1988), trans. A.V. Miller as *Phenomenology of Spirit* (Oxford, 1977). References are given below to the Miller text first, as M followed by the paragraph number(s), and then to the Wessels and Clairmont text, as WC followed by the page number(s); sometimes a more precise line reference to the German text is given as a decimal following the page number.

4 Alexandre Kojève, *Introduction à la Lecture de Hegel* (Paris: Gallimard, 1947), 180–2. Also adopted, for example, by J. Shklar in *Freedom and Independence: A Study of the Political Ideas of Hegel's Phenomenology of Mind* (Cambridge: Cambridge University Press, 1976), for example, 43–4.

5 This is how I have understood Harris's position, based on his lectures on the *Phenomenology of Spirit* and on my understanding of *Hegel's Ladder* (Indianapolis,

Ind.: Hackett Press, forthcoming), an early draft of which I had the privilege of reading. See Q. Lauer, in *A Reading of Hegel's Phenomenology of Spirit* (New York: Fordham University Press, 1976), 113–24 and J.N. Findlay, *Hegel: A Re-examination* (London: George Allen and Unwin, 1958), 100–2 (see following note). Patricia Fagan's 'Philosophical History and Roman Empire' (chapter 1, above) argues that Hegel was a good historian of the Roman world, based on his treatment of stoicism and of legal status; this, however, is a use of these categories to carry out a project in the philosophy of history, rather than a strict interpretation of the roles of these categories within the *Phenomenology of Spirit*.

6 J. Burbidge, 'Unhappy Consciousness in Hegel – an Analysis of Medieval Catholicism?' *Mosaic*, 11 no. 4 (1977–8), 67–80. J. Hyppolite, *Genèse et structure de la Phénoménologie de l'Esprit de Hegel* (Paris: Montaigne, 1946), I, 172–3, 189; his inadequately defined notion of history at I, 214–18, however, makes his position unclear. Despite the position expressed in *Hegel: A Re-examination*, Findlay seems to share the view that the argument is transcendental in his analysis of M230 (on p. 527 of Miller's text).

7 The three forms are articulated in M210, WC 145.29–39. I have presented my analysis in chapter 1 of *The Self and Its Body in Hegel's Phenomenology* (Toronto: University of Toronto Press, 1997).

8 In noting the primacy of unhappy consciousness, I am working in the tradition of such French commentators as J. Wahl, A. Koyré, and J. Hyppolite. See, for example, Hyppolite, *Genèse et structure*, I, 184.

9 See M197, WC 137.35–9.

10 See M200, WC 139.26–31.

11 See M200, WC 139.10–13.

12 See M197, WC 137.39–140.8, M199, WC 138.18–27, and M200, WC 139.5–140.4. See Hyppolite, *Genèse et structure*, I, 172–5.

13 Compare M73, WC 57–8, in the 'Introduction,' which discusses the conception of knowledge as an 'instrument' and the problems that this raises; the two possible unsuccessful strategies for dealing with this bear closely on the problems that I am discussing here.

14 M202, WC 140.15–21, M202, WC 140.36–8, M204, WC 141.24–5. In the 'Introduction,' Hegel compares his own philosophical method with scepticism and, in the context of this discussion, notes as the positive contribution of scepticism that it achieves that transformation whereby 'what first appeared as the object sinks for consciousness to the level of its way of knowing it' (M87, WC 67.32–3). Compare Jay Lampert's discussion in chapter 2, above, regarding what both Hegel and Fichte put forward as the basis of immediate right.

15 M205, WC 142.8–18; Hume, *A Treatise of Human Nature*, Book I, Part IV, sec. VI, 252. I thus disagree with those commentators, including Hyppolite, *Genèse et*

Hegel's 'Freedom of Self-Consciousness'   305

structure, I, 179, and M. Forster, *Hegel and Skepticism* (Cambridge, Mass.: Harvard University Press, 1989), part 1, who maintain that this section of the *Phenomenology of Spirit* addresses only ancient scepticism and not the supposedly less sceptical modern scepticism; on this issue of selfhood I can see no relevant difference and in general am not convinced by the interpretation given to Hume's scepticism. See, on this point, R. Hanna's review of Forster, *Review of Metaphysics*, 43 (1990), 631. I am thus also unsatisfied with R. Pippin's treatment in *Hegel's Idealism* (Cambridge: Cambridge University Press, 1989), 95. A discussion of related issues by a younger Hegel can be found in 'Relationship of Skepticism to Philosophy, Exposition of Its Different Modifications and Comparison to the Latest Form with the Ancient One' in G. di Giovanni and H.S. Harris, eds. and trans., *Between Kant and Hegel* (Albany, NY: SUNY 1985).

16 M205, WC 142.25–8. Compare the dialectic of the thing and its properties in chapter 2, 'Perception,' where a comparable issue of the relation of thinghood as an essential and exclusive oneness to thinghood as a mere locus for the coming together of multiple properties is played out.

17 M205, WC 143.3–5: es spricht das absolute *Verschwinden* aus, aber das *Aussprechen* IST, und dies Bewußtsein ist das ausgesprochne Verschwinden. See Hyppolite, *Genèse et structure*, I, 180–3, especially 182, for a good account of this tension within the sceptic self. Compare the dialectic of the 'now,' M106–7, WC 75.

18 M205, WC 143.9–12: Sein Tun und seine Worte widersprechen sich immer, und ebenso hat es selbst das gedoppelte widersprechende Bewußtsein der Unwandelbarkeit und Gleichheit, und der völligen Zufälligkeit und Ungleichheit mit sich. See M205, WC 142.32–143.12 in general.

I take Lauer's account of the breakdown of scepticism in *A Reading*, 116, to be mistaken. Lauer claims: '[It [scepticism] is self-contradictory, not in the sense that it involves logical contradiction, to which it is indifferent, but in the sense that the way it thinks contradicts the way it lives' – that is, 'it *does* what it *claims* has no validity.' See also Findlay, *Hegel: A Re-examination*, 99–100. It seems to me that this is not Hegel's argument, at least not in the sense that these commentators give to their own words. Lauer seems not to have adequately grasped his own valuable insight that the value of scepticism is its proof that 'only what consciousness produces from within itself counts' (115–16), for this latter point is why Hegel's demonstration of the internal contradiction of scepticism 'counts' whereas this external critique offered by Lauer and Findlay will never overcome the sceptic, since it presupposes a reality to appearances that the sceptic will never accept. Their critique seems unsuccessful both as an argument against scepticism and as a reading of Hegel's text, for both commentators, I believe, have a mistaken view of what Hegel would count as a 'deed' or a 'word.' The whole point of stoicism and scepticism, and the reason they advance the dialectic, is that they are the first forms in which the self-conscious self fulfills the potentiality, implicit in slavery, of recognizing itself in its products – that is, its deeds. The 'deed' of stoicism is precisely to think abstract thoughts (and the sceptic simply universalizes this by recognizing all determinations of consciousness as being such 'deeds' of self-consciousness); the claims of Lauer and Findlay make sense only if one posits a dualism of thought and action that is alien to Hegel's argument. (The 'word' of Hegel's text refers to what scepticism explicitly takes itself to be.) The same criticism can be made of Kojève's claim (*Introduction à la lecture*, 180–1) that the stoic does not do anything; his claim (often repeated by others) that stoicism collapses because it is boring, while based on Hegel's remark at M200, WC 139.38–140.4, is a misunderstanding: what is wrong with stoicism is that the rigorous pursuit of its own principles necessarily leads to scepticism. Shklar's claim (*Freedom and Independence*, 64), that it is an emotional tension that makes or lets the unhappy consciousness take over from the sceptic, seems to me to misunderstand entirely the epistemological issues involved in Hegel's argument.

19 See M82–4, WC 64–5.

20 Typically, commentators consider only inadequate forms of unhappy consciousness and want to limit the use of this term to those forms. In so doing they fail to notice that the third form (discussed below) is not inadequate. It is true that Hegel himself tends to use the expression 'unhappy consciousness' to refer to the inadequate forms, but this is no different from terms such as *Verstand* and *Vernunft* which can function in his vocabulary to name either a particular, limited form of experience or the essence of experience as such.

21 M210, WC 145.29–39. Hegel here articulates the three forms and then goes on to discuss only the first briefly and the second in detail. This second form is itself broken down into three subforms, and it is important not to confuse the third subform here with the third stage described in M210 (a mistake made by almost all commentators on this section, including Hyppolite and Burbidge). The third form articulated in M210 is really the protagonist for the remaining four chapters of the *Phenomenology of Spirit*. It is described in M231, the first paragraph of the 'Reason' chapter, and this paragraph is better read as the final paragraph of chapter 4.

22 Cf. the possibility and necessity of a 'ladder to the absolute' in the 'Preface,' M26, WC 19–21.

23 I notice four interesting features here, each of which is exploited in later idealism. First, the fact of the experience has consequences; this notion that enactment or performance has implications is the basis of transcendental argumentation as it will appear in Kant and Fichte, where the fact of coherent experience guarantees that the conditions that must be in place for there to be coherent experience are actual. This is evident throughout Kant's Transcendental Aesthetic and Analytic; it is the basis of Fichte's familiar refrain in the *Science of Knowledge*, on discovery of an antithesis in the constitutive principles of consciousness: 'The two principles annul one

another ... But if it is annulled, so is the major principle that contains it and with that in turn the unity of consciousness. So it cannot annul itself, and the opposites it contains must be capable of reconciliation.' *Science Of Knowledge*, *Werke*, I, 132, and so on). Second, the *cogito* argument is performed in and as an act of self-reflection, which means that the truth is discovered by a method of phenomenological description in which the two roles are discerned of the consciousness being observed, and the consciousness observing, which will lead to Hegel's 'for itself' and 'for us.' Third, the argument places the reader in the same position as that of the narrator of the text, and so the successful reading of the text involves recognizing that it is one's own consciousness that is being observed. This theme comes to be exploited in Fichte's insistence that the student will grant all of Fichte's arguments: 'I bring you no new revelations. What I can teach you you already know. I cannot deceive you, for you will grant me everyting I say' (*Vocation of Man*, *Werke*, II, 199); it is further exploited in Hegel's insistence that the *Phenomenology of Spirit* must and does provide each single consciousness with a 'ladder to the absolute' (M26, WC 19–21). Fourth, the response to scepticism comes through attention to the unique demands that derive from the determinate form of that being investigated: only if one maintains an 'abstract' scepticism that does not notice what it is doubting but insists instead on the independent, universal validity of doubting can one doubt the existence of the doubter, for as soon as one understands what is being said here – as soon as the doubt has meaning – it becomes impossible. This is the beginning of the insistence on the necessary concreteness of reason.

24 Trans. Donald A. Cress. The emphasis is mine, and the emphasized text reads in the Latin, '*in quibus scilicet repugnantiam agnosco manifestam.*' Here again, the scepticism cannot be maintained in the face of an actual recognition of the determinateness of the object being doubted. This paragraph of Descartes's text sets up the basis for a dialectical argument in the form characteristic of Fichte: two equally compelling but opposed claims are presented; since neither can be rejected and since the conflict cannot be the proper form for their existence, we can be certain that there is a way to reconcile the two.
25 Compare Husserl's discussion of the relation of the empirical and the transcendental 'I' and 'We' in part II, sec. D, of his *Encyclopaedia Brittanica* article, Phenomenology,' trans. Richard E. Palmer, *British Journal of Phenomenology* (May 1971), 85.
26 On this issue, see the second meditation, paragraphs 3ff., and the first part of Arnauld's objections to the *Meditations* (*Fourth Set of Objections*) with Descartes's response.
27 This is the argument that I have taken up in *The Self and Its Body in Hegel's Phenomenology*.
28 Paragraphs 11ff.
29 I am arguing that all the roles that God is made to play in these arguments are

completely consistent and indeed necessary for an argument about transcendental subjectivity. Just at the level of argument, Descartes's position is fine, even compelling, and involves no illicit appeal to any God other than the very concept of reason (hence the accusation that he reasons in a circle from reason to God to reason is a completely true statement that completely misses the point). There remains a question, however, of how Descartes imagined this God: whether he took God to mean something other than reason. On this point I have no strong view, but I would note that in the *Principles* I.51 God already looks a great deal like Spinoza's substance. At any rate, even if Descartes does mean something else, this is logically discardable because the argument does not depend on it; his claim is to be rationally rigorous, and our job is to follow the argument rigorously, so we are compelled by the argument to understand the God of meditations 3 and 5 as reason.

30 See M26, WC 19–21, in the 'Preface' to the *Phenomenology of Spirit*, where recognition of the self in the other is the hallmark of real science. It is because they are all forms of such recognition that 'Reason,' 'Spirit,' 'Religion,' and 'Absolute Knowing' are all included as Section C of the *Phenomenology*.

31 Compare the dialectic of 'external reflection,' *Science of Logic*, trans. A.V. Miller (London: George Allen and Unwin, 1969), 403–4, *Wissenschaft der Logik*, hrsg. E. Moldenhauer und K.M. Michel (Frankfurt: Suhrkamp, 1969) II, 28–40.

32 On this point, Hegel accuses Kant of ultimately being a sceptic. Kant's dialectic is itself portrayed by Kant in the 'Antinomies' as a '*sceptical* method,' while what is clearly a development of this same method is portrayed by Fichte in the second 'Introduction' to the *Science of Knowledge* (and, in turn, by Hegel in the 'Introduction' to the *Phenomenology*) as the direct observation of the truth. See Kant, *Kritik der reinen Vernunft* A423/B451, Fichte, *Werke*, I, 454.

33 This 'check' first appears at the end of the first discourse of the *Science of Knowledge* (on theoretical knowledge), *Werke*, I, 210, and the attempt to resolve the dualism in action is the subject matter of the discourses on the practical that close the *Science of Knowledge*.

34 Here then is the ground for the need, noted by James Crooks in chapter 12, below, that the dialectical method culminate in system.

35 The first three chapters of the *Phenomenology of Spirit* clearly focus on the structures of the object of experience, yet these all translate into structures of what Kant would call transcendental subjectivity; the progress through these three chapters essentially parallels Kant's laying out of the 'layers' of synthesis in the *Critique of Pure Reason*, A98–110. 'Sense-Certainty' begins as the 'synthesis of apprehension in intuition,' and the dialectical argument of the chapter leads us to see that this synthesis already depends on memory and the holding together of sensations within a realm of possibility – that is, 'the synthesis of reproduction in imagination.' This synthesis is the basic 'thesis' of 'Perception,' and the dialectical

argument of this chapter reveals that the recognizable unities that we face are necessarily already the products of a conceptual synthesis, 'the synthesis of recognition in a concept.' Thus the first three chapters move us dialectically from sensation to imagination to understanding, in each case revealing that the earlier presupposes the later. Finally, the chapter on 'Understanding' starts with the thesis of the 'synthesis of recognition in a concept' and argues that this stands on the presupposition of a posited unified field of objectivity (the synthesis of 'the transcendental object = x') and further on the yet more fundamental synthesis of an overarching subjectivity, the unified experience of which is the ground of the unity of the object and all the other syntheses that depend upon it (= the 'transcendental unity of apperception'). Compare Charles Taylor, 'The Opening Arguments of the *Phenomenology*,' in Alisdair MacIntyre, ed., *Hegel: A Collection of Critical Essays* (Notre Dame, Ind.: University of Notre Dame Press, 1976), 151–87, who also considers the transcendental argumentation of the first three chapters.

36 Compare Jay Lampert's discussion of the culmination of property as the need to be stolen in chapter 2, above. Regarding the debate concerning the closure of Hegel's system in David Kolb (chapter 7) and John Burbridge (chapter 8), my argument leads to the conclusion that absolute knowledge is the knowledge that one can never predict the future, in the sense that one must always let the future teach us what it will be, but that one can know for certain that one will be able to learn (and this is the *Aufhebung* of Descartes's argument against the possibility of global scepticism.)

37 I have developed this theme of Aristotle's active empiricism in 'Aristotle's Animative Epistemology,' *Idealistic Studies* 25 (1995), 243–54, and 'Self-Consciousness and the Tradition in Aristotle's Psychology,' *Laval Théologique et Philosophique*, 52 (1996), 777–803.

38 I have benefited from comments by Martin Donougho and Michael Baur; I also thank David Kolb, Kenneth L. Schmitz, and H.S. Harris for their helpful comments on an earlier presentation of this interpretation of the 'Freedom of Self-Consciousness.'

Afterword:
Theme and Variations: The Round of Life and the Chorale of Thought

H.S. HARRIS

As he came to the end of his lectures on the *Encyclopaedia Logic*, Hegel compared it to the religious 'creed' learned in an ordinary, non-philosophical life (see sec. 237, 'Zusatz'). One learns the Credo as a verbal formula in childhood. Already it has a 'story-meaning' for the child: 'God' *created* everything (just as the sunrise 'creates' light, let us say). Then God came down as a man (first he was like me, then like my father); and finally he went back to Heaven, where a lot of dead people, who have lived good lives, are now with him. But his 'spirit' is still here (just as my grandmother, who died only last month, is still with me sometimes when I am in her room). But as the child grows into a seriously committed Christian, and eventually into a thoughtful old (wo)man in the chimney corner, the story takes on a *symbolic* meaning of quite another kind. (In particular, the crucifixion, which my supposed happy child does not even attempt to imagine, becomes the focal image of what God did for us, and we must try to do for him in return.)

Hegel's philosophy is meant to be the logical climax of this life-long process of interpretation. Formal logic he knew by the time he was twelve (I suppose that was before he was 'confirmed,' though I do not know what the custom of his Würtemburg was). He himself endeavoured to teach his still-nascent philosophical logic to boys of fourteen or fifteen. In its fullest exposition, he called it the 'thought of God before the creation' – before the creed-story itself began. Here, then, was a formula of a new kind. This logical creed begins with the thought of 'how to be' and ends with 'method' – with the thought of 'how to think.' Hegel expected those who had just been confirmed (let us assume that, like me, they reached this turning point close to their fourteenth birthday) to participate in God's thinking about thinking and being. Thereafter (in the Real Philosophy) the familiar creed-story is told in its philosophical version. 'The creation of all things visible' becomes 'the resolve' of the self-thinking Idea 'to let itself go' into the outwardness of a being that is not thought; and the creation of the 'invisible' begins with the death of the finite organism and the resurrection of the logical Concept as 'Spirit.'

This double creation appears in scripture, too. The first chapter of John teaches that the Creator was not the Father but the *Logos*, the Son. Hegel's system lets the creation of nature unfold as the 'letting go' of the Father. But when we reach the 'organic' climax of *Naturphilosophie*, we discover that the creation-story is identical with the incarnation-story. The mystery of how we can do the divine thinking (even as early teenagers) is solved by the recollective acknowledgment that we are the beings who actually do think. 'God's' thinking is the thinking of the *logos*, the thinking of 'God made man.' It is the thinking that we must all do in order to be 'thinkers' at all, as a validly universal class – in order to share a common world and communicate effectively with one another about what is 'true' for all of us in it. The first creation by God the Father simply expresses the a priori necessity of the 'order of Nature,' the rational structure of the objective world, without which rational life could not come to be.

'Spirit' itself could not come to be without natural death. That is why the spiritual world is necessarily pictured in our religion, as a beyond. The confirmed Christian is presumed able to imagine the crucifixion. I cannot stay to discuss the 'infinite grief'; but Kierkegaard was wrong in thinking that 'the System' leaves out 'the ethical.' What is important to us here, however, is that the Hegelian interpretation of 'resurrection' directs attention back to the world of experience in which our thinking is done. The Philosophy of Spirit teaches us that there is such a thing (in our experience) as the 'freedom' of thought. We are not logically tied down to the thoughtful interpretation of sense perception, and its elaboration into the 'order of Nature.' In the realm of the 'Spirit' it is not ultimately important whether the child's imaginings about her grandmother are literally 'true' or not. Provided that they are at least reasonable, it may not even be possible to decide whether they are true. The order of nature will always compel our respect; and we must always voluntarily respect the ideal of historical truth, because otherwise we shall be setting ourselves against the objective rationality that is our 'essence' as thinkers. But it is a truth that must be frankly acknowledged, that we do not know what 'did' happen, except so far as we can agree on what 'must have' happened. Beyond that point, there is only belief; and because the essence of rationality is 'freedom that is logically destined to recognize necessity,' 'beliefs' must necessarily differentiate themselves freely.

The old woman in the chimney corner (before she dies) knows that she has forgotten many things. When she tells stories to the children about the 'old days' – tales that *her* grandmother told her – she knows (philosophically) that she must tell them as 'faithfully' as she can. But for things that she has herself forgotten, she makes up replacements without scruple. It is the 'old world,' not the 'facts,' that must be passed on. The child whose interest in history is aroused may well discover that in the recorded memory of the community, quite important matters have a different aspect, but she will be as grateful as ever to grandma and great-grandma.

Already in the creed itself, the teenager thus interested in history can see that the religious 'story' of what God has done is not historical. God the Son, so she repeats in church, 'was conceived of the Holy Ghost, and born of the Virgin Mary.' But she knows already that virgins do not have children, and when she is instructed in the Hegelian logic (or even just in 'natural science') she learns that the objectivity of Reason is not consistent with breaches in the 'order of Nature.' History tells her, however, that in an earlier time her forbears – even the wisest of them – thought that the divine Spirit had to have that sort of arbitrary relation to Nature. If it had to have it, then *a fortiori* it could have it. So, when our budding Hegelian takes stock of the natural impossibility of this supposed relation, she learns something important about the freedom of the human imagination (and the consequently necessary uncertainty of the history that it recollects).

It is certain that her Saviour was not born of a pure virgin; so, in the light of the indubitably historical fact that the creed has been believed, the 'belief of the world' indicates that the Saviour may perhaps not have been a singular historical person at all. Nothing asserted as the work of the Spirit is literally true. Constantine was historical (and his belief was historical); but the 'Donation of Constantine' was not (though belief in it was long-lasting in history). 'The carpenter's son of Nazareth' is believable enough. But do the documents that certify his 'suffering under Pontius Pilate' really have a better claim on our trust than the Donation documents? Our budding historian must see that one could argue that question for ever. But she reads the story of Christ before Pilate, and she realizes that though Constantine's belief in the history was important, hers is not. Pilate's rhetorical question, 'What *is* truth?' points to the fact that even if the story that attributes the question to him is false, the 'truth' that the other character in the story stood for (and stands for) remains crucial.

This insight is what is necessary for the transition from 'religion' to philosophy. Is Hegel the only 'Christian' to maintain that it does not matter to us now whether Constantine's belief was historically sound? Does not every thinking Christian admit that Pilate is more securely historical than the 'carpenter's son' who faced him? (That is exactly why Pilate got mentioned in the creed.) Certainly every thinking Christian agrees that Pilate was asking about something more important than historical fact. If our student – now at the university – reads the *Phenomenology* attentively, she will see that Hegel has carefully constructed the 'appearing of the Absolute Spirit' (in the Manifest Religion) as a 'self-creation out of *nothing*.' The 'belief of the world' recollects the historicity of a story that emerges from the chaotic welter of the Gnostic imagination.

The Gnostics believed in an intermediate realm of daimones.[1] Here then is the one truly divine *daimon*, his divine status certified by his miraculous birth. Everything said about him by Hegel is said in the eternal present, because Luther's interpretation of the witness of the Spirit is essential to this divine status. That this divine man is seen, heard, touched, and so on, is obviously and necessarily independent of whether the carpenter's son was seen, heard, touched historically. This is a miracle of everyday experience that needs no historic testimonies or warrants. Our confirmed Christian sees and touches the sacraments – and she hears the Saviour's own words as she does so. But the historical absurdity of the virgin birth cuts the story of the carpenter's son off from the realm of ordinary, finite historical experience altogether. The Spirit generates itself *ex nihilo*. It is reasonable enough to believe in a real carpenter's son standing before Pilate. But spiritually, once Luther has returned us to Paul's 'Christ liveth in me,' the putative second Joshua does not matter. Dante, beholding Rhipeus (Virgil's 'most just of the Trojans') in Paradise, is already a member of Hegel's 'Christian sect.' Neither of them was ever a 'party of one' in the spirit, whatever their critics may have believed about their situation in the world.[2]

This interpretation of the witness of the Spirit is what makes the Manifest Religion 'absolute.' It is absolute not because its 'faith-content' is capable of 'spiritual' interpretation. Whatever truly deserves the name of 'religion' has that distinction. As far as its content is concerned, the faith in Christ is not merely capable of, but actually subject to, a bad infinity of elaboration and development. Only the other day I learned of the existence of a heretical *Muslim* sect – called the Ahmadis after their founder, who preached his new prophetic revelation in the 1880s – who believe that Jesus did not die on the cross but went to India in search of a lost tribe. There he died at the age of 120 and was buried in Srinagar. Ahmad's revelation – or Mrs Eddy's 'Christian Science' – does not affect the issue. The point about the 'witness of the spirit' is that Paul's (or Luther's) experience of the conjunction of time and eternity absolves us from the need for 'belief' and necessitates the transition to a speculative interpretation of what is 'spiritually' asserted. Thus, though Hegel (like Mrs Eddy and me) undoubtedly believed in the carpenter's son, it is crucial to his interpretation of this 'recollection' that he does not have to believe it. If the connection with a historic event were necessary, the religious experience could not be 'absolute' – since no singular event can be known to be necessary if it is 'historical' – if it has to be 'recollected.'[3]

But now our Christian student, having discovered what her 'faith' means, is ready to become a philosopher properly – in the Hegelian mode. She must leave behind the wisdom of the chimney corner, and the simple faith of parents and friends who have never been troubled about the truth of the gospel record or the identity of Jesus with the *Logos*. The first thing that she will discover now is that among the philosophers the claim 'I know that my Redeemer liveth' seems just as absurd as the claim that he was born long ago to a virgin in the stable at Bethlehem. 'What sort of *knowledge* is *this*?' they will ask. 'How *can* we *know* that we live and move and have our being in God?' Isn't it obvious enough that we live and move on the earth, and in the order of nature?

Hegel himself received a theological education, and he often seems to take it for granted that the problems of Christian theology are the problems of philosophy *tout court*. But this was an absurd opinion even in his time. It served him as an excuse for dismissing any thinker who did not seek to do philosophy systematically as an 'unphilosopher.' But when he became a philosopher he knew that the problem of how the theological assumption of the 'speculative' tradition could be established must be faced. After all, Kant, the greatest thinker of his own tradition, had only just finished overthrowing the claim that we have any theological knowledge at all.

For a *Volkserzieher* this did not matter much. It was enough, in that calling, to clarify what the community actually believed without worrying about the gulf between finite 'knowledge' and social beliefs about 'the Infinite.' But even for a *Volkserzieher* the problem of how to order and relate these beliefs about the Infinite was a pressing one; and Hegel already had enough experience with that problem when he went to Jena to know that the historical development of society held the only answer. Schelling's Identity Theory aimed to show that the critical philosophy of finite experience could be organized to lead to the intuitive understanding of the union of the mind with the whole of nature. But social history showed that there were many variant 'intuitions' of the 'forms of Union.' How can we be sure that any 'intuition' is really 'intellectual,' or if there are many 'universal intuitions' (intellectually shared) how can we know that ours is the best so far?

It is not clear that the thirty-year-old beginner thought that a final solution was possible. Schiller and Hölderlin had given him an aesthetic criterion for the 'forms of life'; for the 'forms of thought' he developed an analogous criterion of an identity of recognition. The 'one true philosophy' takes its conceptual shape according to the 'need of the time.' So a 'true philosopher' can recognize it in every previous age by studying the 'need' of that time; and she can reconstruct it appropriately for her own age in the same way. This was a response to Kant's claim to have brought the hopeless dialectic of the 'Schools' to an end in the 'critical' acceptance of finitude.

But the response was not adequate, because here in Hegel's own age, Fichte had shown how to put Kant's critical theory together speculatively, even before Schelling brought us back to the problem of 'union with nature.' So there *is* progress in philosophy, as well as 'identity.' Where does the progressive movement lead, and what is the rational criterion for it? That is the problem implicit in the *Differenzschrift*. Susan-Judith Hoffmann (chapter 11, above) is right in arguing that the *Differenzschrift* has a reconciliatory-constructive purpose, not just the comparative-critical aim that was so apparent to Hegel's contemporaries (and to most later readers). The Frankfurt 'forms of life' do not (yet) develop from one to another; for the Jews and the Greeks were mutually invisible (and the whole concept depends on cultural autonomy). But Kant-Fichte-Schelling are a developmental series in which 'speculation' is reborn. Looking back on Hegel's development in the perspective that Hoffmann has opened up, the motion of his reflection appears dialectical. The *Differenzschrift* says that Fichte provided a transcendental schema of the speculative standpoint; and Schelling advanced to its 'real' fulfilment in the philosophy of Nature. Consequently, when Fichte provides a 'vision' of his view projected as a 'real' future (in the *Bestimmung des Menschen*), he is cast out among the non-speculative philosophers of 'subjective reflection.' That was the verdict of *Glauben und Wissen*; and the *Naturrecht* essay adds that the real fulfilment is the aesthetic appreciation of an objective 'Idea' that does not return to itself subjectively. But now a new cycle begins. The motion of Hegel's thought does 'return to itself' – and so to Fichte. The 'experience of consciousness' comes to centre stage; and 'Fichtes Verdienst' is to have grasped the pattern of 'self-recognition in otherness' that results in a 'return to self.' For this reason, we can call Fichte the presiding genius of the *Phenomenology*.[4]

In this movement of Hegel's thought, Hölderlin, of course, was there first. Schelling was there in the limelight; and until the *Phenomenology* was published, only students in the lecture room could even surmise that Hegel believed that he was developing the eternal Idea to a stage beyond Schelling.[5] But Hegel brought his doctrine of the aesthetic intuition of 'Nature' with him to Jena from Frankfurt. It is probable that the 'Tübingen Fragment' was inspired by Hölderlin; and the *hen kai pan* was the pre-philosophical form of the 'one eternal Reason.' The Hegelian concept of 'Spirit' was born in Frankfurt; and Nicholas Walker has displayed its process of origin better than Alan Olson did (though he too appreciates the importance of Hölderlin). Olson seems to assume that Hegel simply took over 'the Spirit' from the theological tradition. But actually it was never exclusively 'Christian'; and Hegel was always trying to conceptualize it (as the relation between the human community and its members). Walker brings this out clearly.

It is Hölderlin's ideal of 'Nature' (rather than Schelling's) that is displaced in the Fichte-inspired 'experience of consciousness.' The recognition that spiritual existence involves a 'breach with Nature' (or the metaphysical overthrow of God as 'Substance') is a radical revision of the ideal of 'Union' developed in the Frankfurt texts. But – since 'Spirit' is theologically a 'Person' – we can say that the 'Hellenic ideal' of 'union with Nature' was always foredoomed. The breach with Schelling probably did not seem to Hegel to be as inevitable as that with Hölderlin's poetic vision, because Schelling himself was a philosopher in the Kantian tradition. Schelling believed in 'the Fall'; perhaps he could be persuaded to accept Hegel's interpretation of the 'return to God' in history.

It was only when Hegel rejected the Neoplatonic-metaphysical doctrine of the Fall – first in the *Jena Logic* and then in the *Phenomenology* – that he was forced into an open and unavoidable disagreement with Schelling.[6] But once he recognized 'Fichte's merit' he could no longer accept the intuition (aesthetic and intellectual) of the 'point of indifference' as the goal of speculative philosophy. So, though he was clearly turning one of the most familiar criticisms of the Identity Philosophy against the critics, when he condemned the 'dark night in which all the cows are black,' we must not blink at the fact that the did regard Schelling's doctrine of 'absolute indifference' as radically unsatisfactory. This was the point at which a further development of the new-born concept of 'Speculation' was necessary.[7]

Since the 'point of indifference' can be apprehended only intuitively, Schelling could only 'shoot the Absolute from a pistol.' After struggling for a long time to find an alternative interpretation, I was driven to admit that (as Fackenheim claimed) Hegel meant this barb in the preface to the *Phenomenology* for Schelling. But his comment is a brutally sarcastic climax for an unkind paragraph about the 'introductions to philosophy' offered by others. So George di Giovanni is arguing for the most probable of all addressees when he lays out the case against Fries.[8] I shall certainly support his suggestion in *Hegel's Ladder*. Here again, however, the implicit truth is that the *Phenomenology* is the sort of 'introduction to speculative philosophy' that Schelling himself had not seen to be necessary.

Hamann's position and influence show why this introduction was truly required. The deeply religious soul with an intellectual bent can immerse itself in the tradition 'recollectively,' to the point where it does not need any actual community at all. It is an important fact about the dead, that they do not answer back (except with the words that we supply for them). When we are meditating on 'God's' word, there is no one to answer back – so that any 'conscience' that we may have in the matter is stilled. This was Hegel's complaint about the Beautiful Soul – a complaint that he first raises against the 'prophets' among his romantic contemporaries at the end of his Preface.

Hamann was deeply insightful about language as the *Dasein* of the divine

Spirit; and he laughed at the presumption of those who thought that they could establish a stable conceptual 'system' within the irresistibly flowing continuity of human discourse. The leaps that are shown to be necessary (in the first three chapters of the *Phenomenology*) between the singular *Sachen* with names, the particular *Dinge* with nameable properties, and the universal 'forces' of intelligible 'science' are Hegel's tribute to Hamann's insight. When we reach 'Self-Consciousness' we recognize that the names themselves were produced by the activity of 'Desire' (that is, the 'speculative' meaning of Adam's lordship of all creation except the two Trees). But if our budding philosopher draws from this the moral that Adam's sin should be avoided, and philosophy should be eschewed in favour of a meditative religious scepticism, she has only to read Hegel on Hamann to see what he meant about 'trampling the roots of humanity underfoot' when one refuses to argue.[9] Like Hamann she would find that she had given up the fellowship of those nearest and dearest to her, only to fall into the 'dark night.' The only sensible way to avoid philosophy is to live towards the chimney corner.

If, instead of retreating, the student presses on with her quest for a satisfactory explanation of her faith, she will come (in Hegel's chapter IV) to the laughing sceptics who concede that Hamann is right about language and life but think that we can make a philosophical game of it all. There is no answer to them – for philosophy is a game. The refusal to be satisfied, the offering of counter-arguments, the raising of new problems belong to it. Even someone who can expound Hegel's *Logic* as fluently as John McCumber (chapter 3, above) thinks that perhaps Hamann was right – not in Hamann's spirit, but in that of the laughing sceptic. Hegel's dialectical response is valid only for someone as serious-minded as Hamann himself; for it is true that no 'company of words' can provide the 'comprehensive presentation' of the stoics, until we grasp that it is the identity of Being and Nothing, of Reason and freedom – or of thought as actual thinking – that is to be comprehended. But only a naturally religious soul will experience philosophical scepticism as 'unhappy consciousness.' So I chose my ideal student appropriately.

Alan Olson has noted the Lutheran origins of this first 'religious' Gestalt.[10] But that only makes the transition to 'Reason' harder to comprehend. Olson's view shows how the 'call of the Spirit' to believe what we can in no way understand gets us to the standpoint of 'Faith.' But Hegel clearly wants us to make a transition from Luther's overcoming of rational despair to the rational confidence of Descartes. John Russon's thesis (chapter 13, above) that 'Reason' is a re-enactment of the 'Freedom of Self-Consciousness' is an attractive one. We should expect it to be true (in some sense) both for conceptual reasons – it is the singular self-consciousness that 'has Reason' – and for reasons of historical continuity. Luther overthrew the identification of reason with external authority; and Hegel presents the Enlightenment in the conceptual context of the reformed 'Faith' later on. Whatever view we take of the 'methodical' progression at this point it is clear that we are meant to comprehend the post-Copernican science of nature within the horizon of a 'modern' theology that is 'Lutheran' at least in its inspiration.

The unhappy consciousness of the world coincided with the period during which the saving 'belief of the world' arose.[11] Thus (in my view) the 'Condition of Right' embraces the whole two hundred years that Gibbon allots to the 'artful system' of Augustus; and its inversion into military dictatorship lasted for more than a century. But if we are religious-minded 'believers' (like my ideal student) we can easily prefer Patricia Fagan's reading of the movement (in chapter 1) as all contained in the perceptibly singular 'moment' of the year 68–9. As critical historians we may be sceptical whether the pattern really was providentially fulfilled by the martyrdom of St Paul just as the year began. But Hegel's theory of the 'World Spirit,' and of how religion determines the process of 'recollection,' shows us why such exactly appropriate historical traditions arise. In Pilate's sense of truth, Patricia Fagan's view is 'truer' than mine – unless, as I think, properly 'philosophical history' has to become completely critical once the transition to 'absolute knowing' has been accomplished (and not remain religious-mythic, like Hegel's own 'World History' lectures).

History is only the universal discipline that is conceptually transformed by the philosophical comprehension of time as the communal substance of our singular subjectivity as rational individuals. It began to become apparent in 1914–18 that world history is not 'the judgment of God'; and since 1945 we have known that the face of Death (as the 'Absolute Master') cannot suffer any change of aspect. It cannot be transformed into any shape recognizable as 'justice.' There is nothing here but the 'infinite grief.' It is only a negative moment in the movement of Objective Spirit. Its positive aspect (of 'resurrection' or 'rebirth') belongs to Absolute Spirit only.

Absolute Spirit thus embraces history generally, not just the Platonic triad of Art, Religion, and Philosophy. Everything that we do 'for its own sake' belongs to the sphere of Absolute Spirit. Here is where 'the meaning of life' is revealed; and when our student has successfully sublated the myth of 'Providence,' and understood that 'Absolute Teleology' is so called because it is the true logical shape of her own rational freedom, she will know what to say to the commonsense philosophers who ask how she can possibly know that she lives and moves 'in God.'

Absolute Teleology is the identical conjunction of Reason and freedom. Because of what has happened to the 'judgment of God,' the practical aspect of it is ominous. Everything we do must belong to 'the other' in the future; and we can know nothing of that aspect – except that our expectations are necessarily incomplete, and partly 'mistaken.' Thus we know that we must each die, but we do not know when; and it now appears that we could all die together. There is nothing to be done about this 'fate,' except to 'reverence' it. (That word designates a religious attitude of some sort, but I leave it to others to characterize it more fully.)

For the moment, it is the theoretical (or positively absolute) aspect of 'fate' that interests me. Dante could never have dreamed that his *Comedy* would be interpreted by Auerbach, Donougho (and others, including eventually me, if fate permits) as a poem in which the religious vision is philosophically resolved. He saw this earthly life as the testing ground for the Beyond. So for him, the practical (moral) perspective determined everything else in his vision. For us that perspective is sublated. We can recognize the justice of the view that Francesca's choice was 'wrong.' But to us what appears tragic is that she had no opportunity to learn from her mistake. Of course, Dante felt that too (why else does he faint in the story?), and since he believed in God's justice, I think it is possible to give a strictly this-worldly account of his meaning. The assumption that is basic for this attempt has to be that the poet believes that God has revealed to him only what it is morally useful for us to know, and not the actual fate of anyone in the Beyond. (There are many signs in the *Comedy* that its meaning is dialectical, not historic.)

But, of course, an approach of this kind involves a very different conception of the medieval use of allegory than the flat-footed doctrine of enlightened common sense that Hegel (and Croce after him) spontaneously adopted. Hegel's view of the history of philosophy between Plotinus and Descartes was appallingly crass.[12] If I am right, Dante was a very insightful philosopher of language. He would have agreed with us that language is the *Dasein* of the Spirit – though not, of course, with my strictly immanent reading of Spirit's essence. Dante could do what Glendower claimed; it is for poets and prophets to call spirits from the deep. But philosophical critics must try to give those spirits a benevolent shape (so far as possible).

My student now comprehends the Spirit in its absolute shape. She can take the Hegelian logic and expound it to her philosophical critics as the theory of rational selfhood – the theory of how the singular mortal can exist in the rational substance as the self-knowledge of it. The 'substance' is the human community in its natural world; and its 'subjectivity' is its logically comprehended Spirit – 'the I that is We and the We that is I.' The theory of rational selfhood can be finally stated, she says, because the boundaries of our finite existence are naturally fixed and are known beyond all argument to our own common sense. How the world of absolute Spirit will evolve (or even *that* it will) we cannot know – that is a negative truth that we know absolutely, just as we know that we shall die. There is no final 'long list of categories,' such as Peirce was seeking for many years. Scientific inquiry will transform our concept of nature continually (and may transform it radically). But that concept must continue to be determined by the absolute relation that holds between the ordinary world of sense experience and the supersensible world of Understanding. For the definition of this relation a list of categories longer than Peirce's 'short list' can be determined – and that is what Hegel's Logic purports to be (or should be interpreted as).

This comprehensive context of philosophical inquiry can be recognized by thinkers who remain completely sceptical about the possibility of a systematic map, or about 'dialectic' as the method for making the map. So my student does not need (and will not rationally expect) to convince more than a minority of her colleagues that her 'faith' is now a kind of knowledge. But her perspective on what the unconverted are doing will be very different from that of Hegel in his *History of Philosophy*. I called his view of the medieval thinkers 'crass,' because they were contributing to his 'speculative' concept. We can more readily forgive Hegel's prejudice against everything that sprang from Locke's 'way of ideas,' because Locke did, consciously and deliberately, turn his back on the theological problem. But even Hegel knew that in the 'real philosophy' of the finite world, Locke (and the other theorists of 'subjective reflection') had an important place. Jay Lampert (acting like my ideal student) has examined the 'finite' theorists in the Hegelian perspective – with particular reference to the 'right of property.' But this inquiry could be pursued by someone who was not a 'Hegelian' at all.[13] Such a one may be puzzled by the calm acceptance of contradiction (or inconsistency) at the limits of the finite concept – and may make some misguided criticisms. But that is the common lot of critics (from which Hegelians are not exempted).

In Hegel's perspective, philosophical thought is to be interpreted as the self-conscious expression of its 'world'; and the conscious unity of a cultural world is expressed in its 'religion.' But in our Hegelian world, we have recognized 'self-definition' as our vocation. So we can see that philosophers must have their own problems and that philosophical thought must be assessed in terms of the particular intuitive difficulty with which the thinker was concerned. The 'speculative' tradition has now served its turn. It has bequeathed to us the conceptual ideal of historical objectivity as an achievable standpoint that is higher than the valet's-eye view (and beyond the lordly concept of all ideas as ideological powers in our social struggle). The perspective of the struggle can be applied to it, because it is not beyond dialectical interpretation. For 'absolute teleology' is the ultimate structure of Reason; and therfore the historical tradition is an inexhaustible repertoire of new insights into our own situation (and our freedom). In our own, immediately present context it is a compliment to find one of my own poetic metaphors taken over and developed (by James Crooks in chapter 12). The relevance of his thesis on 'self-measure' to my own argument in this essay is obvious. His conclusion is more aporetic than I like. But I applaud his return to Plato; and his distinction of types of philosophical discourse is insightful. Only we must not confine our attention to the voices that acknowledge a Hegelian inspiration; and we must understand that (if Hegel was right) there will be no recognizable 'Socrates' in the future. We have each to be Socrates for herself. (That is not an aporia, I hope. If we are drawn into becoming philosophers we have some inkling from the first of what our own problem is – and it defines itself as we go on.)

There is some 'counterpoint' in this present essay (but not as much as there ought to be, I fear). I have chosen to evoke rather simpler musical models here. Life is a 'round.' Logically it goes on indefinitely, but only because finite lives must each play a new variation on it. To hear the universal chorale in it is almost as hard as to hear the music of the spheres (and some will cheerfully consign the project to the same category of illusions). But back at the origin of this romantic dream we find the worldly figure of J.J. Winckelmann. It all began with the problem of 'imitating the Greeks.' Goethe, the presiding poetic genius of the whole movement, was inspired by Winckelmann's vision of the Greek achievement. But even in Winckelmann's sense of 'imitation' – so ably expounded by Michael Baur in chapter 4 – Goethe did more than imitate. His Faust brings Helen back to a modern Arcadia. But that was only the focal moment in a far more complex poetic career. Hegel himself was a kind of philosophical Faust. As a schoolboy he discovered Sophocles; as a university student he fell under the spell of the modern Hyperion; and finally as a mature philosopher he saw that his problem was to comprehend the whole experience of spontaneous self-expression and reflective imitation. How now, therefore, shall we later thinkers, inspired by his example, 'imitate' him? The answer is as simple as Winkkelmann's – and closely related. Each does it her own way. We contribute all that we can to the common heritage (like those romantically idealized Greeks) by expressing and enjoying ourselves as strenuously as we can. (The philosopher, repeating one of Grandma's platitudes, thus makes a round of his essay, as he should.)

Notes

1 See the essay of Jeff Mitscherling (chapter 6) in this volume.
2 See the essay of David Kolb (chapter 7) in this volume.
3 The view that the Manifest Religion is 'absolute' because the transition to 'specula-

tion' is (for the first time) necessary solves David Kolb's problem of how any particular religion can be more truly 'absolute' than religion in general. But Kolb is quite right (I think) about the logical implications of John Burbidge's argument that the 'absolute religion' might be manifested in new ways. On that view of its 'absoluteness' there is no logical warrant for holding that the 'shape' we have experienced is 'absolute' at all. Fantasies about the extending of the Christian revelation belong to sentimental literature. They are appropriate for children (as, for instance, in the Narnia stories of C.S. Lewis); but they are only idle amusements for adults (as in his trilogy *Out of the Silent Planet, Perelandra*, and *That Hideous Strength*).

4 For Hegel's comment on Fichte (c. 1804) see *Hegel-Studien*, 4 (1967), 11; for a more detailed discussion of it, see H.S. Harris, '*Fichtes Verdienst*' in *Revue internationale de philosophie* 49 (1995), 79–91.

5 Some students grasped this point when Hegel taught his first course on the history of philosophy – see G. Nicolin, ed., *Hegel in Berichten seiner Zeitgenossen* (Hamburg: Meiner, 1970), report 48, and H.S. Harris, *Hegel's Development II: Night Thoughts (Jena 1801–1806)* (Oxford: Clarendon Press, 1983), 52.

6 *The Jena System, 1804–5: Logic and Metaphysics*, trans. John W. Burbidge and George di Giovanni (Montreal: McGill-Queen's University Press, 1986), 36, *Phenomenology of Spirit*, trans. A.V. Miller (London: Oxford University Press, 1977), sec. 162.

7 I have tried – with some success, I think – to show that Hegel did not mean Schelling to regard himself as the target of the attack; see 'The Cows in the Dark Night,' *Dialogue*, 26 (1987), 627–43, and '*Naturphilosophie* in the Breach between Hegel and Schelling,' *Hegel Jahrbuch* (1989), 9–18. But the displacement of the criticism onto 'Schelling's School' was motivated by Hegel's desire to take Schelling with him in the further development of idealism. Schelling was expected to admit that it was his own way of presenting the 'Absolute Identity' that had inspired 'schematic formalism'; and he made no admission that Hegel's way forward was actually necessary. Like Kant and Fichte faced with their enthusiastic 'developers,' Schelling stood his ground (though he soon went off in a new direction). So the traditional view – well argued by M. Vater in the Introduction to Schelling's *Bruno* (Albany: SUNY, 1984) is objectively valid. Hegel's intention – being frustrated – does not matter.

8 We obviously need to know more about Fries. When will someone make this easier for us by providing a representative body of work in English translation? In the *Logic of Scientific Discovery* (New York: Basic Books, 1959), Popper treats Fries as a significant theorist of scientific method. That ought to have produced some result by now – unless Popper's historical judgment is as bad everywhere else as it is about Hegel.

9 She can save herself some trouble by reading instead John McCumber's essay in

this volume (chapter 3). But I hope that when she goes on to read Hegel's *Logic* she will agree with me that Hegel did 'satisfy the unspoken needs of Hamann.' 'Satisfaction' cannot mean the end of discourse. The 'company of words' can never by magically complete by itself. Only 'the spirit' proceeding between the reader and the words can be 'magical.' That is why Hegel's company of words needs McCumber's words too. McCumber wouldn't wish that otherwise, but he should not write as if that means that Hamann is right to be still dissatisfied. (See further the brief discussion of the Logic below.)

10 See *Hegel and the Spirit* (Princeton, NJ: Princeton University Press, 1992), chap. 1.
11 What John Russon calls the 'transportability' of *Gestalten* is essential to their 'scientific' status. Thus the view of Burbidge that the unhappy consciousness is 'Gnostic' is valid for the *Weltgeist* (in the Religion chapter), even though the singular *Gestalt* in chapter IV is Augustinian at the beginning and Lutheran at the end; see Burbidge, *Hegel on Logic and Religion* (Albany: SUNY, 1992), chap. 20.
12 I was moved at first to say 'astoundingly,' but Hegel was only expressing the prejudice of Gibbon's time about writings that he had not himself read. The few things that he did read – for example, Anselm's *Proslogion* – he judged quite differently.
13 Jay Lampert sometimes writes as if he is not one. He ought to see that for systematic reasons, Hegel cannot begin at the top limit of the concept – with the impossibility of owning spiritual goods. Hegel must begin at the bottom limit – with the natural body that one ought not to 'own.' But Lampert is a Hegelian, because he belongs to a tradition that he is kind enough to say I began. Absolute teleology (or the 'cunning of Reason') has overtaken me here, because this 'beginning' now appears to me to be a historical error. As a philosopher Hegel was logically obliged to be an open-minded pluralist, I think (rather than a guild socialist, as I suggested). But it doesn't matter in the end what Hegel hoped for (or what Lampert and I hope for either). The fertile variety of reason will enforce itself.

Hegel's Works

German Texts

Werke, ed. E. Moldenhauer and K.M. Michel, 20 vols., Frankfurt: Suhrkamp Verlag, 1970–1 (Theorie Werkausgabe).
Gesammelte Werke, ed. Rheinisch-Westfaelischen Akademie der Wissenschaften, Hamburg: Felix Meiner, 1968– .
Theologische Jugendschriften, ed. H. Nohl, Tübingen: Mohr, 1907 (reprinted 1968).
Differenz des Fichte'schen und Schelling'schen Systems der Philosophie in Beziehung auf Reinhold's Beyträge, Jena: Seidler, 1801 (*Gesammelte Werke*, IV 1–92).
'Glauben und Wissen, oder die Reflexionphilosophie der Subjectivität, in der Vollständigkeit ihrer Formen, als kantishe, jacobische, und fichtische Philosophie,' *Kritische Journal der Philosophie*, Tübingen, 2 no. 1 (1802), 3–189 (*Gesammelte Werke* IV, 313–414).
'Über die wissenschaftliche Behandlungsarten des Naturrechts,' *Kritische Journal der Philosophie*, Tübingen: Cotta, 2 no. 2 (1802), 3–88, 2 no. 3 (1803), 1–34 (*Gesammelte Werke* IV, 415–85).
System der Wissenschaft: Erster Theil, Die Phänomenologie des Geistes (Bamberg and Würzburg: Goebhardt, 1807) (*Gesammelte Werke*, IX).
Phänomenologie des Geistes, ed. H.-F. Wessels and H. Clairmont, Hamburg: Felix Meiner, 1988.
Wissenschaft der Logik, 2 vols., Nürnberg: Schrag, 1812, 1816 (*Gesammelte Werke*, XI, XII).
Wissenschaft der Logik, ed. F. Hogemann and W. Jaeschke, Hamburg: Felix Meiner, 1978–81.
Enzyklopädie der philosophischen Wissenschaften im Grundrisse 2nd ed., Heidelberg: Oßwald, 1827 (*Gesammelte Werke*, XIX).

Enzyklopädie der philosophischen Wissenschaften (1830), ed. F. Nicolin and O. Pöggeler, Hamburg: Felix Meiner, 1959.
Grundlinien der Philosophie des Rechts, ed. J. Hoffmeister, Hamburg: Felix Meiner, 1967.
Die Philosophie des Rechts : die Mitschriften Wannenmann (1817/18) und Homeyer (Berlin 1818/19), lvrsg. v. Karl-Heinz Ilting, Stuttgart: Klett-Cotra, 1983.
Begriff der Religion, ed. G. Lasson, Hamburg: Felix Meiner, 1966.
Briefe von und an Hegel, ed. J. Hoffmeister and R. Fleschig, 4 vols., 3rd ed., Hamburg: Felix Meiner, 1969.

English Translations

'*Religion ist eine*: The Tübingen Essay of 1793,' in H.S. Harris, *Hegel's Development: Toward the Sunlight, 1770–1801*, Oxford: Clarendon Press, 1972, 481–507.
'*eine Ethik*: The Earliest System-Programme of German Idealism (Berne, 1796),' in *Toward the Sunlight*, 510–12.
Natural Law (1802), trans. T.M. Knox, Philadelphia: University of Pennsylvania Press, 1975.
System of Ethical Life (1802–3) and First Philosophy of Spirit, trans. H.S. Harris and T.M. Knox, Albany: SUNY Press, 1979.
Faith and Knowledge (1802–3), trans. Walter Cerf and H.S. Harris, Albany: SUNY Press, 1977.
The Difference between Fichte's and Schelling's System of Philosophy, trans. H.S. Harris and Walter Cerf, Albany: SUNY Press, 1977.
The Jena System, 1804–5: Logic and Metaphysics, trans. John W. Burbidge and George di Giovanni, Montreal: McGill-Queen's University Press, London 1986.
Phenomenology of Spirit, trans. A.V. Miller, London: Oxford University Press, 1977.
Science of Logic, trans. A.V. Miller, New York: Humanities Press, 1967.
The Logic of Hegel, trans William Wallace, 1st pub. 1873, London: Oxford University Press, 1963.
The Encyclopaedia Logic, trans. T.F. Geraets, W.A. Suchting, and H.S. Harris, Indianapolis: Hackett, 1991.
Philosophy of Nature, trans. A.V. Miller, with foreword by J.N. Findlay, Oxford: Clarendon Press, 1970.
Hegel's Philosophy of Mind, trans. William Wallace, London: Oxford University Press, 1971.
Hegel's Philosophy of Subjective Spirit, 3 vols., ed. and trans. M.J. Petry, Dordrecht: Reidel, 1978.
Hegel's Philosophy of Right, trans. T.M. Knox, London: Oxford University Press, 1967.

Aesthetics, Lectures on Fine Art, trans. T.M. Knox, London: Oxford University Press, 1975.

Lectures on the Philosophy of Religion, trans. E.B. Spiers and J. Burdon Sanderson, 1st pub. 1895, New York: Humanities Press, 1962.

Lectures on the History of Philosophy, trans. E.S. Haldane and Frances H. Simson, 1st pub. 1894, London: Routledge and Kegan Paul 1963.

Introduction to the Lectures on the History of Philosophy, trans. T.M. Knox and A.V. Miller, Oxford: Clarendon Press, 1985.

Hegel: The Letters, ed. and trans. Clark Butler and Christiane Seiler, Bloomington: Indiana University Press, 1984.

Publications of H.S. Harris

JAMES DEVIN

Books

The Social Philosophy of Giovanni Gentile. Urbana: University of Illinois Press, 1960, XII + 387 pp. (paper 1966). Italian translation (with new introductory essay): *La filosofia sociale di Giovanni Gentile*, tradotto da C. Bonomo e U. Salvi. Rome: Armando, 1973.

Hegel's Development I: Toward the Sunlight (1770–1801). Oxford: Clarendon Press, 1972, XXXII + 574 pp. French translation: *Le développement de Hegel, 1: Vers le soleil, 1770–1801*, traduit sous la direction de Philippe Muller. Lausanne: L'Age d'Homme, 1981.

Hegel's Development II: Night Thoughts (Jena 1801–1806). Oxford: Clarendon Press, 1983, lxxi + 632 pp. French translation: *Le développement de Hegel, 2: Pensées nocturnes – Jena 1801–1806*, traduit sous la direction de Philippe Muller et Eric Vial, Lausanne: L'Age d'Homme, 1988.

Hegel: Phenomenology and System. Indianapolis: Hackett Publishing Co., 1995.

La fenomenologia dell'autocoscienza in Hegel, traduzione e cura di Riccardo Pozzo. Naples: Guerini, 1996 [excerpted from following item].

Hegel's Ladder I: The Pilgrimage of Reason. Indianapolis: Hackett Publishing Co., 1997.

Hegel's Ladder II: The Odyssey of Spirit. Indianapolis: Hackett Publishing Co., 1997.

L'illuminismo francese nella Fenomenologia. Naples: Guerini (in preparation).

Influssi filosofici e letterari nella Fenomenologia. Naples: Guerini (in preparation).

Translations

Giovanni Gentile: Genesis and Structure of Society (translation with introduction, notes, and bibliography). Urbana: University of Illinois Press, 1960 (paper 1966).

G.W.F. Hegel: Difference between Fichte's and Schelling's System of Philosophy, trans. H.S. Harris and Walter Cerf, with introductions and notes. Albany, NY: SUNY Press, 1977.

G.W.F. Hegel: Faith and Knowledge, trans. Walter Cerf and H.S. Harris, with introductions and notes. Albany, NY: SUNY Press, 1977.

G.W.F. Hegel: System of Ethical Life and First Philosophy of Spirit, trans., with notes by T.M. Knox and H.S. Harris, with introductions by H.S. Harris. Albany, NY: SUNY Press, 1979 (paper 1987).

G.W.F. Hegel: Lectures on the Philosophy of Religion, vol. I, edited by P.C. Hodgson and trans. R.F. Brown, P.C. Hodgson, and J.M. Stewart, with the assistance of J.P. Fitzer and H.S. Harris. Berkeley: University of California Press, 1984.

G.W.F. Hegel: Lectures on the Philosophy of Religion, vol. II, edited by P.C. Hodgson and trans. R.F. Brown, P.C. Hodgson, and J.M. Stewart, with the assistance of H.S. Harris. Berkeley: University of California Press, 1987.

G.W.F. Hegel: Lectures on the Philosophy of Religion, vol. III, edited by P.C. Hodgson and trans. R.F. Brown, P.C. Hodgson, and J.M. Stewart, with the assistance of H.S. Harris. Berkeley: University of California Press, 1985.

G.W.F. Hegel: Philosophy of Religion: The Lectures of 1827, edited by P.C. Hodgson and trans. R.F. Brown, P.C. Hodgson, and J.M. Stewart, with the assistance of H.S. Harris. Berkeley: University of California Press, 1988.

G.W.F. Hegel: Lectures on the History of Philosophy, vol. III, trans. R.F. Brown and J.M. Stewart, with the assistance of H.S. Harris. Berkeley: University of California Press, 1992.

Between Kant and Hegel (selected writings in German philosophy after Kant), edited, annotated, and trans. G. di Giovanni and H.S. Harris. Albany, NY: SUNY Press, 1985. [Note: This volume contains excerpts from C.L. Reinhold, S. Maimon, G.E. Schulze, S. Beck, and J.G. Fichte, translated with an introduction by G. di Giovanni; and three essays of Hegel translated with an introduction by H.S. Harris. There is also one essay of Schelling's trans. di Giovanni and Harris together.]

G.W.F. Hegel: The Jena System, 1804–5: Logic and Metaphysics, trans. a group of Canadian scholars, edited by J. Burbidge and G. di Giovanni, with introduction and notes by H.S. Harris. Montreal: McGill-Queen's University Press, 1986.

G.W.F. Hegel: The Encyclopaedia Logic, trans. T.F. Geraets, W.A. Suchting, and H.S. Harris. Indianapolis: Hackett Publishing Co., 1994.

Editing

L.M. Palmer and H.S. Harris, eds., *Thought, Action and Intuition, a Symposium on the Philosophy of Benedetto Croce*. Hildesheim: Georg Olms, 1975, VII, 363 pp.

Series: *The Philosophy of Hegel* (Seventeen books on Hegel's philosophy, reprinted in sixteen volumes). New York: Garland Publishing, 1983.

Chapters in Books

'Introduction' for Giovanni Gentile, *Genesis and Structure of Society*, trans. H.S. Harris. Urbana: University of Illinois Press, 1960 (paper 1966), pp. 1–63 (including Bibliography of Gentile Studies in English).

'Studi sull'attualismo e influenza di Gentile sulla cultura anglosassone' and 'Bibliografia degli scritti gentiliani in lingua inglese,' in *Giovanni Gentile: La vita e il pensiero*, vol. IX. Florence, Sansoni, 1961, 293–333. [Italian translation of parts of previous item]

'Giambattista VICO,' in *Encyclopedia America*, New York, 1962.

'Fichte e Gentile,' in *Giovanni Gentile: La Vita e il Pensiero*, vol. XI. Florence: Sansoni, 1966.

'Pantaleo CARABELLESE,' 'Benedetto CROCE,' 'Giovanni GENTILE,' 'ITALIAN PHILOSOPHY,' 'Bertrando SPAVENTA,' and Ugo SPIRITO,' all in *Encyclopedia of Philosophy*. New York, 1967.

'The Modernity of Franco Lombardi,' in G. Kline, ed., *Contemporary European Philosophy*. Chicago: Quadrangle Books, 1965, 61–87.

'Voluntary Association as a Rational Ideal,' in *Nomos*, the yearbook of the American Society for Political and Legal Philosophy, XI: *Voluntary Associations*. N.p.: Atherton Press, 1969, 41–62.

'The Young Hegel and the Postulates of Practical Reason,' in D. Christensen, ed., *Hegel and the Philosophy of Religion*. The Hague: Nijhoff, 1970, 61–78.

'Benedetto CROCE,' 'Bernardino TELESIO,' and 'Antonio GENOVESI,' all in *Encyclopedia Americana*. New York, 1970.

'The Right Answer to Pontius Pilate,' in R.A. Tursman, ed., *Studies in Philosophy and in the History of Science*, Essays in Honour of Max Fisch. Lawrence, KY: Coronado Press, 1970, 8–17.

'Introduzione all'edizione italiana,' for *La filosofia sociale di Giovanni Gentile* (tradotto da C. Bonomo e U. Salvi). Rome: Armando, 1973, 7–34.

'Another Unknown Page from the Last Months of Hegel's Life,' in L.M. Palmer and H.S. Harris, eds.: *Thought, Action and Intuition*. Hildesheim: Georg Olms, 1975, 126–53.

'The Use and Abuse of Hegel,' in G. Ryle, ed., *Contemporary Trends in Philosophy*. London: Oriel Press, 1976, 223–38.

Introduction for G.W.F. Hegel, *The Difference between Fichte's and Schelling's System of Philosophy*, trans. H.S. Harris and Walter Cerf. Albany, NY: SUNY Press, 1977 (paper 1987), 1–75.

Introduction for G.W.F. Hegel, *Faith and Knowledge*, trans. Walter Cerf and H.S. Harris. Albany, NY: SUNY Press, 1977 (paper 1987), 1–50.

'Gentile's Reform of the Hegelian Dialectic,' in *Il pensiero di Giovanni Gentile*. Rome: Enciclopedia Italiana, 1977, 473–80.

'Hegel's *System of Ethical Life*: An Interpretation,' in G.W.F. Hegel, *System of Ethical Life and First Philosophy of Spirit*, ed. and trans. H.S. Harris and T.M. Knox. Albany, NY: SUNY Press, 1979, 3–96.

Introduction for 'First Philosophy of Spirit,' in G.W.F. Hegel, *System of Ethical Life and First Philosophy of Spirit*, ed. and trans. H.S. Harris and T.M. Knox. Albany, NY: SUNY Press, 1979, 187–204.

'Hegel and Evolutionary Theory' (Comment on T.M. Greene), in W.E. Steinkraus and K.L. Schmitz, eds.: *Art and Logic in Hegel's Philosophy*. New York: Humanities Press, 1980, 150–4. [HSA Conference, 1974]

'The Concept of Recognition in Hegel's Jena Manuscripts,' in D. Henrich and K. Düsing, eds., *Hegel in Jena*. Bonn, Bouvier Verlag Herbert Grundmann, 1980, 229–48. [*Hegel-Studien*, Beiheft 20.)

'Comment on [K. Dove) "Phenomenology as Systematic Philosophy,"' in M. Westphal, ed., *Method and Speculation in Hegel's Phenomenology*. Atlantic Highlands, NJ: Humanities Press, 1982, 41–6.

'La servitude sociale et conceptuelle dans l'élaboration de la *Phénoménologie*,' traduit par Philippe Muller, in Muller, ed., *Religion et politique dans les années de formation de Hegel*. Lausanne: L'Age d'Homme, 1982, 117–39.

'The Social Ideal of Hegel's Economic Theory,' in D. Lamb and L.S. Stepelevich, eds., *Hegel's Philosophy of Action*. Atlantic Highlands, NJ: Humanities Press, 1983, 49–74.

'Giovanni Gentile,' in *Twentieth Century Thinkers*. Chicago: St James Press, 1984.

'... and the darkness comprehended it not. (The Origin and Significance of Hegel's Concept of Absolute Spirit),' in T.F. Geraets, ed., *L'esprit absolu / The Absolute Spirit*. Ottawa, University of Ottawa Press, 1984, 15–37.

'Hegel's Image of Phenomenology,' in K.K. Cho, ed., *Philosophy and Science in Phenomenological Perspective*. The Hague: Nijhoff, 1984, 95–109.

'Scepticism, Dogmatism and Speculation in *The Critical Journal*,' in *Between Kant and Hegel*, trans. and annotated by George di Giovanni and H.S. Harris. Albany, NY: SUNY Press, 1985, 252–71.

Preface and General Introduction for G.W.F. Hegel, *The Jena System, 1804–1805: Logic and Metaphysics*, translation edited by John W. Burbidge and George di Giovanni. Montreal: McGill-Queen's University Press, 1986, xi–xxiii.

'What Is Mr. Earvico Supposed to be "earing"?' in Donald Verene, ed., *Vico and Joyce*. Albany, NY: SUNY Press, 1987, 68–82.

Preface for J. D'Hondt: *Hegel in His Time*, trans. J. Burbidge, with Nelson Roland and Judith Levasseur. Peterborough, Ont.: Broadview Press, 1988, i–iv.

'Hegel und Hölderlin,' in H. Schneider and C. Jamme, eds., *Hegel: Der Weg zum System*. Frankfurt a M.: Suhrkamp, 1990, 236–66.

'L'organon hegeliano di interpretazione,' in N. De Domenico, A. Escher Di Stefano, and

G. Puglisi, eds., *Ermeneutica e Filosofia Pratica*. Venice: Marsiglio, 1990, 131–45.
'Spirito and Pragmatism,' in *La filosofia di Ugo Spirito*. Rome: Istituto dell'Enciclopedia Italiana, 1990, 51–9.
(With T.F. Geraets): 'Translating Hegel's Logic' (introductory essay), in Hegel, *The Encyclopedia Logic*, trans. T.F. Geraets, W.A. Suchting, and H.S. Harris. Indianapolis: Hackett Publishing Co., 1991, xii–xxxi.
'Hegel's *Phenomenology of Religion*,' in John Walker, ed., *Thought and Faith in the Philosophy of Hegel*. Dordrecht: Kluwer, 1991, 89–111.
'Hegel's Intellectual Development,' in F. Beiser, ed., *The Cambridge Companion to Hegel*. Cambridge: University Press, 1993, 25–51.
'Hegel's Image of Phenomenology,' in R. Stern, ed., *G.W.F. Hegel: Critical Assessments*, vol. III. London: Routledge, 1993, 64–77.
'Hegel's System as the Theory and Practice of Interpretation,' in R. Stern, ed., *G.W.F. Hegel: Critical Assessments*, vol. III. London: Routledge, 1993, 311–28.
'Il sistema di Hegel come teoria e pratica dell'interpretazione,' in T.F. Geraets, ed., *Dialettica ed Ermeneutica*, (trans. Giouseppe Orsi). Urbino: Quattro Venti, 1993, 65–78.
'The Naturalness of Natural Religion,' in Stanley Tweyman, ed., *David Hume: Critical Assessments*. London: Routledge, 1995, vol. II, 284–300.
'The Concept of Recognition in Hegel's Jena Manuscripts,' in J. O'Neill, ed., *Hegel's Dialectic of Desire and Recognition*. Albany, NY: SUNY Press, 1996, 233–52.
'The End of History in Hegel,' in Jon Stewart, ed., *The Hegel Myths and Legends*. Evanston, Ill.: Northwestern University Press, 1996, 223–36.
'Theme and Variations: The Round of Life and the Chorale of Thought,' in M. Baur and J. Russon, eds., *Hegel and the Tradition*. Toronto: University of Toronto Press, 1997.
'Croce and Gentile in Collingwood's New Leviathan,' in D. Boucher, T. Modood, and J. Connelly, eds., *Philosophy, Civilization and the Forms of Experience*. Cardiff: University of Wales Press, (in press).
'Hegel's Correspondence Theory of Truth,' in G. Browning, ed., *Hegel's Phenomenology of Spirit: A Reappraisal*. Dordrecht: Kluwer, (in press).
'Gentlemen and Players,' in a *Festschrift* for L. Haworth, ed. Mano Daniel, (publication not fixed).
'The Hegelian Organon of Interpretation,' in Shaun Gallagher, ed., *Hegel, History, and Interpretation (a Festschrift for G. Kline)*. Albany, NY: (in press).
'The Uses of Bradley's Absolute,' to appear in a volume edited by Philip MacEwen. Lewiston/Queenston, Ill.: Edward Mellen (in preparation).

Articles

'"Thematic' Philosophy" (review article), *Review of Metaphysics*, 11 (1957–8), 441–45.

'Hegelianism of the "Right" and "Left"' (review article), *Review of Metaphysics*, 11 (1957–8), 603–9.

'Studi sull'attualismo e influenza di Gentile sulla cultura anglosassone,' with 'Bibliografia degli scritti gentiliani in lingua inglese,' together in *Giornale critico della filosofia italiana*, 13 (1959), 312–42 and 342–52, respectively.

'Logical Pragmatism and the Task of Philosophy in Peirce and Vailati,' *Rivista critica di storia della filosofia* (Milan), 18 (1963), 311–21.

'Giovanni Vailati 1863–1963,' *Dialogue*, 2 (1963–4) 328–36.

'Fichte e Gentile,' *Giornale critico della filosofia italiana*, 41 (1964), 557–78.

'The Legacy of Hegel,' *Monist*, 48 (1964), 112–28.

'What is Living and What is Dead in the Philosophy of Croce?' (review article), *Dialogue*, 6 (1967–8), 399–405.

'Vico after 300 Years' (review article), *Dialogue*, 9 (1970), 410–14.

'Hegel for Today' (review article), *Philosophy of the Social Sciences*, 7 (1977), 303–10.

'Hegel and the French Revolution,' *Clio*, 7 (1988), 5–18.

Introduction and notes for: G.W.F. Hegel, 'Fragments of Historical Studies,' trans. Clark Butler, *Clio*, 7 (1977–8), 112–34.

Hegel: 'On Some Characteristic Distinctions of the Ancient Poets,' translated with notes, *Clio*, 7 (1977–8), 403–7.

Hegel: 'Two Fragments of 1797 on Love,' translated with notes, *Clio*, 8 (1978–9), 258–65.

'The Hegel Renaissance in the Anglo-Saxon World since 1945,' *Eidos* (Waterloo, Ont.) (1978–9), 68–97.

Hegel and Schelling: 'The Essence of Philosophical Criticism,' translated with notes, *Journal of Independent Philosophy*, 3 (1979), 37–45.

Introduction and notes for: G.W.F. Hegel, 'On the Religion of the Greeks and Romans,' trans. C. Seiler, *Clio*, 9 (1979–80), 69–74.

'Much Can Still be Done in the Twilight,' *Owl of Minerva*, 10 no. 4 (1979), 8–10.

'Hamlet's Father's Ghost,' *Bulletin of the Hegel Society of Great Britain*, no. 2, (autumn–winter 1980), 56–8.

Hegel: 'Two Fragments on the Ideal of Social Life,' translated with introduction and notes, *Clio*, 10 (1980–1), 399–406.

'Religion as the Mythology of Reason,' *Thought*, 56 (1981), 301–15.

'Gentile's "The Reform of Hegelian Dialectic." An Introductory Note,' *Idealistic Studies*, 11 (1981), 187–8. (Translation of Gentile by A. MacC. Armstrong follows, 189–213.)

'... and the darkness comprehended it not. (The origin and significance of Hegel's Concept of Absolute Spirit),' *University of Ottawa Quarterly*, 50 (1983), 444–66.

'Hume and Barker on the Logic of Design,' *Hume Studies*, 9 (1983), 19–24.

'From Hegel to Marx via Heidegger' (review article), *Philosophy of the Social Sciences*, 13 (1983), 247–51.
'The Hegel Renaissance since 1945,' *Owl of Minerva*, 15 (1983), 77–106. (Revised version of item 16 above.)
'The Resurrection of Art,' *Owl of Minerva*, 16 (1984), 5–20.
'Les influences Platoniciennes sur la théorie de la Vie et du Désir, dans la *Phénoménologie de l'Esprit* de Hegel,' *Revue de philosophie ancienne*, 3 (1985), 54–94.
'The Naturalness of Natural Religion,' *Hume Studies*, 12 (1987), 1–29.
'Hegel's Science of Experience' (bibliographical survey), *Bulletin of the Hegel Society of Great Britain*, no. 15 (spring–summer 1987), 13–37.
'Hegel's Jena Logic and Metaphysics,' *Owl of Minerva*, 18 (1987), 209–18.
'The Cows in the Dark Night,' *Dialogue*, 26 (1987), 627–43; with 'Postscript (to Symposium on "The Cows in the Dark Night"),' *Dialogue*, 26 (1987), 665–8.
'Le figlie della memoria,' *Rinascità della Scuola*, 12 (1988), 250–61.
'L'istituto italiano per gli studi filosofici e la tradizione filosofica napoletana,' *La Provincia di Napoli*, 10 (Dec. 1988) 126–8.
'Literatura y Religion en la Fenomenologia de Hegel: El Alma Bella (I): La paz de Dios,' trans. Jose Antonio Marin Casanova, *ER* (Revista de Filosofia, Seville), nos. 7–8 (winter–spring 1988–9), 53–103.
'Naturphilosophie in the Breach between Hegel and Schelling,' *Hegel-Jahrbuch* (1989), 9–18.
'The Problem of Kant' (in a symposium on R. Pippin, *Hegel's Idealism*), *Bulletin of the Hegel Society of Great Britain*, no. 19 (spring–summer 1989), 18–27.
'History of the History of Philosophy' (critical study), *Journal of the History of Ideas*, 51 (1990), 115–20.
'Croce and Gentile in Collingwood's New Leviathan,' *Storia, Antropologia e Scienze del Linguaggio*, 5 (1990), 29–42.
'The End of History in Hegel,' *Bulletin of the Hegel Society of Great Britain*, no. 23 (1991), 1–14.
'At Glendon College,' *Behind the Headlines*, 50 (1992), 13–16.
'Fichte's New Wine' (review article), *Dialogue*, 32 (1993), 129–33.
'Come la filosofia "informa il mondo,"' *Scheria*, 2 no. 4 (1993), 5–14.
'Hegel's Correspondence Theory of Truth,' *Bulletin of the Hegel Society of Great Britain*, no. 29 (spring–summer 1994) 1–13.
'Hail and Farewell to Hegel,' *Owl of Minerva*, 25 (1994), 163–71.
'Philosophy and Poetry; The War Renewed,' *Clio*, 23 (1994), 395–407.
'Fichtes Verdienst,' *Revue internationale de philosophie*, 49 (1995), 79–91.
'Magic and Religion in Collingwood's Aesthetics,' *Storia, Antropologia e Scienze del Linguaggio*, 8 (1993), 9–21.

'How Philosophy Instructs the World,' *Laval théologique et philosophique*, 51 (1995), 311–21.
'The World That Has Lost Itself' (review of P. Emberley, *Values, Education and Technology*), *Literary Review of Canada*, 4 no. 11 (Dec. 1995), 13–14.
'Hegel and Adam's Rib,' *History of European Ideas* (forthcoming).

Book Reviews

1951

Luigi Bagolini, *Valutazioni Morali e Giuridiche nella Crisi dell'Etica Individuale*. Siena, 1950. *Ethics*, 61, 330.
Luigi Stefanini, *Metafisica della Persona*. Padua, 1950. *Ethics*, 61, 245.

1955

Agnes Arber: *The Mind and the Eye*. Cambridge, 1954. *Philosophy of Science*, 22, 236.
Ernest Cassirer, *The Platonic Renaissance in England*, trans. James P. Pettegrove. Austin, Tex. 1953. *Philosophy of Science*, 22, 328.
Mary B. Hesse, *Science and the Human Imagination*. New York, 1955. *Philosophy of Science*, 23, 268–9.
Ruth Lydia Saw, *Leibniz*. Baltimore, 1954. *Philosophy of Science*, 22, 327–8.
Georg Simmel, *Conflict and the Web of Group-Affiliations*, trans. Kurt H. Wolff and Reinhard Bendix. Glencoe, Ill., 1955. *Philosophy of Science*, 22, 327.
Mario Untersteiner, *The Sophists*, trans. Kathleen Freeman. New York, 1954. *Philosophy of Science*, 22, 328.

1956

Pantaleo Carabellese, *La conscience concrète*, selection de textes, traduction et introduction par Giuseppe Bufo et Luigi Aurigemma. Paris, 1955. *The Review of Religion*, 21, 92–6.

1958

George Boas, *Dominant Themes of Modern Philosophy*. New York, 1957. *Review of Metaphysics*, 11, 441–5 (review article entitled 'Thematic' Philosophy').
Nathaniel Lawrence, *Whitehead's Philosophical Development*. Berkeley, 1956. *Philosophy of Science*, 25, 141–2.
Jean Pucelle, *L'idéalisme en Angleterre de Coleridge à Bradley*. Neuchâtel, 1955.

Jean Hyppolite, *Etudes sur Marx et Hegel*. Paris, 1955. *Review of Metaphysics*, 11, 603–9 (review article entitled 'Hegelianism of the "Right" and "Left."')
F. Rossi-Landi, ed., *Il Pensiero Americano Contemporaneo I: Filosofia, epistemologia, logica*. Turin, 1958. *Philosophical Review*, 69, 262–5.

1962

J.N. Findlay, *Hegel: A Re-Examination*. London, 1958. *New Scholasticism*, 36, 266–8.
Gian N.G. Orsini, *Benedetto Croce, Philosopher of Art and Literary Critic*. Carbondale, Ill., 1961. *Italica*, 39, 222–5.
Gian N.G. Orsini, *Benedetto Croce, Philosopher of Art and Literary Critic*. Carbondale, Ill., 1961. *Philosophical Review*, 71, 535–7.
Richard A. Webster, *The Cross and the Fasces: Christian Democracy and Fascism in Italy*. Stanford, Calif., 1960. *The Journal of Modern History*, 34, 103–4.

1964

Leslie Armour, *The Rational and the Real*. The Hague, 1962. *Dialogue*, 2, 367–9.
Il Pensiero, 7 (Nos. 1 and 2). Milan, Jan. and Aug. 1962. *The Monist*, 48, 129–32 (review of periodical literature on Hegel).

1967

Benedetto Croce, *Philosophy, Poetry, History*, trans. Cecil Sprigge. Oxford, 1966.
R. Assunto et al., *Interpretazioni Crociane*. Bari, 1965.
Gian N.G. Orsini, *Benedetto Croce, Philosopher of Art and Literary Critic*. Carbondale, Ill., 1961.
R. Franchini, *La teoria della storia de Benedetto Croce*. Naples, 1966. *Dialogue*, 6, 399–405 (review article entitled 'What Is Living and What Is Dead in the Philosophy of Croce?').

1968

Arthur C. Danto, *Analytical Philosophy of History*. New York, 1965. *Philosophical Review*, 77, 508–12.

1970

Giorgio Tagliacozzo, ed., *Giambattista Vico: An International Symposium*. Baltimore, Md., 1969. *Dialogue*, 9, 410–14 (review article entitled 'Vico after Three Hundred Years').

Frederick G. Weiss, *Hegel's Critique of Aristotle's Philosophy of Mind*. The Hague, 1969. *Dialogue*, 9, 251–2.

1971

Günther Nicolin, ed., *Hegel in Berichten seiner Zeitgenossen*. Hamburg, 1970. *Owl of Minerva*, 3 no. 1, 4–5.

1972

G.W.F. Hegel, *Gesammelte Werke. Band 7. Jenaer Systementwürfe II*, ed. Rolf-Peter Horstmann and Johann Heinrich Trede. Hamburg, 1971. *Owl of Minerva*, 4 no. 1, 1–3.

Warren E. Steinkraus, ed., *New Studies in Hegel's Philosophy*. New York, 1971. Jacques D'Hondt, *Hegel et la pensée moderne*. Paris, 1970. *Philosophy and Phenomenological Research*, 33, 278–9.

1974

Giovanni Gentile, *The Philosophy of Art*, trans. and introduction by Giovanni Gullace. Ithaca, NY, 1972. *Philosophy and Phenomenological Research*, 35, 115–17.

William H. Goetzmann, ed., *The American Hegelians*. New York, 1973. *Philosophy and Phenomenological Research*, 35, 117–18.

S. Paul Kashap, ed., *Studies in Spinoza*. Berkeley, 1972. *Philosophy and Phenomenological Research*, 35, 280–1.

Frederick G. Weiss, ed., *Beyond Epistemology* (New Studies in the Philosophy of Hegel). The Hague, 1974. *Owl of Minerva*, 6, 1–3.

1975

Rüdiger Bubner, ed., *Das älteste Systemprogramm*. Studien zur Frühgeschichte des deutschen Idealismus. Bonn, 1973 (*Hegel-Studien*, Beiheft 9). Bonn, 1973. *Hegel-Studien*, 10, 299–305.

Stanley Rosen, *G.W.F. Hegel: An Introduction to the Science of Wisdom*. New Haven, Conn.: 1974. Raymond Plant, *Hegel*. Bloomington, Ind., 1973. Burleigh Taylor Wilkins, *Hegel's Philosophy of History*. Ithaca, NY, 1974. *Philosophy and Phenomenological Research*, 35, 419–23.

Nathan Rotenstreich, *From Substance to Subject*. The Hague, 1974. *Human Context*, 7, 635–7.

1976

G.W.F. Hegel, *Gesammelte Werke. Band 6. Jenaer Systementwürfe I*, ed. Klaus Düsing and Heinz Kimmerle. Hamburg, 1975. *Owl of Minerva*, 8 no. 1, 4–6.

Michel Despland, *Kant on History and Religion*. Montreal, 1973. *Philosophy and Phenomenological Research*, 36, 425–7.

Jean Hyppolite, *Genesis and Structure of Hegel's Phenomenology*, trans. Samuel Cherniak and John Heckman. Evanston, Ill., 1974.

Werner Marx, *Hegel's Phenomenology of Spirit: A Commentary on the Preface and Introduction*, trans. Peter Heath. New York, 1975. Judith N. Shklar, *Freedom and Independence: A Study of the Political Ideas of Hegel's 'Phenomenology of Mind.'* Cambridge, 1976. *Philosophy and Phenomenological Research*, 37, 262–8.

George D. O'Brien, *Hegel on Reason and History*. Chicago, 1975. *Philosophy and Phenomenological Research*, 36, 427–8.

1977

G.W.F. Hegel, *Gesammelte Werke. Band 8. Jenaer Systementwürfe III*, ed. Rolf-Peter Horstmann with J.H. Trede. Hamburg, 1976. *Owl of Minerva*, 9 no. 1, 5–7.

Richard Norman, *Hegel's Phenomenology: A Philosophical Introduction*. London, 1976. *Times Literary Supplement* (5 Aug.), 967.

Charles Taylor, *Hegel*. Cambridge, 1975. *Philosophy of the Social Sciences*, 7, 303–10 (review article entitled 'Hegel for Today?').

1978

N. Badaloni and C. Muscetta, *Labriola, Croce, Gentile*. Rome, 1977. *Canadian Journal of Italian Studies*, 1, 234–6.

Quentin Lauer, *A Reading of Hegel's 'Phenomenology of Spirit.'* New York, 1976. *Clio*, 7, 508–10.

George Lukács, *The Young Hegel*, trans. Rodney Livingstone. Cambridge, Mass., 1976. Howard P. Kainz, *Hegel's Phenomenology Part I: Analysis and Commentary*. University AL, 1976. Lothar Eley, *Hegels Wissenschaft der Logik*. Munich, 1976. *Philosophy and Phenomenological Research*, 38, 575–9.

George J. Seidel, *Activity and Ground: Fichte, Schelling and Hegel*. Hildesheim, 1976. *International Studies in Philosophy*, 10, 236–8.

1979

G.W.F. Hegel, *Phenomenology of Spirit*, trans. A.V. Miller with analysis of the text and

foreword by J.N. Findlay. Oxford, 1977. *International Journal for Philosophy of Religion*, 10, 268–71.
G.W.F. Hegel, *Phenomenology of Spirit*, trans. A.V. Miller with analysis of the text and foreword by J.N. Findlay. Oxford, 1977. *Philosophy and Phenomenological Research*, 39, 443–4.
G.W.F. Hegel, *Philosophy of Subjective Spirit* (3 vols), trans. M.J. Petry. Dordrecht, 1978. *Dialogue*, 18, 600–6.
Wolfgang Bonsiepen, *Der Begriff der Negativität in den Jenaer Schriften Hegels*. Bonn, 1977. *Hegel-Studien*, 14, 331–3.
José Maria Ripalda, *The Divided Nation*. Assen, 1977. *Clio*, 8, 458–60.
Jonathan Robinson, *Duty and Hypocrisy in Hegel's Phenomenology of Mind*. Toronto, 1977. *Clio*, 8, 278–80.

1980

D. Henrich and K. Düsing, eds., *Hegel in Jena*. (*Hegel-Studien*, Beiheft 20). Bonn, 1980. *Bulletin of the Hegel Society of Great Britain*, no. 2, 33–6.
G.R.G. Mure, *Idealist Epilogue*. Oxford, 1978. *Owl of Minerva*, 12 no. 1, 5–6.
Luigi Pareyson, *Fichte: Il sistema della libertà*. Milan, 1976. *Journal of the History of Philosophy*, 18, 97–8.
Merold Westphal, *History and Truth in Hegel's Phenomenology*. Atlantic Highlands, NJ, 1979. *Philosophy and Phenomenological Research*, 41, 239–41.

1981

G.W.F. Hegel, *Gesammelte Werke. Band 9. Phänomenologie des Geistes*, ed. Wolfgang Bonsiepen and Reinhard Heede. Hamburg, 1980. *Owl of Minerva*, 12 no. 4, 5–7.
P.E. Cain, *Widerspruch und Subjektivität*; eine problemgeschichtliche Studie zum jungen Hegel. Bonn, 1978. *Bulletin of the Hegel Society of Great Britain*, no. 3, 35–7.
Werner Hartkopf, *Kontinuität und Diskontinuität in Hegels Jenaer Anfängen*. Königstein, 1979. *Bulletin of the Hegel Society of Great Britain*, no. 4, 32–6.

1982

Crawford Elder, *Appropriating Hegel*. New York, 1981. *Canadian Philosophical Reviews*, 2, 217–19.
David Lamb, *Language and Perception in Hegel and Wittgenstein*. New York, 1980. David Lamb, *Hegel: From Foundation to System*. The Hague, 1980. *Journal of the History of Philosophy*, 20, 441–5.

John E. Toews, *Hegelianism: The Path toward Dialectical Humanism 1805–1841*. New York, 1981. *Owl of Minerva*, 13 no. 4, 5–7.

1983

G.W.F. Hegel, *Vorlesungen über die Philosophie der Religion. Teil I. Einleitung: Der Begriff der Religion*, ed. Walter Jaeschke. Hamburg, 1983. *Bulletin of the Hegel Society of Great Britain*, no. 8, 21–4.

Christopher J. Berry, *Hume, Hegel and Human Nature*. The Hague, 1982. *Hume Studies*, 9, 200–3.

Tom Darby, *The Feast, Meditations on Politics and Time*. Toronto, 1982. *University of Toronto Quarterly*, 52, 563–4.

Gilbert Gérard, *Critique et dialectique: L'itinéraire de Hegel à Jena (1801–5)*. Brussels, 1982. *Owl of Minerva*, 14 no. 4, 1–2.

Philip J. Kain, *Schiller, Hegel and Marx*. Montreal, 1982. *Philosophical Books*, 24, 223–4.

Alexandre Kojève, *Introduction to the Reading of Hegel*, assembled by Raymond Queneau, ed. Allan Bloom and trans. James H. Nichols, Jr. Ithaca, NY and London, 1980. *Philosophy of the Social Sciences*, 13, 247–51 (review article entitled 'From Hegel to Marx via Heidegger').

Quentin Lauer, *Hegel's Concept of God*. Albany, 1982. *Philosophical Books*, 24, 153–7.

Joachim Ritter, *Hegel and the French Revolution*, trans. R.D. Winfield. Boston, 1982. *Philosophical Books*, 24, 224–5.

1984

John Burbidge, *On Hegel's Logic: Fragments of a Commentary*. Atlantic Highlands, NJ, 1982. *Philosophical Review*, 93, 138–40.

M.J. Inwood, *Hegel*. London, 1983. *Philosophical Books*, 25, 209–12.

Gillian Rose, *Hegel contra Sociology*. Atlantic Highlands, NJ, 1981. *Philosophy of the Social Sciences*, 14, 425–6.

1985

G.W.F. Hegel, *The Letters*, trans. Clark Butler and Christiane Seiler, commentary by Clark Butler. Bloomington, Ind., 1984. *Times Literary Supplement* (2 Aug.), 841.

G.W.F. Hegel, *Vorlesungen über die Philosophie der Religion. Teil 3, Der vollendete*

Religion, ed. Walter Jaeschke. Hamburg, 1984. *Bulletin of the Hegel Society of Great Britain*, no. 11, 24–6.

Barry Cooper, *The End of History: An Essay on Modern Hegelianism*. Toronto, 1984. *Dialogue*, 24, 739–42.

Benedetto Croce, *Poetry and Literature*, trans. with introduction and notes by Giovanni Gullace. Carbondale, Ill., 1981. *International Studies in Philosophy*, 17, 97–9.

'A Contribution to the Criticism of Myself.' Response to the review [of *Hegel's Development, 2: Night Thoughts (Jena 1801–1806)*. Oxford, 1983] by Heinz Kimmerle, *Clio*, 14, 433–42. *Clio*, 14, 442–7.

1986

G.W.F. Hegel, *Three Essays: 1793–1795*, ed. and trans. with introduction and notes by Peter Fuss and John Dobbins. Notre Dame, Ind., 1984. *Philosophical Review*, 95, 113–15.

F.W.J. Schelling, *Bruno, or, on the Natural and the Divine Principle of Things*, ed. and trans. with introduction by Michael G. Vater. Albany, NY, 1984. *Owl of Minerva*, 18, 71–4.

William Desmond, *Art and the Absolute: A Study of Hegel's Aesthetics*. Albany, NY, 1986. *Cithara*, 26, 60–1.

Dieter Henrich and Christoph Jamme, eds., *Jakob Zwillings Nachlass. Eine Rekonstruktion (Hegel-Studien*, Beiheft 28). Bonn, 1986. *Bulletin of the Hegel Society of Great Britain*, no. 13, 25–9.

Giacomo Rinaldi, *Saggio sulla metafisica di [E.E.] Harris*. Bologna, 1984. *Idealistic Studies*, 16, 262–3.

1987

Joseph C. Flay, *Hegel's Quest for Certainty*. Albany, NY, 1984. *Philosophical Review*, 96, 469–72.

Donald Phillip Verene, *Hegel's Recollection: A Study of Images in the Phenomenology of Spirit*. Albany, NY, 1985. *International Journal for Philosophy of Religion*, 21, 126–8.

1988

Richard Bellamy, *Modern Italian Social Theory* (Ideology and Politics from Pareto to the Present). Stanford, Calif., 1987. *Ethics*, 99, 176–7.

Stephen Priest, ed., *Hegel's Critique of Kant*. Oxford, 1987. *Canadian Philosophical Reviews*, 8, 107–9.

Publications of H.S. Harris 343

1989

David Kolb, *The Critique of Pure Modernity: Hegel, Heidegger and After*. Chicago, 1987. *Philosophy and Phenomenological Research*, 49, 752–5.

Vincent A. McCarthy, *Quest for a Philosophical Jesus: Christianity and Philosophy in Rousseau, Kant, Hegel and Schelling*. Macon, Ga., 1986. *International Journal for Philosophy of Religion*, 22, 62–4.

David M. Parry, *Hegel's Phenomenology of the 'We.'* New York, 1988. *Bulletin of the Hegel Society of Great Britain*, no. 20, 52–4.

Adriaan T. Peperzak, *Philosophy and Politics: A Commentary on the Preface to Hegel's Philosophy of Right*. Dordrecht, 1987. *Philosophy of the Social Sciences*, 19, 396–8.

Terry Pinkard, *Hegel's Dialectic*. Philadelphia, 1988. *Canadian Philosophical Reviews*, 9, 460–2.

Riccardo Pozzo, *Hegel: 'Introductio in philosophiam.'* Florence, 1989. *Bulletin of the Hegel Society of Great Britain*, no. 20, 48–50.

Peter G. Stillman, ed., *Hegel's Philosophy of Spirit*. Albany, NY, 1987. *Philosophy of the Social Sciences*, 19, 118–20.

Norbert Waszek, *The Scottish Enlightenment and Hegel's Account of 'Civil Society.'* Dordrecht, 1988. *Hegel-Studien*, 24, 215–18.

1990

Jacques D'Hondt, *Hegel in His Time (Berlin, 1818–1831)*, trans. John Burbidge. Peterborough, NY, 1988. *Dialogue*, 29, 602–3.

Maurice A. Finocchiaro, *Gramsci and the History of Dialectical Thought*. Cambridge, Mass., 1988. *Idealistic Studies*, 20, 259–60.

C.D. MacNiven, *Bradley's Moral Psychology*. Lewiston, NY, 1987. *Owl of Minerva*, 22, 96–8.

Antimo Negri, *Hegel nel Novecento*. Rome, 1987. *Idealistic Studies*, 20, 85–6.

D.D. Roberts, *Benedetto Croce and the Uses of Historicism*. Berkeley, 1987. *Journal of the History of Philosophy*, 28, 145–6.

Giovanni Santinello, ed., *Storia delle storie generali della filosofia* [Part III]. *Il secondo illuminismo e l'età Kantiana*, 2 vols. Padua, 1988. *Journal of the History of Ideas*, 51, 115–20 (critical study entitled 'History of the History of Philosophy').

A. Wylleman, ed., *Hegel on the Ethical Life, Religion and Philosophy*. Louvain, 1989. *Bulletin of the Hegel Society of Great Britain*, nos. 21–2, 92–4.

1991

Lawrence Dickey, *Hegel, Religion, Economics and the Politics of Spirit 1770–1807*. New York, 1987. *International Journal for the Philosophy of Religion*, 29, 123–5.

H.-F. Fulda and R.-P. Horstmann, eds., *Rousseau, die Revolution und der junge Hegel.* Stuttgart, 1991. *Bulletin of the Hegel Society of Great Britain*, nos. 23–4, 112–16.

Kunio Kozu, *Das Bedürfnis der Philosophie.* Bonn, 1988. *International Studies in Philosophy*, 23, 127–8.

Andrew Seth and Richard B. Haldane, eds., *Essays in Philosophical Criticism.* London, 1883; reprint, Bristol, 1990. *Bulletin of the Hegel Society of Great Britain*, nos. 23–4, 106–8.

1992

G.W.F. Hegel, *Elements of the Philosophy of Right*, ed. Allen W. Wood and trans. H.B. Nisbet. New York, 1991. *Canadian Philosophical Reviews*, 12, 26–7.

Johann G. Fichte, *Early Philosophical Writings*, trans. and ed. D. Breazeale. Ithaca, NY, 1988. *Owl of Minerva*, 23, 193–5.

Brigitte Falkenburg, *Die Form der Materie: zur Metaphysik der Natur beim Kant und Hegel.* Frankfurt a M., 1987. *International Studies in Philosophy*, 24, 100–1.

Annemarie Gethmann-Siefert, ed., *Philosophie und Poesie*, 2 vols. [Festschrift for Otto Pöggeler's sixtieth birthday]. Stuttgart, 1988. *Idealistic Studies*, 22, 255–6.

Angela Schinaia, ed., *Carteggio Gentile – Maturi (1899–1917).* Florence, 1987. *Idealistic Studies*, 22, 254–5.

Richard Tursman, *Pragmaticism or Objective Idealism? Peirce's Theory of Scientific Discovery.* Bloomington, Ind., 1987. *Idealistic Studies*, 22, 256–8.

Kenneth R. Westphal, *Hegel's Epistemological Realism.* Dordrecht, 1989. *Philosophy of the Social Sciences*, 21, 512–15.

1993

David MacGregor, *Hegel, Marx and the English State.* Boulder, Col., 1992. *Bulletin of the Hegel Society of Great Britain*, nos. 27–8, 68–73.

Frederick Neuhouser, *Fichte's Theory of Subjectivity.* Cambridge, 1990. *Dialogue*, 32, 129–33.

Alan M. Olson, *Hegel and the Spirit.* Princeton, NJ, 1992. *Bulletin of the Hegel Society of Great Britain*, nos. 27–8, 50–2.

1994

Myriam Bienenstock, *Politique du jeune Hegel (Jena 1801–1806).* Paris, 1992. *International Studies in Philosophy*, 26, 108–9.

Stephen Houlgate, *Freedom, Truth and History.* London, 1991. *Philosophy of the Social Sciences*, 24, 517–19.

Edward C. Moore, ed., *Charles S. Peirce and the Philosophy of Science*. Tuscaloosa, Ala., 1993. *Transactions of the Peirce Society*, 30, 1046–54.

1995

Peter Emberley, *Values, Education and Technology*. Toronto, 1995. *Literary Review of Canada*, 4 no. 11, 13–14.

Philip M. Merklinger, *Philosophy, Theology, and Hegel's Berlin Philosophy of Religion, 1821–1827*. Albany, NY, 1993. *Review of Metaphysics*, 48, 914–15.

Terry Pinkard, *Hegel's Phenomenology: The Sociality of Reason*. Cambridge, 1994. *Bulletin of the Hegel Society of Great Britain*, no. 32, 33–40.

Andrew Shanks, *Hegel's Political Theology*. Cambridge, 1991. *Philosophy of the Social Sciences*, 25, 135–7.

Robert C. Solomon and Kathleen M. Higgins, eds., *The Age of German Idealism*. Routledge History of Philosophy, vol. VI. New York, 1993. *Journal of the History of Philosophy*, 33, 525–7.

Merold Westphal, *Hegel, Freedom, and Modernity* Albany, NY, 1992. *Owl of Minerva*, 26, 201–3.

Contributors

H.S. Harris is Distinguished Research Professor of Philosophy (emeritus) at Glendon College, York University, Toronto.

Michael Baur, assistant professor in the School of Philosophy at The Catholic University of America, in Washington, DC, received his PhD from the University of Toronto. He is currently secretary of the Hegel Society of America and is working on a translation of Fichte's *Foundations of Natural Right* for Cambridge University Press.

John Burbidge is professor of philosophy at Trent University, in Peterborough, Ontario; past president of the Hegel Society of America; and author of *On Hegel's Logic: Fragments of a Commentary* (New York: Humanities Press, 1981), *Hegel on Logic and Religion: The Reasonableness of Christianity* (Albany: SUNY Press, 1992), and *Real Process: How Logic and Chemistry Combine in Hegel's Philosophy of Nature* (Toronto: University of Toronto Press, 1996). H.S. Harris was the external examiner for Burbidge's doctoral dissertation. They collaborated with Kenneth Schmitz, George di Giovanni, and others in translating Hegel's Jena Logic and Metaphysics of 1803–4 (Montreal: McGill-Queen's University Press, 1986) and chapter 6 of the *Phenomenology of Spirit*.

James Crooks is associate professor and chair of the Department of Philosophy at Bishop's University, in Lennoxville, Quebec. He received his PhD from the University of Toronto in 1989. His interests are in ancient philosophy and contemporary continental philosophy, and his recent publications include 'Speaking in Our Own Voices: Plato's "Protagoras" and the Crisis of Education,' *Paideusis* (1994), and (with R. Bontekoe) 'The Interrelation of Moral and Aesthetic Excellence,' *British Journal of Aesthetics* (1992).

Contributors

Martin Donougho, associate professor of philosophy at the University of South Carolina, received his doctorate from the University of Toronto. (H.S. Harris was external examiner for the oral defence.) He has written on Hegel's philosophy of art, on aesthetics generally, and on such thinkers as Adorno, Derrida, and Foucault. He has completed a translation of Hotho's transcription of Hegel's 1823 *Lecture on Aesthetics*.

Patricia Fagan is currently a PhD candidate in the Department of Classics at the University of Toronto. Her dissertation, 'Horses: A Case Study in the Similes of the Iliad,' uses interpretive methods derived from post-Kantian philosophy to interpret the significance of various central metaphors to the meaning of the *Iliad* as a whole.

George di Giovanni has published widely on topics and figures connected with Kant and his age. In cooperation with H.S. Harris and others, he has also translated texts of Hegel and of authors from the period between Kant and Hegel. He has just completed a volume on F.H. Jacobi that includes translations of texts, critical notes, and commentaries. He has also translated and edited, in cooperation with Allen Wood, Kent's writings on religion and natural theology. He is professor at McGill University, Montréal.

Susan-Judith Hoffmann is a graduate of the Guelph-MacMaster Doctoral Program in Philosophy. Her first contact with H.S. Harris was in 1988, when he very kindly agreed to meet with her to discuss an early version of the paper published in this *Festschrift*. She was recently awarded a Deutscher Akademischer Austauschdienst Fellowship to work in Tübingen on a book-length study of Wilhelm von Humboldt's contribution to hermeneutics.

David Kolb received his PhD from Yale University, has taught at Fordham University, the University of Chicago, and is currently Charles A. Dana Professor of Philosophy at Bates College in Lewiston, Maine. He is the author of *The Critique of Pure Modernity: Hegel, Heidegger and After* and of *Postmodern Sophistications: Philosophy, Architecture, and Tradition*, both from the University of Chicago Press. He has edited *New Perspective on Hegel's Philosophy of Religion* (Albany: SUNY Press) and is the author of articles on Hegel, Heidegger, Plato, and questions about modernity and post-modernity in philosophy, architecture, and hypertext.

Jay Lampert is assistant professor of philosophy at the University of Guelph. He is the author of *Synthesis and Backward Reference in Husserl's Logical*

Investigations (Dordrecht: Kluwer Academic Publishers, 1995) and of articles on Hegel, Husserl, and other figures in the history of philosophy.

John McCumber is professor of philosophy at Northwestern University in Evanston, Illinois. He is the author of *The Company of Words* and *Poetic Interaction: Language, Freedom, Reason.*

Jeff Mitscherling is associate professor of philosophy at the University of Guelph. He has published numerous papers in ancient philosophy, eighteenth- and nineteenth-century German philosophy, phenomenology, philosophical hermeneutics, and aesthetics, as well as *Roman Ingarden's Ontology and Aesthetics* (Ottawa: University of Ottawa Press, 1996). He joined the Central Ontario Hegel Translation Group in 1978, just as the group was proceeding to revise H.S. Harris's preliminary translation of the *Jena Logic*.

John Russon is assistant professor of philosophy at the Pennsylvania State University. He received his PhD in philosophy from the University of Toronto in 1990. His first book, *The Self and its Body in Hegel's Phenomenology*, is published by the University of Toronto Press. He has also published articles on Hegel, ancient philosophy, nineteenth-century philosophy, and phenomenology.

Nicholas Walker, formerly of Magdalene College, Cambridge, is involved in research in German literature and philosophy. He is an officer of the Hegel Society of Great Britain and co-translator of volume XXIV/XXX of Heidegger's *Gesamtausgabe*.